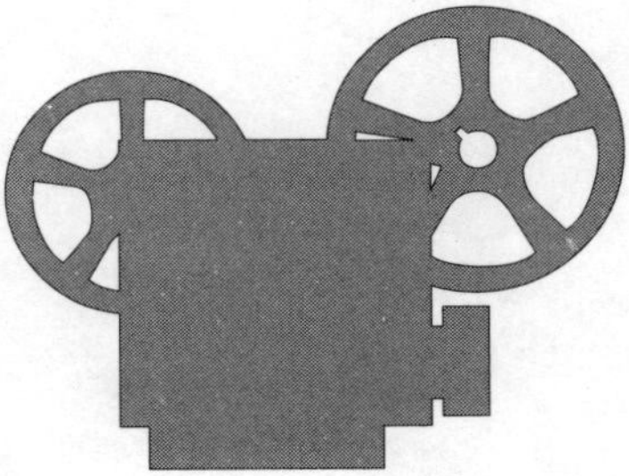

Bollyworld

Bollyworld

Popular Indian Cinema through a Transnational Lens

Editors
Raminder Kaur
Ajay J. Sinha

SAGE Publications
New Delhi | Thousand Oaks | London

First published in 2005 by

Sage Publications India Pvt Ltd
B-42, Panchsheel Enclave
New Delhi 110017
www.indiasage.com

Sage Publications Inc
2455 Teller Road
Thousand Oaks, California 91320

Sage Publications Ltd
1 Oliver's Yard, 55 City Road
London EC1Y 1SP

Published by Tejeshwar Singh for Sage Publications India Pvt Ltd, phototypeset in 10/12 Goudy Old Style by Star Compugraphics Private Limited, Delhi and printed at Chaman Enterprises, New Delhi.

Library of Congress Cataloging-in-Publication Data

Bollyworld: popular Indian cinema through a transnational lens/editors, Raminder Kaur, Ajay J. Sinha.
p. cm.
Includes bibliographical references and index.
1. Motion pictures—India—Social aspects. 2. Motion pictures—India—Foreign influences. 3. Motion pictures, Indic. 4. India—In motion pictures. I. Kaur, Raminder, 1967– II. Sinha, Ajay J., 1956–
PN1993.5.I8B595 791.43'0954—dc22 2005 2005004208

ISBN: 0-7619-3320-4 (Hb) 81-7829-450-8 (India-Hb)
0-7619-3321-2 (Pb) 81-7829-451-6 (India-Pb)

Sage Production Team: Sunaina Dalaya, Rajib Chatterjee and Santosh Rawat

Contents

List of Illustrations

Acknowledgements

The editors would like to thank all the contributors to this volume for their time, energy and thoughts in making this volume possible. Also to Omita Goyal and Mimi Choudhury for their wholehearted support and to Sunaina Dalaya for her meticulous editorial hand in this book project at Sage. Thanks also to the Research and Graduate Support Unit at the University of Manchester for help in funding the publication of the illustrations, and the 'Border-Crossing' Initiative of the Association for Asian Studies, which generously funded international travel of participants for the conference panel in Chicago in 2001 in which the project was originally conceived. Thanks also to Pushpamala N. for generously providing the image for the cover.

1

Bollyworld: An Introduction to Popular Indian Cinema through a Transnational Lens

RAMINDER KAUR AND AJAY J. SINHA

Mere juta hai Japani, yeh patloon Englistani,
Sar pe lal topi russi, phir bhi dil hai Hindustani

(My shoes are Japanese, my trousers Englistani,
On my head is a red hat from Russia, and yet my heart is Hindustani)

—song from the film, *Shri 420*
(*The Gentleman Cheat*, dir. Raj Kapoor, 1955)

Mahatma Gandhi, the champion of Indian *swadeshi* and non-violent nationalism, and Charlie Chaplin, the comic extraodinaire of the silent cinema, two of the unlikeliest bedfellows, met in London in 1931. In spite of certain socialist similarities between them, their meeting was a little fraught. Chaplin was nonplussed and a little surprised to discover what seemed to him to be Gandhi's 'strange apathy to anything technological/industrial'. Gandhi's dedication to the cottage industry and his ideals of non-violence did not impress Chaplin. Still, the film star was moved by Gandhi's motivation and commitment, or what he called his 'will of iron' (Biren Das Sharma, 1993: 135).

This 'will of iron' was a temperament shared by the South London-born actor, enough for him to fight against all the odds and leave an indelible mark on cinematic history, so much so that two decades later, India had its own cute vagabond hero with a peculiar walk, Raju, played by the phenomenal Raj Kapoor. Sauntering down the road, with a knapsack on his shoulder and singing like there was no tomorrow in *Shri 420*, Raju lyrically asserts that, even though he is a walking advertisement for various national products—his Japanese shoes, English trousers and Russian hat—at heart he remains an Indian.[1] A song that put 'Englistan' firmly on the lexical map, it is essentially about material made elsewhere, but a heart made in India. It is a narrative about the production of nationalism through its intricate entanglement with the global, that even though the Indian nation is swamped with all kinds of foreign influences and products, this does not need to undermine the strength of patriotism.[2] It is the case that 'Indianness' is produced in relation to difference, rather than simply being the outcome of the autochthonous processes. It is this more transnational focus—often overlooked in nation-oriented accounts—that this volume on Indian cinema addresses. The question it explores is: how and in what ways did global dynamics take on such a regionalist or nationalistic veneer in the history of Indian cinema; and, how do movies from the subcontinent continue to interact with their global counterparts in their multifarious forms?

For Gandhi and many other freedom fighters, cinema was associated with the hedonistic ways of the West. The West, of course, signified not only a place corresponding to the economically powerful countries of western Europe and the USA, but what Stuart Hall (1992: 277) outlines as a concept that: (*i*) characterises societies into different categories;

[1] The film's title is drawn from Section 420 of the Indian Penal Code, under which cheats and frauds are prosecuted. The sentiments of the song have contemporary legacies as with the pop star, Alisha's, 'Made in India', and the song, 'I love my India' in the film, *Pardes* (dir. Subash Ghai, 1997). See Uberoi (1998: 330) for commentary on the latter.

[2] As Sumita Chakravarty proposes: 'This was the Nehru era and being national also meant, in some sense, to declare oneself to be international' (1993: 203). Similarly, the philosopher, Jonathon Reè (1992) elaborates on how nationality can only be conceived of in a context of internationality. Signifiers only make sense in relation to their opposites, others and differentials. Reè states: 'in the same way that (Kristeva has proposed, and most literary theorists have accepted) individual texts can function only within a field of general intertextuality, so individual nations arise only within a field of general internationality; or in other words, that the logic of internationality preceded the formation of nations' (1992: 9).

(*ii*) describes a set of images; (*iii*) provides a model of comparison; and, (*iv*) functions as an ideology. In relation to Indian cinema,

> the West is not so much a place, or even a culture, as [it is] an emblem of exotic, decadent otherness, signified by whisky, bikinis, an uncontrolled sexuality and what is seen as lack of 'respect' for elders and betters, and (from men) for womanhood (Thomas, 1985: 126).

For others, however, films were not canvases for decadence, but represented potentials for social change. As K. Ahmed Abbas argued against Gandhi:

> My own father never sees films and regards them as an imported vice from the West. I respect his opinion even though I may not be able to share it [...] We want more decent people to take interest in this industry, so that it becomes an instrument of social good rather than a *tamasha*. But these people may be discouraged and kept away if you and other great men like you continue to count the cinema among such vices as gambling and drinking (*Filmindia*, October 1939, cited in Bandyopadhyay, 1993: 130).

As film historians are all too aware, Dhundiraj Govind Phalke (later Dadasaheb Phalke) paid little attention to concerns about the moral depravity of cinema.[3] The oft-cited story goes that the original impulse to make an Indian feature-length film came as Phalke sat and watched a short documentary, *The Life of Christ*, at P.B. Mehta's America-India Cinema in Bombay. Sitting in the dark, he mused on how wonderful it would be to produce a film about Indian gods and with Indian actors. Phalke brought a different notion of the West into play, one relating to available technologies for cinematic magic. Three years later, in 1913, India's much acclaimed first feature film, *Raja Harishchandra*, opened to fascinated audiences in Bombay's Coronation Cinematograph.[4]

---

[3] Phalke once stated: 'Those who are susceptible to depravity do not need cinema or theatre to mislead them. There are numerous other factors which lead to immorality' (cited in Chakravarty, 1993: 38).

[4] Some prefer to highlight R.G. Torney's *Pundalik* about a Maharashtrian saint as the first indigenously produced movie, released on 8 May 1912, at the Coronation Cinematograph in Bombay (Rangoonwalla cited in Chakravarty, 1993: 34–35). However, as the film was shot by an Englishman, it does not appear in many nation-oriented histories.

National teleologies regarding Phalke are all too evident in the historiography of Indian cinema. They have been recently criticised by scholars for eclipsing both the regional variations and international connections that Phalke and his contemporaries demonstrated in their films (Hughes, 1996; also see Jain in this volume). Additionally, Phalke's Hindu mythologicals did not have an even affect on all parts and people of India, particularly if one considers the reluctance of Muslims to view movies about Hindu deities (ibid.: 179, 185). Moreover, foreign films were much more widely distributed in the country than Hindu mythologicals. Indians did not just watch Parsi theatre or folk plays and diligently follow the religious epics, they were also open to a feast of films from all over the world, particularly America and Britain. About 90 per cent of all films screened in India were from abroad until the late 1920s. Indeed, the critic Rajaji, opining in 1942, wrote: 'I have not seen more than half a dozen films in my life. Perhaps it was my misfortune that the Indian ones I saw proved boring' (cited in Bandyopadhyay, 1993: 156). It was only the arrival of sound technology in the 1930s that 'freed the Indian language film from competition with imported films' and led to the expansion of the Indian film market (Chakravarty, 1993: 38).

Our narrative must, therefore, consider a criss-cross of relationships, and account for the personnel involved in film production, the spread of technologies, the distribution of films amongst a varied audience, and a constant traversing of all these elements through countries and subcontinental regions. Not only was film technology imported from Europe, but by 1914, Phalke was invited to London to screen *Raja Harishchandra* along with two other feature films, *Mohini Bhasmasur* and *Satyavan Savitri*.[5] This East-West manoeuvre was a lyrical response to the touring agent Maurice Sestier's first ever screening of the Lumière Brothers' short clips in the Watson Theatre in Bombay in 1896. Clearly, whether it be through a consideration of the available films, their inspiration, storylines, technological know-how, or the exchange of personnel, India's popular film history cannot be written without exploring the *constructions* of the 'national'—this is a project that reached intensified heights particularly in the post-Independence years when Hindi language commercial cinema quickly came to be seen as the 'national' cinema of India. This volume

[5] Phalke's work was praised as much by London-based film critics as it was by the Indian press for its focus on Indian mythologies (Chakravarty, 1993: 37). This is another instance where the contours of nationalism collide with the interests of the Orientalists.

attempts a departure and breakthrough from these paradigms of nationhood that have dominated the studies of Indian cinema.

Our argument, however, is not that Indian cinema is shadow puppetry of the West, but rather that the changing notions of the West might themselves be used to fix and unfix national narratives.[6] As Rosie Thomas comments:

> ... Indian cinema has, throughout its long history, evolved as a form which has resisted the cultural imperialism of Hollywood: the form has undergone continual change and there has been both inspiration and assimilation from Hollywood and elsewhere, but thematically and structurally, Indian cinema has remained remarkably distinctive (1985: 116).

Whatever technological, narrative and aesthetic dimensions were incorporated into films, they presented a relationship of *difference*, providing a parallel to Partha Chatterjee's (1986) arguments on Indian nationalism, namely, that it borrowed from elsewhere, continued to dialogue with the outside, and eventually became a force to be reckoned with both inside and outside of its bordered territories.

If Hollywood represents the homogenising effect of American capitalism in global cultures, a study of Bollywood allows a unique opportunity to map the contrasting move of globalisation in popular culture.[7] Bollywood's integration with film studies has brought it closer to the conceptual frameworks developed for Hollywood narratives (audience voyeurism, narrative techniques, and so on), and consequently Hollywood's cultural capitalism is mapped, consciously or unconsciously, onto that of India's commercial cinema. One fundamental difference between Hollywood and Bollywood is that the former pushes world cultures towards homogenisation, whereas the latter introduces in those cultures a fragmentary process. Hybrid in its production since its beginnings, the circulation of India's commercial cinema through the globe has led to the proliferation and fragmentation of its fantasy space, as its narrative and spectacle beget diverse fantasies for diasporic communities and others.

---

[6] Patricia Uberoi (1998) has shown the changing notions of the West in her analysis of the films of the 1990s.

[7] Bombay was officially designated Mumbai in 1995. However, the two terms continue to be used interchangeably in popular parley. The authors here have their particular preferences too.

In its very (sometimes) contentious name, Bollywood cinema indicates the crossing of borders. The hybrid term refers to India's commercial Hindi film industry, based primarily, but not exclusively, in the city of Bombay, now officially designated as Mumbai since 1995.[8] It has a complex history, but much like Hollywood, this commercial industry has hegemony over the diverse, regional cinema in India, and circulates globally, from Japan to the US, through a transnational distribution network as well as video piracy. Hence the neologism, *Bollyworld*, to refer to Indian cinema through a transnational lens, at once located in the nation, but also out of the nation in its provenance, orientation and outreach. Bollyworld may be taken in at least three senses: first, to allude to the inherently hybrid constituency of Bollywood yet also an index of variant senses of Indian identity; second, the global distribution of Bollywood movies and a conveyor of 'Indianness' to diverse audiences; and third, as a means of negotiating both Indianness and its transformation, particularly when representing and being received by diasporic populations.[9]

This volume sets out to describe this fundamentally fragmentary character of Bollywood through case studies, or what Stephen Greenblatt (1991) has called 'anecdotes'. Greenblatt describes anecdotes as surprising encounters for a traveller who otherwise knows which highway of history to take. Against grand, totalising narratives, such as those of progressive history, or in his phrase, 'history that knows where it is going' (ibid.: 2), Greenblatt's notion of anecdotes presents the world as a succession of singular, brief, contingent experiences that may imply a larger pattern of history but will never show that pattern fully to the reader. We hope this volume provides some analytical terms through a record of encounters that intervene and modify the 'highway' of a national cinema.

The anecdotal approach proposed here provides the best opportunity to construe the world of popular culture itself as fragmentary and dialogical clusters of variegated and entangled cultural discourses. Unlike Hollywood narratives, which are basically studied as textual constructions with an internal cohesiveness and audience address, the chapters in this volume treat India's commercial cinema as 'globalized intertexts', made visible in specific narratives or deployed as visual and eroticised spectacles at specific

[8] Accordingly, the contributors to this volume have chosen to describe this cinema which developed over the decades in their own particular ways—popular Indian, Bombay, Hindi, commercial cinema or simply, Bollywood. We, as editors, want to hold on to the diversity that is implied in the cinema's multiple identities.

[9] See also Brosius' (this volume) more specific use of the term, Bollyworld, to consider film worlds amongst German Pakistanis residing in Frankfurt.

cultural intersections in different parts of the world. Bollywood cinema provides an exceptional example with which to examine global flows without always positing western provenance.[10]

Sea Changes

The latter-day popularity of the Indian film industry has taken many by surprise. An English colleague recently commented: 'It seems that the whole world is going mad about Bollywood.' After decades of intellectual neglect, film critics are now claiming it as 'the new cool in international cinema' (Banker, 2001: 7). Such proclamations are certainly not too far removed from the truth. For instance, *Ashoka* (dir. Santosh Sivan, 2001) posters festooned London Underground stations as Warner Brothers decide to leverage on the renewed interest in Bollywood with their Indian star-studded West End opening. This was accompanied by a launch of the film at the Venice International Film Festival and a release in Tokyo. *Lagaan: Once upon a Time in India* (*Tax*, dir. Ashutosh Gowarikar, 2001) was nominated for an Oscar four decades after the nomination of the first Indian popular movie, *Mother India* (dir. Mehboob Khan, 1957). Amitabh Bachchan was voted the film star of the millennium on BBC Online News in 2000, beating old veterans such as Sir Lawrence Olivier and Sir Alec Guinness. *Moulin Rouge* (2001), the musical epic set in nineteenth century gay Paris, was feted by the mainstream cinema-going public—its director Baz Luhrmann clearly paying his debts to the eastern splendours of Indian popular film. A year later, Daisy von Scherler Mayer tries a similar fusion formula for her film, *Guru*, which was high on the cringe-factor scale. In the film, the pop band Basement Jaxx explored the rather simplistic trials and tribulations of an Indian couple in love, dancing at every opportunity in tune to their chart hit *Romeo* of 2001. London's and Manchester's department superstore, Selfridges, decorated their numerous floors like Bollywood actress' bordellos in the spring of 2002.

---

[10] It is not as if globalisation is a contemporary phenomenon which some of the literature leads one to believe: for instance, Uberoi talks about the 1990s as 'the age of globalisation' (1998: 331). Rather, in a formerly colonised country such as the subcontinent, globalisation has a discrepant yet phenomenal trajectory characterised by changing contours of trade, political rule and alliances, and cultural encounters. On theoretical arguments about the contemporary, diverse and fragmented nature of globalisation, see Appadurai (1990). On arguments about earlier manifestations of world systems and globalisation, see Wallerstein (1983) and Robertson (1992) respectively.

Figure 1.1
Selfridges shop window, London, 2002
Source: Photograph courtesy Raminder Kaur.

Andrew Lloyd Webber decided that it was time that London's West End looked East with the production of *Bombay Dreams* (2002)—a Bollywood extravaganza previously attempted by the London-based theatre group, Tamasha with their stage production of *Hum Aapke Hain Koun...!* (*Who am I to You...,*) in 1999 called *Four Weddings, Forty Songs and a Funeral*. Bollywood production crew trips overseas for song shoots are becoming more the norm than the exception.[11] Film enthusiasts are quick to point out how audiences abroad have even revived the flagging interest of Indian-based audiences in particular films. This was the case with *Dil Se* (*From the Heart*, dir. Mani Ratnam, 1998), the first Bollywood movie to hit the top 10 British films list (see Kaur, this volume), and *Taal* (dir. Subhash Ghai, 2000) which featured in the US top 20. Institutions such as London's Victoria and Albert Museum, for the first time, presented Bollywood posters in their exhibition, *Cinema India: The Art of Bollywood* as collectors' items, corresponding with the phenomenal rise in value of

[11] Some have set up their own offices abroad to handle overseas distribution, a notable case being Yashraj Films established in London and New York in the late 1990s (see Dwyer, 2000: 147).

this once disposable art form.[12] And, trailing the contours of popular culture, academic courses on Indian cinema have sprung up with a vengeance since the 1990s.

Such a scenario is a far cry from the earlier decades. Rosie Thomas comments on the curiously mixed reception of the classic film, *Mother India*, by western audiences in the 1950s. If taken seriously at all, the film was subjected to criticism according to the canons of western realism. She goes on to argue:

> Western critics are perhaps not completely to blame, for they take their cues from the Indian upper-middle class intelligentsia and government cultural bodies, who have a long tradition of conniving at this denunciation and, somewhat ironically, themselves insist on evaluating the popular films according to the canons of European and Hollywood film-making (Thomas, 1985: 118).

For India's various diasporas, however, connections with Indian cinema replaced its incomprehension (see Brosius, Halstead, Hansen and Kaur, in this volume). Historically, the mass migrations from the subcontinent during the post-World War II years paved the way for subsequent cultural flows between East and West, South and North. The Asian presence in various outposts around the world slowly began to acquire a new public profile; one that was distinct from the monocultural conditions of the workplace in those countries. Hindi films were (and still are) an important element of this diasporic South Asian public culture. Their consumption by an eager diaspora helped sustain a link with 'the old country', however much it was predicated on fantasy and modified by contingent realities. Meanwhile, their redemptive narratives offered a useful caveat to their embattled audiences who, in everyday life, struggled under the twin yoke of workplace discrimination and old-country expectations.

However, this is not to posit the diasporic reception as simply a post-Independence phenomenon. Even in the past, South Asians travelling to USA, Canada and England to study, work, or as tourists have been keen spectators of films relating to India, whether produced in India or the West (Chowdhry, 2000: 21). Outposts where indentured labourers were sent, such as Fiji (Mishra, 2002: ix–xxiii), Mauritius, Guyana and countries in southern and eastern Africa were more substantial sites of

---

[12] See the accompanying book, *Cinema India: The Visual Culture of Hindi Film* (Dwyer and Patel, 2002).

emergent Bollywood film cultures (see Hansen and Halstead, this volume). N.L. Rangia, writing on his trip to the Far East in 1931, provides a remarkable insight into the many problems that tended Indian film distribution abroad in its early years:

> Before my arrival, there were already three pictures in Strait Settlements. The first one, a Telegu talkie, *Prahlad*, which was shown not with much success; the second one was *Raja Harishchandra* (Tamil); and the third was *Nurjehan*, a silent film. At that time the Tamil talkie was being shown at Penang. Scenting [sic] my presence with films in S.S. one of these two distributors despatched his silent film to Java lest I might reach Dutch East Indies with Indian pictures for the first time [...] In Federated Malay State, there were very few wired theatres, and that is why it was not possible for me to go there with my talkie .... Indians in S.S. and F.M.S. were really glad to see Indian films and several Indian gentlemen called on me to get some idea of the cinema business and to interest themselves in motion picture exhibition. Most of the cine theatres were under the Chinese .... These Chinese people would not agree to give more than two days for exhibition with difficulty. I secured three days in mid-week (Rangia, *Filmland*, 17 November 1934).

The travel of films and film personnel to diasporic outposts draws attention to Indian film's global reach. It is well known that non-Indian populations in numerous other parts of the world, extending from Latin America to Africa and the Middle East, the former USSR and even China, also cheered and applauded popular Indian cinema throughout the twentieth century. Whether it be for its sheer spectacle, action stunts, beautiful people, poignant songs, or perhaps the anti-Hollywood stance, Bollywood cinema has left more than a mere mark in cinematic history—a subject that has received scant attention in the existing literature, excepting occasional reflective comments. For instance, Yves Thoraval (2000: ix) reveals some intriguing vignettes in his reminiscences:

> Later, I lived in Cairo during the early '70s, in order to gather material for my thesis on the history of Egyptian cinema, and was able to enjoy the pleasures of forgetting everything, as I immersed myself in the music and dances of 'made in Bombay' films, which were shown in halls in the city centre, a kind of 'mini-Broadway'. Commercial Indian cinema has had a marked influence on Egyptian cinema, and during

the International Film Festival held in Cairo in 1991, the presence of the Hindi film superstar Amitabh Bachchan caused riots and then police had to be called in to control the crowds [....]

Moreover, during my travels of the last three decades, to places as diverse as Iran, the Maghreb, Indonesia, Salalah in Oman, or Mukalla in South Yemen—where the film was projected on a concrete wall withered away by salt from the nearby Indian ocean—or Kassala in Sudan, Asmara in Eritrea, Uzbekistan, Cambodia, or Syria—how many evenings, which would otherwise have passed idly, were enlivened by an open air screening of a 'B' grade Indian film? For, these countries were for a long time 'missionary post' territories for the Indian cinema industry ...!

Brian Larkin's study of how the Hindi film was received by the Hausa people in Nigeria provides further perspective. Indian films began to be distributed in the country in the 1950s, and:

> [t]o this day, stickers of Indian films and stars decorate the taxis and buses of the north, posters of Indian films adorn the walls of tailors' shops and mechanics' garages, and love songs from Indian film songs are borrowed by religious singers who change the words to sing praises to the Prophet Mohammed (Larkin, 1997: 406).

As with other countries in the Middle East, and the pre-glasnost Eastern bloc, Indian films provided an alternative to what is overwhelmingly seen as the oversexed and individualistic premises of Hollywood movies. By engaging with Indian films, Hausa youth could rework Indian films within their own culture 'without engaging with the heavy ideological load of "becoming Western"' (ibid.: 410).[13]

Such fascinating insights into a globalised cultural economy of Indian film through distribution, migration, and localisation, are emerging only recently as legitimate subjects of academic research.[14] This volume synthesises some of that research and investigates Indian commercial cinema

[13] See also Larkin's chapter in this volume on the influence of Hindi cinema on Hausa popular culture.

[14] To make up for their former paucity, a spate of growing literature on Indian cinema has become available in the last few decades, including biographies of key film-makers, such as on Guru Dutt, Yash Chopra (see Kabir in references); accounts of significant films such as *Awara* (*The Vagabond*, dir. Raj Kapoor, 1951), *Sholay* (*Flames*, dir. Ramesh Sippy, 1975) and *Mother India*; overviews of themes and narratives (for example,

with what might be described as a compound lens—exploring not just its distributive and consumptive networks, but also the kaleidoscope of inspirations and aspirations of cinema for its Indian makers and viewers who have been participating from the very beginning in complex regional, national and global networks described by the contributors to this volume.

Tracking Bollywood Cinema and its Networks[15]

The meeting between Chaplin and Gandhi might have been a bit of a non sequitir, but it highlights the awkward, sometimes productive convergence of two of the most dominant cultural–political formations of the early twentieth century—the global spread of celluloid and the force of nationalism throughout the formerly colonised states. However, Indian nationalism and the concomitant growth and spread of Indian cinema should be seen both from more regional and more transnational perspectives. To date, too much emphasis has been placed on Bollywood's 'Otherness', in terms of its unique formulae, and its dependency on ritual and mythology (see, for example, Inden, 1999; Kakar, 1980; Mishra, 1985; Nandy, 1999). Much of the literature has also centred on pan-Indian aesthetics drawn from sources such as folk-theatre, folk tales and epics like the Ramayana and Mahabharata. For instance, Vijay Mishra prefers to locate an understanding of popular cinema in the epic texts, folk plays, Parsi theatre and Indian lithographic prints (2002: 4–15). Although recognising Indian cinema's transcultural debts, M. Madhava Prasad dedicates his volume to a cogent study on the nationalist ideologies running through popular cinema: 'I study cinema as an institution that is part of the continuing struggles within India over the forms of the state' (1998: 9). Similarly, Sumita Chakravarty acknowledges 'hybridity [as] a

---

Chatterjee, Dissanayke and Sahai, Mishra, Thomas and Vasudevan); cinema's role in public culture (see Appadurai, Dickey, Dwyer and Pinney, and Nandy); the politics of cinema with regard to state ideology and national identity (for example, Chakravarty, Bharucha and Prasad), historical accounts of cinema (see Barnouw and Krishnaswamy, Chabria, Ganti, and Rangoonwalla); and, essays on cinema in journals such as *Journal of Arts and Ideas* and *Indian International Centre Quarterly*. Articles have also begun to appear discussing the relationship with South Asian diasporas and Bollywood film, but they tend to be predominantly focused on post-1990s phenomena (for example, Gillespie, Inden, Kaur, and Uberoi). See the bibliography for further details.

[15] This was the title of a panel out of which some of the chapters in this volume emerged. It was organised by Ajay Sinha for the Association for Asian Studies meeting in Chicago, 2001.

fact of cinematic life' (1993: 13) but focuses for the large part on how cinema has become the 'sole model of national unity' (ibid.: 310), and how this reveals the ambivalence of nationalism as propagated through film narratives.[16] On a related point, Tejaswini Niranjana (1994, 1995) critiques the Hindu nationalist bias in films such as *Roja* and *Bombay* which purport to be about Hindu–Muslim secular brotherhoods. These studies may well be a reaction to earlier evaluations of popular Indian cinema according to Eurocentric paradigms—as indeed, Chidananda Das Gupta (1991) ends up demonstrating with his standard of cinematic realism—but in doing so they overlook the larger terrain that transcends the indigenous and the national.

We offer a third analytical alternative, namely, to note the interdynamic relationships between the local and the global, the national and the international, and even the national and the intra-national. Our emphasis on networks is designed to draw attention to the audio-visual and cultural economies in which cinema participates, and the flow of representational capital and technologies of production on which it draws. We propose that there are multiple sites of productive economies, linking Bollywood cinema to a broader network of transitional societies as well as diasporic communities. The contributions to this volume explore such networks as they achieve density in particular locations.[17] Our emphasis on tracking (using a cinematic metaphor of camera movement as it follows its subject) suggests attempts to follow, anecdotally, the paths of Bollywood's own movements, and characterise the configurations that emerge at various sites of intersection within a global flow of images.

This volume asks the following questions: how did Indian cinema become a national vehicle and acquire national status? How does its journeys through the rest of the world inflect the imaginings of a nation? A focus on the Indianness of popular film alone is to eclipse the industry's imbrication in modernity/ies, and world history/ies within which modernity

[16] See Banerjea's chapter (this volume) on a reworking of Chakravarty's argument to highlight the transnational elements of the national imaginary. On a related point, Ravi Vasudevan's interests also lie in 'cinema's account of a modern national culture' (1995: 84), but he also goes on to look at the close connections between Hollywood and Indian cinema in the 1940s. This is in terms of filmic conventions, thematic comparisons and also middle-class audiences who were just as likely to watch Hollywood movies as they were Indian ones.

[17] See Kajri Jain's chapter (this volume) for her invocation of Deleuze and Guattari's work to look at nodal concentrations in rhizomatic networks enabling lateral linkages across heterogeneous categories as a paradigm with which to consider the various inspirations and influences on film productions.

might be taken to be: 'a (more-or-less) pliable sign, [drawing]...a multitude of distinct voices into a worldwide conversation, a multilogue' (Comaroff and Comaroff, 1993: viii). This multilogue perspective focuses on the specificities of Indian popular cinema and investigates how Bollywood films came into being and how they are in relation to a wider arena of sources, inspirations and influences. This perspective also focuses on the impact of Bollywood on global audiences themselves. This volume draws upon various fields (including social anthropology, cultural studies, film analysis and art history) in an attempt to provide interrelated modalities of the interpretation of this multifaceted filmic production. The different chapters discuss the tensions between locality, nationality and internationality through the prism of Indian popular films. The aim is not to present nations and their cultures as bounded entities (Wolf, 1982), but to analyse the production and reception of film through its inscription in a mesh of relationships in terms of a transfer of technology, skills, personnel, representative conventions and ideas.

We propose to situate Bollywood within a more interactive worldview, based on a flow of technologies, or what Stephen Greenblatt (1991) has called, in a different context, the reproduction and circulation of mimetic capital. In adapting Karl Marx's idea to representation and mimesis, by capital Greenblatt implies

> a stockpile of representations, a set of images and image-making devices that *accumulated*, or 'banked' in, as it were, archives, collections, and cultural storehouses, until such time as these representations are called upon to generate new representations. Images that matter, that merit the term capital, acquire reproductive power, maintaining and multiplying themselves by transforming cultural contacts into novel and often unexpected forms (ibid.: 6).

Capitalism only provided the enabling condition for the proliferation and circulation of such images in spectacular and global proportions. The significance of Greenblatt's economic view of images for this volume might be that filmic representations are not merely a reflection or product of social relations, but rather social relations themselves, linked to group understandings, hierarchies, and conflicts in other areas of cultures in which they circulate. With the reframing of the problematic, this volume cannot, of course, provide a comprehensive history of every significant episode on this global–national–local landscape. The contributions to this volume only home in on some indicative moments that demarcate prominent changes in the character of globalisation throughout the twentieth century. The contributors have taken complementary, different and even opposing views, generating discussions that we, as editors, have facilitated. The book is divided into three overlapping sections—Topographies, Trans-Actions and Travels. Each of these is discussed in detail ahead.

Topographies

This section concentrates on the globalised audio-visual economies within which the technology and aesthetics of India's commercial cinema developed. This is a period that spans the silent movies from 1913 to the advent of the sound movies or the 'talkies' from 1931 onwards. Despite colonial strictures, transnational liaisons were not uncommon. Rosie Thomas' chapter looks to such relationships with a comparative focus on the actresses—Devika Rani, the demure and beautiful Brahmin woman, and Fearless Nadia (aka Hunterwali), the thigh-slapping adventurer who reigned from the 1930s to the 1950s, 'a Tarzan, Zorro and John Wayne all rolled into one' (Sahai, 2000: 5).[18] Thomas highlights their ambivalent relationship with the nation and the 'outer-nation'. Kajri Jain's chapter takes an emphatically 'biographical' approach to the two pioneers of Indian cinema, D.G. Phalke and Baburao Painter, in order to describe within a shared genealogy, a relay of various visual idioms—painting, print, photography, and theatre—that traverse the regional, national and international in two entirely different ways in an early moment of Indian cinema. Her main point is to situate the specificity of locality in any discussion on transnationalism. Whereas Phalke, situated in Mumbai, represented a high-caste artistic proclivity, Baburao Painter, situated in Kolhapur, was from a lower caste, artisan tradition. Gayatri Chatterjee, in her chapter, explores the dynamic globalised visual culture of performances, paintings, chromolithographs, magazines,

[18] Men too were compared with stars from abroad. Master Vithal, a professional wrestler, styled himself somewhat on Douglas Fairbanks. The latter's *Thief of Baghdad* (1928) was the most popular film of that decade, and with its Arabian ambience it particularly appealed to Muslim viewers (Thomas, 1987: 305). Other adventure films where language was not a deterrent included *The Adventures of Robin Hood, Tarzan, Tarzan and his Mate* and *King Kong* (Chowdhry, 2000: 13–14). Whilst the kind of adventure and comedy provided by the likes of Charlie Chaplin, Buster Keaton and Harold Lloyd movies was lapped up with delight in the subcontinent, Indian actors fulfilled a romance with the 'exotic' abroad. Sheikh Iftekhar Rasool better known as the 'Valentino of the Far East' went to work abroad in 1923, beginning first in Britain, then moving on to France, and eventually, after the success of the Arabian Night extravaganza, *Scheherezade* (1928), Hollywood.

calendars and even board games that reflected the development of early cinema in India. Her analysis leads to a close reading of films themselves. By way of contrast, Shuddhabrata Sengupta's chapter analyses Bollywood films from the point of view of the cameramen, who develop cinematography at the interface of competing aesthetic codes between the 'local' and the 'international', the available technologies, and the political economy of film-making.

Trans-Actions

The dominant theme of this section is to propose that the 'national fantasy' of Indian commercial cinema is an unstable construction, produced by Bollywood narratives and recycled within a globalised world. The chapters in this section do not study film as national texts, as might be evident in a difference between Prasad's (1998) and Koushik Banerjea's (in this volume) treatments of Amitabh Bachchan action movies. Prasad sees in these films a 'moment of disaggregation' within India's own cultural politics. Banerjea, in contrast, treats them and their fantasy of angry underclass, as a local adaptation of internationalised action films from Hong Kong, Europe and the US. In other words, if Prasad studies these films as texts in their national context, Banerjea studies these films as local, intertextual, manifestations of globalisation.

The other chapters in this section also do the same by folding the national fantasy of Indian cinema into a globalised world. The role of women is particularly pertinent for epitomising much of the contradictions surrounding nationhood and foreignness, and the moral (yet vicariously desirable) and immoral woman. Geetanjali Gangoli explores the relationship of women in film to notions of cultural propriety and nationhood. With an analysis of films from the last five decades, she notes how the equation of woman as nation, as scholars such as Ravi Vasudevan (1995: 99) propose, is too reductive. Instead, she examines its supposed antithesis, the 'vamp'. The category can be seen in at least three discrete yet connected ways: the vamp as Anglo-Asian; the vamp as marginal Indian, yet westernised; and, the vamp as a metaphor represented in the body of the contemporary heroine yet carrying an Indian 'soul'.

This section concludes with Sudhanva Deshpande's focus on cinema of the 1990s, noting the change of characterisations, plots and aesthetics that have characterised post-liberalisation cinema in a media-saturated world. The developments reflect not only technological availability, but also the changing aspirations of film-makers with the production of family romances such as *Maine Pyar Kya* (*I Have Fallen in Love*, dir. Sooraj R. Barjatya, 1989), *Hum Aapke Hain Koun...!* (dir. Sooraj R. Barjatya, 1994), *Dilwale Dulhania Le Jayenge* (*The Brave Heart Will Take the Bride*, dir. Aditya Chopra, 1995) and *Kuch Kuch Hota Hai* (*Something or Other is Happening*, dir. Karan Johar, 1998) to meet a new 'imagined' global audience consisting of diasporic communities and a growing pool of mainstream audiences in the West. The plethora of movies vindicate Ashok Banker's observations that: 'The new consumer boom has turned the country into one enormous Mall...yet there was an even greater longing for all things ethnic and traditional' (2001: 74). Whilst the ornamental gloss of consumption is craved, 'traditional' values based on family honour and female chastity appear to remain intact.

Travels

This final section of the volume maps, more fully, the effects of contemporary globalisation—this time following the desires and demands of both international capitalism as well as India's diasporic populations. This is in context of the end of the Cold War, the breakdown of the former Soviet empire, increased economic liberalisation, the institutionalisation of multiculturalism, particularly in the European countries, and the stronger voice of migrant Indian populations across the world. Allied to this is the wider audio-visual grammar available to the Indian middle classes via satellite and cable television and the more feasible prospect of foreign tourism, which has become increasingly affordable—some of which is also funded by diasporic relatives.

The chapters in this section focus on the reception of Indian cinema in the 1990s with ethnographic case studies based in Germany, Guyana, USA, South Africa, Nigeria and Britain. Overall, they shift attention from the technologies of cinematic production to the sites of reception. Christiane Brosius attends to the dynamics of identification and fantasy amongst diasporic Asians in Frankfurt, Germany who either retail or watch Indian videos. This is compared with an analysis of Internet users' commentaries on popular Indian cinema. In her chapter, Narmala Halstead takes a 'twice-migration' focus with a consideration of Indian film reception in Guyana and in New York amongst Guyanese Indians. She concentrates on the imaginings of India as conveyed by Bollywood and its ambivalent incorporation into diasporic identities and values such as 'shame' and 'respect'. This is in the context of a wider diet of English-language films and television programmes.

Thomas Blom Hansen's chapter considers the unprecedented popularity of *Kuch Kuch Hota Hai* amongst Durban-based Indians in post-apartheid

South Africa. The film's impact is discussed in relation to the new forms of identities that Indians in South Africa are forging in the public sphere, in the midst of a precarious tension between the 'gaze of the other'—the white culture which is considered the mainstream norm—and the black majority which is seen as threatening. Whereas Hansen reports that Indian cinema is not avidly consumed by the black populations in South Africa, Brian Larkin's chapter presents a contrasting scenario—the mass popularity of Indian cinema amongst the Nigerian Hausa people. He looks at the mediation of popular Indian cinema and its influence on Sufi songs available amongst the Hausa and considers how this informs a debate about morals and modernity. Finally, with the example of the film *Dilwale Dulhania Le Jayenge* (*The Bold will take away the Bride*), Raminder Kaur demonstrates that audience reception in England is not as straightforward as Bollywood producers and film enthusiasts might assume: here film ratings and audience numbers are too hastily translated into a discourse on NRI (Non-Resident Indian) nostalgia. She then goes on to describe how popular Indian cinema has monopolised the images of the diasporic Indian, such that films and representations in general made by those very diasporic Indians now appear 'inauthentic'.

Tales of Fantasies

I've been interested in Bollywood films for years .... It's the fairy story thing. We see a lot of blood and car chases here. Bollywood is bigger than Hollywood. I always thought as a kid may be if they made Bollywood movies with a blend of Indian, American and British stars, then you've got the world.

Interview with British actor Ray Winstone on The Kumars at No. 42, *BBC2, 2002*.

The spectacle of cinema is unsurpassable. It provides pleasure to various sections of the population—all hues, cultures, languages and classes. Many non-Indians have also flirted with the notion of becoming an 'Indian star', that is, making it in Bollywood.[19] Throughout its history, white people have always figured in Indian cinematic scapes—at airports, in wild clubs or simply as decorative wallflowers. But rather than play ciphers of privilege

[19] See also the fictional works by Luke Jennings (1993), Clive James (1996) and Justine Hardy (2002) inspired by the Indian film industry, and Chris England's (2002) autobiographical work based on his experiences as part of the *Lagaan* cast.

and lax morals, they are increasingly coming to the fore as providers of entertainment, whether it be as dancers or as characters with or without speaking parts. With the success of *Lagaan*, the English actress Rachel Shelley has become an 'exotic' fair beauty for many a red-blooded Indian male, and it looks as though Sophie Dahl is also set to do the same with her acting debut in a Bollywood film titled *The King of Bollywood* (dir. Piyush Jha, 2004). Other non-Indian actors too have tried their luck in the industry, most often in retrospective nationalist films about the colonial era. Indeed, hundreds of westerners choose to stand in long queues hoping to be picked up for the next blockbuster, particularly in Bombay's traveller ghetto, Colaba, where they are used to add a cosmopolitan flavour to the city's ceaseless celluloid production line.

> Steve, a student from Manchester, came for a day and ended up filming for two weeks: 'I thought I was being hired for a day to hang around in the background', he said, 'but the director said that I should play a soldier. The film was about freedom fighters in the 1930s, so I was a baddie, and I had to say things like, 'Hey you, stop right there,' and 'We've got him, sir, he's hiding in the hut.'
>
> Chris, another English traveller, had spent a day promenading up and down a street set of Victorian Calcutta, dressed in a monocle and bowler hat and accompanied by a woman carrying a caged canary. He had to complement her on the majesty of the bird. 'Taking the piss on film is obviously their revenge for the Raj', he said. (*Guardian Guide*, April 27–May 3, 2002: 9).

However staple the diet and familiar the formula, Bollywood is gradually attracting all kinds of new audiences for various reasons in its continuous quest to monopolise global cinema. The predominance of young lower class males in cinema halls up and down the subcontinent as was the case in the decade of the 'angry young man' no longer applies. Nowadays one is likely to see families driving into the multiplexes in their flashy BMWs, or studious conference-goers and curious travellers trying to get to the bottom (and indeed, the top) of Indian cinema.[20] But this is not just to

[20] Scholarship shows the cultural politics of the new global 'attraction' of Bollywood. Examples include Patricia Uberoi's (2003) analysis of *Hum Aapke Hain Koun...!* which depicts a 'clean' (traditional!) Indian family that marks the advent of a new 'imagined community' of middle class affluence, as opposed to the 'masses' for whom Bollywood films were earlier made. See also Ajay Sinha (2002) for a close reading of the film *Lagaan*

blandly celebrate such universalising currents as a happy-clappy indication of transcultural rapprochement, but also to enquire into the premises that have led to the changing role, status and relationships of Indian popular cinema with various constituencies throughout the last century.

References

APPADURAI, A. 1990. 'Disjuncture and Difference in the Global Cultural Economy', in M. Featherstone (ed.), *Global Culture*. London: Sage Publications.

BANDYOPADHYAY, S. (ed.). 1993. *Indian Cinema: Contemporary Perspectives from the Thirties*. Jamshedpur: Celluloid Chapter.

BANKER, ASHOK. 2001. *Bollywood*. Herts: Pocket Essentials.

BARNOUW, E. and S. KRISHNASWAMY. 1980. *Indian Film*. New York: OUP.

BHARUCHA, R. 1994. 'On the Border of Fascim: Manufacture of Consent in *Roja*', *Economic and Political Weekly*, 4 June, pp. 1389–95.

CHABRIA, S. (ed.). 1994. *Light of Asia: Indian Silent Cinema, 1912–34*, New Delhi: Wiley Eastern.

CHAKRAVARTY, S. 1993. *National Identity in Indian Popular Cinema, 1947–87*. Austin: University of Texas Press.

CHATTERJEE, GAYATRI. 2002. *Mother India*. London: BFI.

CHATTERJEE, PARTHA. 1986. *Nationalist Thought and the Colonial World: A Derivative Discourse?* London: Zed Books.

CHOWDHRY, PREM. 2000. *Colonial India and the Making of Empire Cinema: Image, Ideology and Identity*. Manchester: Manchester University Press.

COMAROFF, JOHN and JEAN COMAROFF (eds). 1993. *Modernity and its Malcontents*. Chicago: The University of Chicago Press.

DAS GUPTA, C. 1991. *The Painted Face: Studies in India's Popular Cinema*. New Delhi: Roli Books.

DAS SHARMA. 1993. 'Indian Cinema and the National Leadership', in Samik Bandyopadhyay (ed.), *Indian Cinema: Contemporary Perspectives from the Thirties*, pp. 135–40, Jamshedpur: Celluloid Chapter.

DICKEY, S. 1993. *Cinema and the Urban Poor in South India*. Cambridge: Cambridge University Press.

DISSAYANAKE, W. and M. SAHAI. 1992. *Sholay: A Cultural Reading*. New Delhi: Wiley Eastern.

DWYER, RACHEL. 2000. *All You Want is Money, All You Need is Love: Sexuality and Romance in Modern India*. London: Cassell.

DWYER, RACHEL and CHRISTOPHER PINNEY. (eds). 2000. *Pleasure and the Nation: The Politics and Consumption of Popular Culture in India*. New Delhi: OUP.

DWYER, RACHEL and DIVYA PATEL. 2002. *Cinema India: The Visual Culture of Hindi Film*. New Brunswick, N.J.: Rutgers University Press.

ENGLAND, CHRIS. 2002. *Balham to Bollywood*. London: Hodder and Stoughton.

---

for a complicity, achieved 'visually', between Bollywood and the affluent, globalised, middle-class consumers of cricket.

Gandhy, Behroze and Rosie Thomas. 1991. 'Three Indian Films Stars', in Christine Gledhill (ed.), *Stardom: Industry of Desire*. London: Routledge.
Ganti, Tejaswini. 2004. *Bollywood: A Guidebook to Popular Hindi Cinema*. New York: Routledge.
Gillespie, Marie. 1995. *Television, Ethnicity and Cultural Change*. London: Routledge.
Greenblatt, Stephen. 1991. *Marvellous Possessions: The Wonder of the New World*. Oxford: OUP.
Hall, Stuart. 1992. 'The West and the Rest: Discourse and Power', in Stuart Hall and G. Bram (eds), *Formations of Modernity*. Cambridge: Polity Press.
Hansen, Thomas Blom. 1996. 'Recuperating Masculinity: Hindu Nationalism, Violence and the Exorcism of the Muslim "Other"', *Critique of Anthropology*, 16(2): 137–72.
Hardy, Justine. 2002. *Bollywood Boy*. London: John Murray.
Hughes, Stephen Putnam. 1996. *Is There Anyone Out There? Exhibition and the Formation of Silent Film Audiences in South India*. Ph.D., Department of Anthropology, Chicago, Illinois.
Inden, R. 1999. 'Transnational Class, Erotic Arcadias and Commercial Utopia in Hindi Films', in Christiane Brosius and Melissa Butcher (eds), *Image Journeys: Audio-Visual Media and Cultural Change in India*, pp. 41–66, New Delhi: Sage Publications.
James, Clive. 1996. *The Silver Castle*. London: Jonathan Cape.
Jennings, Luke. 1993. *Breach Candy*. London: Hutchinson.
Kabir, N.M. 1996a. *Talking Films: Conversations on Hindi Cinema with Javed Akhtar*. New Delhi: OUP.
———. 1996b. *Guru Dutt: A Life in Cinema*. New Delhi: OUP.
Kakar, S. 1980. 'The Ties that Bind: Family Relationships in the Mythology of Hindi Cinema', *India International Centre Quarterly*, 8(1).
Larkin, Brian. 1997. 'Indian Films and Nigerian Lovers: Media and the Creation of Parallel Modernities', *Africa*, 67, pp. 406–40.
Mazzarella, William. 2004. *Shovelling Smoke: Advertising and Globalisation in Contemporary India*. Durham: Duke University Press.
Mishra, V. 1985. 'Towards a Theoretical Critique of Bombay Cinema', *Screen*, 26(3&4), pp. 133–46.
———. 2002. *Bollywood Cinema: Temples of Desire*. London: Routledge.
Nandy, A. (ed.). 1999. *Secret Politics of Our Desires: Innocence, Culpability and Indian Popular Cinema*. New Delhi: OUP.
Niranjana, Tejaswini. 1994. 'Integrating Whose Nation? Tourists and Terrorists in *Roja*', *Economic and Political Weekly*, January 15: 79–82.
———. 1995. 'Banning 'Bombay': Nationalism, Communalism and Gender', *Economic and Political Weekly*, June 3: 1291–92.
Prasad, M.M. 1998. *Ideology of the Hindi Film: A Historical Construction*. New Delhi: OUP.
Rangia, N.L. 1934. 'Indian Films in the Far East', *Film Land*, 17 November, in Samik Bandyopadhyay (ed.), *Contemporary Perceptions from the Thirties*, pp. 129–32, Jamshedpur: Celluloid Chapter.
Reè, J. 1992. 'Internationality', *Radical Philosophy*, 60: 3–11.
Robertson, R. 1992. *Globalization*. London: Sage Publications.
Sahai, Malti. 2000. *Bollywood Nostalgia*. New Delhi: Roli Books.
Sinha, Ajay. 2002. 'Fascist Aesthetics in Bollywood Cinema: Case of *Lagaan*,' Paper presented at the 31st Annual South Asia Conference, Madison, Wisconsin, October.
Thomas, R. 1985. 'Indian Cinema: Pleasures and Popularity', *Screen*, 26(3&4): 116–31.

Thomas, R. 1987. 'Mythologies and Modern India', in William Luhr (ed.), *World Cinema since 1945*, pp. 301–29, New York: Ungar Publication Co.

———. 1990. 'Sanctity and Scandal: The Mythologisation of *Mother India*', in M. Binford (ed.), *Quarterly Review of Film and Video, Special Issue on Indian Popular Cinema*, pp. 11–30.

Thoraval, Yves. 2000. *The Cinemas of India (1896–2000)*. New Delhi: Macmillan.

Uberoi, Patricia. 1998. 'The Diaspora Comes Home: Disciplining Desire in DDLJ', *Contributions to Indian Sociology*, 32(2): 305–36.

———. 2003. 'Imagining the Family: An Ethnography of Viewing *Hum Aapke Hain Kaun...!*' in Pinney and Dwyer (eds), *Pleasure and the Nation*, pp. 309–51, New Delhi: OUP.

Vasudevan, Ravi. 1995. '"You Cannot Live in Society—and Ignore it": Nationhood and Female Modernity in *Andaz*', *Contributions to Indian Sociology*, 29(1&2), pp. 83–108.

———. (ed.). 2000. *Making Meaning in Indian Cinema*. New Delhi: OUP.

Wallerstein, I. 1983. *Historical Capitalism*. London: Verso.

Wolf, E. 1982. *Europe and the People Without History*. Berkeley: University of California.

Part I

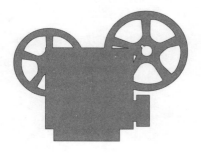

Topographies

2

Not Quite (Pearl) White: Fearless Nadia, Queen of the Stunts

ROSIE THOMAS

It was June 1935, on a dark monsoon-lashed Bombay night that J.B.H. Wadia was taking one of the biggest gambles of his film production career. His new venture, *Hunterwali* (*Woman with the Whip*, dir. Homi Wadia, 1935), was premiering at the Super Cinema in downtown Grant Road. The film had been an unprecedented six months in the making and cost more than Rs 80,000 but no distributor had come forward to buy it. Rumours in the industry suggested it was a turkey: the film starred a large blonde-haired muscle woman with fearsome fighting skills who thrashed Indian men into the ground—on the face of it an unlikely proposition for Indian audiences at the height of the nationalist movement. J.B.H. and his partners had been reduced to pooling their own resources to secure a release. Extravagant pre-publicity had reeled in the crowds for the opening night. It was now down to their new star, Fearless Nadia, aka Mary Evans, in her role as a masked avenging angel, to deliver the goods. Playing a swashbuckling princess in disguise, she roamed the countryside on horseback sporting hot pants, big breasts and bare white thighs and, when she wasn't

---

The author, in this chapter, has referred to Mumbai, Kolkata and Chennai by their former names—Bombay, Calcutta and Madras.

swinging from chandeliers, kicking or whipping men, she was righting wrongs with her bare fists and an imperious scowl. By the time Nadia hitched up her sari and cracked her whip in the third reel, declaring: '*Aaj se main Hunterwali hoon*'[1] the audience was cheering. Within days the Wadias knew they were sitting on a goldmine: the film ran to packed houses for more than 25 weeks and became the major money-spinner of the year. Fearless Nadia became a sensation across the country and unofficial merchandising followed: Fearless Nadia whips, belts, matchboxes and playing cards appeared and her famous yell '*hey-y-y*' became a catch phrase (see Figure 2.1). Nadia went on to secure a reputation as one of the biggest female stars of the Indian screen of the 1930s and early 1940s.

In the same year, just outside Bombay in rural Malad, an urbane Brahmin beauty, Devika Rani, and her charismatic husband, producer Himansu Rai, were launching a visionary new studio enterprise, Bombay Talkies. Already the toast of London high society for her debut as a glamorous oriental princess in Rai's Anglo-Indian co-production, *Karma* (*Fate,* dir. J.L. Freer-Hunt, 1933), Devika Rani quickly established her own and Bombay Talkies' reputation at home with the phenomenal box-office and critical success of *Achhut Kanya* (*Untouchable Girl,* dir. Franz Osten, 1936). This premiere was a grand affair at Bombay's Roxy Cinema, boasting a glittering cosmopolitan audience which, legend has it, included Nehru. Devika Rani's role as a doe-eyed tragic heroine, an untouchable village belle trapped in a doomed romance, was seen as a social comment on caste iniquities, establishing her as a major icon of Indian cinema and the other top female star of the era.

The two women could scarcely have been more different: where Nadia was big, buxom, blonde and blue-eyed, a white-skinned former circus artiste, who had been the darling of the soldiers in the north-west frontier, Devika Rani was a conventional Indian beauty. Petite, almost childlike, with long dark hair and large velvety brown eyes, she was upper class and upper-caste, educated at South Hampstead High School and Royal Academy of Dramatic Arts (RADA), and widely known to be a grandniece of Tagore. While Nadia and her director (later to be her husband), Homi Wadia, moved in the world of Bombay clubs and horse-racing, and openly admired and adapted the popular comic book fare of Hollywood action serials and comedies, Devika Rani and her husband and director, Himansu Rai, moved amongst the European cosmopolitan elite, learning their craft at Berlin's UFA studios and drawing their inspiration—and many of their

[1] Trans. 'From today I am [to be known as] the woman with the whip.'

Figure 2.1
Fearless Nadia: Booklet cover from *Lootaru Lalna* (1938)
Source: Wadia Movietone Pvt. Ltd.

technicians—from German cinema. Where Devika Rani was the aristocrat who made her screen reputation through playing an outcaste, Nadia was the outcaste who played the princess. The two star personae—neither of them the most likely of nationalist icons and both of them speaking poor Hindi—are in interesting ways inversions of each other. In examining the late colonial period, we might see the two as complementary exotic fictions, speaking to the project of defining Indianness whilst simultaneously exploding the idea of Indian cinema as isolated from the rest of the world.

Nadia, in her heyday, was the queen of the box office. It was, however, Devika Rani who became 'the first lady' of Indian cinema, celebrated by the critics and fêted throughout Europe. Until recently Devika Rani dominated the histories of Indian cinema of this period as the embodiment of good, serious and patriotic cinema, her films seminal in establishing the genre of Indian film melodrama.[2] Nadia, despite her extraordinary popularity with the mass audience, both in India and throughout the diasporic distribution networks of South East Asia, the Middle East, the Caribbean and Africa, was virtually unknown in Europe or America and had been largely erased from official Indian cinema histories until recent years.[3] However, following her death in 1996, and fuelled by the 2002 Bollywood boom, interest in Nadia is growing. A Hollywood bio-pic is in development, collections of postcards of her film posters are on sale and her films are being digitally remastered and sold to international television and archives. Meanwhile, Devika Rani has, for the time being, largely disappeared from view—relegated to a dusty pedestal within the hall of fame of Indian cinema history.

Focusing on the intriguing figure of Fearless Nadia, this chapter explores the construction of one form of modern Indian femininity in the late colonial period, examining Nadia within the film production context of 1930s Bombay and, in passing, drawing comparisons with her shadow persona, Devika Rani. It asks why Nadia was chosen by the Wadias and why she was so popular with her contemporary audiences, in particular, and how the Wadia brothers dealt with her whiteness/Otherness and negotiated the points of tension in her image, especially in the context of the nationalist movement. It asks to what extent she simply 'copied' Hollywood stunt stars such as Pearl White and how these role models were 'Indianised'. It also considers why Nadia became so peripheral to later histories of Indian cinema and why the Wadias' films were given so little status, particularly in

[2] See, for example, Mishra (2002: 17–18).

[3] Barnouw and Krishnaswamy (1980: 110), for many years the key authoritative work on Indian cinema, made no reference to Nadia at all, despite a brief mention of *Hunterwali*. Mishra et al. (1989: 52), also fail to mention Nadia in their list of Indian imitators of Hollywood stunt stars and then proceed to claim, somewhat contentiously, that the imitations of Hollywood '*never really produced a star as text*'.

relation to studios such as Bombay Talkies. Finally, it speculates about why Nadia seems so interesting to us now and, paradoxically, so contemporary.

The chapter begins with a brief history of the Wadia studios and the interests and aspirations of the brothers themselves, set within the context of early cinema and the nationalist movement. It moves on to examine the Nadia persona in greater depth, arguing that the films produce her as a modern Indian woman through a complex process which refers to Hollywood (not quite Pearl White), cosmopolitan Indian modernity, and the warrior women of India's *virangana* tradition. The argument is illustrated though the examination of her classic *Diamond Queen* (dir. Homi Wadia, 1940). Finally, the Wadias' oeuvre is considered in the context of debates on mimicry and nationalism and it is suggested that, given their eclectic vision of Indian modernity, J.B.H. Wadia's lifelong quest for respectability was inherently doomed within the framework of mainstream nationalist discourse. However, the hybridity and playful impersonations of the Wadia brothers' films were major factors in their contemporary success and are what, today, reverberates—for better or for worse—with global popular culture.

Early Years of Indian Cinema

It has been well documented that the arena of Indian cinema in the early decades of the century boasted very real exchanges between Bombay and the cinemas of both Hollywood and Europe.[4] Indian audiences had been exposed to Hollywood from the earliest years: the stunt and action films and serials of stars such as Pearl White, Ruth Roland, Charlie Chaplin, Eddie Polo, Douglas Fairbanks ran to full houses throughout the 1920s, when four out of five films screened were foreign and Douglas Fairbanks' *Thief of Baghdad* (dir. Raoul Walsh, 1924) was the decade's most popular film. Hollywood stars—including Fairbanks—visited Bombay and producers such as Ardeshir Irani forged their own links with Hollywood personnel.[5]

---

[4] *The Report of the Indian Cinematograph Committee, 1927–28*, together with its four volumes of evidence, gives a rich flavour of this era. For summaries of this material see Barnouw and Krishnaswamy (1980: 39–58) and Chowdhry (2000: 13–21).

[5] Hollywood technicians were in Bombay years before sound arrived. See diaries of Harold Sintzenich, one of D.W. Griffith's cameramen, posted in Bombay between 1928 and 1930 by Eastman Kodak to advise local talent on modern film and processing techniques (Barnouw, 1980: 102). See also Sengupta, this volume.

Phalke's vision of producing the first Indian feature film was famously inspired by a viewing of *The Life of Christ* and a desire to promote Indian religion and culture. Rajadhyaksha has documented how, in doing this, Phalke established the template for a nationalist aesthetic (1980: 20–67). Alongside the Hollywood influences, a parallel stream was fed by European cinema. Phalke himself made three trips to Europe and, between 1922 and 1924, Himansu Rai trained with Pabst and Pommer at Germany's most prestigious studio, UFA. Rai later brought his bride-to-be, Devika Rani, to Berlin in order for her to begin her own art direction apprenticeship, working first as Marlene Dietrich's make-up assistant and later attending acting master-classes under Pabst. In 1933, after a successful run of Indo-European co-productions, Rai decided they should return to India. They brought with them a cohort of German technicians, including Franz Osten and Joseph Wirsching, to work at Bombay Talkies and train the local talent. Inspired by the ideals of the nationalist movement to bring international glory to India's heritage and build a world-class film industry, Rai told Devika: 'Let us learn from these people, but let us put the knowledge to work in our country.'[6]

Throughout the years, Indian cinema has shown a remarkable resistance to Hollywood cultural imperialism. Since it could build its own distribution networks capable of sustaining the industry—within India and throughout much of Asia, the Middle East and Africa—its conventions could develop without conforming to the expectations of wider international audiences. Gradually, a form evolved which combined borrowings from world cinema with a range of other cultural influences: traditional entertainment forms, notably village dramatisations of the mythological epics and also, more directly, urban nineteenth- and twentieth-century Urdu Parsee theatre which itself adapted Shakespeare and Victorian melodrama. Whilst most film-makers have openly borrowed some elements from Hollywood and elsewhere, successful films always 'Indianised' such borrowings through integration within what evolved as Indian conventions (Thomas, 1985, 1995). The Wadias' films exemplify this process.

[6] Information on Devika Rani draws primarily on a January 1989 interview with the author. This quotation also appears in Barnouw and Krishnaswamy (1980: 98).

Wadia Brothers

Beginnings

Like many young men growing up in the early decades of the twentieth century, the brothers Jamshed and Homi Wadia were avid movie fans, eagerly consuming the Hollywood westerns, comedies, stunt films and serials which ran to packed houses across the subcontinent.[7] In 1926, aged 25, Jamshed (widely known and referred to as J.B.H.) scandalised his respectable Parsee family, master shipbuilders to the East India Company, by throwing up a promising career in law and banking to become a freelance writer and director for the silent movies. Homi, 10 years his junior, soon joined him, working first as his assistant at the Devare Film Laboratory at Kohinoor Studios, then as his 'trusted lieutenant' and partner in Wadia Brothers' Productions, perfecting his camera and editing skills and soon directing his first silent film, *Diler Daku* (*Thunderbolt*, dir. Homi Wadia, 1931).

Between them the Wadia brothers showed remarkable populist flair and a run of successful silent films, all written by J.B.H., proved that big money could be made in the movies. The release of *Alam Ara* (*Beauty of the World*, dir. Ardeshir Irani, 1931), India's first sound film, caused some panic amongst other Bombay producers but J.B.H. quickly linked up with Parsee entrepreneurs and industrialists—M.B. Billimoria and the Tatas—who offered to set him up with his own studios and a distribution office for both Indian and foreign films. Wadia Movietone was launched in 1933.

Their first sound film, *Lal e Yaman* (*Ruby of Yemen*, dir. J.B.H. Wadia, 1933), was a melodramatic Arabian fantasy, a musical which drew its storyline and visual style from Parsee theatre: J.B.H. had shrewdly invested in the talent of Joseph David, the acclaimed theatre director who had written *Alam Ara*. The film was a major hit and on the proceeds of this and other early successes Wadia Movietone was soon able to build impressive studios in the well-heeled Parel area of Bombay, in the grounds of the Wadias' ancestral home, Lovji Castle. This became a major business

[7] Information on the early days of the Wadias draws on J.B.H. Wadia's own writings (1955, 1980a, 1980b), the author's 1986 interview with Homi Wadia, the documentary *Fearless: The Hunterwali Story* (prod./dir. Riyad Vinci Wadia, 1993), Riyad Wadia's unpublished 1994 research dossier, together with other papers he kindly provided.

enterprise, run along factory lines, which by the mid-1930s had around 600 people on the payroll, ranging from carpenters and cleaners to its top stars. Homi, reminiscing, described the discipline as 'like a school': when the ten o'clock bell rang, stars clocked in along with everyone else and a register was called to check for absences. Those not needed on set would rehearse or go home or, in the case of the stunt artistes, work out in the studio gym. Studio production specialised in comedy, stunt and action films, and orientalist fantasies.

As one of the top studios in town, J.B.H. made sure it was on the itinerary of visiting VIPs, and a stream of Hollywood producers, directors, technicians and stars came to meet him. When his boyhood hero Douglas Fairbanks hit Bombay, J.B.H. gave him a royal welcome. The visit was so successful that Fairbanks agreed to sell the Indian distribution rights of his evergreen 1920 hit, *Mark of Zorro*, to Wadia Movietone's distribution arm. J.B.H. knew the movie well. He had already adapted it for Indian audiences in the silent era as *Diler Daku*. Shortly afterwards he had reworked it again, this time with a swashbuckling female lead for the studio's 'beautiful and doll-like' Bengali star, Padma, resplendent in mask and sword in the film *Dilruba Daku* (*The Amazon*, dir. A.H. Essa, 1933).

When Nadia arrived in Bombay in 1934, the studio was buzzing. Foreign dignitaries were welcome guests and J.B.H. openly acknowledged the influence of Hollywood film-makers, but the studio also prided itself on its home-grown talent: local musicians, theatre writers and self-taught film technicians. The ambience fitted well with Nadia's own culturally heterogeneous background.

Nadia had been born Mary Evans in Perth in 1908[8] to a Greek mother and British father, arriving in India in 1911 with her father's army unit. Following his death on the French battlefields in 1915, her mother, a one-time belly dancer, decided to settle in Bombay where her daughter became a weekly boarder at Claire Road Convent School. In 1922 they joined an uncle, an army vet in Peshawar, and Mary spent an idyllic adolescence learning dancing, horse riding and other outdoor skills from her army friends. She was also an enthusiastic movie fan, enviously enjoying the

[8] Previous articles, including my own, have invariably put her birth date as 1910—a fiction Nadia herself promoted. Information on Nadia's life story is drawn primarily from Nadia herself through conversations and an interview with the author and Behroze Gandhy in February 1986. Additional material is drawn from Karnad (1980) and Riyad Vinci Wadia (1993, 1994) as indicated.

exploits of Pearl White in *Perils of Pauline* and Ruth Roland's *Adventures of Ruth*. Back in Bombay in 1926 with a baby son, Bobby, who was politely referred to as her 'brother', she needed work. Finding shop life at the Army and Navy Stores too dull and law office work stultifying, she decided to take up her hobby, dancing, professionally. She toured the country first with Madame Astrova's Russian ballet troupe, making her name as an acrobat, singer and dancer. After a brief stint with Zarko's Circus she became a vaudeville singer and dancer touring army and civilian clubs and cinemas, where she sang playback to silent stars or performed risqué songs in Hindustani. After flirting with a number of names, including the highly inappropriate Carmen Miranda—'... quite ridiculous, I didn't look at all Spanish'—she became Nadia, a name suggested by an Armenian fortune-teller who promised it would bring her fame and fortune. Mary was pleased because 'Nadia ... was accepted as being both Indian and foreign enough' (Karnad, 1980: 86). In 1934, her screen potential was spotted by the manager of Regal Theatres, Lahore, Mr Kanga, who offered to introduce her to his old friend, J.B.H. Wadia.

In the week that Mr Kanga brought Mary Evans out to the studio, J.B.H. had just re-released Fairbanks' *Mask of Zorro* and was waiting to see how the experiment of adding a sync sound track and dialogue dubbed in Hindi went down with Indian audiences. Nadia recalls her first visit:

> I was very nervous when Kanga told me he had organised a meeting with these Wadia brothers. While I had never heard of them myself or seen any of their films, my friends on hearing about my audition said that they were a reputable firm. I remember catching the tram .... Parel was a very posh area and the studio was located right next to the Governor's Palace of that time ... [and] was surrounded by miles of green paddy fields .... I recall wearing this lovely blue sun dress that I had treated myself to and this white fedora with a sunflower arrangement. When I got off the tram Mr Kanga was waiting for me in his bright red Chrysler and we drove in through the large wrought iron gates [of] the studio .... I had expected to see tin sheds as I had previously seen when I had gone to see some shooting at the Imperial Studio in the silent days but here was this massive mansion of stone, very imposing and all (Wadia, 1994: 29).

The meeting was a success. The brothers were clearly captivated by her sense of fun, charming lack of deference and plucky 'can-do' attitude, as well as her obvious stage talents: singing, dancing, gymnastics and a wonderful curvaceous body that she displayed with little inhibition. She was hired at Rs 150 per month on condition that she passed a screen test.

J.B.H. clearly had qualms about introducing a buxom, blue-eyed, blonde as an Indian heroine. Nadia herself noted that he seemed surprised when she arrived: 'I don't think he expected me to be quite so large or fair.' The screen test seven days later was apparently disastrous, her Hindi diction laughable. However, the dubbed re-release of *Mark of Zorro* had already started to make money, encouraging J.B.H. in his plans for a sound remake of *The Amazon*. Nadia might be just the leading lady he was looking for. She was told she would have to work hard with a voice coach on her Hindi, to change her name and to wear a wig or dye her hair: 'otherwise people will think you are a buddhi'.[9] She claims she did try an auburn tint but it went lighter than before so she decided to let it be. But she flatly refused a black wig with long plaits: 'Look here Mr Wadia, I am a white woman and I'll look foolish with long black hair.' She also refused to change her name to the Hinduised Nanda Devi: 'That's not part of my contract. Nadia rhymes with Wadia and besides ... I'm no devi.'[10]

J.B.H. decided to try her out with a tiny role in his *Desh Deepak* (*Light of the Homeland*, dir. J.B.H. Wadia, 1935), an orientalist costume melodrama being shot at the studios with Joseph David. Although she had only three minutes of screen time, Nadia's sequence—as a skimpily clad slave girl and nationalist supporter—hit the cinemas in full colour. Wadia had organised hand colouring on 25 prints, emphasising her golden curls, bright blue eyes and ample flesh spilling out of a tight choli and diaphanous golden sarong. As a slave market auctioneer details Nadia's considerable physical charms, the camera obliges us with cut-away close-ups on her teeth, her mouth, her eyes. J.B.H. had already decided on the two features that, together, would sell Nadia to Indian audiences: a voluptuous white body and populist nationalism. Audiences went wild and fan mail started pouring in, especially from the north-western provinces where she already had a reputation as a stage performer.

With her additional success as Princess Parizad in the musical melodrama *Noor e Yaman* (*Light of Yemen*, dir. J.B.H. Wadia, 1935), a small role in which she had to speak, sing, dance and cry, J.B.H. felt confident enough to let her take the lead in his *Amazon* remake. Openly inspired

[9] Trans: *buddhi* means old person. In conversation with the author.
[10] Trans: *devi* means goddess. In conversation with the author.

by both *Mark of Zorro* and *The Perils of Pauline*, the script was called *Hunterwali.* Twenty-four-year-old Homi Wadia was chosen to direct this, only his second 'talkie' film. Shooting began as soon as a gap appeared in the studio schedules and, carried away by enthusiastic reports from the floor and impressive rushes, J.B.H. extended the production period from six weeks to six months as songs and a romantic sub-plot (starring another actress) were added. However, when the film was finished his business partner, Billimoria, got cold feet about Nadia, considering her feisty persona too risky in the Indian context: 'An Indian woman doing all that fighting—the public may not like it—we must sell the picture.' Fortunately for the Wadias there were no serious takers and they were forced to release the picture themselves thereby retaining for Wadia Movietone one of the biggest box-office hits of the decade.

Nationalist Politics

Over the next few years a run of stunt and action films—with and without Nadia—enriched the studios, which produced around six films a year. Nationalism and the freedom movement had been a constant subtext of the early Wadia films, including *Hunterwali.* Like many in the film industry, the Wadias were early Congress supporters and these beliefs underpinned their films. Although strict British censorship forbade overt references to the freedom movement, film-makers of the 1930s and 1940s would slip casual references to Congress songs and symbols into the soundtrack or screen. A princess rescuing an oppressed kingdom from a wicked foreign tyrant would have obvious resonances in 1930s India.[11] Nadia saw her role—on screen and off—as supporting the nationalist movement and stated explicitly: 'In all the pictures there was a propaganda message, something to fight for, for example for people to educate themselves or to become a strong nation' (Gandhy and Thomas, 1991: 14).

Socially responsible themes were becoming de rigueur at this time for producers who wanted critical status. The 1936 box-office and critical success of Devika Rani's *Achhut Kanya* had upped the stakes and, while Wadia Movietone's reputation for 'cheap' films for the 'masses' was unassailable, Bombay Talkies—and other studios making socials, such as

[11] In 1984, J.B.H. Wadia openly admitted: 'a revolt against a tyrannical king or a minister for Azadi (freedom) was nothing if not against the British Raj, although indirectly ....' quoted in Chowdhry (2000: 97).

Prabhat—were considered more 'respectable'. J.B.H. responded to *Achhut Kanya* with a jokey twist on the caste theme in *Hurricane Hansa* (dir. R.N. Vaidya, 1937) in which Nadia plays a harijan[12] girl who transforms her name from 'harijan Hansa' to 'Hurricane Hansa', dons her trademark mask and takes revenge on a villain who had destroyed her family.

Inspired by the ideas of the radical Bengali Marxist and humanist, M.N. Roy, J.B.H. left the Congress Party and in 1938 became a founder member of Roy's Radical Democratic Party.[13] As his political commitment increased, J.B.H. became increasingly frustrated with his film-making. While he wanted to follow his peers and make socials, his business partners had no intention of killing the golden goose—theirs was the most profitable studio of the day. Reluctantly they allowed J.B.H. one non-stunt film a year. His formal experiment *Naujawan* (*Youth*, dir. Aspi, 1937), billed as the first Indian sound film without songs, had been a flop. He now focused on infusing his stunt films with social issues: Nadia starred in *Lootaru Lalna* (*Dacoit Damsel*, dir. Homi Wadia, 1938), taking on the explosive issue of Hindu–Muslim unity, and in *Punjab Mail* (dir. Homi Wadia, 1939), attacking the class system and championing women's rights.[14] The influence of M.N. Roy's humanist ideas became increasingly visible, culminating in *Diamond Queen* (dir. Homi Wadia, 1940), which dealt with women's emancipation and presented the tough and capable Nadia for the first time without her whip and mask. This film hit the jackpot of combining box-office glory with the critical acclaim J.B.H. so desired, prompting even the usually acerbic *Filmindia* to praise: 'a thought-provoking film that enlightens as it entertains'.[15]

With *Diamond Queen*'s success—and the fact that wartime film-stock rationing limited studios to two films per producer—Homi Wadia was promoted from director to producer. J.B.H. became actively involved in the war effort, chairing the Film Advisory Board and making pro-war

[12] Trans: *harijan* means *child of god*. It was Gandhi's name for untouchables.

[13] Roy was a charismatic activist and political intellectual who had travelled widely throughout Europe, the Soviet Union and the Americas. At one time a leading figure in the international communist movement and a confidante of Lenin, he became disillusioned equally by the Communist Party and the Congress Party politics, and attempted to forge a new democratic humanism.

[14] J.B.H. Wadia (1980a: 93–94) wrote: 'When I became a filmmaker I tried to equate (sic) my conscience by weaving the screenplays of some of my early talkies around the problem of emancipation of Indian womanhood,' referring to the Nadia films as 'the genre which was much maligned and least understood by many "all-knowing" film critics and producers of social films'.

[15] Baburao Patel in *Filmindia* editorial, 1940.

documentaries.[16] Wadia Movietone became increasingly schizophrenic as the two brothers followed their own paths. Homi Wadia, flush with the success of the latest Nadia films, pursued ever more extravagant production values. For *Bombaiwali* (*Woman from Bombay*, dir. Homi Wadia, 1941) and *Jungle Princess* (dir. Homi Wadia, 1942) he constructed fine sets and brought in a host of new special effects technicians—clever local boys such as Babhubhai Mistry—to build a 40-foot jungle model for an ambitious storm in the jungle and to introduce high-speed car chases. However, J.B.H.'s authorial hand on script and screenplay simultaneously reduced the number of stunts and increased the 'plausibility' and social themes of these stories. The industry believed the stunt film was dead and the comparatively small profits made by these two films appeared to confirm the view. Primarily to augment their raw stock allocation, the brothers set up Basant Pictures in 1942, initially geared to producing more socials. Notionally Homi Wadia's company, J.B.H. was in fact a silent partner.

However, J.B.H.'s central obsession was his radical project *Raj Nartaki* (*Court Dancer*, dir Madhu Bose, 1941), a prestige production on which he was relying for the intellectual and critical credibility that still eluded him. Starring celebrated classical dancer, Sadhana Bose, and top thespian, Prithviraj Kapoor, J.B.H. boasted this was the first Indian film shot simultaneously in English, Bengali and Hindi. His final coup was to secure it as a 100 per cent English language film and to also secure a US and European distribution deal through Columbia in Hollywood. The film undoubtedly helped to redeem his reputation with the Bombay intelligentsia but, although it recouped its costs across three language versions, a crisis was brewing at Wadia Movietone. While J.B.H. wanted to pursue the now fashionable social melodramas, Homi Wadia and Bilimoria wanted to go aggressively for box-office hits. In the autumn of 1942 the company was split. With the box-office failure just months later of Basant's first film, *Mauj* (*Wave*, dir. Homi Wadia, 1943), a social drama in which the Wadias experimented with Nadia playing a vampish femme fatale, J.B.H. suggested cancelling the stars' contracts. At this point the brothers fell out, their differences apparently irresolvable.

Homi Wadia, ever loyal to Nadia, who was by now also his long-term lover and unofficial partner, decided to concentrate on making the most of his assets: the stunt star contracts. He decided to follow a hunch that

[16] Following M.N. Roy's lead, J.B.H. argued that this should be seen as a workers' war to defeat world fascism and India should cooperate with the British, opposing the Congress policy of boycotting the war effort until India was free.

what a sizeable section of the audience really wanted was the old whip-cracking Nadia. He suspected that if produced cheaply enough the films could make money. Produced on a shoestring, *Hunterwali ki Beti* (*Daughter of Woman with the Whip*, dir. Homi Wadia, 1943) was an immediate success and Homi Wadia had found his formula. Cheap, quickly-made action, stunt and jungle films followed and Basant Studios went from strength to strength with such films as *Flying Prince, Tigress, 11 o'clock, Baghdad ka Jadoo* (*The Magic of Baghdad*) and *Circus Queen*. Meanwhile, J.B.H.'s fortunes at Wadia Movietone dwindled and by 1946 he had to sell his studio buildings to his old rival, V. Shantaram. The brothers had by now teamed up again and, following the 1947 success of *Ram Bhakt Hanuman*, discovered a lucrative market niche in quality mythologicals which sustained Basant for many years, while Homi Wadia continued to knock out cheap action films for Nadia until she retired in 1956.

Two Visions

The split between the Wadia brothers is invariably characterised as the clash of two visions: Homi Wadia, the shy, conservative, technical genius and astute business brain who left school at the age of 16, who unashamedly loved lowbrow entertainment and despised intellectual pretensions; J.B.H. Wadia, M.A, L.L.B, the self-assured, cultured, radical humanist, a teacher and writer who craved critical acclaim and international recognition. The situation was, in fact, more complex as J.B.H. was himself torn between the high ideals of his political and intellectual passions and his own love of Hollywood entertainment and brilliant understanding of the popular Indian imagination.

This perceived conflict between 'respectability' and 'popularity'—or profit—echoed between the professionals and the business community, the two emergent and competing forces of urban India, and permeated contemporary thinking. On release, the press had applauded Wadia Movietone's distinctly melodramatic *Lal e Yaman* for being a 'serious drama' rather than a 'cheap' stunt film. Rajadhyaksha has described how Bombay film melodrama became 'the privileged form of representation' for the nationalist consciousness (1996: 408–9).[17] In the Indian context,

[17] 'Melodrama in the cinema, from the early 1930s, has consistently written into its various proliferations ... the transition of a "national" culture into the creation of a State: the loss of an ideal, the paradigms for belonging' (Rajadhyaksha, 1994: 26).

melodramatic 'socials' became equated with 'realism' and harnessed to the nationalist project with a mission to project images not of what is, but of what India *should* be. As Chakravarty puts it: 'Realism is the masquerading moral conscience of the Indian intelligentsia in their assumed ... role of national leadership ...' (1993: 81). By the 1950s further discrimination in the shape of post-independence government censorship, which according to K.A. Abbas 'did not look favourably on magic and fighting scenes', virtually wiped out the stunt genre (ibid.: 61). Film history was rewritten to celebrate the golden age of 'realist' 1930s socials. Bombay Talkies eclipsed Wadia Movietone. Only in the 1990s has re-evaluation of the stunt film begun to acknowledge its importance in the development of storytelling, editing and mise en scène in Indian cinema.[18]

At stake were two different visions of the nationalist project—and two different relationships to modernity and the West. 'India is most truly national when it is international' Nehru famously wrote, but the tug between national self-definition and global modernity could be articulated in different ways. J.B.H. straddled the two. Like the European educated Congress intellectuals of the 1930s he saw the nation-building project as comprising humanist social reform at home and a proud display of modern India's classical heritage abroad. Modernity meant a national self-definition which drew on the roots of a 'pure' tradition, setting these within 'modern' European social values: a humanistic and scientific worldview. This worthy vision valued 'realist' melodramas on social issues and orientalised classical dance films for European audiences.

However, J.B.H. also understood market forces and saw that popular passions would be the seed for new modernities which could not be neatly controlled from the centre. He valued aspects of the West that the intellectuals dismissed as Hollywood 'trash', as well as popular Indian entertainment forms. It appears that he brilliantly understood hybridity and recognised that national identities would be forged through playful negotiation, rather than simply imposed from above. This vision of modern India drew comfortably on global popular culture but looked to its home markets, rather than the international stage, for its validation.

Whilst wholeheartedly celebrating the remarkable achievements of Indian film-makers, J.B.H. unashamedly paid homage to the Hollywood

---

[18] See Rajadhyaksha, 1994: 33–34; Chabria, 1994: 15; and Shyam Benegal's interview in *Fearless: The Hunterwali Story* (Wadia, 1993).

pioneers of technical skills and storytelling conventions naming, amongst others, Charlie Chaplin, Douglas Fairbanks, Harold Lloyd and D.W. Griffiths (Wadia, 1955: 4–12). He also openly acknowledged the influences of character and storyline—Nadia was billed as 'India's Pearl White', John Cawas as 'India's Eddie Polo'[19]—and spoke uninhibitedly about *adapting* such films as *Mark of Zorro* and the Tarzan series for Indian audiences. This might be seen as an example of the mimicry we associate with the sites of the anti-colonial struggle, but it was also sharp marketing: these were huge brand names and the Wadias understood their value. At the same time, they knew how to 'Indianise'—in subject matter and in form. Their films were, at their core, sites of negotiation of a new Indian modernity: alongside Hollywood they drew on Urdu Parsee theatre (via Joseph David), Indian myth and legend, and contemporary political debate.

Whilst both visions of modern India acknowledged the transnational, the first was largely premised on an essentialised Indian cultural tradition, while the second better recognised the hybridity and fluidity within the porous borders of this modern 'India'. The former leaned towards melodrama as a film form, the latter action, comedy and masquerade. As Mishra has noted, stunt films are: 'the only form [in Indian cinema history] that arguably escapes from [melodramatic] staging' (2002: 36). The Wadias' films embodied an ongoing tension between these two forms and the two visions of the transnational arena. Fearless Nadia was constructed within the framework of this dual vision.

Nadia Persona

Nadia was undoubtedly the Wadias' most brilliant discovery and creation. If they were looking for an Indian heroine, she was not an obvious choice and at first sight perhaps the strangest aspect of the Nadia phenomenon was that, despite her obvious whiteness, she was so easily accepted as an Indian heroine in films that were read by many audiences as anti-British allegories.

From the very first her ethnicity was an issue for the Wadias and Indianising her was a conscious project: hair colour, name, Hindi diction were all areas they sought to control. Interestingly, while J.B.H.'s original concern had been that Nadia might appear too European for Indian audiences, on *Hunterwali*'s release Billimoria was worried that audiences might reject

[19] This continued a well-established tradition of many studios of the silent and early sound era, see Wadia (1980a: 94).

her for behaviour inappropriate to an *Indian* woman.[20] A number of strategies were used to 'fix' her identity as Indian. Taking no chances, *Hunterwali* prefaces its action with a written title: *Brave Indian girl who sacrificed royal luxuries to the cause of her people and her country*. As the films went on she was increasingly referred to as 'Bombaiwali' (*the woman from Bombay*), connoting cosmopolitan sophistication and modernity, thereby justifying her apparent transgressions of traditional Indian female dress codes and mores, whilst retaining her as an all-Indian heroine. A certain fluidity did accompany her physical appearance in posters and on screen: although she was adamant about refusing a wig, in posters her hair was sometimes hand-coloured light brown and, in black and white films, shadows could render her colouring ambiguous. The mask, itself, helped weaken the visual impact of her ethnic identity. In fact, in the context of the nationalist movement, Nadia's heroism and support of the underdog was almost enough in itself to place her on the Indian side. Girish Karnad recalls:

> The single most memorable sound of my childhood is the clarion call of Hey-y-y as Fearless Nadia, regal upon her horse, her hand raised defiantly in the air, rode down upon the bad guys. To us school kids of the mid-forties Fearless Nadia meant courage, strength, idealism (1980: 86).

However, her western looks were undeniably part of her exotic appeal and in choosing her the Wadias were involved in a careful calculation. Billing her as India's Pearl White, they could attract to their films all the glamour of the Pearl White brand and exoticism of the 'white mem' whilst simultaneously constructing an all-Indian Nadia. Played cleverly, they could have it both ways, conflating two traditions: the Hollywood stunt queen (and by implication the whole Hollywood stunt genre—her persona referred as much to Fairbanks as to White) and the legendary Indian warrior woman. Through these a cosmopolitan modern femininity could be forged.

The Wadias did not invent the masked fighting woman. This was a well-established convention of the silent cinema—both Indian and Hollywood—and Wadia's *Dilruba Daku*, *Hunterwali*'s immediate predecessor, was

[20] British censorship in the 1920s was keen to protect the image of white women. This had been one of the key reasons for setting up the Indian Cinematograph Committee in 1927. 'Much harm has been done in India by the widespread exhibition of Western films .... The majority of the films ... degrade the white woman in the eyes of the Indians', the ICC Report of 1927–28, quoted in Barnouw and Krishnaswamy, 1980: 43.

part of a contemporary vogue for warrior women, known as *viranganas*. Kathryn Hansen (1992: 188–98), in her study of *Nautanki* theatre, describes how historical and legendary figures from various eras and different parts of India (from Razia Sultana to Lakshmibai, Queen of Jhansi) fed the imagery and stories of a significant body of work within popular theatre and early cinema, as well as folk songs, comic books and calendar art. The *virangana* prototype describes a good queen, who takes over the throne when a male kinsman dies, leads her people into battle dressed as a man, displays astonishing military skills, and dies defending her kingdom against invaders. The key image—a turbaned woman on horseback brandishing a sword above her head—has been enthusiastically exploited by female politicians, notably Indira Gandhi, over the years.

The British government censorship of overt references to the nationalist movement fuelled the popularity of *virangana* stories in all forms of popular entertainment between 1910 and 1940, as figures such as the Queen of Jhansi had become a focus for nationalist activism (ibid.: 194). Thus, fictionalised biographies of historical and legendary female warriors as well as fictional warrior queens, princesses and female outlaws became popular staples of early cinema.[21]

Hansen suggests that the distinction between *sat* and *sati* is the key to understanding what she refers to as 'this startling counterparadigm of Indian womanhood' (ibid.: 189). The *virangana*, usually dressed as a male, is seen to operate within the widest sphere of morality, the upholding of justice and truth (*sat*), which is more usually associated with men, rather than *stridharma*, the traditional female sphere of (*sat*), which proposes passive/suffering, sexual fidelity and chastity for the *sati* (the woman who embodies *sat*). As the *virangana*'s status derives from her own noble deeds rather than her relationship to a man, she is allowed an independence denied other women. Four aspects of this counterparadigm are relevant to Nadia.

Body

'[T]he *virangana* ideal commends physical training and active deployment of the body in combat' (ibid.: 189). Nadia's proud display of a muscular and athletic body, her fighting skills, and championing of exercise and gym

[21] For lists of these films, see Chowdhry, 2000: 120–21; Hansen, 1992: 195. For description of the 1931 silent film, *Diler Jigar*, see Rajadhyaksha, 1994: 25–40.

sessions are pure *virangana*. Like her American counterparts, Pearl White and Douglas Fairbanks, she was always admired for doing all her own stunts[22] and was, from the first, identified with her body and its power, in a way that heroines such as Devika Rani (who frequently suffered and died—the *stridharma* ideal of the *sati*) were not.

Moral Strength

'The *virangana* arrives not simply when force is required but when moral order needs to be restored' (Hansen, 1992: 192). Nadia always occupies the position of moral strength within her films—she rights wrongs and restores order and justice, being introduced from her first *Hunterwali* appearance as a 'protector of the poor and punisher of evildoers'.

Sexual Freedom

'Because her virtue is not reducible to the sexual transactions of the female body, physical relations cannot impugn her truth' (ibid.: 189). In the *virangana* tradition, sexuality is irrelevant—women can have lovers without being defined by their sexual transgressions. Whilst her sexuality was not explicitly marked within the films' diageses, Nadia's on-screen sexual and erotic appeal was enormous—she could carry off an (almost) nude bathing scene in *Hunterwali* and still be seen by fans as 'voluptuous but prim' (see Figure 2.2).

Cross-dressing

'The *virangana* ... in these dramas claims male positions for the female body; she rides on horseback, wears male dress, wields weapons ordinarily carried by men' (ibid.: 192). Nadia regularly wore masculinised clothing, especially in confrontations with the villains, reinforcing her placement

[22] In the case of White and Fairbanks this has been exposed as studio marketing: both regularly used stunt doubles, especially in their later years (Wise and Ware, 1973: 215–19). Nadia and Homi Wadia insisted that Nadia did all her own stunts. If true, this marks a real difference with Hollywood. Coming out of a vaudeville tradition, it was particularly important to their public image and marketplace value that the stars could 'really' do these stunts.

Figure 2.2
Still from *Hunterwali*
Source: Wadia Movietone Pvt. Ltd.
Note: Nadia could carry off an (almost) nude bathing scene in *Hunterwali* (1935) and still be seen by fans as 'voluptuous but prim'.

within the sphere of *sat* rather than the more limited *stridharma.* This ranged from riding breeches and hacking jackets to sailor suits or Fairbanks-style cloaks and swords. However, Nadia invariably played a split persona, with either a double life (*Hunterwali*) or the complex Bombaiwali construction (*Diamond Queen*), so she also regularly wore a sari—the ultimate signifier of Indian femininity.[23]

Even the Wadias underestimated the extent to which the *virangana* ideal underpinned and legitimised Nadia's persona, discovering to their cost how limited a range of roles she could play. Whilst she could champion the cause of the oppressed on almost any issue—from caste to class, from anti-communalism to women's issues—she was never allowed to show weakness. 'Nadia cannot cry' one distributor exclaimed, insisting an emotional scene in *Mauj* be cut from the final film. Moreover, whilst she could wear clothes that revealed more female flesh than any other Indian actress

[23] However, this was frequently the Maharashtrian sari—nine meters long and with much greater freedom of movement—which also refers to the *virangana* tradition of Maharashtrian horsewomen.

of her day and her image was undeniably erotically charged, her appearance as a 'vamp', smoking, drinking and flirting as part of a double role in *Muqabla* (*Competition*, dir. Batuk Bhatt and Babubhai Mistry, 1942), was not a box-office success. She was emphatically coded as the 'good girl', but only within the conventions of *virangana* morality. A telling anecdote describes how, in later years, a churlish Homi Wadia responded to his brother's request that he direct a mythological film for him with the retort: 'only if Nadia plays Sita', a calculatedly provocative suggestion as the Ramayana heroine, Sita, is the embodiment of *stridharma*, becoming a *sati* by walking into fire to prove her chastity.

In an earlier essay examining the contradictions within the star persona of Nadia, I had proposed two answers to the question of her popularity as an icon within a nationalist context despite her whiteness (Gandhy and Thomas, 1991: 110–16). First, as a white woman her status was liminal—the threat of her physical prowess could be contained and her sexuality could be vicariously 'consumed'. Her whiteness, simultaneously recognised and disavowed, undoubtedly underpinned the ambivalent frisson of her erotic appeal, the classic colonial miscegenation fantasy. Second, her identity was fixed within the films' diegeses through identifying her not with whiteness but with the cosmopolitanism and modernity of the 'Bombaiwali'. What the Wadias spotted was the potential to build Nadia as a *virangana* for a modern world. The Wadia films are importantly a reverie of potency within modernity and Nadia was, throughout the films, associated with a gamut of signifiers of western technology: cars, planes and, importantly, trains.

Partha Chatterjee has described how developments within the nationalist movement of nineteenth-century Bengal created the figure of a 'new Indian woman'. Identified with spiritual qualities symbolised by the 'home', she could preserve the purity of an essentialised Indian culture whilst allowing Indian men to operate in the westernised 'world' of rationality and technological progress (1989: 622–33; also see Chatterjee, 1993). Although this formulation empowered middle-class women to benefit from education and equality in the workplace as well as to champion social reform, the power of (at least mainstream versions of) the new nationalist woman lay ultimately in embracing a more limited and essentialised femininity, and was consequently comparatively constrained. This was a different model from the *virangana* counterparadigm which implied recognition of gender ambivalence and multiple models of femininity. The distinction is relevant to the comparison between Nadia and the stars of the melodramatic social films, notably Devika Rani.

Whilst Devika Rani's modernity constructed her as both a cipher for humanist values and fount of purity within an orientalised 'tradition', Nadia's was firmly situated within the (male, western) world of technological progress, where she was unambiguously in control, whether driving a car or riding the roof of a hurtling train. Fearless Nadia was frequently shown running triumphantly along the tops of trains, fist-fighting her male tormentors, parading burly men high above her shoulders before chucking them to their deaths on the tracks below (see Figure 2.3). Whilst Devika Rani's attempts to challenge traditional orthodoxies in *Achhut Kanya* left her crushed under the wheels of an oncoming train, Nadia, championed the oppressed and effected change in the world from the giddy heights of the train roof, empowered rather than crushed by technology.

Figure 2.3
Miss Frontier Mail
Source: Wadia Movietone Pvt. Ltd.

The significance of both stars as key icons of the era emerges through Qurratulain Hyder's autobiographical *Memories of an Indian Childhood* (2001). Devika Rani is remembered for her family background, *Achhut Kanya* being one of the few films Hyder's parents allowed her to watch on the grounds that: 'India had at last entered the era of cultural revolution because Gurudev's [Tagore's] own niece had become a cinema actress' (Hyder, 2001: 213). Meanwhile 'Miss Nadia of *Hunterwali* fame' was a cultural reference point against which children compared the skills of a local circus Well [sic] of Death motorbike queen. In what appears as a dichotomy between substance and performance, Devika Rani's significance stemmed from her social status as an upper middle-class Brahmin—*who she was*—and Nadia's from her body and its skills—*what she could do.*

Diamond Queen

Diamond Queen, often celebrated as the Wadias' best film, and probably the most seamless fusion of the brothers' two visions, offers fascinating insights into the balancing act that was the Nadia persona. It was the seventh in the Diamond Thriller series which began with Homi Wadia's first sound film, *Veer Bharat* (*Indian Warrior,* dir. Homi Wadia, 1934). *Hunterwali* had been the second and audiences were by now fond of its cast of side characters: the faithful horse, Punjab ka Beta (Son of the Punjab), a baby Austin car christened Rolls Royce ki Beti (Daughter of Rolls Royce) and Moti, the naughty dog.

In *Diamond Queen,* Nadia plays Madhurika, a modern cosmopolitan girl who returns to her small town, Diamond Town, after five years of education in Bombay. She finds the people terrorised by villain Kedarnath and his gang, who have taken over the kingdom during the 10 years that the good prince has been abroad. Their corrupt and decadent regime sabotages local literacy campaigns, steals taxes from the poor and threatens the chastity of local women. Madhurika links up with Diler, a bandit with a heart of gold who has his own reasons for seeking revenge, to expose Kedarnath's corruption and restore order. With the help of her friends including Miss Radha (the pretty school teacher) Radha's father Sevakram (a respected elder of the community) and Prince Ranjit Singh (who has disguised himself as a westernised bumbling fool in order to find out the truth about Kedarnath's rule) Madhurika defeats the villains and allows the good prince to return and rule benignly. In the process she espouses the causes of women's independence, education and physical exercise programmes.

Madhurika is undoubtedly the film's central pivot. Although Diler's life story—his boyhood and his marriage—bookends the film, Madhurika is the Diamond Queen of the film's title and also the focus of the villain's wrath. 'I fear bandit Diler less than the free and fearless Madhurika—her poisonous thinking will spread through Diamond Town unless we get rid of her,'[24] Kedarnath snarls from his palatial den. Madhurika motivates the action and *she* ultimately kills Kedarnath.

Madhurika is visually constructed within *virangana* codes. We first meet her through a sequence of eroticised body parts emphasising her physical strength: a close-up of a white fist, swiftly followed by a muscular arm which lands a sharp punch in the face of the lascivious brute who is threatening to abduct Miss Radha. The camera moves to Madhurika's feet as she crushes a male hand attempting to grab a fallen knife, then pans slowly up her body—wide black trousers, taut across her large hips, tight white blouse and big bosom, natty neck-scarf and brooch—eventually revealing a regal blonde dominatrix, high cheekbones, aquiline Greek nose, tight blonde curls. When she has disposed of the villains—kicked, thrown and spectacularly de-trousered—she greets her father and friends' astonishment at the way she's changed in Bombay with a smile and the casual throwaway: 'I've been training in a women's gym.'[25]

Madhurika unequivocally upholds the moral order. She punishes villainy and protects and rescues the vulnerable good: virtuous young women who epitomise Indian traditional arts and culture (Miss Radha), tortured animals (her horse, Punjab ka Beta), benevolent wise old men (Sevakram), and the community itself that has been cheated for years by their corrupt rulers. Whilst Diler enthusiastically supports Madhurika, seeing her as a potential partner in his own lone campaign to rid Diamond Town of its corrupt rulers, as well as a future lover and wife, she primly rejects his criminal methods. Demurely draped in a white embroidered sari and sporting a halo of backlit blonde curls,[26] she entreats him to give himself up to the law. 'A criminal cannot arrest a criminal,' she gently cajoles. Only when he has paid his dues in jail will she consider marrying him. Throughout the final assault on the villains, Madhurika is at the helm: she organises her gang, draws up the plans, is at the driving wheel throughout the car chase and finally wrestles Kedarnath to his death on top of a hurtling tonga, Diler looking on admiringly.

Comparison with Nadia's Hollywood counterparts, notably the Pearl White character in the *Perils of Pauline* serials, is relevant here. Although

---

[24] Dialogue translations from UK's Channel 4 2002 transmission of *Diamond Queen*.

[25] Implicit here are references to other films in which Nadia is seen working out in her gym—which apparently stimulated a keep-fit craze at the time.

[26] Richard Dyer describes how backlighting developed in Hollywood largely to ensure that blonde hair looked blonde on orthochromatic stock, as a welcome consequence producing the blonde white woman's 'heavenly' 'effulgent dazzle' (1997: 124).

Nadia was always accompanied by a male hero, usually John Cawas, for romantic interest, we see here that Nadia was primarily a fighter and rather more than Pearl White's plucky daredevil stunt woman. Nadia was always the primary agent of the villains' demise and as likely to rescue her hero as be rescued. Invariably, a second heroine, in this case Miss Radha provided the focus for romance, emotion, and song and dance in Nadia's films.

Two narrative threads run through *Diamond Queen*, both set up in an intriguing opening scene in which the mother, father and boy child, Diler, are having dinner in their simple hut in a rural paradise. The utopian family romance is shattered when the father's treacherous business partner, Kedarnath, bursts in and, wanting their gold-mining spoils for himself, shoots both parents. In the ensuing scuffle between the boy Diler and the villain Kedarnath the hut catches fire but Diler escapes, having promised his dying father he will take revenge. The rest of the film unfolds 16 years later.

An opening reel which sets up the action—and polarities of good and evil—in the hero's childhood is usual within Indian cinema conventions. Here we find a schematic equilibrium and disruption: happy family life in harmony with nature is disrupted by the villain's greed and insensitivity to family and friendship loyalties. However, in *Diamond Queen*, unusually, a second discordant note also surfaces. As the boy Diler excitedly chatters about the freedom he has to roam and play in the jungle, his mother, most uncharacteristically for the genre, complains: 'you may enjoy it but it's hard work for me'. We discover they are about to leave the jungle paradise because she will no longer tolerate her unequal workload, raising the spectre of women challenging their traditional subservient roles.[27]

These two narrative threads need resolution: treachery and greed must be punished by destroying the villains, and a viable model of contemporary Indian womanhood must be held together. Whilst in most films the boy hero grows up to effect narrative resolution, here the eruption of women's issues changes things: neither Diler, nor any of the other men in this film, can fully restore order. Only Madhurika has the physical and moral power to resolve both threads.

Madhurika sets out her stall in her first scene. When the disgruntled boor she has just pulped complains of the insult to his virility: '*mai mard*

[27] The subsequent fire in which both parents die is played out in quasi-melodramatic mode which suggests an immediate punishment.

hum, mard',[28] Madhurika retorts with what, within the 1940s context, appears an astonishing:

> Hey mister, don't think today's women are so weak they'll submit to the brutality of men ... if India is to be free, women must be given their freedom ... if you try and stop them you'll face the consequences.

Thread one is told through action scenes which push the narrative forward, where Madhurika, in her most masculinised outfits, challenges the tyranny of the villains. These include scenes of greatest tension: fights, car chases, and choreographed swashbuckling, building excitement through skilful editing and intercutting storylines. Madhurika wears eroticised, westernised clothes: trousers and blouse in two key scenes, riding breeches and hacking jacket in a third, whilst for the only other major showdown with the villains she wears the knee-length black dress in which she kills Kedarnath. In these revealing costumes she performs all her most physically demanding feats, whilst simultaneously commanding the moral authority of the film—Douglas Fairbanks meets the *virangana* queen.

Thread two unfolds predominantly through spectacular excess[29]—songs, love scenes, slapstick—a combination of melodrama and comedy. A mostly sari-clad Madhurika challenges, negotiates with and supports a range of ineffectually 'modern' Indians: her father, Diler, Miss Radha, Sevakram and Prince Ranjit—all in varying degrees sympathetic to radical reform but unable to make this happen without Bombaiwali, Madhurika. The success of the film's ideological project depends, to some extent, on how skilfully this thread is integrated into the body of the film and resolved within the moral order.

Two of the film's four songs openly advocate nationalist, reformist messages about education and exercise, and are barely contained within the diegesis. At a literacy campaign concert the lovely schoolteacher, Miss Radha, performs a classical Indian dance to a song, exhorting the townspeople to: 'forge ahead a path of reading and writing ... for ... the pen is mightier than the sword', while her father, a socially-enlightened community leader, lectures his audience: 'education is the first step to freedom ... vital to solve the country's problems ... knowledge is power'. Later, in

[28] Trans: 'I'm a man, a [real] man.'

[29] This is a tendency rather than an absolute distinction as the opposition between narrative momentum and spectacular excess is not as strong in Hindi film as Hollywood, the former being more of a 'cinema of attractions'.

Miss Radha's school playground, quasi-militaristic rows of children stretch, bend and march to patriotic music, a final Busby Berkeley-style top-shot revealing a swastika formation.[30] The song's words proclaim:

> Thank the Lord for exercise, all hail god Hanuman—to exercise is to live in bliss, always be courageous, banish weakness, be brave and strong ... let strength be your weapon—the pride of the nation is the power of its people.

Other encounters play through comedy, notably the scenes where modern femininity is at issue, particularly the sequences of Madhurika with her father, and more ambivalently modern friends. Her father, incensed by her clothes and insistence on a love marriage and an independent life beyond his authority, becomes a running joke, a rather ridiculous, reactionary old goat, who is mocked by the townsfolk, cheeked by Madhurika, and is unable to see the error of his ways or accept his 'free and fearless' daughter. The good Prince Ranjit, disguised as a 'foreign returned' buffoon in stripy blazer, brolley and absurd black specs, suffers Madhurika's playful slapstick put-downs, as she deftly throws him over her sari-clad shoulder or trips him up, until he finally redeems himself—through humility, generosity, Madhurika's support and Radha's love—and turns into a benign and enlightened ruler, deserving of his kingdom.[31] There is also a comedy subplot which provides a surreal shadow of, and comment on, the main action through half a dozen comic characters who, in nonsensical vein, discourse on colonialism and women's rights.

Two romantic sub-plots also contribute to this thread. In one love scene with Diler, a glamorous Madhurika in a dramatic black sari and bindi, her tight dark-looking curls profiled against a spectacular waterfall, shows the modern Indian woman in control as she leans to kiss Diler before the camera quickly pans away across the rocky landscape to find her father, anxious for a showdown: 'Is this how you use your education?' Miss Radha and Prince Ranjit's romance is played more conventionally, through misunderstandings and a melancholic love song, but is no less an exploration of the boundaries of modern relationships between the sexes.

---

30 The swastika here refers to the Indian peace symbol, not Nazi Germany, though in the 1940s context there might be a curious ambivalence as some Indian National Congress supporters (not J.B.H. Wadia) supported Hitler on the basis that Britain was their common enemy.

31 There are also textual references to the playful god Krishna, as the name he adopts for his disguise is Krishna Kumar (Prince Krishna).

Ultimately, the two threads just about work together to contain the radical ideas within a traditional moral order. Madhurika's apparent transgressions of traditional values are justified by a greater moral and political vision than her father's. Despite her rebelliousness, she ultimately saves the community and gets married, although the farcically schematic nature of this coupling—Madhurika seated in white sari and bindi beside a miraculously transformed bandit Diler, who now wears a western suit and tie, with Miss Radha and Prince Ranjit in traditional Hindu wedding clothes beside them—is underlined by two comedy couples larking about on a tree behind them, a gentle parody of the main action.

However, it is the tag 'Bombaiwali' which does most to legitimise and redeem Madhurika's rebelliousness and fix a revised model of contemporary Indian feminine identity. She may be as 'foreign' as Pearl White and Douglas Fairbanks and as 'traditional' as India's warrior women, but she is ultimately Bombaiwali, the epitome of Indian cosmopolitan sophistication and modernity, and a fiery nationalist to boot (see Figure 2.4). The excessive potency—and ambivalence—of her image warrants further exploration.

Figure 2.4
Still from *Diamond Queen*: Bombaiwali Madhurika (Fearless Nadia) meets Bandit Diler (John Cawas)
Source: Wadia Movietone Pvt. Ltd.

Mimicry Parama Roy, drawing on the work of Homi Bhabha et al. on colonial mimicry, argues that, if we are to understand the formation of Indian national identities, we need to examine not just Anglicisation but the variety of forms of impersonation and mimicry that exist alongside this. She aims to 'open up the field of identity formation and nation formation to a more heterogeneous model than that of Anglicization' and suggests that:

> [impersonation] is ... central to the ways in which nationalism imagines itself: hence the production of the nation is almost invariably mediated ... through such practices as Gandhi's impersonation of femininity, an Irishwoman's assumption of Hindu feminine celibacy, or a Muslim actress's emulation of a Hindu/Indian mother goddess (Roy, 1998: 4).

The Wadias were, at one level, brilliant Anglicising mimic men. Hollywood was their acknowledged role model and J.B.H., on at least one occasion, produced orientalist fare for European approval. However, their films were also rich vehicles for far wider forms of mimicry and impersonation. Fearless Nadia directly reverses (and broadly challenges) the mimicry of Anglicisation: white woman mimics Indian woman. But her persona is also a conflation of other impersonations: white woman mimics white man (Douglas Fairbanks), white woman (Pearl White), Indian woman (Jhansi ki Rani—the *virangana*), and Indian man (masked heroine disguised as a man).

In hiring Nadia, J.B.H. had demonstrated an astute, if unstated, understanding of the potential fluidity offered by Nadia's whiteness. White memsahibs had been a popular exotic feature of Urdu Parsee theatre since the early years of the century and, in the context of the nationalist movement of the day, his decision was not inherently risky. Many nationalist men had white European wives or followers—both of M.N. Roy's wives were white westerners, whilst Vivekananda's most loyal disciple, Nivedita, was an Irish woman. Parama Roy, in tracing the relationship between Vivekananda and Nivedita, describes how he recruited her in London in 1897, as 'a real lioness, to work for the Indians, women especially' (ibid.: 121), firmly believing that no man or Indian woman could do the job: a western woman had to 'become' a Hindu woman in order to educate Hindu women. She argues:

> Of all the figures in the Colonial scene—western man, Indian man, western woman and Indian woman—it seems that it is only the

western woman whose identity is available—for the Indian man—as relatively open, mobile, malleable. She is distinct from the Indian woman, whose identity has to be, in the nationalist context, fixed quite as much as the Indian male's is. What we have here is the familiar process of (colonial) mimicry performed in reverse, and for the Indian nationalist male; (Hindu) nationalism demands at this point its mimic woman (Roy, 1998: 123).

The parallels with the Nadia persona are interesting: Nadia was a white woman impersonating an Indian (invariably coded as Hindu) woman, whose mission was to educate and 'save' Indian women (and oppressed men). She was white but not white—and white but not (Pearl) White. But also, as Roy says of Nivedita, she was not quite/not white (or even not quite not quite/not white). While, Roy contends, Nivedita partially substitutes for Indian woman, her racial difference is crucial, for this: 'guarantees ... the Indian male's .... Indianness and masculinity' (ibid.: 122). A white woman impersonating an Indian (Hindu) heroine allows the Indian male to constitute himself at the centre of the project of nationalism. Did the Wadias want their mimic woman in order to construct themselves as Indian nationalists? More interestingly, how did this ambiguity/ambivalence play within the films?

Nadia's regular co-star was John Cawas, a strongman of Parsee background known for intrepid feats of bravery and brawn and a muscular body on which admiring cameras lingered. Winner of the 1930 all-India bodybuilding competition, he was already famed for such astonishing world records as carrying a Chevrolet containing four passengers on his bare back. His was a masculinity far removed from the effeminate Hindu male ideal of Gandhian nationalists. His appeal tied in with the wrestling subculture around the monkey god Hanuman, but Cawas was also billed as 'India's Eddie Polo' as well as overtly identified as 'India's Tarzan' thanks to the Wadias' *Toofani Tarzan* (*Tempestuous Tarzan*, dir. Homi Wadia, 1937) which had launched both India's jungle genre and Cawas' solo star career.[32] As in the Nadia films, Hollywood (and in this case Edgar Rice Burroughs) is openly drawn upon, but skillfully Indianised, opposing the corruption of the (westernised) city with the innocence of the (ur-Indian) rural jungle—well-worn themes of the nationalist movement. Cawas' Tarzan is a romantic savage, and lost grandson of westernised city folk. Having shown his family the original wisdom and happiness they have

[32] This was not his first film. He had been second hero in *Hunterwali.*

lost—at one point literally providing a bridge for them to walk to safety by spanning a treacherous ravine with his taut body—he is ultimately 'saved', ready to be returned to modern Indian society. The Tarzan figure inflects all subsequent Cawas roles, not least *Diamond Queen*'s opening scene where the boy Diler extols the virtues of jungle life. This produces a fascinating set of displacements and impersonations: Cawas was a Parsee Indian man playing a Hindu Indian man who plays a 'savage' which mimics a fictional American/British aristocrat who impersonates a savage. Nadia then plays white mimic woman to his multiple mimic man, raising the question of how far she was a factor in fixing Cawas' almost hysterically potent Indian masculinity.

Nadia's persona is complex as, although she was white, she was known to have grown up in India. There was considerable fluidity around 'Indianness' at that time and visual markers were (and still are) often ambiguous. Nadia described the struggles over her own identity while growing up:

> [At school] I was always considered to be English. However Mummy was Greek and spoke English with a heavy Greek accent. Many of my friends would tease me about this and I felt very embarrassed ... I guess you could say that I was never too sure as to where I belonged, though I never thought of myself as un-Indian. Many people used to call me Anglo-Indian, even though I was not born in India (Wadia, 1994: 12–13).

When she first arrived at Wadia Movietone, workers expressed anxiety about how to address her: 'You see she was a white mem and we at the studio were not sure how to react', although they soon relaxed when her unpretentious ways made her one of the gang. It was only later, especially after 1945, 'without the machinery of the studio to protect her' (ibid.: 62) that we get reports that she was singled out for malicious gossip on account of her skin colour—equated with loose morals—and her status as an unmarried mother. Wadia Movietone had been a particularly comfortable environment for Nadia. Owned by westernised Parsees, workers included a generous representation of Parsee, Muslim and other non-Hindu communities. J.B.H., discussing his films' feminist themes, admitted that, at least in his early days:

> I was ... out of tune ... with the overall Indian way of life .... As an insular [Westernised] Parsee I had not taken any interest in the pattern of family conventions of Hindus or Muslims ... for the world

> of me I could not understand ... why or how women subscribed to the male chauvinist ideology which infested the so-called social film ... (Wadia, 1980a: 93).

Whilst the reality of India was—and still is—a hybrid society, a key imperative of the nationalist project was to negotiate the boundaries of the imagined community that was to become the homogeneous 'nation'. As Somnath Zutshi (1993) puts it:

> The key element in this process (of nationalism) is the separation of 'ourselves' from the Other, 'the outsider', since what nationalism is crucially about is the matter of boundary/border setting .... Before political/geographical borders can be drawn on a map, psychological, social and cultural borders have to be erected ... [T]he question 'Who are we?' is constantly being reformulated in terms of the alternative 'How are we different from them?' (p. 83).

Films and their stars provide a terrain for such negotiation—within the broader arena of 'public culture'. Christopher Pinney, developing Arjun Appadurai and Carol Breckenridge's seminal argument, usefully characterised public culture as 'a nexus of overlapping discourses and interests that exist in a state of inter-ruptive tension' (2001: 14). The melodramatic 'realist' social offers one model of negotiating national identity, tending to resolve and disavow ambivalence, hiding the exclusions necessary to define an essentialised tradition. With a more inclusive and hybrid model of Indian modernity the focus changes. The Nadia persona—in all its complexity—is a figure at play within a liminal zone of fluid racial, ethnic, gender and religious categories, where multiplicity and heterogeneity are celebrated. In the Wadias' stunt films the key players explore new identities through mimicry and impersonation, 'fixed' only temporarily to help disguise the inherent instabilities of the border and the anxieties about what, within mainstream nationalism, is being repressed.

There were undoubtedly many reasons for the Wadias' failure to find 'respectability' through their films, not least sheer snobbery: their primary audiences were proletarian and the films were unabashed commercial 'entertainment'. However, the Wadia films and their characters would have represented sources of profound anxiety for the nationalist project and some of their popular appeal may have derived from precisely the frisson that this engendered. Where Bombay Talkies was headed by Hindu aristocrats who could place themselves firmly at the centre of the nationalist project, the Wadias represented all that was peripheral: Parsees, Muslims, Christians and 'white trash'.[33] As J.B.H.'s attempts to fix his films within the nationalist mainstream grew ever more hysterical ('right on' themes, high-minded lectures, films without songs and films with classical music and dance), he lost his audience. It was only when Homi Wadia pulled the films back from social melodrama—to playful mimicry which explored and reveled in the gamut of modern Indian identities—that the films once again succeeded with their subaltern audiences, especially the proletarian and Muslim masses.

Within the Wadia oeuvre the Nadia films represented a small but significant stream, at their best the most satisfactory resolution of the brothers' competing visions of cinema and nationalist identity. Whilst J.B.H. would have hated being immortalised by his 1986 obituary headline, *'King of the Stunt Film Dead'*, the importance of Nadia's stunt films is now undeniable. In comparison with Devika Rani, the liberal, modern, cosmopolitan beauty, Nadia was—for better or for worse—a thoroughly postmodern hybrid woman/man. Whilst Devika Rani ended up under the train, dead on the tracks, Nadia remains on its roof, an ebullient *virangana* in a modern world. Whilst Devika is now more or less lost to time, Fearless Nadia—whip held aloft, thigh-high boots dug into her trusty steed, Punjab ka Beta's flanks—looks set to ride the global media once again, this time as a Hollywood bio-pic star, returning to Hollywood a version of its earlier self that is not quite Pearl White, ready to do new work within the cultural flows of a postcolonial late capitalist world.

Acknowledgements

Many thanks to Behroze Gandhy whose interest in, and collaboration on, much of the original research on Nadia and the Wadias has been invaluable. Thanks also to Kathryn Hansen and Christopher Williams for comments on the draft and to Aarti and Laxmi in the Documentation Centre of the National Film Archive of India.

I wish to dedicate this essay to the memory of Riyad Vinci Wadia who gave generously of his time and expertise to answer my questions and comments on the draft, and whose vast knowledge of the subject is, sadly, irreplaceable.

[33] Ravi Vasudevan, describing the complexities of emergent Hindu hegemony in the 1930s Bombay industry, points out that '... the religious identity of producers, directors and actors was being related to the on-screen narrative and in fact was seen to constitute a critical social and political level to the narrative' (2000: 156).

References

Appadurai, Arjun and Carol Breckenridge. 1988. 'Why Public Culture?', *Public Culture*, 1(1): 5–10.

Barnouw, Erik. 1980. 'Shards of the Silent Era', *Cinema Vision India: The Indian Journal of Cinematic Art*, 1(1): 102.

Barnouw, Erik and S. Krishnaswamy. 1980. *Indian Film.* New York: OUP.

Chabria, Suresh (ed.). 1994. *Light of Asia: India's Silent Cinema 1912–1934*. New Delhi: Wiley Eastern.

Chakravarty, Sumita. 1993. *National Identity in Indian Popular Cinema: 1947–1987.* Austin: University of Texas Press.

Chatterjee, Partha. 1989. 'Colonialism, Nationalism and the Colonialized Women: The Contest in India', *American Ethnologist*, 622–33.

———. 1993. *The Nation and Its Fragments: Colonial and Postcolonial Histories.* Princeton: Princeton University Press.

Chowdhry, Prem. 2000. *Colonial India and the Making of Empire Cinema: Image, Ideology and Identity.* Manchester: Manchester University Press.

Dyer, Richard. 1997. *White.* London and New York: Routledge.

Gandhy, Behroze and Rosie Thomas. 1991. 'Three Indian Film Stars', in Christine Gledhill (ed.), *Stardom: Industry of Desire*, pp. 107–31, London: Routledge.

Hansen, Kathryn. 1992. *Grounds for Play: The Nautanki Theatre of North India*. Berkeley: University of California Press.

———. 2000. 'The *Virangana* in North Indian History: Myth and Popular Culture', in Alice Thorner and Maithreyi Krishnaraj (eds), *Ideals, Images and Real Lives: Women in Literature and History*, pp. 206–19, Mumbai: Orient Longman.

Hyder, Qurratulain. 2001. 'Memories of an Indian Childhood', in Amit Chaudhuri (ed.), *The Picador Book of Modern Indian Literature*, pp. 206–19, London: Picador.

Karnad, Girish. 1980. 'This One is for Nadia', *Cinema Vision India: The Indian Journal of Cinematic Art*, 1(2).

Mishra, Vijay. 2002. *Bollywood Cinema: Temples of Desire.* New York and London: Routledge.

Mishra, Vijay, Peter Jeffery and Brian Shoesmith. 1989. 'The Actor as Parallel Text in Bombay Cinema', *Quarterly Review of Film and Video*, 11(3): 49–67.

Pinney, Christopher. 2001. 'Introduction: Public, Popular and Other Cultures', in Rachel Dwyer and Christopher Pinney (eds), *Pleasure and the Nation: The History, Politics and Consumption of Public Culture in India*, pp. 1–34, New Delhi: OUP.

Rajadhyaksha, Ashish. 1980. 'Neo-traditionalism: Film as Popular Art in India', *Framework*, 32/33: 20–67.

———. 1994. 'India's Silent Cinema: A "Viewer's View"', in Suresh Chabria (ed.), *Light of Asia: India's Silent Cinema 1912–1934*, pp. 25–40, New Delhi: Wiley Eastern.

———. 1996. 'Indian Cinema: Origins to Independence', in Geoffrey Nowell-Smith (ed.), *Oxford History of World Cinema*, pp. 398–409, Oxford: OUP.

Rajadhyaksha, Ashish and Paul Willemen. 1994. *Encyclopaedia of Indian Cinema*. London: British Film Institute.

Roy, Parama. 1998. *Indian Traffic: Identities in Question in Colonial and Postcolonial India.* Berkeley and Los Angeles: University of California Press.

THOMAS, ROSIE. 1985. 'Indian Cinema: Pleasures and Popularity', *Screen*, 26 (3–4): 116–31.
———. 1995. 'Melodrama and the Negotiation of Morality in Mainstream Hindi Cinema', in Carol Breckenridge (ed.), *Consuming Modernity: Public Culture in a South Asian World*, pp. 157–82, Minneapolis/London: University of Minnesota Press.
VASUDEVAN, RAVI. 2000. 'The Politics of Cultural Address in a 'Transitional' Cinema: A Case Study of Indian Popular Cinema', in Christine Gledhill and Linda Williams (eds), *Rethinking Film Theory*, pp. 130–64, London: Arnold.
WADIA, J.B.H. 1955. *Looking Back on My Romance with Films*. Bombay: Jayant Art Printer.
———. 1980a. 'Those Were the Days', *Cinema Vision India: The Indian Journal of Cinematic Art*, 1(1): 91–99.
———. 1980b. 'JBH in Talkieland', *Cinema Vision India: The Indian Journal of Cinematic Art*, 1(2): 82–83.
WADIA, RIYAD VINCI. 1993. *Fearless: The Hunterwali Story*. Documentary, produced and directed by Riyad Vinci Wadia.
———. 1994. *Unmasked: The Life and Times of Fearless Nadia*. Unpublished research notes, Wadia Movietone Private Ltd.
WENNER, DOROTHEE. 1999. *Zorro's Blonde Schwester*. Berlin: Ullstein Buchverlag.
WISE, ARTHUR and D. WARE. 1973. *Stunting in the Cinema*. London: Constable and Company.
ZUTSHI, SOMNATH. 1993. 'Women, Nation and the Outsider in Contemporary Hindi Cinema', in Tejaswini Niranjan, P. Sudhir and V. Dhareshwar (eds), *Interrogating Modernity: Culture and Colonialism in India*, pp. 83–142, Calcutta: Seagull Books.

3

Figures of Locality and Tradition: Commercial Cinema and the Networks of Visual Print Capitalism in Maharashtra

KAJRI JAIN

This chapter situates itself at the interface between Indian commercial cinema and the contemporary genre of mass-produced images known in India as 'calendar art' or 'bazaar art'. Bazaar prints take the form of posters, actual calendars, and smaller prints called 'framing pictures', and are mostly—though by no means all—religious icons; we might think of them as the South Asian equivalent to the pictures of saints and votive images found in many Catholic cultures. These have been mass-produced on the subcontinent in one form or another since around 1857, when the first lithographic presses were set up in Calcutta. As might be expected from a phenomenon that dates from the anti-colonial insurgency of 1857, these printed images have been integral to the rise of a nationalist consciousness in India, through their representational work of figuring the nation—as cartographic entity, as mythic origin, as woman. But these prints have also served to inscribe what Benedict Anderson (1983) has famously called

The author, in this chapter, has refered to Mumbai, Kolkata and Chennai by their former names—Bombay, Calcutta and Madras.

'imagined communities', functioning in India as the pictorial equivalents to Anderson's newspapers and books through their pan-national circulation as objects of common recognition, enabled by the rise of 'print capitalism'. To this extent, most of the work that has been done on calendar art has been concerned with the various aspects of nationalism (example, Pinney, 1997, 1999; Uberoi, 1990), as is the case with work on other aspects of the Indian 'culture industry', and particularly the commercial cinema (Chakravarty, 1993; Dwyer and Pinney, 2001).

Recently, with the rise of satellite and cable television in the subcontinent and the close and fluid links of South Asian culture industries with an increasingly assertive South Asian diaspora, a great deal of attention is being focussed on the way in which popular cultural forms, and again especially the commercial cinema, are negotiating questions of transnational identity (example, Gillespie, 1995; Inden, 1999; Mishra 2002; Uberoi, 1998). This negotiation is particularly apparent in Hindi film narratives from the mid-1990s onwards, in their formal aspects and in their performance of self-reflexivity. These features of the 'Bollywood' cinema are closely articulated with its address to a transnational South Asian middle class and corresponding changes in modes of production and distribution. Scholarly attention to these recent processes of global border-crossing has led to, or coincided with, a retroactive recognition of the various ways in which the Indian (not just Hindi) commercial cinema has been a transnational phenomenon almost throughout its history, whether this be a matter of its appropriating and adapting foreign elements, techniques and narratives, or of Indian films being shown in Africa, the Middle East, Greece, Turkey, China, South East Asia, Russia and Eastern Europe since the 1940s and 1950s.

I want to suggest, however, that the scholarly focus on nationalism, and now on transnationalism, while entirely appropriate and productive from one perspective, has tended to obscure other processes occurring at more 'local', sub-national levels, which also articulate with these larger national and transnational contexts. As I hope to show, attention to these other processes enriches the problematics of 'border-crossing' by demonstrating how the question is not simply one of interaction and exchange between pre-defined, static, and monolithic 'cultures', but of encounters that actively *produce* identitarian categories such as national/Indian, western, international, regional, local, communal and so on (on the 'production of locality' see Appadurai, 1995). These processes become apparent on examining the genealogy of pan-national cultural forms such as calendar art and commercial cinema in a manner that conducts some border-crossing of its own: tracing their development in relation to a wider visual 'culture industry' in nineteenth- and twentieth-century India, and the links between their visual idioms as well as those of other contemporaneous forms such as fine art, advertising, illustrated magazines and comic books. In particular, thinking together the technologies, aesthetics and political economies of image-production in the earlier part of the century reveals the ways in which transnationally-derived formal means and national markets are harnessed to the consolidation of caste, regional and/or linguistic as well as national identity. This chapter seeks to foreground some of these processes in the regional context of the western Indian state of Maharashtra, of which Bombay (Mumbai) is the capital, and its early twentieth-century mix of continuing feudal patronage, bureaucratic–institutional consolidation and commercial–industrial development.[1] Examining these earlier moments in the growth of an 'indigenous' capitalist sector might nuance our understanding of the post-liberalisation political scenario, and of phenomena such as the explosion of television broadcasting in the vernacular languages. But also, what is at stake here is the intellectual investment in what might variously be called the vernacular, subaltern or provincial histories of the post-colony as opposed to metropolitan, diaspora-centred concerns—although this is a contentious distinction that necessarily has a performative rather than a theoretical salience.

In mapping something of this 'sub-national' terrain onto an otherwise transnational set of concerns I approach the commercial cinema as a node in what Gilles Deleuze and Felix Guattari (1977, 1987) call a rhizomatic network, whose ceaseless proliferations make various kinds of lateral linkages across heterogeneous categories. The strength of a rhizomatic approach is that it allows us to simultaneously hold in view different registers of efficacy. Thus, for instance, calendar art images, whether as religious icons, as commodities, or as calendars that are given away as gift-cum-advertisements, insist on being valued in their capacity as objects whose efficacy resides in their specific material presence as much as in their meaning. Most analyses of visual culture emphasise the effects and affects that flow from the meanings of objects or from their work of representation; here, however, I want to foreground those that flow from their production and circulation, from the networks they inscribe (local,

[1] 'Maharashtra' is something of a retrospective term in this instance—it was not declared a state until 1 May 1960, when the Marathi and Gujarati speaking areas of the erstwhile Bombay Presidency were separated. However the concept of Maharashtra as a Maratha state had existed in the western Indian imaginary since the reign of Shivaji.

national and transnational), and the forms of sociality and mobility that they enable. This is why I proceed by stringing my narrative in this chapter rather unfashionably along a series of representative figures—artists, in fact: producers rather than texts or consumers. My aim here is not to revive the idea that authorial intention provides a privileged key to reading a text, even though I am concerned to recognise the part that some of these under-acknowledged figures have played in South Asia's cultural history. Nor is it to discredit the essential procedure of close formal analysis. On the contrary, my hope is that such readings might be further enhanced by viewing these figures and their products as nodes that *embody* the intersections between visual media within the culture industry, between economic contexts of production, and between political agendas. The thread that links these figures is their mobilisation of mythic and religious material, which is often aligned with an 'Indian' or 'traditional' image-making practice. The use of such materials in cinema and print has lent itself to a variety of aesthetic and political strategies in both embodying and constructing—or in other words performing as well as representing—the categories of location and tradition. As the following representative figures demonstrate, however, non-indigenous or 'transnational' techniques, forms and ideas have also been integral to the figuring of various levels of location.

I shall begin at the origin of Indian cinema with the pioneering film-maker Dadasaheb Phalke (1870–1944), who made one of the first feature films in India or indeed anywhere in the world, *Raja Harishchandra*, in 1913. An oft-quoted excerpt from an essay by Phalke, signalling the impact of European cinema on his nationalist motivations, describes how he was inspired to go to England and buy a movie camera after seeing a film on the life of Christ:

> While the life of Christ was rolling fast before my eyes I was mentally visualizing the gods Shri Krishna, Shri Ramachandra, their Gokul and Ayodhya .... Could we, the sons of India, ever be able to see Indian images on the screen? (Rajadhyaksha, 1993: 49).[2]

Film scholar Ashish Rajadhyaksha (1993) and art critic Geeta Kapur (1993) have made links between Dadasaheb Phalke and another seminal figure, the painter and early entrepreneur of chromolithography or colour

[2] It is not clear whether this *Life of Christ* was the Pathe film from 1902 or Alice Guy's 1906 film for Gaumont.

printing, Raja Ravi Varma (1848–1906). First, there was a direct connection: one of Phalke's many jobs, after working as a theatrical scene painter, a photographer, a draughtsman and a magician's assistant, was as a lithographic transfer artist at the Ravi Varma Fine Art Lithographic Press in Malavali, between Bombay and Pune, producing popular chromolithographic prints on mythological, historical and iconic subjects. Indeed, after that, and before becoming a film-maker, Phalke ran his own printing press. Ravi Varma had started his press in Bombay in 1894, in financial partnership with Govardhandas Khatau Makhanji, who might well have been the elder son of Khatau Makhanji, a leading member of Bombay's Bhatia trading community and the founder of the Khatau Mill in 1874, now the cornerstone of a major business house.[3] Varma's was not the first chromolithographic press in India, but it expanded the existing market for prints to the point where it could legitimately be called a mass market, with pan-national distribution through agents and a new breed of picture merchants and framing shops.[4]

This arena of circulation enacted and inhabited the nation-space in one register, while Varma's images figured a national cultural imaginary in another. Varma's prints prefigure Phalke's cinematic enterprise in that his press played a leading role in bringing religious and mythic imagery into a pan-Indian public sphere, as part of a growing nationalist discourse on Indianness and civilisation. In so doing, it conventionalised a visual vocabulary for the mythic past, its costumes, gestures and mise-en-scène, drawing on a rich mix of elements including Parsi and folk theatre, European neoclassicism and history painting, and the South Indian Tanjore painting tradition (Figure 3.1). Ashish Rajadhyaksha firmly situates Phalke's cinematic project within a similar nationalist frame, again citing Phalke when he writes: 'My films are *swadeshi* in the sense that the capital, ownership, employees and stories are *swadeshi*' (Rajadhyaksha, 1993: 66).[5] But Phalke's nationalism was not just a matter of the means of production:

[3] Apart from the compatibility of dates, his involvement with the Ravi Varma press would be consistent with Tripathi and Mehta's account of the Khataus, which characterises them as cautious participants in industry at that stage, still somewhat overshadowed by the trading ethos from which they emerged, and preferring to ride on the initiatives of others than to take bold entrepreneurial risks of their own (Tripathi and Mehta, 1990).

[4] Some of the early picture merchants included Anant Shivaji Desai in Bombay and the Delhi firm Hem Chander Bhargava (established in 1900), S.S. Brijbasi in Karachi (established in 1927), Harnarayan and Sons of Jodhpur, and Nathmal Chandelia of Calcutta and Jaipur (the last two are mentioned in Ambalal, 1987).

[5] The *swadeshi* movement sought to oppose colonial rule through self-sufficiency in manufacture.

Figure 3.1
Arjuna and Subhadra by Raja Ravi Varma, Oil, 1896
Source: Maharaja Fateh Singh Museum Trust, Baroda.

both Rajadhyaksha and Kapur also highlight the formal challenges that faced both Phalke and Varma in finding 'Indian images', or in other words a visual idiom that might figure forth or actualise the necessarily virtual genealogy of a newly-constructed Indian national subject. Central to this challenge was the disjuncture between nationalism's imperative of bringing this Indian subject into the post-Enlightenment civilisational narrative of a teleological 'history', and its location of the essence of Indianness in a timeless, mythic realm that must be recast as the origin of the vector of that history. Their visual solutions to this 'representational dilemma' (Kapur, 1989) deployed an illusionism of technique—magical special effects in the case of Phalke, and the selective adoption of European perspective and three-dimensional modelling in the case of Varma—alongside a compelling 'frontality' in framing, and a sense of ritual ornamentation and rhythm, that evoked a devotional engagement with the iconic image ('frontality' is a term used by Geeta Kapur to characterise popular aesthetics in India; see Kapur, 1993: 20).

The narrative impulse in the historicisation of mythic scenarios in Varma's paintings often gave way in his prints to a more explicitly iconic mise en scène. In Phalke's case, while the use of mythic material literally invokes the ritual relationship to the iconic image, Kapur argues that by the 1930s, with the *bhakti* biographical or 'saint film' genre, the mythic or iconic is mediated to 'secular effect' through the use of a specifically cinematic language for a productive, metaphoric narrative of social praxis.[6] While I would essentially endorse Kapur's and Rajadhyaksha's reading of both Phalke and Varma as harnessing illusionist techniques to a frontal imperative, I would want to contest the over-reliance on the category of frontality, which enables Kapur to draw a direct lineage from Phalke to the saint films, pioneered by Vishnupant Damle and Shaikh Fattelal of the Prabhat Film Company: from Phalke's *Raja Harishchandra* or *Kaliya Mardan* to Damle and Fattelal's 1936 classic *Sant Tukaram*, about the life of a seventeenth-century Maharashtrian poet-saint (see Chatterjee, this volume).

[6] Here, Kapur is using the work of Paul Ricoeur to think about myth as narrative fiction, so that on the one hand cinematic illusionism cannot be reduced to realism, nor can the filmic use of iconicity be reduced to a manifestation of religiosity-as-ideology. To this extent, Kapur presupposes an opposition between religion as ideology on the one hand and as tradition, culture or aesthetics on the other—which gets mapped onto a distinction between institutionalised religion and the personalised practices of *bhakti* or devotion that have often been associated with egalitarian social movements: an opposition which is arguably untenable.

Kapur discusses *Sant Tukaram* as an instance of the secular, socially transformative or radical potentials of the cinematic mediation of mythic material. I want to suggest, however, that there is an important missing link between Phalke and the Prabhat Film Company, which is elided in the formalist identification of common cultural sources and a generalised 'popular' frontal aesthetic as sites of continuity. This missing link is my next figure or node in the network: the carpenter, sculptor, painter, photographer, set designer, film technician and director from Kolhapur, Baburao Mestri (1890–1954), better known as Baburao 'Painter'.

Baburao Painter and his cousin, Anandrao, can legitimately be placed on a continuum with Prabhat Film Company. Damle and Fattelal, who founded Prabhat with V. Shantaram, had been assistants to Anandrao in his set-design work for Marathi drama companies, and apprentices and collaborators of Painter when he started the Maharashtra Film Company in 1919; Damle and Painter had assembled their own camera in 1918. I would contend that the lower-middle class and/or working-caste backgrounds and local alliances of Painter, Damle, Fattelal and Shantaram might have something to do with the radical edge and affective charge of the 'saint films', and the channelling of cinema's narrative mediation of mythic material towards a transformative social vision. Painter, Anandrao and Fattelal all came from artisan backgrounds, a significant context for their skills in painting and the design and construction of sets, and for their adoption of informal modes of training. Fattelal, for instance, was apprenticed to the celebrated local Kolhapur painter, Abalal Rahiman, in contrast to Phalke, who had attended art schools in Bombay and Baroda. But in terms of form, too, as Pramod Kale (1979) has argued, there is a distinction to be made between Phalke's technomagical virtuosity and the relatively realist idiom with which Painter pursued his more explicitly political themes.

Apart from shooting documentary footage of an Indian National Congress session in 1918, Painter's second feature, *Sairandhari* (1919), was based on the controversial play *Kichakavadha* that had been banned by the colonial government for its political allegorisation of an episode from the Mahabharata (Kaur, 2003: 73; Pinney, 1999: 215–16). The film, too, was censored for the graphic violence of the scene where the character Bhima (who represents the nationalist leader Tilak) kills Kichak. Painter's *Savkari Pash* (1925), about a peasant's exploitation by a greedy moneylender, is seen as establishing the genre of the social melodrama. From all accounts, Painter had a painterly *and* craftsmanlike approach to cinema, working slowly from elaborate storyboards and making sophisticated technical innovations in order to achieve precise visual effects; he pioneered artificial lighting, fades and the use of filters and coloured backdrops to provide the right shades of grey (Kale, 1989; Mandare, 1995; Rajadhyaksha and Willemen, 1994). He also designed his own sets and, of course, painted the posters for his films.

Both Phalke and Painter were inspired by the radical Maharashtrian anti-colonial leader, Bal Gangadhar Tilak—indeed Painter actively sought and received his blessing, inviting him to his first film premier—but each articulated differently with the many facets of Tilak's nationalist agenda. Phalke's *swadeshi* vision was a pan-national one, as epitomised in the name of his company, Hindustan Cinema Films; while Painter's Maharashtra Film Company, and then Prabhat, reflected their more local alliances. Painter and Prabhat had strong backing from within Kolhapur itself: they were supported by the successful singer, Tanibai Kagalkar—a female professional with personal wealth—and the gold and silver merchant, Kulkarni. But also, the local Maratha rulers, Chhatrapati Shahu Maharaj, his successor Rajaram, and Rajaram's sister the Rani of Dewas, lent them resources like palaces, costumes, animals, and soldiers for their shoots, as did the Rani of Jath, who apparently lent the Prabhat crew 400 spotless cows to shoot *Gopalkrishna*. Rajaram is said to have arranged battle scenes and personally supervised their shooting. Kolhapur provided a conducive environment for the entry of men from craft backgrounds into this new medium of industrial art, at least in part because of Shahu Maharaj's explicitly anti-Brahmin and, therefore, anti-Tilak agenda. Opposed to what he saw as a Brahmin–Vaishya capitalist nexus represented by Tilak, Shahu Maharaj sought to forge a 'soldier'-worker alliance: thus his attempts to develop professional opportunities for artisan castes, which translated into patronage for painting and sculpture, and then for the cinema (Kale, 1989: 1511–12).[7]

Thus, if what made the early cinema viable was partly the fascination of its technological novelty and partly its adoption of the familiar forms of mass address developed by vernacular devotional movements, there were varying currents within the mytho-political stream, ranging from social realism to political allegory to techno-magical attraction. These variations were inflected not just by differing visions of nationalist reform, but by the political–economic configuration of the sites at which these struggles were carried out. Lithographs, too, followed a similar pattern of variation, catering to a pan-national Puranic or mythical imaginary as

[7] Painter, however, was a supporter of Tilak, who (as mentioned earlier) he invited to his first film premier.

well as to specific local and regional cults or pilgrimage sites, and ranging from clearly political references to, say, the Cow Protection agitation, through more veiled anti-colonial allegories, to what Christopher Pinney has described as more 'subliminal', and thus more 'innocent' depictions of an idealised nation space (Pinney, 1997: 840). Here, Pinney refers to the mythic landscapes in the icons painted by artists attached to the Krishna shrine at Nathdwara in Rajasthan, which were taken up for printing by the Brijbasi brothers of Karachi and Mathura in 1927 and are still in circulation to this day.

As the film industry grew in Bombay, Calcutta and Madras (as they were formerly known), it provided opportunities for aspiring artists from all over the country, for work on make-up, sets and art direction, publicity banners and 'showcards' (painted posters placed in theatre lobbies and windows). A number of artists who went on to work for the more lucrative and stable calendar trade centred on the south Indian town of Sivakasi in the 1960s started out in the film line, some of them attracted to the industry after studying at the art schools in these cities (for 'fine art' alone would not earn them a living). K. Madhavan, who studied at the Madras School of Art, did sets and banners for the Gemini Studios in the 1940s; S. Courtallam, also from the Madras School of Art, learnt the art of make-up in Madras in the 1950s from 'Haribabu', a leading make-up man of the time, who had himself studied at the Calcutta School of Art. (And just to gesture towards another rhizomatic strand here, Courtallam also briefly put his make-up skills to work for the state, creating disguises for police detectives.) The extraordinary Ram Kumar Sharma (b. 1923), a self-taught artist from Meerut, came to Bombay in 1941, eventually becoming an art director at Filmistan from 1952–60. Ram Kumar worked for calendars for a while, and a number of calendar artists, including J.P. Singhal, Ved Prakash and Courtallam were his apprentices; however he lost interest and went back to film.[8] However, the most celebrated of them all was a graduate from Bombay's J.J. School of Art who began his commercial career in 1939, painting MGM showcards for Bombay's Metro theatre: S.M. Pandit, cited as an influence and a source of inspiration by almost all the calendar artists I have spoken to.

Pandit (1916–91), was born into an artisan family from Gulbarga (in present-day Karnataka);[9] his very first teacher, Shankar Rao Allandkar,

[8] This is when I met him a few years ago while he was working on the television series, *Ashoka the Great*.

[9] Pandit's grandfather had been a *kansagar* or manufacturer of copper vessels; his son describes their community as 'Vishwakarma' (the god of crafts). Information on Pandit

had been trained at the J.J. School of Art (hereafter JJ), and had a sideline designing showcards for Gulbarga's Lakshmi Theatre. Pandit's intense desire to master naturalist techniques took him through three different art schools: the Madras School of Art, Bombay's JJ and Nutan Kala Mandir, also in Bombay. His teachers were also mostly Indian art school products practicing a version of western academicism. His headmaster at JJ was M.V. Dhurandhar (also, incidentally, from Kolhapur), a successor to Ravi Varma in his use of naturalist techniques to depict Indian mythological, historical and literary themes. Dhurandhar and Pandit index the persistence in Bombay of what many calendar artists call 'realism'. Unpacking the way this complex, loaded term is used in this context warrants a separate paper; suffice it to say, that if in the early decades of the twentieth century, 'realism' was aligned with western-style academicism, in opposition to the neo-traditionalist Bengal Renaissance and its quest for an 'Indian' art style, it has later come to represent a strong alternative current for many painters, including some trained at art schools, but often from craft backgrounds, who are unable to reconcile themselves with what they see as the fraudulence of 'modern art'.

Pandit's passion for 'realism' and his skill in portraiture were well suited to the film posters on which he founded his commercial career. Around 1938, he and two others set up the Young Artists Commercial Arts Studio in Bombay, designing the publicity for Franz Osten's 1938 Bombay Talkies film *Bhabhi*, and becoming the first Indians to create showcards featuring stars like Greta Garbo, Norma Shearer and Joan Crawford for MGM, whose publicity had until then come from the USA (see also Sengupta, this volume). Film posters were usually done in oils on cloth (like stage backdrops), a slow technique requiring a good deal of control. Instead, Pandit began to use the quicker-drying gouache (still on cloth), while retaining the illusionist techniques associated with oils, an innovation which became his trademark. Pandit continued to design posters when he left Young Artists to join Ratan Batra's advertising agency, which catered to several of the new indigenous industrial houses, including textile mills like Mafatlal, Kohinoor and Khatau (a name which came up earlier in the context of Ravi Varma). Around this time, Pandit met Baburao Patel, the editor of *Filmindia* magazine (an English-language film monthly, started

---

based on an interview with his son, K.S. Pandit, and his wife, Nalini Pandit, Gulbarga, December 1995, also V.T. Kale (1989); Shriram Khadilkar, 'Aata Keval Swatah Satheech Painting Karnar' (Now I Shall Only Paint for Myself), interview with S.M. Pandit, *Maharashtra Times*, 24 August 1991; and Shirish Pai, 'Chitrakaleche "Pandit"—S.M. Pandit' ("Pandit" of Fine Arts—SM Pandit), *Loksatta* (*'Kala Kunj' section*), 28 January 1989.

in 1935), who asked him to design *Filmindia*'s covers, and also became a channel for contracts from the film industry (Figure 3.2). By 1944, Pandit had set up his own studio called Studio S.M. Pandit in Bombay's Shivaji Park, producing film publicity for Prabhat Studios, Raj Kapoor, and Sohrab Modi among others. His visitors here included Baburao Painter.

Figure 3.2
Cover of *Filmindia* magazine, August 1953, Studio S.M. Pandit
Source: K.S. Pandit.

One of Pandit's assistants was a young, self-taught artist from Goa by the name of Raghubir Mulgaonkar (1922–76), whose work appeared in *Filmindia* under the signature of Studio S.M. Pandit: he is said to have done much of the publicity artwork for V. Shantaram's first Bombay film, *Shakuntala* (1943).[10] By 1945, Mulgaonkar had set up his own studio, expanding into illustrations for books and magazines. Both men continued to work for *Filmindia* in a characteristic style similar to Hollywood posters of the 1930s and 1940s (particularly those of MGM)[11] carrying their glamorous appeal, dramatic expressiveness and bold, graphic composition across to their other work, including the mythological paintings which have proved to be their most popular and influential legacy.

Pandit's turn to mythology came in the early 1950s, when the proliferation of offset presses brought high-volume colour printing within affordable reach of companies seeking to consolidate their image in a newly independent India.[12] The Bombay Fine Arts Press and Nagpur's Shivraj Fine Arts Press supplied both Pandit and Mulgaonkar with a steady stream of work doing mythological paintings for advertisements and calendars. Perhaps the most famous of Pandit's images was a Ravi Varma-inspired painting of Sita pointing out the golden deer to Ram, used by the Parle confectionery and soft drink company on a calendar and packaging (a later Pandit painting for Parle features Nala and Damayanti above a range of Parle products, including a toffee tin bearing the same Ram-Sita image; see Figures 3.3a and 3.3b.

The influence of Hollywood film posters is particularly evident in the treatment of his characters' faces and expressions, a soft-skinned, pink-cheeked, dewy-eyed, 'made-up' look, with highlights bouncing off their lips and hair—or in his depictions of Shiva as a bluish, muscular Tarzan-type hero clad in a leopard skin (Figure 3.4), and a Disney-like detailing of flowers and animals. Mulgaonkar took this soft-focus look a step further with his use of the airbrush, a technique which eventually cost him his life (he died of lung cancer); see Figure 3.6.

[10] This is somewhat controversial, as this was a job which many people see as a particular triumph for Pandit; the claim that Mulgaonkar did the artwork is made by his brother, G.D. Mulgaonkar.

[11] As distinct from the film posters of RKO, Paramount or Warner Brothers, MGM's were characterised by their brightness and simplicity, often featuring portraits of the stars against simple monochrome backgrounds (Edwards, 1985: 68).

[12] The first offset press was set up in Calcutta in 1930; however from the 1950s, a number of machines were imported relatively cheaply from Eastern bloc countries like the German Democratic Republic which accepted payment in rupees. (Interview with P. Dharmar, National Litho Press, Sivakasi, December 1994.)

Figure 3.3a
Nala-Damayanti by S.M. Pandit. An advertisement for Parle company
Source: K.S. Pandit.

Figure 3.3b
Ram-Sita on a toffee tin by S.M. Pandit
Source: K.S. Pandit.

All these works depart from the stylised, frontal depictions and elaborate ornamentation of the Varma-Phalke-Prabhat era, as well as from the more iconic framing pictures like Brijbasi's (Figure 3.5). Indeed, the Nathdwara calendar painter, Indra Sharma, said that often publishers would seek him out rather than Pandit because Pandit's gods were too realistic, too much like ordinary men and women.

If this more narrative impulse was partly to do with the influence of film posters, in Mulgaonkar's case it also tied in with another context for his mythological work: his illustrations for a new genre of vernacular Marathi-language magazines, which were hugely popular from about 1946 to 1976. These were the annual 'Diwali specials', with titles like *Alka*, *Ratnadeep*, *Ratnaprabha*, *Mangaldeep*, *Deepawali* and *Deeplakshmi*.[13] These were intended as family fare, catering to a vernacular '*rasik*' sensibility[14]—a kind of relaxed, sensual aesthetic—with stories, poems, articles on theatre, film, science, religion and culture, character sketches of illustrious personalities, satire, cartoons, and above all, offset printed black and white and colour plates on art paper. Mulgaonkar's illustrations included the life of Krishna, the Ramayana, Kalidasa's *Meghdoot* and *Geet Govind*, biographies of Marathi stage star Bal Gandharva, Shivaji and Gautam Buddha, the saint poets, and various manifestations of the Indian women as *nayikas* (actress) like Pavitra or Mangala, as well as the usual Radha, Sita and so on. He also illustrated advertisements; the back covers of Mulgaonkar's own publications advertised a Nasik-based chemical company called Bitco, which also commissioned him to do a series of paintings for the Krishna temple at Muktidham in Nasik. Like the pan-national magazines for 'neo-literates' such as *Kalyan* from the Geeta Press, Gorakhpur, or the later *Navneet* and *Bhavan's Journal* (started in the early 1950s by the novelist, K.M. Munshi, under the auspices of the Bharatiya Vidya Bhavan), the popular Marathi magazines of the 1950s and 1960s were sites for the delineation of an Indian modernity where 'Indian' religion and culture, often formulated in opposition to a decadent, materialistic 'West', negotiated its relationship with the discourses of science, technology and progress and the practices of commercial and industrial capital; they often carried articles on the lives and philosophies of prominent industrialists, as well as meditations on, for instance, space exploration, the ideas of Einstein or satires on the western influences on modern youth.

[13] Similar Diwali special issues were produced in several other Indian languages as well, including Hindi, Gujarati and Tamil.

[14] A *rasik* is one who partakes of *rasa*, meaning enjoyment or flavour, connoting aesthetic pleasure in a manner more akin to the earlier Greek meaning of *aesthesia* with its emphasis on the senses.

Figure 3.4
Shiva Ashirwad (Shiva's Blessing)
by S.M. Pandit, offset print (50×36),
published by Calco, Bombay

Figure 3.5
Shiva Gouri by Indra Sharma,
print (17×12), published
by S.S. Brijbasi and Sons

Figure 3.6
Bharat Janm (The Birth of Bharat) by R.S. Mulgaonkar (21×27.5 approx.)
Source: Deeplakshmi magazine.

But these magazines that proliferated after Independence operated out of different articulations of power and locality: the Bharatiya Vidya Bhavan was a nationalist institution with the backing of one of the country's most powerful industrialists, G.D. Birla; the Marathi magazine *Kirloskar*, started in 1920 by another industrial giant, attempted to forge a kind of Maharashtrian 'Protestant ethic' with its slogan of 'inspiration-industry-success'[15] while Diwali annuals like *Ratnaprabha* depended on smaller local capitalists like Bitco, or another manufacturer of tooth powder, Porwal and Company of Pune. The regional *rasik* flavour of the Diwali specials aligned itself with the popular culture industry in a way that the more reformist high moral tone of the theological *Kalyan* and the culturally purist English-language *Bhavan's Journal* tended not to. Neither of the latter, for instance, gave much credence to film as a cultural form. Interestingly, *Kalyan* is an early instance of the Indian culture industry's address to a transnational diaspora: from 1934 the Geeta Press also produced an English version, the *Kalyana-Kalpataru*, for overseas Indians.

A more recent example of this phenomenon, which also precedes Bollywood's current address to a cosmopolitan Indian middle class, is the *Amar Chitra Katha* comic series, which transmuted mythological imagery into yet another medium. Started in 1967 by Anant Pai, its stated aim was to provide children with reading that would reacquaint them with the Indian classics (a need brought home to Pai by the inability of a little boy on a TV quiz show to name Ram's mother).[16] The first comic in the series, *Krishna*, was produced in English, and although many titles have been translated into most major Indian languages English remains the most popular, with Hindi the only other significant Indian language. This pan-Indian form was mainly consumed by a fast-growing audience of middle-class, literate

[15] Pramod Kale cites the *Kirloskar* magazine as a possible inspiration to V. Shantaram in his 'rags to riches' success (Kale, 1989: 1515). The *Kirloskar* carried articles on 'scientific, social and industrial matters ... (and) was seen by the reading public not merely as the messenger of a business group and its products, but also as an instrument of social change' (Tripathi and Mehta, 1990: 139). Its success encouraged the Kirloskars to start *Stree*, for women, and *Manohar*, an artistic and literary magazine, both in Marathi. Interestingly, Laxmanrao Kirloskar, the founder of the Kirloskar industrial house, had attended the J.J. School of Art; his first job was as a mechanical drawing teacher at the Victoria Jubilee Technical Institute (VJTI) in Bombay. He was assisted in the early stages of his entrepreneurial efforts (producing ploughs) by his friend from VJTI, Balasaheb Pantapratinidhi, who provided a factory site in his principality at Aundh (which later grew into the township of Kirloskarwadi).

[16] Information on *Amar Chitra Katha* is from Frances W. Pritchett (1995), John Stratton Hawley (1995), and from an interview with Ram Waeerkar, illustrator on the *Amar Chitra Katha* series, Bombay, December 1995.

English-speakers in India and, by the 1980s, a large diasporic readership keen to stay in touch with its roots. *Amar Chitra Katha* soon came to be used, and subsequently to view itself, as an authoritative source on the 'classics', quickly accruing a hypertrophy of textual elements—footnotes, glossaries and so on—bound volumes of the comics are found in many Indian school libraries. Here again, as in the cinema, we see a tension between the visual imperative of narrative 'realism' and the increasing burden of authority that *Amar Chitra Katha* has taken on as a vehicle of 'tradition'. *Amar Chitra Katha*'s first illustrator, Ram Waeerkar, spoke of his frustration when Anant Pai, a stickler for *shastric* textual accuracy, insisted that male gods like Ram and Krishna could not be depicted as muscular action heroes. Waeerkar, a largely self-taught artist, had picked up his knowledge of male anatomy by copying from the Tarzan comics, but given Pai's strictures he tempered this influence with that of Vijay Bhatt's Ramayana films of the 1940s.

Despite such differences between these cultural products and their modes of address, however, it would be unproductive to map their readership onto specific caste or class fractions, for more often than not people would encounter several of these forms, and negotiate between the overlapping or conflicting cultural modalities they made available. In other words, just as I have been looking at the producers of mass-cultural artefacts as nodes in a network, consumers also embody junctures between multiple modes and registers of reception—and indeed, as I have argued elsewhere (Jain, 2003), between what might otherwise appear to be incommensurable frames of value and efficacy.

Even as mythic and magical idioms have imparted certain formal characteristics to the popular visual field, there are also significant distinctions to be made within this arena. One of the things I have tried to show here is how mythic visuality in cinema and print has been available to a range of players and cultural-political agendas, and the *multiple* ways in which its formal idioms have been shot through with a tension between narrative and frontality, between historical teleology and iconic stasis, between Pandit's MGM-style 'realism' and Indra Sharma's iconicity. But if, despite these heterogeneities and tensions, this realm of popular print culture seems at times to be homogeneous, with evident similarities across the visual media, I have also tried to show how this has often had to do with the fact that sometimes the same people have been working across a broad spectrum of commercial opportunity. While these remarkable artists, often from craft backgrounds, seldom gained recognition in the elite realm of fine art, they regularly achieved material success and social mobility through their work behind the scenes. To deploy Deleuzo-Guattarian terminology once again, this might be seen as a deterritorialising movement enabled by print capitalism. However, it is a movement whose reterritorialising obverse has been the re-harnessing of this print culture, and the mythic imaginaries it produced, by nationalism and by capital's postcolonial compact with absolutism.

References

AMBALAL, AMIT. 1987. *Krishna as Shrinathji: Rajasthani Paintings from Nathdwara*. Ahmedabad: Mapin.

ANDERSON, BENEDICT. 1983. *Imagined Communities: Reflections on the Origin and Spread of Nationalism*. London: Verso.

APPADURAI, ARJUN. 1995. 'The Production of Locality', in Richard Fardon (ed.), *Counterworks*. London: Routledge.

CHAKRAVARTY, SUMITA. 1993. *National Identity in Indian Popular Cinema, 1947–1987*. Austin: University of Texas Press.

DELEUZE, GILLES and FELIX GUATTARI. 1977. *Anti-Oedipus*. Trans. Robert Hurley, Mark Seem, Helen R. Lane. New York: Viking Books.

———. 1987. *A Thousand Plateaus: Capitalism and Schizophrenia*. Trans. B. Massumi. Minneapolis: University of Minnesota Press.

DWYER, RACHEL and CHRISTOPHER PINNEY (eds). 2001. *Pleasure and the Nation*. New Delhi: OUP.

EDWARDS, GREGORY J. 1985. *The International Film Poster*. London: Columbus Books.

GILLESPIE, MARIE. 1995. *Television, Ethnicity, and Cultural Change*. London: Routledge.

HAWLEY, JOHN S. 1995. 'The Saints Subdued: Domestic Virtue and National Integration in *Amar Chitra Katha*', in Babb and Wadley (eds), *Media and the Transformation of Religion in South Asia*. Philadelphia: University of Pennsylvania Press.

INDEN, R. 1999. 'Transnational Class, Erotic Arcadis and Commercial Utopia in Hindi Films', in Christiane Brosius and Melissa Butcher (eds), *Image Journeys: Audio-Visual Media and Cultural Change in India*, pp. 41–66, New Delhi: Sage Publications.

JAIN, KAJRI. 2003. 'More than Meets the Eye: The Circulation of Images and the Embodiment of Value', in Sumathi Ramaswamy (ed.), *Beyond Appearances?: Visual Practices and Ideologies in Modern India*. New Delhi: Sage Publications.

KALE, PRAMOD. 1979. 'Ideas, Ideals and the Market: A Study of Marathi Films', *Economic and Political Weekly*, XIV(35): 1511–20.

KALE, V.T. 1989. *S.M. Pandit: A Biography*. Bangalore: Karnataka Lalithakala Academy.

KAPUR, GEETA. 1989. 'Ravi Varma: Representational Dilemmas of a Nineteenth Century Indian Painter', *Journal of Arts and Ideas*, 17–18: 59–80.

———. 1993. 'Revelation and Doubt: Sant Tukaram and Devi', in Tejaswini Niranjana, P. Sudhir and Vivek Dhareshwar (eds), *Interrogating Modernity: Culture and Colonialism in India*. Calcutta: Seagull Books.

KAUR, RAMINDER. 2003. *Performative Politics and the Cultures of Hinduism: Public Uses of Religion in Western India*. New Delhi: Permanent Black.

MANDARE, SURYAKANT. 1995. *Vishwakarma*. Pune: Purandare Prakashan.

MISHRA, VIJAY. 2002. *Bollywood Cinema: Temples of Desire*. London: Routledge.

PINNEY, CHRISTOPHER. 1997. 'The Nation (Un)Pictured? Chromolithography and "Popular" Politics in India: 1878–1995', *Critical Inquiry*, 23: 834–67.

———. 1999. 'Indian Magical Realism: Notes on Popular Visual Culture', in Gautam Bhadra, Gyan Prakash and Susie Tharu (eds), *Subaltern Studies X: Writings on South Asian History and Society*, pp. 201–33, New Delhi: OUP.

PRITCHETT, FRANCES W. 1995. 'The World of *Amar Chitra Katha*', in Babb and Wadley (eds), *Media and the Transformation of Religion in South Asia*. Philadelphia: University of Pennsylvania Press.

RAJADHYAKSHA, ASHISH. 1993. 'The Phalke Era: Conflict of Traditional Form and Modern Technology', in Tejaswini Niranjana, P. Sudhir and Vivek Dhareshwar (eds), *Interrogating Modernity: Culture and Colonialism in India*. Calcutta: Seagull Books.

RAJADHYAKSHA, ASHISH and PAUL WILLEMEN. 1994. *Encyclopedia of Indian Cinema*. New Delhi: OUP and BFI Publishing.

TRIPATHI, DWIJENDRA and MAKARAND MEHTA. 1990. *Business Houses in Western India: A Study in Entrepreneurial Response, 1850–1956*. London: Jaya Books.

UBEROI, PATRICIA. 1990. 'Feminine Identity and National Ethos in Indian Calendar Art', *Economic and Political Weekly*: 41–48.

———. 1998. 'The Diaspora Comes Home: Disciplining Desire in DDLJ', *Contributions to Indian Sociology*, 32(2): 305–36.

4

Icons and Events: Reinventing Visual Construction in Cinema in India

GAYATRI CHATTERJEE

In this chapter, I look at various sources behind modes of visual and narrative (re)configurations in Indian cinema. Like national cinema everywhere, 'traditional forms' as well as 'foreign influences' flowed into the making of 'Indian cinema'; but of interest to a student of cinema are some specific and fascinating features of Indian films that require proper attention. I emphasise two prominent aspects that mark the reconfiguration and formation of cinema in this country. The first is the constant interplay of the *iconic* and *narrative* images. The other is the frontal address of religious and erotic imageries from past traditions as they are reinvented for cinema's contemporary audiences through cinematic elements such as mise en scène and editing.

The *Iconic* Image

The usual way of recognising or describing the *iconic* image in cinema or in painting is that the figure in the image is frontally placed, with the body and face, or only the face and facial features in full view. Making important connections

The author, in this chapter, has refered to Mumbai, Kolkata and Chennai by their former names—Bombay, Calcutta and Madras.

between painting and cinema, Ashish Rajadhyaksha and Geeta Kapur described the iconic image and its full-frontal address as the most distinctive features of Indian cinema (Kapur, 1987; Rajadhyaksha, 1987). They argued that images of actors facing the camera and looking towards it (if not right into it) could be likened to traditional iconic images. It is now time to look at other possibilities within what we perceive as the cinematic iconic image. As we will see, there are departures to every case we make; for example, a face in an iconic image can also be in profile.[1]

I suggest, in relation to film and painting, that:

1. The iconic image stands out on the frame. It is always foregrounded. The figure seems to lie on the surface of the image, creating a flattening effect, with no spatial background. Neither composed around a focal centre nor along diagonals, the image—including faces, figures and events—is distributed over the entire surface. The pictorial surface is the surface of the world. In painting, different events could take place on the same surface, which is divided variously. For example, different colour fields could be used to distinguish events. Peripheries of the pictorial image also come into prominence. Unlike a painting, however, an iconic film image could have depth or can be created in depth.
2. The pictorial iconic image is essentially still and immobile, as if frozen.[2] A striking difference between the pictorial and cinematic icon is that the latter can actually involve a moving figure, since movement of figures and objects can be captured by the movie camera. In other words, a moving image can also be iconic, as we will later see in some detail.
3. An image in a cinematic shot could go on for several minutes, as in the case of the film *Sant Tukaram* (dir. V. Damle and S. Fattelal, Marathi, 1936) where two images of a motionless deity and the devotee-hero take up 160–200 feet of film (about 2–3 minutes duration). Existing over real time, even a still image in motion pictures necessarily contains both, the component of *time* and *movement*. The movement integral to the medium itself renders

[1] In medieval Jain paintings, for example, iconic images are often shown in profile, unless the image is that of a god or a realised soul. These are also distinct in that the face can be in profile but both eyes are made equally visible. The profile or the three-quarter (of the face) is popular in Mughal and other court art.

[2] Some iconic figures might invoke motion or mobility of objects, human or animal figures (like the figure of the goddess Kali is perennially caught in the midst of full motion).

the cinematic icon different from images in other mediums, as exemplified by the difference between the following two experiences: a photograph of a face we might gaze for full 3 minutes and a film image of a face running in front of us for 3 minutes.[3]

Iconic Image from Traditional Sources to Cinema

Iconic images have their source in past material, and so are already known and familiar to the film's spectator either in the form of a narrative or a discourse. An iconic image is an image spectators already hold in their minds, but where meanings and stories lie frozen. When used in a film, such an image acquires new meanings, and a new story is initiated by the use of an icon through the process of editing. When an image is preceded or followed by another image, the aspects of time and motion 'set free' the frozen narrative of a pictorial icon. To understand the trajectory of the image from earlier cultural material to the new filmic one, and to illustrate the diverse sources behind a single iconic representation in film, let us begin with an image that has been popular since the beginning of the last century.

A woman is on her way to worship or perform puja at a temple. She wears a white or saffron-coloured sari, her open hair freshly washed flows down her sides and back. She carries a plate of flowers (and other paraphernalia needed for worship) balanced on her left (or right) palm raised shoulder high. Paintings with such images were most common in Bengal, usually captioned *pūjārinī*—a new word coined for a new image.

Perhaps it is Rabindranath Tagore who introduced the word *pūjārinī* with a long poem thus titled (1899). The poem is about a female court dancer who defies royal orders by praying at the Buddha's stupa, and is thus killed. Later, in 1926, Tagore wrote a play, *Nautir Puja*, which ends with the woman singing and dancing before being executed. Among other contemporary writers, notable is also Bengal's 'rebel poet' Kazi Nazrul Islam's long romantic poem on the *pūjārinī* image. Songs composed on the topic of the temple-going woman-worshipper soon became popular through 78rpm gramophone discs and the radio. Puja-*nritya* or puja-dances,

[3] Actually, several factors decide frontality—like the lens. A frontal image is one taken by a normal lens. A face captured by a wide-angled lens or caught from a very low angle will not be thus defined.

accompanied by songs or instrumental music, were to be extremely popular all across the land.[4]

Interestingly, while the masculine form *pūjāri* means a priest in Bengali, its feminine form is used only to mean 'the wife of a priest', not a woman-priest (perhaps because women traditionally have no right to worship). So, this particular usage of *pūjārinī* as a *woman-going-to-the-temple* is a modern creation—not to be found in dictionaries, but in art and literary practices only.

In Marathi, the word *pūjārinī* exists with a pejorative connotation and does not normally mean a woman-worshipper.[5] Interestingly, the Maharashtrian image pre-dates that in Bengal. A sculpture by Govind Mhatre (1898) on permanent exhibit at the J.J. School of Art in Bombay has an English title *To the Temple*, and a Marathi title (Sanskritised, compounded word) *mandira-patha-gāminī* or 'on the way to the temple'. Tagore had written two articles full of excitement and admiration on this piece of sculpture, however, whether he began coining the image and term after seeing Mhatre's work (or its photograph) cannot be determined.

Significantly, men too worship at temples, but there is no similar image of a temple-going male-worshipper. Also, for the period under consideration it was rare for a woman to go anywhere alone; even now they usually go to the temple with others—men, women and children. These representations are thus about the individuality of women, manifesting desire for modernity and the modern subject.

For antecedents to this image we could go to miniature and other medieval paintings. Particularly common are the images of goddess Parvati worshipping Shiva. Figures of ascetic women occur in the *rāgamālā* paintings too, where each Ragini (melodic pattern marked as feminine) is a heroine or *nāyika*. These paintings are marked by the Indian habit of seeing woman as sacred or erotic, engaged in devotion and renunciation (*bhakti*) or revelling in dressing up and love play (*shringāra*). Small iconic etchings and paintings of the *pūjārinī* and photographs (models were

[4] We were learning them in Bengal in the 1950s. Shanta Gokhale informs that in her childhood in Bombay, she had learnt a dance composition along with a Bengali song from a teacher from Sri Lanka, who came to teach Candy dance to school children. Pushpa Bhave similarly reiterates, through her personal example, the enormous popularity of this Bangla song in the city of Bombay.

[5] Women-worshippers or *pūjārinīs* do conduct worship services in some particular sects in Maharashtra, which are not respected by the mainstream society. Interestingly, a film *pūjārinī* from 1935 by Nandlal Jaswantlal and with E. Billimoria and Sulochana has the English subtitle *Dancer of the Temple*.

dressed up for this purpose) ornamented serialised Indian novels in the early teens and twenties of the twentieth century, marking the transition of visual themes into the print medium, and later into cinema.

The representation of a heroine on her way to the temple often became the opening shot in films from all regions in the early decades of cinema. It is the first image of the Hindi version of *Devdas* (dir. P.C. Barua, Hindi/Bengali, 1935).[6] So, since the Silent Era of Indian cinema, a pictorial and poetic image, made familiar to the reader/spectator through various trajectories, becomes an 'iconic' representation, and is used liberally for telling filmic stories.

Narrativity

The heroine of *Devdas*, Parvati, enters the film narrative as an iconic figure of the woman-worshipper—the *pūjārinī*. Rising from bottom frame, her back towards the audience, she walks away from the camera, which then tracks-in forward. As she turns towards the camera, the mise en scène (the combination of camera position, distance and movement in relation to the character within a frame) itself produces a close-up. Thus, the idea implied in captions such as 'On the way to the temple' is realised here through the technology of the motion picture, making the (moving) image of Parvati going for worship an icon as we have defined it. The momentary close-up pushes the icon towards the storyline. Parvati is distracted upon hearing a song in a male voice (off-screen): 'O friend/lover, come and reside in my heart/mind' (*baalam aan baso more man mein*). She turns around again, walking away from the camera. Listening to the song, she stops in the middle ground, and then exits from the left of frame. This lyrical shift implies within the mise en scène that the iconic woman-worshipper is now waylaid by the call of a man, forgetting what she had set out to do. Parvati goes to Devdas, a childhood friend, a man she loves and worships.[7] And thus begins the story of the film.

---

[6] Today, we take this to be the beginning of the Hindi version. The only (heavily damaged) copy of the Bengali version is kept at the Bangladesh Archive; its beginning is missing.

[7] Urmila Bhidekar points out that the motif of a woman setting out for the temple but going off to meet a lover is common. She provides a suitable example, a famous *khayāl bandish*, or classical-music lyrics by Inayat Khan:

jhanana jhanana jhana-nana-nana bāje bichhuwā.
piyā ke milan ko chali jāt apne mandar so, māi.

It is important to note here how smoothly the iconic image initiates the story-telling process, playing along with what we call the *narrative image*. Films are made up of a constant juxtaposition of both kinds of images. Surely, iconic and narrative film images can be distinct and distinguishable. There can also be interim images anywhere between *iconicity* and *narrativity*. The mixing and mingling of all different kinds of images further the story, and generate meaning and emotions. Naturally, all this happens variously, according to individual directors' predilections, or trends particular to each decade or production house. But the study of visual composition and its interrelationship with narrative matters gives us a better insight into cinema in India, shifting some of the imbalance that is caused when we look only at stories, characters or stereotypes in a film (and relegate them to any single genre).

One Figure: Two Figures

Religious icons contain single or dual figures. For example, Radha and Krishna can be represented singly or together. Images of this divine dyadic relationship are captioned *jugalmūrti* (coupled image). These gods might both look out towards us or they might look at each other. The icon of coupled figures prevails in Indian cinema as *two-shot* compositions. In Barua's *Devdas*, for example, Devdas is sitting by the river with a fishing rod. Parvati steals behind the idling youth, and tickles his ears with a long blade of grass. This teasing of her childhood friend is now a 'two shot' or a shot containing two faces of two characters (see Figure 4.1 on p. 96).

It is noteworthy that the film's hero and heroine, Devdas and Parvati, are *never* filmed in shot counter-shot, only singly or in two shots. The first sequence of the film contains a truly remarkable mise en scène. The camera tracks a full 180 degrees, so that the respective position of the man and the woman is reversed in one single shot. While the effect of this is an *image change* and changed position of characters, such an axis-jump is not created by separate shots, as is usually done. There is no *cut* or separation of the lovers. Rather, the lovers continue to be shown as a duo or *jūgalamūrti* in a two-shot composition.

---

pūjā karan ko nikasi ghar se haun akeli nār,
chaunkata Ināyat bār bār

Figure 4.1
Devdas: Two-shot composition showing Devdas and Paro

Iconic Film Image: Their Source and Social Life

Films are an integral part of the larger social life of images in modern India. Recently, Christopher Pinney and others have written widely about India's popular visual culture. Though more interested in chromolithography and photography, Pinney occasionally refers to cinema, as when he addresses chromolithographs as 'cinema's inter-ocular bedfellow' (Pinney, 2002: 355). Earlier, Rajadhyaksha traced the source of iconic images in cinema to calendar art and credited painter Raja Ravi Varma and his press in Malavli, Maharashtra, for having influenced early film-makers like D.G. Phalke. Phalke had worked in the Ravi Varma Press and so the influence from chromolithograph to film is seen as direct and immediate (see Jain, this volume).[8]

[8] The story of influences is never simple. A familiar image from *Kaliya Daman*—the shot of child Krishna standing on the hood of the serpent-king, Kaliya, as four Queens pray to the child-god—compares well with, and could have come from, a lithographic print by Bamapada Banerjee. I thank Tapati Guha-Thakurta for showing this image from our childhood, as it is in the collection of the Centre of Studies of Social Sciences (CSSS) collection, in Calcutta.

Pinney places chromolithographs in two groups: 'the calendar' ones and those 'to be framed'. I will begin with the latter and call it the 'poster' (a term that is in current use). Printing lithograph and oleograph posters as wall adornments was a vibrant activity from the mid-nineteenth century onwards. Established artists either worked for, or supplied their artwork to, litho-presses. Prints were available in great many styles and a wide range of sectarian and secular topics, covering iconic figures of gods and goddess to representations of events and narratives attached to them. Secular topics included natural scenery, men and women from different walks of life and society, cityscapes and architecture, images of national leaders and 'Mother India'.[9] With the advent of cinema (but before the establishment of the star system) posters carried scenes from films.

A recently acquired chromolithograph entitled *tukārāmāche swargārohan* or *Tukaram's ascent to the heavens* is yet to be dated and so is not possible to say whether it was made before or after the release of the film *Sant Tukaram*.[10] The image is similar to the last shots in the film depicting Tukaram's demise and bodily ascension to the heavens. However, the first instance of a litho print of a Tukaram image to my knowledge belongs in a book, *Tukaram gatha*, by W. Frazer (1923). The hero of the silent film, *Tukaram* (dir. G. Shinde, 1929), bears striking resemblance to this image and the hero of the 1936 film *Sant Tukaram* resembles Tukaram figures in those earlier versions. Thus, images grow familiar and popular in the interactions between popular print and cinema.

Drawn either by artistic aspiration or financial necessity, members of traditional artist–artisan families (*chitrakār, patua, kalākār*), engaged in the modern craft of woodblock cutting and litho-oleograph printing in cities, brought past knowledge into the new profession including film. For example, D. Damle and S. Fattelal, the makers of *Sant Tukaram* were both trained in painting and other artisanal skills.

Chromolithograph and oleograph posters were bought by the trading community, aristocracy and the nouveau riche. These still adorn walls of havelis (mansions) and palaces in Rajasthan, Madhya Pradesh or Uttar Pradesh: it is possible to see them now, as tourism has made many such homes available to the public. A large percentage of these posters were

---

[9] The nation imagined as a mother was depicted as a woman in various garb, iconography and moods. At times she is by herself, at times she is inscribed within the map of the Indian peninsula, and at times she is accompanied by figures of national leaders or her vast population.

[10] Registration No. 764, printed under the aegis of Anant Shivaji Desai and at the Raja Ravi Varma Press.

printed in Calcutta, suggesting the national spread of localised print products. Also, artists from one region were invited in another. For example, M.G. Dhurandhar, popular for illustrations in Marathi books and journals, also provided images for Bengali journals like *Pravāsī* and *Bhāratī*.[11] Reproductions of Raja Ravi Varma's paintings or the works of Bengali painters, Abanindranath Tagore, Asit Haldar and Bamapada Banerjee were very popular all over India, and lesser artists also enjoyed wide circulation.

Such circulating images are grafted on to films, making the medium extremely *hybrid*. A goddess image particular to one region travels to another along with devotees and pilgrim groups. The representation of the goddess Kali, which is particular to Bengal, can be seen all over Maharashtra, Tamil Nadu and Kerala. Perhaps, Swami Vivekananda's visit to south India and the foundation of a temple at Cape Comorin or Kanyakumari spread the worship of his guru Ramakrishna of the Dakshineshwar temple, along with Goddess Kali of that temple. In the early decades of cinema, south Indian films made in Calcutta and Bombay further provided the means for the national circulation of this local deity.[12] Also, in the 1940s, Bengali technicians were brought over to Madras in large numbers to begin the studio system there. Thus, Tamil studio films such as *Demon Land* (AVM Pictures/A.V. Meiyappan, Tamil, 1948) used several literary, artistic and musical motifs along with the Bengali style representations of Kali.[13]

Beyond the interaction of local and national, the most important contribution to the film and print medium's *hybridity* must be attributed to Euro-American sources. British, Dutch, French, Portuguese and Danish missionaries and educators founded the print medium in India, to which several foreign painters and engravers also made their contributions. On the one hand, Christian icons, relics and medallions that sailors and traders brought into India from Europe and America (Bean, 2001) influenced the print medium considerably. On the other, prints with Christian representations made in India were touched with Hindu and Islamic styles.

---

[11] I thank Tapati Guha-Thakurta for providing help in going through the collection at CSSS, Calcutta.

[12] Another search could show just the reverse; that the image travelled *to* Bengal, instead of away.

[13] Interestingly, much of the cultural material in this film, made a year after Indian independence, had been of nationalist import, yet the film ultimately aims at establishing a strong Tamil identity. I thank Indira Peterson for her help in viewing this film.

The Human/Divine Figure in the Age of Trade and Commerce

Influences from Europe and America changed Indian ways of depicting the human/divine body. This happened not only through paintings, but also through sculptured figurines, such as marble copies of neo-classical sculptures that adorned elite houses and offices. Traditionally, god sculptures were made out of dark wood such as ebony or rosewood, and stones such as jasper or *basanite* (the stone goldsmiths traditionally used to test gold with). Metal images too were of a darker hue. Medieval paintings typically showed gods and goddesses in different colours that were considered part of their iconography. When porcelain images made in Dresden became popular, gods and goddesses became fairer, and adopted poses and postures different from earlier conventions. Truly dramatic is the transformation of Lord Krishna, the dark blue god, who suddenly turned 'white'.

Coloured advertisements and commercial labels contributed in a very definite way to the introduction of certain facial and bodily features and gestures. Not only did they further 'fair skin', they also created a taste for it in popular culture. Women with European facial and anatomical features, and fair skin, began an alternative chain of identifications. Carrying marks like 'printed in Germany', they also provided an extra-national attraction and validity.[14] Native models and actors would hereafter copy poses and postures from these images.

During the Silent Era (and until the 1940s), a large number of Eurasian, Jewish and Armenian women joined Indian film studios. Appearing under Indian or Arabic names, they brought on to the screen the 'desirable woman-types' (see Thomas and Gangoli, this volume). Even in the films of south India, where the prevalent skin colour is dark, female protagonists were often required to be, or shown as, 'fair'.

Art and Artisanship, Work and Worship and Play

This history of changing visual taste is coterminous with the history of urban migration, including the rapid growth in production and consumption of all mediums and cultural practices we are looking at. The popularity of cinema grows out of new desires, curiosities

[14] Manufacturers advertised, 'Buy only after checking the labels' in order to curb the spread of spurious products manufactured by competitors.

and needs. These needs were first fulfilled by god posters. Displaced from one's village and village deity, people from the same village or language group gathered in their adopted towns and cities to form *bhajan mandalis* or religious singing groups in front of framed images of gods (Singer, 1972). The modes of worship also changed significantly with the growing need to worship in the privacy of one's own home. This contributed to the popularity of poster images. Furthermore, the earlier habit of worshipping only one deity, whether it was a personal deity, family deity, village deity or the deity worshipped by the king of the land, gave way to the habit of worshipping a crowd of gods and goddesses. Now one perhaps felt better equipped to fight the many demons of the city, calling upon both known and unknown gods, who could gather in one's domestic space in the form of god posters.

Work and worship combined in novel ways. The new work environment was adorned with a range of posters and calendars. Also, new concepts of leisure and games followed the new job conditions. The Indian 'Snakes & Ladders' and other dice games were by-products of the print medium that could be studied against stories of urban hope and anxiety, failure and success. Alternating between opportunities in the heavens for spiritual gain or for guilty pleasures freely available in the new cities, each rung of the ladder or each halt in a game called *Golak-dhām* (the heavenly abode of Lord Vishnu) was marked by vivid captions and illustrations. One climbed to the feet-of-Vishnu or fell at prostitute quarters.[15]

Adding to the transformations engendered by such varied printed products before cinema is another highly interesting Bengali phenomenon, *The Directory and the Almanac,* which I will discuss in some detail. Copies of the British and American *Almanac & Directory* had come to India in the eighteenth century, and the first indigenous one appeared in 1818–19. The nomenclature, *Directory & Panjikā,* used for these is a good indicator of that period of *mélange* hybridity. The almanac section of a 1915 edition of *P.M. Bagchi's Panjikā & Directory* printed at the Bagchi Press, Calcutta, is a veritable tome[16] containing Hindu as well as Islamic (and Christian) religious calendars as well as information concerning myriad rites and rituals, must-dos, taboos, and other injunctions. The directory section is a document of tremendous growth of a modern city,

[15] A copy of the *Golak-dhām* I recently acquired unfortunately lacks all of this early splendour—visual and linguistic.

[16] It is preserved in the private collection of Jayant Bagchi of P.M. Bagchi Press, Calcutta. I thank him for giving me access to it. The other popular Bengali almanac was the *Gupta Press Panjikā*.

providing information about Calcutta's streets and houses, court fees and names of advocates, rail and steamer fare rates and timings.[17] It carries advertisements (with ample text and visual material), cooking recipes and lists of songs on gramophones (with complete lyrics). Catering scantly to villages, it also provides agricultural advice. The traditional and modern, *deshi* (of the homeland) and *videshi* (foreign), urban and rural, sacred and profane, rational and irrational—all became strange bedfellows on this hotbed of urban activity.

The advertisements in the almanac exhibit an *encyclopaedic* spirit, at times providing pictures of *all* the items the business house had for sale or had ever sold. Through such a catalogue they advocate a culture of plenty. Many remember the almanac for the gigantic pictures of cabbages and cauliflowers. Almanacs also carried images of modern day anxieties: advertisements guaranteeing miraculous cures for sexual inadequacies and loss of energy; sadhus, tantrics or other magic men proclaiming the magical feats they could perform to help people fulfil desires, find lost objects, seduce a lover or tame an enemy. Plenitude and excess, euphoria and anxiety, utopic and dystopic mindsets are the hallmark of these reference books.

The use of the almanac brought real change in the life of a householder, who now did not have to consult a priest for knowing religious dates, observance rules and other related matter. Almanacs also provided game opportunities: for example, by consulting a diagram one could learn one's fortune for the month. Some divination games were combined with the game of chance, entertaining children, who spent hours pouring over these—singly and in groups.

All regions had some version or another of this tome. Maharashtra had the *pancāng* written like the leaf manuscript of earlier times. Small in height but greater in length, they had to be placed on wooden stands. These too were illustrated and carried articles by astrologers (but no advertisements). Today, the region has the popular *kālnirnaya* in the form of a calendar, with advertisements but no illustrations.[18]

Requiring renewal each year, the *Directory & Almanac* became lucrative business for publishers, who proceeded to publish both fiction and nonfiction in them. Almanacs carried detailed announcements of forthcoming

[17] During the time I was growing up in the early 1950s, the directory section was gradually decreasing and it ultimately got dropped altogether.

[18] Pioneered by the Kālnirnaya Press, this term in this region has become a generic term for the Hindu calendar—a sub-category of almanacs, where each month is contained on one page.

publications—in-house ones and those from other publishers. At times, over half a dozen pictures accompanied the synopses, and the reader was promised 'more such pictures in the book'.

Book Illustrations

To appreciate the travel of images across various mediums, it is important to look at the phenomenal spread of the print medium amongst the middle class from the nineteenth century. I persist with the example of Bengal, where N.B. Halhed brought out *Grammar of the Bengali Language*, in 1778, using Bengali movable types for the first time. Panchanan Karmakar was the first Bengali to be trained in printing and engraving. The first illustrated Bengali book *Sachitra Anandamangal*, in 1816, carried six prints by Rupchand Roy. By 1799 there were about 368 titles, many heavily illustrated. Journals with illustrations began to appear after 1818. The most telling example is a popular fairytale book, *Thākurmār Jhuli*, by Dakshinaranjan Mitra Majumdaar, in which the author had himself done the illustrations but provided the names of all his engravers as a mark of their growing importance in this period of illustrated books (Kesavan, 1985).[19]

Book illustrations exhibit visual tendencies—especially naturalism and perspective, proscenium stage-setting and dramatic use of architecture—also visible in films. There are remarkable instances of crossover in theme and content between cinema and book illustrations and posters. For instance, a popular print image entitled *Prostitute and Police Constable* also appears in a Prabhat Studio bi-lingual film, *Maanus/Aadmi* (*The Man*, dir. V. Shantaram, Marathi/Hindi, 1939).[20]

Tactility of the Image

With such cultural exchanges, images seem to grow less rarefied. They are not merely to be looked at or adored, but touched, held, bought, gifted or possessed, worshipped, or simply hung on walls. While considering the camera as a vehicle for the mechanical reproduction of images, Walter Benjamin observed: 'Every day the urge grows stronger to *get hold of an object at very close range* by way of its likeness, its reproduction' (Benjamin, 1936; emphasis added). In reproducing all kinds of images, the print medium brings the image home, making it part of quotidian life. Benjamin's proposition

[19] My own copy is the sixteenth edition by publishers Mitra and Ghosh.
[20] One such painting is in the R.P. Gupta collection, CSSS, Calcutta.

that the flooding of art objects and images through mechanical reproduction leads to the decay of the 'aura' of art has recently come under question (Pinney, 2002). Michael Taussig (1993) has brought the issue of 'optical tactility' to the forefront of understanding the modern age of reproduction, which I apply to the Indian example.

The question in India (as indeed, in many colonial/post-colonial situations) is complicated. Growing mimetic tendencies following the print medium and the camera do not slacken the ties with traditional non-mimetic, non-analogous, ways of representation. Rather, traditional icons are put to mimetic use. Also, an image with less 'aura' might suddenly acquire a new shine, for example, a calendar print may be turned into an object of worship at the end of the calendar's utility.

Taussig begins with Benjamin's insight into mimesis, and uses Benjamin's citation of Hegel, who writes: 'Pulling you this way and that, mimesis plays a trick of dancing between the very same and the very different.' Hegel describes mimesis as the 'movement of becoming another' or looking for 'pure self-identity in otherness'. Taussig calls this self-identification 'alterity'. The modern impulse in the age of mechanical reproduction of images and words is to grasp and possess that *Other*. This might not imply full knowledge and comprehension; but the impulse continuously grows.

Mimesis creates a continuous looping of images between the fully auratic and the quotidian, sacred and profane, producing an unstable site for the formation of selfhood and alterity. In the case of Indian cinema, the process of selfhood and alterity is best described by two elements: the organisation of the look and darshan.

Darshan

Film scholars such as Ravi Vasudevan (2000) have suggested that the aspect of gaze in worship or darshan be used as a tool for analysing Indian films. Hindu discourses (in Bhakti as well as in earlier texts) see images as ways of understanding and getting familiar with the *Other*. It has been explained that the pleasure generated by the image lies in gazing at one's god (or one's king), and being gazed back. This happens through the eyes (and the act of seeing), as well as the entire body (and all the senses). Darshan thus must be seen as something that involves both, the eyes and the body. Darshan is clearly operative where the figure in an image is positioned in a frontal manner, looking out of the frame in the general direction of the audience. But darshan in film also involves a more complex organisation of the look that differs from a printed god poster.

The Organisation of the Iconic Look

Different scholars have used the phrase 'organisation of the look' in different ways. But I use this phrase for teaching the film-maker cameraman's practice of deploying the actors' eyes and the act of their looking while shooting a scene.[21] The film-maker/cameraman team must take into account how the eyes of particular actors should be vis-à-vis the camera. The team must ask: should the look be contained within the frame or spill out; what angle should the eyes make with the camera lens; could they look into the camera? This is compounded by whether the characters are to look, or not look, at each other. The deployment of the eyes means a certain positioning of the face and the body vis-à-vis the camera. Let us look at the example of a film where the entire body comes to be important in the organisation of the look.

The opening passage of *Sant Tukaram* (1936) provides a very good example of re-figuration of the iconic image in cinema. It is about Tukaram (1610–48), one of the most important saint-poets belonging to the Bhakti movement in Maharashtra.[22] The film opens with the title cards accompanied by a composition by Tukaram. After the titles end, there begins the first shot showing a full-frontal image of the deity Panduranga, also addressed as Vitthala—the principal deity of people following Bhakti in Maharashtra. The song from the title cards continues over this shot/image.

Vitthala (always of black stone and meaning one who stands on a brick) stands erect, arms akimbo, body and eyes directed in full-frontal address. This opening shot does not establish any story or character, but locates the film within the tradition of Bhakti. The image is shot against a blank

[21] Here, I am interested only in this ontological aspect of films as a formal device. I suggest the study of this is absolutely necessary for the proper understanding of a film; this would lead to greater formulation, theorisation and understanding of the ideological aspects of cinema.

[22] The tradition of religious reformation and practice known today as the Bhakti movement grew since the eleventh century and spread all over the subcontinent, but in many different forms. Its practitioners intensely pursued personalised forms of worship. The movement saw a tremendous rise of vernacular literature, music and the performing arts as well as painting, sculpture and architecture. In Maharashtra, all the important figures of the movement were also poets and were addressed as *sant*.

wall, without a prop or background. It is not clear where the deity is situated. It might as well be an image of a god poster that audiences may carry in their heads, and not a physical deity placed in some temple. The shot remains on the screen for about a minute and a half. Nothing happens. There is no change in image size or angle, no movement of figure and camera, except at the very end, when the camera tracks-in slightly. Effectively, the long duration makes this shot a 'meditative shot'. The song, running through the entire length of the title cards as well as this shot heightens the simulation of a devotee's look of adoration at the god-of-worship (*ārādhya devatā*).

This is the opening shot of the film, when the audience has not yet settled down into the experience of viewing. Yet, the prolonged shot captures their attention, bringing to cinema their habit of casting a prolonged look at a deified image. Thus, directors Damle's and Fattelal's choice of mise en scène creates a special instance of the act of film viewing. The moments underlying this shot are not narrative moments. They belong purely to the *scopic* aspect of worship recreated within cinema.

It is true that the use of a frontal shot with figures looking out at the audience occurs widely in other cinemas as well. In European avant-garde film, such shots represent deliberate breaks within the film's narrative moments, and have been linked to the process of Brechtian alienation.[23] In contemporary documentary, such a shot heralds the denial of the possibilities of illusion, inviting an audience to fully engage with the issue instead.[24]

Studies of isolated shots in films, however, might not always lead to satisfactory comparison. Even an iconic shot must be discussed in the context of the preceding and/or the following shot in a sequence. Our eyes, locked now in an exchange of gaze with an image, must look at another image in the moment following. In the second shot of *Sant Tukaram*, we see a devotee with sandalwood paste markings on his face, sitting crossed-legged on the ground, with eyes closed, musical instruments in hand. From the iconography and from the film title, we assume that the man is Tukaram. This too is a long-held shot continuing for over 200 feet

[23] In this context, Jean-Luc Godard's ways of alienating the audience from habitual identification (thereby deriving visual and narrative pleasures) are the most famous. Some of these devices are: having actors directly acknowledge the camera, introducing inter-titles within sound cinema, verbal or other linguistic but extra-diegetic inputs, discontinuous editing patterns (including jump cuts) and elliptical narrative structure.

[24] A documentary using images of a person talking to the camera is called 'talking head films'. Thomas Wagh has suggested the phrase 'talking group films' for Indian films.

of running time without any movement of actor or camera. There is not even the last track-in movement, as in the previous case. The song that began with the start of the film continues on the sound track, but now Tukaram is shown singing it. Out of over 3,000 verses attributed to the poet, the choice of verse for the song is apt for accompanying the *meditative* stance of these images: *Pānduranga dhyāni, Pānduranga mani* (I meditate upon [the figure] of Panduranga; his thoughts fill my mind). The continuity of this song gives the worshipper as well as the worshipped an iconic status.[25]

To see the beginning of *Sant Tukaram* is to revisit the practice of showing the iconic image along with song accompaniments in musical and other performative modes in various regions of India. Vertical or horizontal scroll-paintings, *phad* or *pat*, are unfurled to the accompaniment of songs about figures and events represented. At times the performance is held at night, the scroll is fully opened and tied across a wall and the relevant portions illuminated as the song unrolls. The shadow puppetry or *chitrakathi* of western India involving light and shadow is another example of pre-cinema in India, where images and songs (words and music) all combine in order to tell a story (Chabria, 1994: 3).[26]

To Look is to Relate

Both the images initiating *Sant Tukaram* are iconic images, where the concept of darshan can be applied, but the second image differs from the first. The figure of actor Vishnupant Pagnis is composed in slight perspective, placed at an angle (about 30 degrees) to the camera. While there was no spatial placement of the deity in the first shot, in the second the background

[25] Separately or together, word and image form a system of symbols in the world of discourse and praxis. A god has several names or *nāma* and can reside in any; a god has *rūpa* or form (along with iconography). Both are worshipped separately and together. Action and event or *karma* is a third element giving further rise to name and form. Narration is the 'telling' and representation the 'showing' of name, form and event or action. The trajectory of the word Sita shows it as: a proper noun meaning a plough; a story character, *born* when a plough is dug into the earth; the heroine of an epic. How these practices, specialised to different literary practices and exclusive to different social or religious groups, become popular cultural phenomenon spreading over wider circles, is socio-cultural dynamics we have noted but have yet to study with greater attention.

[26] During a conversation Dilip Chitre pointed out that one unique feature of the *chitrakathi* is the play of image, light and shadow which often alternates with the narrative/musical parts instead of being simultaneously conducted. No doubt, each case demands individual attention.

details are roughly worked out. There are farming implements, suggesting that Tukaram could be in his house. But there is also a pillar, suggesting that he could be at some temple. The juxtaposition of these two long-duration shots of the divine followed by the devotee does not crank-start the process of location and narration. We cannot definitively say that Tukaram is worshipping before his god at his family temple in Dehu. If the process of editing has brought together two distinct images, it is not for narrative but some other purpose.[27] We could say that Tukaram is not physically before his god, even if he may be close to him. Or we could say that the two are always together, and we as the audience relate to them as always linked. Together, they form a dual icon.

In the tradition of Bhakti in India (however not unique to Bhakti) *bhakta* (devotee) and *bhagvān* (god) are both *objects* of adoration. We look at them singly and separately or together. We look at the relationship between them, and their relatedness as a single instance. So, the film creates a triangular relationship between *bhakta*, *bhagvān* and 'audience'—the spiritual aspirant (Cutler, 1979: 19–27). Bhakti literature, paintings and performative modes are replete with the use of this triangulation.

The angular placement of the Tukaram figure opens up a space each member of the audience can take up. Thus, importantly, these two images are not merely scopic, but ones that allow us to bring into the screen space our corporeality as spectators. The two opening shots of *Sant Tukaram* do not initiate a story. They do not tell us, 'Once upon a time there was a man, Tukaram, a devotee of Vitthala (or Panduranga), and look this is how one day he was sitting in front of his deity at the family temple at Dehu.' Rather, they bring us physically near the god and the *bhakta*; providing the experience of *sānnidhya* or nearness.

At the end of the second shot of the film we hear the same song, but now sung in a different style altogether (belonging to the contemporary theatrical tradition of *sangeet-nātak*). The villain, Salomalo, stands and sings in the midst of a gathering inside a temple, and then claims the song to be his own composition. The camera now begins to move immediately. There are shot changes, initiating the process of editing. Dialogues break into the song, and there are exchanges between actors conducted in shot/counter-shot technique. In other words, only now the story starts, and the set of interlinked shots produces a 'narrative image'. Significantly,

[27] Importantly, all this and the long shot-duration of these two initial shots makes them autonomous shot-sequences. I see the oft occurrence of such shots as an important feature of Indian films.

the music director of the film, Keshavrao Bhole, has chronicled much of what they thought while doing this film. He writes, 'Our film began with the villain Salomalo.'

Showing and Telling

Director Sheikh Fattelal had intended to 'tell the world about Tukaram', and to *tell*, one needs to *show*—especially, if the telling is conducted through the medium of cinema.[28] So, what we see in the beginning of the film is both the mobilisation of cinema's *scopic* effect in order to initiate the process of *telling* a story and the mobilisation of some characters (the God too is a character) in a series of relationships (between them, between us and each of them, between us and their relatedness). We are looking at many ways of *showing* and *telling* as a play between iconicity and narrativity. This pair, showing and telling or *dikhāna* and *batāna* so influences spoken languages that in Hindi, for example, a film screening is *picture/film dikhāna* or *picture batāna*. Even for a song, one could say 'tell me the song' or *gānā batāo*.

A look at Hindu religious literature from the Puranic period and onwards would further this particular understanding of iconicity and narrativity (elements of this duality are found in Jain literature and some schools of Buddhist literature as well). There are two definite sections to religious literature. One is the *staba* or *dhyān-māla* devoted to the praise of the god or the goddess. Here, various predicates, physical indicators and attributes of the gods are described with embellishment, imagination and exaggeration. This portion, I suggest, is the linguistic equivalent of an iconic image. The other section is devoted to narration or recounting events and actions associated with the goddess; this section can be called: *kathā* or *upākhyān* (story/tale), *itihāsa* (narrative, but now used in the sense of history), and *carita* (hagiography). The two sections can be repeated many times over the span of a book. The connection between the iconic and the narrative is played out in every mode of artistic practice in Bhakti.

Interestingly, pre-modern images often had inscribed within them words, sentences or verses. Syllables and words have been part of symbolic–representational practices in several religious cults. Later in the chapter, we will return to further enquiries into the word when it is audio, and the

[28] The reverse, to show is to tell, is equally true as seen in the examples of the 'pre-cinema audio-visual shows'.

word when it is visual. Such a discussion opens up other areas of investigation. For example, in manuscript writing, images illustrate or illuminate a text. When we come to the age of mechanical reproduction of words and images, and their large-scale proliferation, print technology provides added momentum to word and image combinations.

Image and Discourse

The credit titles of *Jogan* (dir. Kidar Sharma, Hindi, 1951) are written on a medieval style manuscript or *punthi*, for the film draws a connection between the medieval poet-saint Meera Bai and the film's heroine, who is a poet as well. But the film itself begins with the hero and not the heroine.

The hero Vijay had left his village for the city of Bombay and is back now with the intention of selling his ancestral home. The initial two shots establish a lazing and ambling hero, much like Devdas.

1. After the credits, the film opens with the view of a river. Vijay enters from right-of-frame—in extreme long shot. Lazing by the river, he throws a stone into the water. A song in the soundtrack follows this little silence and the visual splash.
2. The next is a mid-length shot with the same camera angle but reduced distance. We get a closer look of the hero. Vijay hears the song and looks to the right-of-frame.

The next five shots, including a dissolve, generate the feeling of an event:

3. A silhouette image of a temple, indicating the song is coming from that direction.
4. Vijay keeps throwing stones in the river and listening.
5. The next shot returns to the temple image, but now there is a tilt-down of the camera. Over that, there is a dissolve including the following: the temple interior, a group of men and women gathered around the *sannyāsini* Meera devi in white, playing on a string instrument (*ektārā*) and a cymbal (*tāl*).
6. An extreme long shot; Meera devi is positioned in the right-of-frame, along with the audience. The camera tracks-in and we get a better view of her. This shot establishes an audience viewing position; as it were, the audience enters this narrative space.

The proper beginning of the *event*, as it were, follows:

7. The exterior to the temple door in extreme long shot: Vijay enters frame, from left-of-frame and stops outside the door.
8. A tight close-up of the heroine in a full-frontal image—Meera devi is singing with eyes downcast. She turns her head to the *left-of-frame*—the image rests at her profile. She looks up slowly, as if aware of his presence.

The spatial logic that binds a story is brought into jeopardy:

9. But, the hero has not yet entered the temple; another shot of Vijay at the temple door (same image size and composition).
10. Another shot as in no. 6 (the song continues).
11. An extreme close up of Vijay's profile: his head is to *the right-of-frame*.
12. Meera devi's profile is still towards left-of-frame and she slowly lifts her eyes, as if to look at Vijay. Shots 11–12 and their juxtaposition suggest the protagonists are in close proximity, looking at each other.
13. The camera cuts to the hero standing outside the door (extreme long shot). The spell is broken; they cannot be looking at each other, for they are not in the same space—she inside, he outside.

14–18. Five shots repeat the play between the two faces in close-up (with little variation in image style and content).

The audience now fully anticipates a relationship between the two. Remarkably, the usual shot/counter-shot mode of classical cinema is not employed in this passage containing the hero and heroine. There is a narrativisation that establishes their relationship—*he* is going to meet *her*; but there is also the attempt to establish *the discourse of the look*. It has been argued that most audiences might not 'get' the aforementioned facts, but rather find pleasure in their favourite actors drawn in the assumed relationship of look—and love. This chapter cannot take up that point and provide for further elaboration of spectator position and reception.

The film would continue to pose questions as to whether the two characters should *look* at each other, talk and get to know each other—or refrain from all contacts. In his village, Vijay meets, and is tremendously drawn towards, the woman-renouncer, Meera devi. He wants to understand her asceticism, which is also a way of confronting and containing his own sexuality. Vijay's intrusion into her life, in turn, triggers off in the woman recollections of her feudal past. She too confronts her inner demons, those that did not leave her even after she took her vows. The drama of the film lies in determining what kind of relationship they could form or will have. We will now leave the sequence.

19. Vijay, still at the temple door (as in shots no. 9 and 13), turns back and moves away.
20. There is a track-back motion of the camera—an exact reverse of the track-in (introducing Meera devi in the temple) in shot no. 6.

The initial track-in and this subsequent track-back fixes audience position or point of view—it is as if they enter and leave this particular narrative space, this event/non-event, and leave. Importantly, the close-ups do not simulate respective subjective viewing positions of the actors, as in classical Hollywood narration, or a strict alignment of audience's identification with this or that protagonist.[29] The section initiates a particular discourse of icon within the film narration (see Figures 4.2a and 4.2b on p. 112).

The use of the profile in *Jogan* reminds us of the pictorial traditions wherein a face in profile is also a frontal image. While deployed within the mimetic technology of film, the profile relates to the earlier tradition of iconography in which gods, appearing in profile, full-frontal, or other intermediary views, emerge not mimetically but through symbolic systems relating to a nexus of religious and cultural discourses. Film mimetically relates its mise en scène and characters to those iconic representations. The love of divine couples such as Krishna and Radha or Shiva and Parvati (the latter adding a note of domesticity) gave rise to a host of representational and narrative modes relating to romantic love in cinema. Matters of word and image are often indicated through an Islamic reference. Indeed, the inter-titles of silent cinema bear marks of Islamic calligraphic influences rather than Hindu manuscript styles.[30]

[29] Such mise en scène is not visible in the other sequences with other characters.

[30] All films carried inter-titles in Urdu; in some the credit titles too were in two languages, English and Urdu. In one scene of the film, Devdas reads a letter in Urdu script.

Figure 4.2a
Jogan: Nargis (close-up profile)

Figure 4.2b
Jogan: Dilip Kumar (close-up profile)

Vaishnav Bhakti seems to have influenced several films of the period we are studying.[31] Films like *Vidyapati*, *Devdas*, *Jogan* and many others are marked by straight borrowing of representational and discursive elements from Bhakti. But we must note that such borrowal is also invariably problematised. In the case of *Jogan* we see an inner critique of the act of *looking* as it is cultivated within Bhakti.

Vijay goes for darshan of the woman renouncer; going to see her is literally a 'visit to the temple'. But that is also an act of transgression. After the song is over Vijay soliloquises (through a voice-over): 'My steps do not normally falter from entering the house of a singing woman (*gānewāli*). Why are they trembling now, as I am about to enter a temple?' Vijay regularly visits the house of a courtesan singer, but he is always in control of his libido. Now he needs to confront fully the question of his sexuality; he feels he can only do that by asking Meera devi the nature of *her* renunciation. She must have gained wisdom and calm through meditation and chanting, and so it is her duty to set right his emotional/moral quandary. But his presence and constant queries set in motion unresolved libidinal impulses and other desires in Meera devi. She is reminded of her past as Surabhi, the daughter of a feudal overlord, who wrote poetry, sang songs, painted pictures and dreamt of marrying a modern man—a writer or an artist. The film is an attempt at a cinematic (re)presentation of the traditional discourse of desire and renunciation of desires—*pravṛtti* and *nivṛtti*—through constant verbalisation of the duality of *body* and *eye* or *body* and *soul*.

The song Meera devi sings is attributed to the legendary Bhakti saint-poet of the sixteenth century, Meera Bai: 'Remove the cloth covering your face; only then will you see/get/find your Beloved' (*ghungat ke pat khole re tore piyā milenge*). The unclear gender of the Beloved makes the song relate to both the sexes. The song is attached to traditional discourses about looking as a cognitive and hermeneutic act: to look is to know and understand. To understand a god is to find/get/see him or her. But, the hero's look at the woman is bereft of this quality; he cannot *understand* what he is *looking* at. His *look* ultimately destroys what he wanted to see.

[31] Since the eleventh century, there has been a widespread rise of cults and groups, individuals and schools initiating an individuated mode of worship, altering and keeping within earlier religious traditions. This largely meant the worship of any of the three: Krishna—alone or with consort Radha; Shiva—singly or with consorts like Parvati; and, Durga, Kali, etc.—alone or with her consort Shiva. Known popularly as the Bhakti movement, this was accompanied by tremendous growth of vernacular language, performative modes, art and music.

The heroine too fails to rise to the occasion, meet his gaze and her own self-esteem. At the end of the film Meera devi dies 'consigning her body to the fires of yogic practice', leaving behind for Vijay her book of poetry, the evidence of her soul.

Thematically the film is important, as it very clearly discusses the conflicts of modernity in India. In this chapter, we looked at the formal devices through which film makes modernity palpable to its audience. The mimesis of the iconic image is crucial in understanding the way film addresses the desire for modernity to its audience.

The Bottom Frame

In D.G. Phalke's *Shri Krishna Janma* (1919), there is a remarkable scene in which baby Krishna climbs a tree situated in the extreme right-of-frame. The figure rises from the bottom of the frame and for a couple of seconds is difficult to locate him on screen.[32] Phalke's *Kāliyā Mardan* (1922) has villagers and Krishna's family members gathered by the river Yamuna looking at baby Krishna's disappearance into the river, their heads and faces occupying about a quarter of the frame from the bottom. The bottom frame is a cinematic creation that stands for, or represents, the place of the audience to whom the iconic image addresses.

The bottom frame, marking the frontal address of the film, is perhaps the most distinctive of cinematic devices used in Indian cinema. Proscenium-type entry of characters from the right or left-of-frame is an important ingredient of the classical narrative cinema. The logic of the right and left frame entry helps in the logic of continuity or chronology of events in the dramatic-analytic mode. This logic is congruent with other editing modes, such as eye-line matching, shot/counter-shot cutting patterns, and the rules of axis-jump we discussed earlier. The adherence

[32] Edwin's Porter's *The Great Train Robbery* (1903) is much discussed in the context of the frontal address and a character's direct look into the camera in the beginning and end of the film. American films of the 1920s, in particular, begin with the use of iconic images—a triptych—a panoramic shot of Nature, a house cradled in the bosom of Nature, and a family residing in the house. *Way Down East* (dir. D.W. Griffith, 1923), *Tolla'ble David* (dir. Harold King, 1928), *Seven Chances* (dir. Buster Keaton, 1929) are some examples of the triptych. In *Seven Chances*, for example, the-family-to-be, man and woman (and a dog) stands outside the house positioned in a full-frontal manner (the end brings back this iconography). This triptych (in American cinema), Nature-Home-Family, came out of a common metaphor for the nation-state—the family. Equally popular in latter decades would be City-Home-Family and reveal further the discursive nature of the icon.

to all these rules makes a classical Hollywood film so perfectly 'understandable' and easy to follow. We have been seeing how Indian films have been doing quite a few different things. The use of a bottom-frame entry for characters is very rare in global cinema and this mode of mise en scène (and editing) surely needs to be studied.

As Indian cinema fully adopts the Institutional Mode of Representation (IMR) or the Hollywood classical cinema methods, right and left entry is used when a linear storytelling and delineation of events is being achieved. Most film-makers, however, continue to use the bottom frame for the entry of a character into the discursive space, as in Raj Kapoor's films such as *Aag* and *Awāra* (Chatterjee, 1992/2003). Another film-maker, Ritwik Ghatak (active from the 1950s through to the mid-1970s) made extensive use of the bottom frame. Cameraman Mahendra Kumar describes how Ghatak instructed him during the shootings and made sure that such images were precisely planned. Ghatak personally arranged the actors, orchestrated the actor's body, face position, eyes (or the fact of their looking) and movement (body, face, eyes) vis-à-vis the camera. In the opening shot of Barua's *Devdas*, we already saw the woman-worshipper Parvati entering the film narrative from the bottom frame.

The use of the bottom frame is important to understand because it brings us back to the visual culture of indigenous artisans and artists, whose work enters the films of today. When a painter stands in front of an easel and paints a picture, the gaze travels towards the vanishing point. In this case, there would also be the demand for perspective, and depth of field. On the other hand, I suggest, when a painter is squatting on the ground (or sitting on a mat) and the paper is placed on the ground (or a low stool), the pictorial surface appears flat, and the bottom frame or the bottom layer becomes important.[33] In discussing the prominence attached to the bottom frame, we return to the relationship between the production of miniature paintings in relation to the eye and the body of the squatting artist (and by extension the audience).

The bottom frame also has a resonance for the viewer. While writing this article, I happened to be watching Mani Kaul's *chef d'oeuvre*, *Siddheshwari* (Hindi, 1987), a film that most successfully recreates or revokes the feel of a miniature painting (many of the points I have raised in this article are illustrated in it). I watched the film sitting on the floor

[33] There are several film clips of the painter Nandalal Bose shown applying his brush in upward strokes while painting.

(the carpeted theatre of the National Film Archive of India and its tradition of removing footgear before entering, which made it convenient for me to do so). A poignant sequence shows the Sarod maestro, Pandit Narayan Mishra, lying on the bed and playing his instrument most beautifully, despite the unusual supine position. The camera lingers for about three minutes, and then the shots cut back and forth between a close-up of his face and the full torso in long shot. Last, the camera pulls back, so that his feet, earlier outside the frame, now become visible in extreme bottom frame. The camera rests on that image for a little while. The first time I had seen the film, I had asked Mani Kaul if the camera was touching the guru's feet, and Kaul only smiled. But the experience at least illuminates the fact that the bottom frame may have been designed to incorporate the cultural habit of people who may have watched a film in a village while sitting on the ground.

This chapter demonstrates some of the ways in which the visual field of cinema in India reconfigures in modern technological terms the pictorial surface of pre-modern images. Literary, artistic and performative modes and expressions from the past and contemporary sources come into play in this process of reconfiguration. And all this happens within the context of diverse globalised cultures, rendering the medium of cinema ultimately very 'modern'. The centrality of the gaze invests the visual image with an aura, but to bring in the 'body' of the viewer within the filmic discourse is to do other things. This chapter shows that the gaze need not be the only way of analysing film. The question of embodied 'looking' makes film study a plural enterprise, taking into account the complex visual and cultural nexus interrelating film and its audience.

References

ASHIT, PAUL (ed.). 1993. *Woodcut Prints of Nineteenth Century Calcutta*. Calcutta: Seagull Books.

BEAN SUSAN. 2001. *Yankee India: American Commercial and Cultural Encounter with India in the Age of Sail 1784–1860*. USA: Peabody Essex Museum & Mapin Publishing.

BENJAMIN, WALTER. 1936. 'The Work of Art in the Age of Mechanical Reproduction', in Hannah Ardent (ed.), *Illuminations*, New York: Schoken.

BRUNO, GIULIANA. 1993. *Streetwalking On a Ruined Map: Cultural Theroy and the City Films of Elvira Notari*. Princeton University Press.

CHABRIA, SURESH (ed.). 1994. *Light of Asia: Indian Silent Cinema 1912–34*. Pune/New Delhi: National Film Archive of India/Wiley Eastern Ltd.

Chatterjee, Gayatri. 1992. *Awara*. New Delhi: Wiley Eastern. Reprint 2003, New Delhi: Penguin Books.

Cutler, Norman. 1979. *Song of the Road*. University of Chicago Press.

Kapur, Geeta. 1987. 'Mythical Material', *Journal of Arts & Ideas*, 14.

Kesavan, B.S. 1985. *History of Printing and Publishing in India: A Story of Cultural Re-awakening*. New Delhi: National Book Trust.

Pinney, Christopher. 2002. 'Indian Work of Art in the Age of Mechanical Reproduction: or What Happens When Peasants "Get Hold" of Images', in Faye D. Ginsburg, Lila Abu-Lughord and Brian Larkin (eds), *Media Worlds: Anthropology on New Terrain*, University of California Press.

Rajadhyaksha, Ashish. 1987. 'The Phalke Era: Conflict of Traditional Form and Modern Technology', *Journal of Arts & Ideas*, 14–15.

Singer, Milton. 1972. *When a Great Tradition Modernizes: An Anthropological Approach to Indian Civilization*. University of Chicago Press.

Taussig, Michael. 1993. *Mimesis and Alterity: A Particular history of the Senses*. New York: Routledge.

Vasudevan, Ravi. 2000. 'The Politics of Cultural Address in a "Transitional" Cinema: A Case Study of Popular Indian Cinema', in C. Gledhill and L. Williams (eds), *Reinventing Film Studies*, London: Arnold.

5

Reflected Readings in Available Light: Cameramen in the Shadows of Hindi Cinema[1]

SHUDDHABRATA SENGUPTA

The history of cinema is also a history of its practitioners, and yet practitioners rarely find a place in the histories that are written of cinema.[2] Cinema represents, perhaps more than any other art form, the coming together of different practices, skills and kinds of technical knowledge within the framework of an industrial organisation of artistic production. And yet, all of this seems to retreat into the fine print of the final credit-roll in deference to the big names on the marquee—of the stars, the directors, the composers—of the ones that the mainstream discourses of cinema

[1] This article is based on the materials gathered in the course of a four-year long research project titled 'The History and Practice of Cinematography in India', undertaken by the Raqs Media Collective, Delhi (Jeebesh Bagchi, Monica Narula and Shuddhabrata Sengupta), and C.K. Muralidharan (Cinematographers' Combine, Mumbai) between 1997 and 2001. The project was supported by the India Foundation for the Arts, Bangalore. The author acknowledges that many of the ideas and observations contained in this text emerge from the discussions between the Raqs Collective and C.K. Muralidharan, and in the interviews with several working and veteran cinematographers done in the course of the project. An online archive of the research project is to be found at the Sarai website, www.sarai.net. (See web resources, bibliography.)

[2] The extant literature on cinema in India, including standard histories, critical texts and works of an encyclopaedic nature are, by and large, silent about cinematography and

history, film theory and the 'gossip factories' have all become accustomed to bestowing with an 'authorial' function.

Cinema as a finished product, as the prisoner of a 'can', is easy to stick labels on, that mark it out as 'Indian' or 'Bollywood' or 'Western', and also as the 'property' of those recognised as its authors. But cinema (or any other media form) as process, as something constantly being undone and remade defies the claims of authorial and cultural fixity. From its very inception, the domain of practice in cinema is an instance of different kinds of borders being crossed, and the constant repositioning of practitioners and of their work across new thresholds. What are these borders and thresholds? This chapter, which bases itself on materials gleaned from the life histories (from a series of interviews) of a few key figures in the history of cinematography in India is an attempt to map some of these thresholds and borders, and to point at the locations in practice where they might have been transcended—to create one of the richest corpuses of imagery in the history of world cinema.

The lives of those who have practiced the art of cinematography in a country like India are witness to the fact that the history of cinematographic practice is one of movements between and across nations, cultures, spaces, métiers and sensibilities. It is a story of violinists who end up as cameramen, of German expressionism's impact on Hindi cinema, and of Indian technicians who pioneer trends in lighting worldwide, and of a constant dialogue between technology, aesthetics and visual culture. In recognising this fact, I also feel compelled to see echoes in the way in which the trajectories of the evolution of a *practitioner's sensibility* in my own work (in partnership with that of my colleagues in the Raqs Media Collective) is one that constantly questions the idea of a 'bounded' or 'bordered' practice, and keeps straying from one arena to another, from practice to reflection, from the moving image to movable type, from documentary video to media installations, and from the very local to the very global. This propensity to cross borders is one of the things that my colleagues and I have learnt from the histories of the *practice* of the moving image, and the reflections that underpin this chapter are by way of

---

cinematographers. A notable exception to this singular neglect of cinematography is Gayatri Chatterjee's recent book on Mehboob Khan's *Mother India* (2002) which does go into some detail in terms of discussing the cinematography of the film and the contribution made by the cameraman, Faridoon Irani. Nasreen Munni Kabir's (1997) study of Guru Dutt also contains some references to, and citations of, V.K. Murthy. There are a few articles and interviews that have appeared in specialist magazines, and lately, some web pages that do recognise the contributions made by cinematographers to cinema in India. For a comprehensive listing, see the bibliography that accompanies this chapter.

recompense for that debt. Here, it is my intention to gesture towards the vitality of some of these acts of moving across borders that I have found so exemplary in the history of cinematographic practice. In that sense, this work represents a settlement of a few key personal debts.

While the Raqs Media Collective's and Muralidharan's research project on the history and practice of cinematography in India, encompassed both the art house as well as the commercial cinema in Hindi, Bengali and south Indian languages, this chapter looks specifically at what we consider to be certain key moments and practitioners in the mainstream Hindi commercial cinema. Neither the research project, nor this work lay any claim to comprehensiveness, but are to be seen as points of entry for further work and reflection and research on issues that need urgent attention.

The Servant with the Lantern

A door opens on what is obviously a stormy night, and a man with a lantern, perhaps a servant in a ruined mansion, illuminates the way in for two strangers, sheltering from the rain (the opening sequence of *Madhumati*, dir. Bimal Roy, 1958). (See Figure 5.1.)

Figure 5.1
The lantern scene: The opening sequence of *Madhumati*

I like to think of this scene, of the act of holding up the light, of the casting of shadows, of the hide-and-seek of darkness and light, and of the obvious tensions between visibility and invisibility, as a metaphor for the circumstances of the lives and labour conditions of those who work to create images, with their eyes, their minds, their hands and with those incredibly cruel and complex machines called cameras, lenses, lights, cutter stands, filters, printers and developers. To think about these lives and these circumstances is to make reflected readings in available light.

The heat, the fatigue and the stench of a studio, a location or a laboratory are always obscured by the magic lantern of the cinema. I would like to call attention to the servants who come in from the shadows with the light, who are sometimes perhaps ironically called 'masters of light'. I like to think of the servant with the lantern as an old forgotten cameraman, the strangers as the public, and of the abandoned mansion with its missing pictures and portraits as the decaying edifice of cinema history.

This scenario, made up of shadows and lantern bearers, is a scene from a black and white classic from the early 1950s cinema culture that flourished in what was then called Bombay. The people who worked on the making of this image are significant for a variety of reasons. The film is *Madhumati*, the screenplay by a young Ritwik Ghatak, later to become the troubled signature of epic melodrama in Calcutta (now known as Kolkata), and responsible for some of the most arresting image-making in the history of cinema in India. The direction is by Bimal Roy, a pioneering cameraman (and later director) with the New Theatres in Calcutta, and the cameraman is Dilip Gupta, one of the great survivors of the vicissitudes of the history of cinema in India.

The only time that I have met Dilip Gupta was not far from his 90th birthday, in the summer of 1997 in a small apartment in suburban Mumbai, at the beginning of our research. Over the course of the next four years (1997–2001) that we worked on this project, interviewing many of the Indian film industry's most significant cameramen, we became aware of a narrative of amnesia and delayed remembrance, of fading prints and damaged negatives, of archives that collect absences, of a sudden rush to buy the television rights to old classics when it became clear that the monster of television needed to feed off retro chic and nostalgia. We came to know of cameramen who created images of astounding beauty and were forgotten when it came to authorial recognition, and we began to see the relationship between the ritual obeisance to the hoary tradition of Indian cinema and the studied neglect of the living history of practitioners and technicians.

Let us take the case of Dilip Gupta himself, who began his career as a cameraman in 1927 in silent cinema. He lived, worked and trained in Hollywood, worked extensively on trick films at Walt Disney studios and then came back to India to join a burgeoning cinema industry. In the 1920s and 1930s to talk about Bombay or even Hindi cinema was premature, the production base of cinema was pan-subcontinental with studios creating work for a South Asian as well as a larger Central Asian, East Asian, African and Caribbean market. Cinema in India has had a global reach and market from its very inception. This diversity of markets and audiences then was echoed in a cosmopolitan workforce, with cameramen, technicians, actors and actresses and directors from all over undivided India (with a preponderance of Bengalis, Punjabis, Parsis, Tamils, Maharashtrians and Malyalis), but also from parts of Germany, Italy, America, even Iran—working in a transient migratory mass between the major production centres of Calcutta, Bombay, Madras, Pune and Lahore. Particularly in cinematography, German and American technicians continued to have a significant presence in both Bombay and Madras cinemas till the mid to the late 1950s.[3]

Shortly after the opening sequence in *Madhumati*, we see the hero, Dilip Kumar, explore the mansion, with a candle in his hand: this moment epitomises the cross-currents that fertilised cinema practice at that time in Bombay (Figure 5.2).

[3] The career of Franz Osten most clearly epitomises the cosmopolitan nature of cinema production in India in the first three decades of the twentieth century. He began working with Emelka Studios, Munich, and was approached by Himanshu Rai to direct *The Light of Asia* in 1925. The Rai–Osten partnership lasted into the late 1930s, and together they started Bombay Talkies in 1934. Notable films directed by Osten include *Shiraz* (1928); *A Throw of Dice* (1929); and *Karma* (1933), among others. Osten gathered around him a team of mainly German co-workers and technicians such as Bertl Schultes (assistant director), Willi Kiermier and Josef Wirsching (cameramen). Josef Wirsching was to stay on and work in India for several decades, and shot part of Kamal Amrohi's epic *Pakeezah* (1971) starring Meena Kumari.

The influence of German film culture on the film industry in India was also particularly strong because of the number of technicians and film-makers such as Himanshu Rai, Bimal Roy and Promothesh Baruah who spent time training themselves in various aspects of film technique, especially cinematography in the 1930s in Germany.

Other émigré film-makers and technicians working at the same time included the Iranian Abdolhossein Sepanta, who made the first Farsi-talking film (*The Lor Girl*, 1934) in Bombay; the Italian sound recordist T. Marconi, the American cameraman and director Ellis. R. Dungan who worked in the Tamil film industry, photographing and directing significant films like *Sathi Leelavathi* (1936), *Iru Sahotharargal* (1936), *Ambikapathi* (1937), *Kalamegham* (1939), *Sakunthalai* (1940), *Meera* (1945), *Ponmudi* (1950) and *Mantirikumari* (1950). The Italian director Eugenio de Liguoro and the French Camille Legrand, both

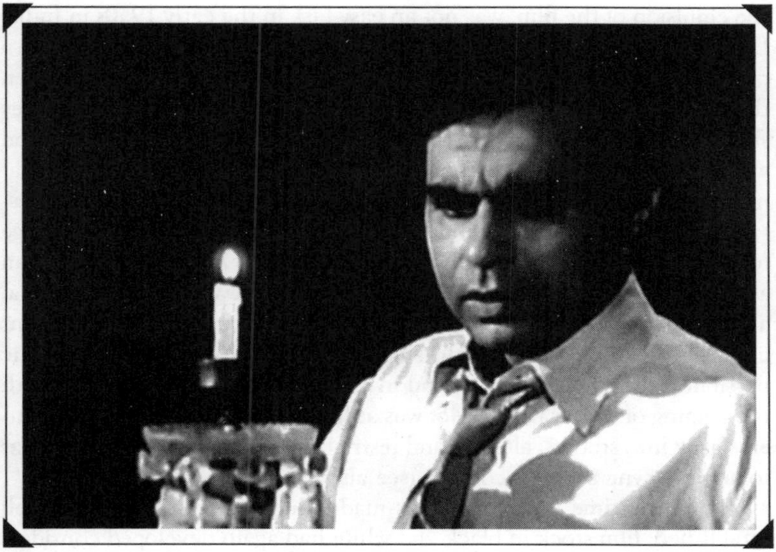

Figure 5.2
Dilip Kumar and the candle: *Madhumati*

The roadmap, which takes Dilip Gupta to the distinctive (almost gothic) visual signature of this scene, displays styles of film noir as well as German expressionism. It is difficult (and risky/presumptuous) to identify the influence of specific films. One can, in general terms, say that the visual vocabulary of German expressionist image-making was influential because of the presence of key features such as the use of high contrast lighting, strong shadows, accentuated use of diagonals in the framing, and an attention to 'atmospheric' characteristics, particularly in terms of lighting design. Rather than zero in on the links between individual films, it would be more accurate to draw attention to a set of 'family resemblances' that link the visual field of German expressionist film-making and the cinema of the 1930s, '40s and the early '50s in India.

What is particularly remarkable in *Madhumati* is the attention paid to the mise en scène, and the almost luxurious indulgence of candlelight, resulting in rich black and white tones and the play with light itself. To achieve this candlelight effect, to effectively almost risk near darkness on

of whom worked for J.F. Madan's 'Madan Theatres' in Calcutta, along with several other European technicians, and who directed the mythologicals *Nala Damayanti* (dir. de Liguoro, 1921), *Ramayan* (dir. de Liguoro, 1922) and *Ratnavali* (dir. Legrand, 1922).

the emulsion of the film, was not an easy task in the early 1950s in India. Dilip Gupta would recount with boyish glee the delight of daring to use a practical (an actual light source) on the person of an actor. He had taken the candlestand and wired the actor, Dilip Kumar, so that in certain key shots the actual electrical bulb concealed in the housing of the candlestand would throw an adequately candle-like penumbra of light as Dilip Kumar moved about. Tremendous control with cutters and reflectors was necessary in a scene like this to avoid a multiplicity of shadows and yet manage to evoke a candlelit feeling. What someone like Dilip Gupta had as an asset was the liberty and creative freedom of the heyday of silent cinema; a time when location shooting and exposures taken with low or ambient light where able to create and suggest extremely evocative cinematic possibilities. The coming of sound in 1931, as with the later period with the coming of colour from 1948, was at first a handicap, forcing the cameras back into studios, altering and restricting framing to a frontality so as to achieve sync sound recording (see also Chatterjee, this volume).[4]

Yet by the time *Madhumati* was made, dubbing was viable and well established, film stock in black and white had again developed considerable exposure latitude—that is, it began to allow for a fair bit of contrast in the tonal range. This had the effect of liberating cameras and actors to move and allowing the frame to become once more a dynamic entity, repositioning mise en scène as a central objective of the film's aesthetic goals. These features were beginning to be exploited by people like Dilip Gupta (who could return to a silent film style expressionist aesthetic in fragments of this film) and as we shall see, soon by Guru Dutt's cameraman, V.K. Murthy.

Clear Light in the Mirror

V.K. Murthy was perhaps the most remarkable cameraman of his generation working in Bombay at that time. Murthy, whose active mind continues to be a neglected archive of film history, was a teenage runaway who came to Bombay to become a hero (a recurrent motif in cameramen's personal biographies). He ended up being a studio hand, by sheer accident

[4] The first sound film was *Alam Ara* (dir. Ardeshir Irani, 1931). The first colour film was *Ajit* in 1948, However, it was shot in 16 mm Kodachrome and blown up to 35 mm. The first colour 35 mm films to be shot in India were both made in 1952—*Aan* (dir. Mehboob Khan) and *Jhansi ki Rani*. The first cinemascope film was *Kaagaz ke Phool* (dir. Guru Dutt, 1959).

became a student at a polytechnic that happened to offer courses in cinematography along with plumbing, carpentry and cobblery, and returned to work as an orchestral violinist at a Bombay studio. Whilst in the studio, he accidentally solved a minor technical flaw in camera loading that was vexing a group of senior assistant cinematographers. The director of photography in that film noticed what looked like original acumen, but which Murthy himself says was simple mechanical training from his polytechnic days, and Murthy was taken on as an assistant. He gradually learnt to work in the extremely segregated, hierarchical, almost caste-conscious atmosphere of the studio. This was apparent in the varying degrees of those who could touch which part of the camera, the lens of filters being a case in the politics of untouchability of paranoiac proportions. It was also apparent in the constant struggle to access rudimentary pieces of information like the aperture setting for a given shot. In Murthy's own words:

> I remember that in the early days as an assistant, the very simple fact of which exposure setting we could use for a given light situation in any shot was shrouded in mystery. Cameramen would always, rotate the aperture setting ring away from the correct position after a shot, so that their assistants would never know. These were the days when most assistants were untrained apprentices, and all that lay between an apprentice and his master was the mystery of the f stop number.[5]

He goes on to talk about how a famous cameraman had humiliated him on coming too close to the camera and how in an ironic and perverse play of destiny, the same cameraman had to once beg him for work when Murthy was an established professional and the one-time master a man past his prime.

It was in these unlikely circumstances that a man like V.K. Murthy could attract the attention of a young dèbutante film director called Guru Dutt. Both Guru Dutt and Murthy represented that liminal world of transients who found the film industry an ideal refuge for their talents and personalities. Neither had formal education, nor much by the way of artistic experience, yet this pair went on to make some of the most arresting images in Indian cinema. Murthy went to London once, to observe the

[5] V.K. Murthy, interviewed by Raqs Media Collective and C.K. Muralidharan, Bangalore, December 1999.

shooting of *The Guns of Navarone* in 1960. He was sent by Guru Dutt. When we asked him during an interview whether he recommended anything to Guru Dutt on his return from this 'study trip', he told us that he asked Guru Dutt to raise the wages of all the spot boys and the camera crew, indicating that better work could emerge once people were paid better and the crew had a more egalitarian ethos, which is what he had seen in London.

Kaagaz ke Phool (*Paper Flowers*, dir. Guru Dutt, 1959) may well be seen as the high point of this artistic collaboration. As a film about the film industry and largely set within the locale of a film studio, it allowed for elaborate set pieces that capitalised on a 'behind the scenes' atmosphere of movie-making. However, it has been suggested that this elaborately self-reflexive sensibility is precisely what was responsible for the film's inability to find commercial success.

For a film industry that is so obsessed with itself and which is so productive, it is quite surprising how few films reflect back, even if in passing, on film-making itself. I can count a handful: a pedagogic one-reeler by Phalke on film-making itself, *Manus* (*Man*, dir. V. Shantaram, 1939); *Kaagaz ke Phool*; *Nayak* (*The Hero*, dir. Satyajit Ray, 1966); *Bombay Talkie* (dir. James Ivory, 1970); *Guddi* (*The Doll*, dir. Hrishikesh Mukherjee, 1971); *Rajnigandha* (*Tube Roses*, dir. Basu Chaterjee, 1974); *Bhoomika* (*The Role*, dir. Shyam Benegal, 1981); *Rangeela* (*The Colourful Character*, dir. Ram Gopal Varma, 1995); and *Zubeida* (dir. Shyam Benegal, 2001).

Compare this list to the number of films on aspiring singers or dancers and which feature either recording studios or dance halls and you will realise what I mean by the fact that there is a clear logic of actually rendering the process of making films invisible. Technology, technicians, light boys, these are elements that take away from the magic of the movies and so must be kept hidden as far as possible. *Kaagaz ke Phool*, in tracing the travails of a film-maker and his refusal to compromise on the integrity of his craft, can be read also as a story of the pressures that bear on the image-making process, a predicament that was particularly familiar to V.K. Murthy.

The set piece where the heroine, played by Waheeda Rehman, accidentally walks into a film set and is captured on film remains remarkable also because it actually shows us a cameraman. Along with the rest of the crew, Guru Dutt (playing the director, and in a sense, himself) is the mustachioed man sitting next to the camera on the crane and the cameraman is played by V. Ratra, who was Guru Dutt's earlier cameraman. Playing the part of the assistant, a slim, bespectacled man is V.K. Murthy himself

(Figure 5.3). Incidentally, Murthy did act as Ratra's assistant on *Baazi* (*The Bet*, dir. Guru Dutt, 1951) and a couple of earlier Guru Dutt films that were produced under the Navketan Studios banner.

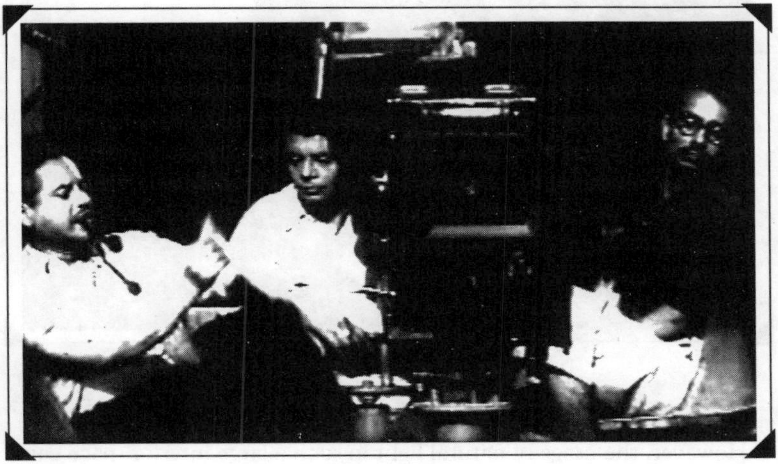

Figure 5.3
Guru Dutt, Ratra and V.K. Murthy in *Kaagaz ke Phool*

This sequence is remarkable in that it shows us elaborately staged crane shots in progress, and a crew at work. By doing so, it brings a quite rare attention to the ambience of a film shoot itself. It is as if, for the first time, the technicians in the film industry were themselves registered as the subjects of cinema. Murthy fondly recalls *Kaagaz ke Phool* as Guru Dutt's gift to his (Murthy's) craft and skill. By being the first cinemascope film it was a definite technical challenge, and the nature of the narrative itself demanded a constant tussle with light in all its aspects.

This is particularly true of a key sequence of the film, where Waheeda Rehman and Guru Dutt meet on the empty studio floor, lit by a single shaft of sunlight (see Figure 5.4 on p. 128). Here, the decision to use natural light, in an interior setting, was particularly apposite, as it made for a dramatic lighting pattern, well-suited to the emotionally charged encounter that was to take place between the two characters, and yet it made perfect sense in terms of the natural ambience of an empty shooting floor, bereft of all the paraphernalia and artifice of the world of film-making. At the same time, it called attention to the 'materiality' of film-making by its explicit bareness by saying this is what a studio floor looks like when the lights are switched off, and the sets and properties packed away.

Figure 5.4
Waheeda Rehman shot by mirrored sunlight in *Kaagaz ke Phool*

However, the usage of natural light in such a large interior space came with its own challenges and difficulties, and Murthy's inventiveness is evident in the way he met and surmounted these challenges. Let me quote again from his interview:

> After the shooting we used to sit together and talk in the afternoon in Mehboob Studios. Sunlight used to come down through the exhaust fan high above, close to the ceiling. All the dust in the studio would catch as motes in that shaft of light. I said to Guru Dutt—isn't it beautiful. He said could you do this? I said I'll try and at that time the idea I had was to focus a giant spotlight which was available at Shantaram's studio. This had a problem though, the highlight used to come but it was divergent light not parallel wave. I got that, but was not satisfied. One day I was sitting outside in the sun, one make-up man was playing with a mirror, chasing reflections on a wall. I saw that and thought, 'Damn it, that's what I need, not a spot light.' So, I got the carpentry department to make two big mirrors, some four feet tall. I placed them outside the studio and had sunlight strike on them at such an angle that it would hit the exhaust fan from the outside, then another big mirror was placed on the catwalk inside the studio, and that would direct the shaft of light in a diagonal pattern straight across the studio. So, we got sunlight not on location,

> but inside the studio floor. It was quite something, na. Till then nobody had used sunlight inside the studio not even in Hollywood films.[6]

What combination of circumstances made this moment of cinema possible? I do not think the explanation can be sought in terms of the creative geniuses of Guru Dutt or V.K. Murthy alone. First, there is the fact of sitting after a day's work and chatting and watching the light play in the afternoon: something that could only be possible between two people who were full-time employees in an old-fashioned film studio. Second, there was the possibility of trying things out, and of legitimate dissatisfaction with the results—not something that you can do in a film that needs to be canned in less time than it takes to clap a clapperboard. Third, there was the existence of a regular carpentry department and artisans who shared a relationship of trust, who made not only big made-to-order mirrors if need be, but also went on to make parabolic reflectors, from Murthy's design (something he later found patented, advertised and sold on the pages of the magazine *American Cinematographer*).[7]

All these factors were possible in a regime where films were made out of studios by a team of collaborators. Where actors, directors, technicians and production staff were part of an integrated unit, who knew one another, had a modicum of respect for each other's professional skills and had the time to spend with each other on a regular basis. Once the studio system collapsed and films became vehicles for stars, the importance of the team diminished. The collapse of the studio system can be roughly dated in tandem with the rise of the superstars, particularly Shammi Kapoor, Rajesh Khanna and Dharmendra, who were able to negotiate individual contracts that effectively undermined the power and prestige of the film studios, replacing them with the network of the star—the producer, the financier and the distributor. This was a gradual process, but the first traces of it can be seen from the early 1960s onwards. The studio system was more or less finished by the late 1960s. Along with this collapse, the cameraman's worth became measured by whether or not he could

[6] V.K. Murthy, interviewed by Raqs Media Collective and C.K. Muralidharan, Bangalore, December 1999.

[7] The *American Cinematographer* is the official journal of the American Society of Cinematography—a guild of camera professionals in the (mainly Hollywood based) motion picture industry. It has been widely recognised as the leading professional magazine in the field of cinematography and digital image-making. The online version of the magazine is available at http://www.theasc.com/magazine/index.htm.

enhance a leading lady's profile, and not by his innate skill or willingness to work with others to create a new kind of image. A rigid compartmentalisation of practice, contrary to the collaborative work ethos that had briefly flowered in the production teams around key figures like Guru Dutt and Murthy, or Bimal Roy and Dilip Gupta, or Raj Kapoor and the Mistry brothers, developed. Teams were broken up and partnerships forged over long years between art directors and cameramen, and assistants and studio hands were fragmented by a new 'shift' based system, which worked to the convenience of stars and their ability to manipulate shooting dates, rather than the requirements of a production schedule.

Along with this phenomena came new slow speed colour film, which initially had low exposure latitudes, poor contrast ratios, and which forced a retreat back to conventional lighting and framing, just as two decades earlier, sound had forced another retreat in the development of the visual possibilities of cinema. Further, an intensive regime of strict control over the import of raw stock, lighting equipment, cameras and accessories, as a result of inordinately high import duties (which marked the decades of the 1950s and 1960s, continuing well into the 1980s), meant that cinema industry was starved of fresh resources. It would not be far-fetched to state that a more or less constant artificially induced shortage of materials (due to state policies) actually led to a greater control over film production in the hands of financiers with links to organised crime, and to the sharp decline in the studio system.

While these assertions remain at present largely speculative, they indicate lines of enquiry that need to be opened up so that we can come to a more concrete understanding of the material circumstances of the history of film production in India. Films from the early 1960s onwards had a dull, plastic, disembodied look. Guru Dutt virtually destroyed himself with bouts of depression just as his screen persona had done in *Kaagaz ke Phool* and Murthy was left without Guru Dutt films or Guru Dutt himself to provide a scaffold for his creativity.[8] In his advancing years, Murthy became an efficient cameraman of lacklustre films, that neither had the intense luminosity nor the rich darkness of the best films of the 1950s. A brief new shimmer of light came when Satyajit Ray's pioneering cameraman, Subrata Mitra, came to Bombay, first to work with Merchant–Ivory

[8] Guru Dutt took his own life in 1964. Estranged relationships (particularly with his wife Geeta Dutt) and the commercial failures of his most ambitious film projects (notably, *Kaagaz ke Phool*) are attributed to be the reasons for his depression which combined with alcohol abuse, rendered him suicidal.

films[9] and then to make the stunningly beautiful and pastoral Raj Kapoor-Waheeda Rehman starrer, *Teesri Kasam* (*The Third Promise*, dir. Basu Bhattacharya, 1966). Mitra used his bounced lighting technique, perfected during his years with Ray, to great effect to create a soft gentle even sunlit feel that was lyrical in its evocation of afternoons, of the soft light of lanterns in fairgrounds and campfires, of dappled sunlight on a bullock cart. Mitra, in *Teesri Kasam*, does things with north Indian mid-afternoon light and the dust of a fairground that I have never seen since (see Figure 5.5).

But Subrata Mitra, whom the Spanish cameraman, Nestor Almendros,[10] considered as his personal master, could not survive Bombay, and had to return as a virtual exile from film-making to Calcutta. He was considered too slow, too finicky in his insistence that the lighting be perfect. No one ever dared complain if a star delayed shooting by never turning up on set,

Figure 5.5
Muted exteriors: *Teesri Kasam*

[9] The Merchant–Ivory partnership, in it's early 'Indian' days in some sense echoes the cosmopolitanism of the film production culture of the 1930s. Mitra, as cameraman, and Ruth Prawer Jhabvala, as scriptwriter, brought their own energies into this mix, which resulted in chamber pieces like *Householder* (1963), *Shakespearewalla* (1965), *The Guru* (1969) and *Bombay Talkie* (1970).

[10] Nestor Almendros shot several films for Francois Truffaut and Eric Rohmer, including *The Wild Child* (dir. Truffaut, 1969) and *My Night At Maud's* (dir. Rohmer, 1969). For an anecdotal recounting (by Govind Nihalani, cameraman and director) of Almendros acknowledging his debt to Mitra, see http://www.fortunecity.com/greenfield/bigmama/37/id53.htm.

but a cameraman who takes a little longer to light was simply unwilling to be tolerated by the industry in Bombay. Consequently, drab, flat films followed one after another.

From Slaves of Light to Midgets with Light Bulbs

Having glossed over the two decades of the 1960s and 1970s, which to my mind were cinematographically insignificant as far as the mainstream commercial film industry was concerned,[11] I now proceed to the 1980s, and to the revitalisation of colour cinematography due to availability of faster film stock in larger quantities—especially as a result of the loosening of import restrictions on film stock. Ashok Mehta, a cameraman whose life story in Bombay began again as a runaway teenager, and encompassed everything from someone who sold boiled eggs on the street to a canteen boy in a film studio to a light boy and finally to one of the most respected cameramen working today, was one of the practitioners who returned to a spirit of play with light and darkness in mainstream Hindi film, and in colour. This is particularly evident in the 'jewel scene' in *Utsav* (*The Festival*, dir. Girish Karnad, 1984)[12] when Rekha, playing the courtesan Vasantasena takes off her jewelry to the astonished gaze of Shekhar Suman playing Charudatta (Figure 5.6). Here too, what is particularly noticeable is the usage of candlelight, strongly reminiscent (although in a completely different register, and in colour) of what Dilip Gupta was trying to achieve in the1950s. The camera by now has a clearly defined position as the revealing agent of the beauty of the star.

Ashok Mehta went on to became a master of the glamorous look, and he remains in demand for his ability to transform song sequences into vehicles of desire. This is particularly evident in the famous 'Choli ke Peeche Kya Hai' (What Lies Behind the Bodice) song in *Khalnayak* (*The Antagonist*, dir. Subhash Ghai, 1993) which actually follows a progression from relative darkness to very bright light (see Figure 5.7). Here, of course, Ashok Mehta has stopped playing any games with visibility. He has become the slave of light—of bright iridescent rainbow coloured luminosity that smacks us straight in the eye. The amount of light in kilo wattage to make

[11] However, this period did produce the maverick personality of K.K. Mahajan, experimental cameraman of the Indian new wave, who worked especially with film-makers like Mrinal Sen and Kumar Shahani.

[12] Girish Karnad's cinematic interpretation of a well-known Sanskrit play—*Mricchakatikam* (*The Little Clay Cart*).

Figure 5.6
The jewel scene in *Utsav*

Figure 5.7
'Choli ke peeche kya hai'

that scene work is perhaps the daily output of a small power plant. Even the drums have lights in them. This explosion of illumination is the hallmark of today's Hindi cinema, a reflection in perverse ways of both substandard projection facilities in most cinema halls as well as the dependence of cinema on the glowing cube of the television set. The brighter the colour, the longer the finger stays away from the remote button.

It would not be incorrect to say that the 'song and dance sequence' is the one space within the body of a mainstream Hindi film where a cinematographer gets to call the shots. The lavish costumes, the increasingly exotic locales and the presence of a huge production infrastructure makes the song sequence the cinematographer's special domain—a space where he knows dazzle is called for. A new aesthetic, filtered via music television entered the Hindi cinema in the early to mid-1990s. After years of being in the shadows, cameramen were in demand again, they started to command huge fees, became near stars with their names now being printed on cinema posters. Although this trend began in the south, especially with cameramen like P.C. Sriram, who shot quite a few early Mani Ratnam films,[13] it rapidly spread to Mumbai and charismatic personalities like Ashok Mehta and their almost miraculous life histories contributed to the new iconic stature of the cinematographer.

Anil Mehta, a younger cameraman who represents the new generation of film institute trained cinematographers who were once looked down upon as difficult but are now sought after as efficient light-masters, commented on the changing look and feel of the Hindi film:

> Films have started to look more and more like products or advertisements. It is something that people are consciously trying to do; one would be lying if one were not to say that. Because of the spread of television the advertising industry has grown tremendously in size and so have the kind of budgets to make the films. A lot of talent has also gone into the advertising world. But, there are also a lot of international references, and this has brought about a visual qualitative shift. Kids now say, 'I love to watch advertisement films', which is a huge thing to say.
>
> The mainstream Hindi film industry had a very strong visual style right up to the sixties, where the visual quality was influenced by

[13] Especially, *Mouna Ragam* (*Silent Symphony*, dir. Mani Ratnam, 1986); *Nayagan* (*Hero*, dir. Mani Ratnam, 1987); *Agni Nakshatram* (*Fire Star*, dir. Mani Ratnam, 1988); and, *Anjali* (dir. Mani Ratnam, 1990).

> European and Russian films. In the seventies, however, this changed completely! Think of Prakash Mehra and Yash Chopra—their films looked fairly shoddy. I think this had to do with the Amitabh Bachchan icon. His presence was enough in the film! I think some of the shoddiest films in Indian cinema history were made around him. Later, with the advertising boom, visual quality began to be an issue again.
>
> But this meant that all the attention went into the mounting of the films. The same story could have been told in a much smaller house with much fewer cost and less fabric, but no that won't do. But this mounting factor is a huge thing in the industry. It's a huge thing to an extent that it makes your film sell or not sell and forces everything to be more lavish and colourful. Light becomes a commodity. Colour becomes a commodity. Volume becomes a commodity. Something to be consumed almost instantly. So the more lavish and more colourful, the better it is. See that is what makes all the films look the same now again, with varying degrees of skill, that is all.[14]

This statement by Anil Mehta gestures towards a whole set of contrary forces at work. On the one hand, the 'star' consumes all the attention, and so the camera merely becomes a recording instrument, an index of the star's radiance. The world of practice in the Hindi cinema becomes isolated and insular, leading to a certain creative stagnation. When, under pressure from television, and a renewed proximity to global media forms, a new 'advertising' induced attention to visuality is resorted to, what becomes an issue is how lush the screen can be made to look. Hence, cinematographers beginning from the late 1980s have begun to command a new power within the film unit. Cinematographers' fees have gone up, technical skill and professionalism has begun to be recognised, and the film industry has begun, at last, to realise the worth of technical training. However, this trend basically aims at making the screen 'shine', it leads to demands for 'virtuoso' camera work, large sets and increased expenditure on lighting and decor. This is the era of the big budget spectacle, shot in global locations, banking on a new global audience for Hindi cinema (see Deshpande, this volume).

While the frame is lush and opulent, it is debatable as to whether this necessarily represents a deepening of the cinematographer's engagement

[14] Anil Mehta, interviewed by Raqs Media Collective and C.K. Muralidharan, Bangalore, Mumbai 2000.

with form or with his craft. It is as if the solution to aesthetic issues is provided by throwing money at them. While the increased clout and resources that the cameraman can lay claim to within the film unit is indeed a positive development after decades of being relegated to a marginal status, it does not necessarily translate into a respect for the integrity of a cinematographic vision independent of the necessity of furnishing the spectacle that mainstream contemporary Hindi cinema constantly aspires to be. Once again, what is not necessarily given much thought to is the possibility of cinematography as a form of expression in its own right.

Hum Dil De Chuke Sanam (*We Have Given Away Our Heart, Darling*, dir. Sanjay Leela Bhansali, 1999), a Salman Khan, Aishwarya Rai and Ajay Devgun starrer, is a good example of the new opulent kind of Hindi film shot with big budgets across global locations. A song sequence in the film (the '*dhol baje*' or 'Drum Sounds' song) is an interesting instance of what a cinematographer can now muster in order to give the spectacle its due (see Figure 5.8).

For this song sequence, Anil Mehta mounted an acrylic platform some distance above the studio floor and rigged a battery of lights totaling 75 kilowatts mounted on long rods. The lighting set up for the floor alone had its own generator and its own main cable. The light was bounced onto the pit, which was painted white so that it shone, and reflected

Figure 5.8
The '*dhol baje*' song: *Hum Dil De Chuke Sanam*

through the acrylic sheets on to the bodies of the dancers, from below, without casting shadows. The resulting effect, in Mehta's words was: '... it was as if the whole floor was glowing'. It grew so hot in this set that the bulbs kept getting spoilt. To ensure that the shooting could proceed without too many interruptions as a result of overheated bulbs a blower had to be kept in place and a midget positioned within this contraption so that he could change bulbs at will, even as the takes were being canned.

Imagine being a midget surrounded by 75 kilowatts and having dancers stamping overhead while you sit cramped under a false floorboard, changing lamps, always millimetres away from electrocution. I invoke this figure of the midget and the light bulbs because I think it is necessary to take it into account if we are to arrive at any understanding of how images are produced in the cinema industry. Ultimately, what we see on screen is a result of certain material conditions of production, and of the place of cinematographic practice within the economy and micro-politics of the cinema-producing apparatus. While the cinematographer in Hindi cinema may have come a long way from being a slave of light to becoming the grand vizier, the camera, and the lighting set up remains in a sense imprisoned in the palace, captive to the demands of the spectacle. And so long as the midget changes the light bulbs in the dungeon below the dancer, cinematography will remain a prisoner.

The atelier of the cameraman, that messy studio floor with its cabling, its scaffolds, its grease, its heavy machinery and its nightmarish production schedule is one that the film historian and film theorist of Indian cinema have by and large never stepped into. They have rarely crossed the border to the terrain of trying to understand the conditions of practice. The tools of their understanding, far removed from the concrete realities of the industrial production apparatus of cinema are forged in the parlours of abstracted narrative analysis and an ahistorical aestheticism that has more to do with folkloristics than it has to do with film studies. Perhaps this is the burden of coming from an overstated, hyper-glamourised, sexy, film culture. Who wants to talk about work, labour, production, machines, technology, power and knowledge when we can do a little detour into the semiotics of the navel twitch in a song sequence, and speculate about the construction of 'frontality' in framing without trying to understand the reasons why a camera has to suddenly become immobile when a new kind of film stock is introduced, or agonised over?

To think, or to discuss the process of 'writing with light' is to attempt a clumsy transposition of voices and registers from what shines on screen to what lies behind its brilliance. What I have tried to do in this chapter is to attempt a foray across the borders that lie between understanding aesthetic decisions in cinematographic practice, and a material understanding of the work process of an industrial art form—with the help of a few fragments of the personal histories of working lives. We need many more such border-crossings, more audacious and detailed acts of critical reflection on practice than the sketchy transgression that I have been able to undertake here. Perhaps such acts, which can occur only if there is an alive and continuing conversation between researchers, theorists, critics and practitioners *about practice*, may lead to a small measure of liberty for the midget changing light bulbs in the dungeon, and free the practice of cinematography in India to undertake more modest yet liberating tasks, within, at the margins and outside the grand palace of the spectacle of the mainstream Hindi film.

Select Bibliography

ALMENDROS, NESTOR. 1986. *A Man With A Camera*. London: Farrar, Strauss & Giroux.

BANERJEE, HAIMANTI. 1985. *Ritwik Kumar Ghatak: A Monograph*. Pune: National Film Archive of India.

BANERJEE, SHAMPA (ed.). 1982. *Ritwik Ghatak*. New Delhi: Directorate of Film Festivals, National Film Development Corporation.

BARNOUW, ERIK and S. KRISHNASWAMY. 1980. *Indian Film*. Second edition. New York: OUP.

BHATTACHARYA, RINKI. 1994. *Bimal Roy: A Man of Silence*. South Asia Books.

CHABRIA, SURESH. 1994. *Light of Asia: Indian Silent Cinema, 1912–1934*. New Delhi: Wiley Eastern.

CHATTERJEE, GAYATRI. 2002 *Mother India*. London: BFI Film Classics, and New Delhi: Penguin India.

GANGAR, AMRIT. 1999. 'The Look of the Image', *Cinemaya*, Winter, 46: 4–10.

KABIR, NASREEN MUNNI. 1997. *Guru Dutt: A Life in Cinema*. New Delhi: OUP.

LONG, ROBERT EMMET. 1997. *The Films of Merchant-Ivory*. New York: Harry N. Abrams.

MERCHANT, ISMAIL. 2002. *My Passage from India: A Filmmaker's Journey from Bollywood to Hollywood*. London: Viking Books.

MITRA, SUBRATA. 1989. 'Convocation Address in Film & Television Institute of India', unpublished.

———. 1995. 'Inaugural Speech at the founding of Indian Society of Cinematographers', unpublished.

RANGOONWALLA, FIROZE. 1973. *Guru Dutt: A Monograph*. Pune: National Film Archive of India.

RAJADHYAKSHA, ASHISH and PAUL WILLEMEN. 1994 [1999]. *Encyclopaedia of Indian Cinema*. London: British Film Institute/New Delhi: OUP.

TORGOVNIK, JONATHAN and NASREEN MUNNI KABIR. 2003. *Bollywood Dreams: An Exploration of the Motion Picture Industry and it's Culture in India*. London: Phaidon Press.

VASUDEVAN, RAVI (ed). 2001. *Making Meaning in Indian Cinema*. New Delhi: OUP.
WESTERN INDIA CINEMATOGRAPHERS ASSOCIATION (WICA). 1993. *Indian Cinematography*. Mumbai: WICA.

Interviews

AZMI, BABA. Interview in *Lensight: Journal of the Film & Television Institute of India*, Vol. II, No. III, July 1993, pp. 4–10.
BABU, K. RAMACHANDRA. Interview in *Lensight: Journal of the Film & Television Institute of India*, Vol. IV, No. II, April 1995, pp. 4–7.
GUPTA, DILIP. Interview in *Lensight: Journal of the Film & Television Institute of India*, Vol. III, No. II, April 1994, pp. 21–28.
MATHUR, R.D., A.K. BIR, ALOK DAS GUPTA, BARUN MUKERJEE, JAYWANT PATHARE, KAMAL BOSE, PRABHAKAR PENDHARKAR, KAILASH SURENDRANATH, K.S.M. RAO, RAJAN KOTHARI, R.V. RAMANI and RAMCHANDRA BABU. Interviews in *Lensight: Journal of the Film & Television Institute of India*, Vol. II, No. IV, October 1993, pp. 4–9, 83–116.
PRADHAN, BINOD and RAJENDRA MALONE. Interviews in *Lensight: Journal of the Film & Television Institute of India*, Vol. III, No. IV, October 1994, pp. 18–22, 79–84.
SIVAN, SANTOSH. Interview in *Lensight: Journal of the Film & Television Institute of India*. Vol. IV, No. III, October 1998, pp. 182–87.

Webliography

Web Resources on Cinematography in India

Cameraworking: Materials for the History of Cinematographic Practice in India—(Raqs Media Collective & C.K. Muralidharan): http://www.sarai.net/cinematography/camera.htm
Interviews with Indian Cinematographers: http://www.sarai.net/cinematography/pages/interviews.htm
Interview with V.K. Murthy (Raqs Media Collective & C.K. Muralidharan): http://www.sarai.net/cinematography/pdf/interviews/vk_murthy.PDF
Interview with Ashok Mehta (Raqs Media Collective & C.K. Muralidharan): http://www.sarai.net/cinematography/pdf/interviews/ashok_mehta.PDF
Anil Mehta (Raqs Media Collective & C.K. Muralidharan): http://www.sarai.net/cinematography/pdf/interviews/anil_mehta.PDF
A Timeline of Cinematography in India (Raqs Media Collective): http://www.sarai.net/cinematography/pages/timeline.htm
Bibliography on Cinematography in India (Raqs Media Collective): http://www.sarai.net/cinematography/pages/biblio.htm
Vasudevan, Ravi: *Looking At Production Stills*: http://www.sarai.net/cinematography/pictures/raviv.htm

Upperstall.Com —'A Better View of Indian Cinema': www.upperstall.com
Website on Franz Osten: http://www.wupper.de/sites/unnet/files/franz_osten.html
Website on Himansu Rai: http://www.upperstall.com/people/rai.html
Jamsetji Framjee Madan and the Madan Theatre Empire: http://www.3to6.com/final_retro/featurejamsethjiframjee.htm
Subrata Mitra Website—by the Indian Society of Cinematographers: http://www.fortunecity.com/greenfield/bigmama/37/index.htm
Govind Nihalani recalls Nestor Almendros talking about Subrata Mitra as an inspiration: http://www.fortunecity.com/greenfield/bigmama/37/id53.htm
History of Merchant Ivory Films: http://www.merchantivory.com/about-mip.html
Interview with Ashok Mehta on 3to6.com: http://www.3to6.com/final_techtalk/washokmehta.htm

Web Pages of Referenced Films

Madhumati (dir. Bimal Roy, 1958): http://www.upperstall.com/films/madhumati.html
Manus (dir. V. Shantaram, 1939): http://www.upperstall.com/films/manoos.html
Kaagaz ke Phool (dir. Guru Dutt, 1959): http://www.upperstall.com/films/kaagazkephool.html
Bombay Talkie (dir. James Ivory, 1970): http://www.merchantivory.com/bombay.html
Nayak (dir. Satyajit Ray, 1966): http://arts.ucsc.edu/rayFASC/*nayak.html
Guddi (dir. Hrishikesh Mukherjee, 1971): http://www.rediff.com/entertai/2002/may/02dinesh.htm
Rangeela (dir. Ram Gopal Varma, 1995): http://www.uiowa.edu/~incinema/rangeela.html
Zubeida (dir. Shyam Benegal, 2001): http://www.upperstall.com/zub.html
Baazi (dir. Guru Dutt, 1951): http://www.upperstall.com/films/baazi.html
Teesri Kasam (dir. Basu Bhattacharya, 1966): http://www.upperstall.com/films/teesrikasam.html
Utsav (dir. Girish Karnad, 1984): http://www.uiowa.edu/~incinema/utsav.html
Hum Dil De Chuke Sanam (dir. Sanjay Leela Bhansali, 1999): http://www.uiowa.edu/~incinema/humdilde.html

Part II

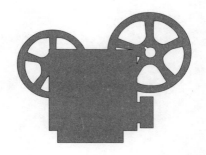

Trans-Actions

6

Sexuality, Sensuality and Belonging: Representations of the 'Anglo-Indian' and the 'Western' Woman in Hindi Cinema

GEETANJALI GANGOLI

What are you reading?' London based Preeti to Indian Bharat
'The Bhagvad Gita,' replies a Bharat indifferent to Preeti's charms.
'Gita? Who is Gita? Is Gita the name of the heroine of the novel that you are reading,' Preeti replies.

Purab aur Paschim
(*The East and the West*, dir. Manoj Kumar, 1970)

'Just because I have grown up in London, I haven't forgotten my culture, don't forget that.' London returned Tina after singing a Hindu devotional song, 'om jai jagdeesh hare' effortlessly and devotedly during her ragging after joining a college in India.

Kuch Kuch Hota Hai
(*Something or Other is Happening*, dir. Karan Johar, 1998)

These excerpts from two Hindi films set almost 30 years apart reveal interesting aspects of life in India and what it means to be constructed as

Indian. In both films, 'Indianness' has been created in comparison and contrast with the West and is often unproblematically reconstructed as Hindu. However, while in the 1970s, the West and the East were projected as polarised oppositions; contemporary films in the age of globalisation locate the East and the West in the same person—or they seem to.

There is much literature on representations of vamps (Kabir, 2001; Kasbekar, 2001) and heroines in Indian films (Uberoi, 1999). Studies also include the representation of the westernised Indian as 'English speaking, sexually permissive and indifferent to family allegiances' (Vasudevan, 2002). This chapter focuses not on the literal vamp but the representation of the vamp and the western(ised) woman in Hindi films through the 1970s to the present in at least three discrete, yet connected ways: the vamp as Anglo-Asian;[1] as marginal Indian, yet westernised;[2] and, the vamp as metaphor represented in the body of the heroine.

Anglo-Asian women represented in Hindi films were seen as 'liminal' as compared to Indian (read Hindu) women (see also Thomas, this volume). A casual reading of Hindi films in the 1950s and 1960s demonstrates that Anglo-Indian women were able to not only partake in the film world, but were also seen as more accessible.[3] This was manifested in two ways. One, in their actual presence in the films (Kabir, 2001: 54–55). Second, in the kind of roles offered to them. In other words, the vamp/prostitute division has been somewhat fuzzy. Literary projections of Anglo-Indian women follow a similar pattern—they are projected as promiscuous, sexually active, disrupting the colonial agenda or as pathetic victims of displacement and boredom (Sen, 2000: 12–32). In the films examined here, we find that Anglo-Indian or non-Indian/western women are similarly represented as sexual beings in a way that 'Indian' women are not. However, in Hindi films, the frame of reference is not the colonising man, but the post-colonial Hindu man.

Films made in the 1990s look at the issue of transnationalism differently (see also Deshpande, this volume). Patricia Uberoi points out that in the 1990s a new series of films were made positioning the Non-Resident Indian

---

[1] *Teesri Manzil* (*The Third Floor*, dir. Vijay Anand, 1966) was one of the many films that Helen acted in as a vamp and an Anglo-Indian woman.

[2] Films like *Shree 420* (*Mr 420*, dir. Raj Kapoor, 1955), brings out the difference between the virtuous working class heroine, Nargis, and the westernised vamp, Nadira.

[3] Anglo-Asian women have been a part of the Indian film industry since the very beginning of film features—around the 1920s. A possible reason for this is that 'respectable' Indian women deemed the industry as unrespectable.

(NRI) as hero, testifying to the liberalised economy of the 1990s (Uberoi, 1999: 183). While Uberoi focuses on 'family values' as being markers of Indianness for the NRI, I suggest that the 'ideal' family is created by replacing the vamp with the heroine with vampish attributes who gets tamed into an 'ideal' Indian woman, either through sexually aggressive behaviour—called 'eve-teasing' in India—by the hero; or more subtly, through love.

The issue here is not whether Hindi films in this instance or another reflect reality, but what they create as acceptable to viewership (Kakar, 1990).[4] Recent work by Asha Kasbekar reminds us that cinema is based on scopophilia (the pleasure of looking) and examines the cultural negotiations with regimes of power that must take place to successfully present the woman as an erotic spectacle. She explores ways that film-makers have used to legitimise the spectacle of the vamp of the 1950s and the 1960s and the 'modern, independent heroine' of the 1970s and the 1980s (Kasbekar, 2001: 286–308). However, cinema does more than reflect existing values in society. It also plays a vital role in creating, legitimising and entrenching identities. By constructing the Anglo-Indian and the westernised as the 'other', the boundary between 'us' (the moral east/good Hindus) and 'them' (the immoral west/the Anglo-Indians) is more sharply etched out. It also aids in integrating a group and transgressing conflicts within the group. It fulfils perhaps another important role—converting unconscious envy against the articulate and urbane westernised woman to resentment and anger. This can perhaps serve as a partial explanation for the sorry end that meets most westernised women and Anglo-Indian vamps in popular Hindi films. Thus, it offers a message to those selves—women in this case—within the group that may not want to conform to the stated norms of the one or the other role. Devaluing the other therefore provides a potential levelling device for women of all or lower strata.

The audiences of most films are seen as Hindu or, at least, honorary Hindus, both by film-makers and in some cases by the judiciary. In 1989, the Bombay High Court heard a case involving a Hindi film, *Pati Parmeshwar* (*My husband is my God*, dir. Madan Joshi, 1989). The film was denied a certificate on the grounds that it violated Guideline 2(IV-a) of the

[4] Kakar argues that the common reaction by critics of dismissing Hindi films as being unrealistic is condescending and based on a restricted understanding of what realism means. Realism includes not only the demonstrably factual but also the psychologically real, or acceptable.

Cinematography Act, 1962, which states that 'visuals, words depicting women in ignoble servility to men, or glorifying such servility as a praise worthy quality of women are not represented'. The film depicted the heroine as a woman constantly servile to her husband, accepting and glorifying the violence meted out to her by him and his family. In one scene that feminists and women's organisations particularly took objection to, the protagonist carries her sick husband to a prostitute's house arguing that she was duty-bound to carry out his wishes. The producer of the film held that the refusal of the Censor Board to grant a viewing certificate violated his freedom of speech and expression under Article 19(1)(a) of the Constitution.

Three of the four judges that heard the case held that the projection of the leading actress did not violate the guidelines. Justice Pratap stated that far from being servile, the heroine exhibited a praiseworthy commitment in saving her marriage, and the violence suffered by her was seen by him as 'ennobling'. Justice Aggarwal held that the characterisation of the heroine did not violate the relevant section of the Act, as servility is not 'ignoble, but worthy of praise'. Justice Shah did not find the characterisation 'ignoble' or 'indecent' since he reasoned that a primarily Hindu audience would see the film. Only one judge disagreed with this reading of the film. He reasoned that the film violated the relevant guideline, as the heroine was depicted as servile in a demeaning manner (Jaisingh, 1989: 6).

I am not concerned here with issues such as the film-maker's freedom of choice or the role of the state in cinema. Those are important questions that are dealt with elsewhere (Prasad, 1998: 123–46). My concern is with the issue of the representation of the ideal Hindu woman as a suffering and devoted wife (*pativrata*), for whom serving her husband and husband's family (*sasuraal*) and putting up with humiliation at their hands is not merely an ordinary duty, but a sacred obligation. Servility and humiliation in the marital home are, therefore, constructed as 'ennobling' and 'worthy of praise', especially when displayed by Hindu women. Further, the judgement marks the film as viewable by a Hindu audience, whose shared cultural attitudes to women would see this projection as positive and empowering.

As opposed to the well-documented images of the wife/mother figure in academic literature on Indian films (Kakar, 1990; Mazumdar, 2000: 246; Vasudevan 2002), this chapter focuses on the images of the sexually active and/or sensual young woman. These include representations of the Anglo-Indian woman, the Christian woman, the modern westernised woman and the NRI woman. I do not suggest that these 'categories' of women form a continuum in 'real' life. However, in popular Hindi films, they can and do form a continuum of experiences and representations of a 'type' of woman, the other of the Hindu middle-class woman, the good wife and mother.

The chapter is divided into three sections, one that looks at the representation of Anglo-Indian characters in films made in the 1960s and 1970s. I also look at an ambivalently constructed marginal Indian woman in another popular film of the 1970s. Next, I examine and contrast these with the projection of a NRI woman in a film made in the late 1990s. How has the construction of foreignness and the West shifted in the 20 years under study? I have chosen to focus on a range of films—*Teesri Manzil*, 1966; *Purab aur Paschim*, 1970; *Julie* (dir. K S Sethumadhavan, 1975); *Dewaar* (*The Wall*, dir. Yash Chopra, 1975); and, *Kuch Kuch Hota Hai*, 1998. These films represent different but connected themes into the question of representation of the western(ised) woman. *Teesri Manzil* and *Poorab aur Paschim* projects the western woman as Anglo-Indian, vampish, sensual and attractive. The westernised woman both contrasts with the more conventional 'Hindu' heroine and is central to the theme of the film. The male-oriented films made in the 1970s such as *Deewaar* typically dealt with the relationship between the male protagonist and his virtuous mother and loving brother, and the romantic lead, in the form of a westernised—though not necessarily western—woman is somewhat less important in the theme of the film, at least in an initial reading. The films made in the 1990s, such as *Kuch Kuch Hota Hai* deal with the Indian woman located in the West, who maintains her 'Indianness' in a foreign environment (see also Hansen, this volume). All these films locate the normative family structure as Hindu and North Indian.[5] This is not only a chronology but provides three moments within the history of Indian cinema that talk about the construction of desire and the West.

[5] There are of course some notable exceptions—the 'Muslim socials' of the 1970s such as *Pakeezah*, the story of a courtesan, and 'action' films like *Coolie* (dir. Manmohan Desai, 1983) and *Muqaddar Ka Sikandar* (*The King of Fate*, dir. Prakash Mehra, 1978) where the male protagonist, played by Amitabh Bachchan is a Muslim. However, the latter films are only implicitly informed by Muslim culture in a non-obvious and 'natural' manner.

The Anglo-Indian Woman as a Sexual Metaphor: Mainstream and 'Alternative' Cinema

As we have seen, Indianness/Hinduness is reflected in and legitimised through the projection of women in films. The ideal Indian/Hindu woman, represented by the heroine, the hero's mother and/or sister is quintessentially Hindu and is compliant with the wishes of the hero, embodying the male/patriarchal view. In contrast, the vamp is Anglo-Indian or 'westernised', most often sexually promiscuous and knowing, as opposed to the 'innocent' heroine.[6] Thus, the vamp is located as being the outsider to 'Indianness' and to Indian norms and traditions.

It is no understatement to state that the Anglo-Indian woman represents unbridled sexuality in popular Hindi films. While popular Hindi films do not often state with finality when a character is Anglo-Indian, there are markers that any regular and clued-up viewer can read effectively. In films made in the 1950s and 1960s, the markers are names, the appearance and the costumes worn by the characters, and the persona.

Helen often played the Anglo-Indian woman in the 1950s and the '60s. Her 'mixed' parentage—English and Indo-Burmese—helped her to 'look' the part. She played the vamp, sexually promiscuous, scheming to seduce the hero and to ruin him. In the grammar of the film, she stood for all that the chaste heroine is not. A film-maker says of Helen, 'She was a provocative figure and her persona truly intrigued me. She was a Bollywood movie star who was playful, glamorous ...' (Ali, 2001). Helen's scheming was however, ultimately unsuccessful and most often she was punished for her sexual misdemeanors, by the hero's rejection and sometimes, her death.

An interesting example is *Teesri Manzil*, a tightly scripted murder mystery, where the hero, Shammi Kapoor, playing a hotel crooner, is framed in the murder of the heroine, Asha Parekh's sister. Helen plays a dancer employed in the same hotel, attracted to the hero.[7] In contrast with Asha Parekh, who is dusky, dark-haired and clad in *salwar kameezes*—Helen is blonde and westernised in appearance. Interestingly, Helen plays a sexually promiscuous character in the film that shows few signs of 'feminine' vulnerability, unlike the heroine.

[6] John Berger argues that innocence can mean both refusal to enter into a conspiracy, in this case, a sexual conspiracy—and ignorance, of her sexuality and the excitement that sexual knowledge can lead to (Berger, 1972: 32).

[7] It is important to remember that a hotel dancer is considered to be sexually available, and generically a prostitute in the syntax of Hindi films.

In *Teesri Manzil*, Helen plays a central, almost parallel romantic role. She is lively, beautiful and unabashedly sexual, as opposed to the softer sensuality of Asha Parekh. Helen 'throws herself' at the hero, thus transgressing an important gender role—that of the woman being the recipient of male attention and aggression, and the man the pursuer. This fits into the stereotype of western women—as sexually aggressive and promiscuous. Interestingly, the stereotype recasts itself in another way, that of the 'whore with the golden heart', Helen is killed by a bullet meant to kill the hero, dying in his arms. Her dramatic death partially redeems her identity as a whore and a quasi-Indian. Her death is both a punishment for her sexuality and an attempt to make amends for it.

Given India's history of colonialism, constructing the Anglo-Indian and the western woman in the context of the 1960s and early 1970s as vamp/prostitute is simultaneously an act of defiance and an assertion of cultural superiority. It aims to 'other' the westernised woman as immoral and sexually accessible to the Indian man. This contrasts with the experience of Indian men under colonialism. On the one hand, under colonial rule, Anglo-Indian sex workers were not accessible to Indian men (Ballhatchet, 1980); on the other, they were the untouchable wives and daughters of the rulers. Anglo-Indian women, whether as wives or prostitutes, were therefore unavailable to Indian men and were meant only for the sexual consumption of white men.

In these early years of independent India, the middle classes, at least, continued to experience the euphoria of freedom from colonialism, a belief in the intrinsic supremacy of 'Indianness' (Rushdie, 1991: 47–52). This was reflected, perhaps, in the films under question through the projection of Anglo-Indian women as morally and spiritually inferior to the Indian/Hindu man and woman. The quintessential Indian woman was therefore the repository of chastity and the man, the repository of masculine values, who tames the feminine West. What is unstated—but by no means absent—is the sexual fascination of Indian men for Anglo-Indian and western(ised) women.[8]

The desire of sexually possessing an Anglo-Indian woman may remain in the realm of fantasy for many Indian men, but are often acted out by men visiting brothels in urban India. Clients express a preference for sex workers who 'appear' westernised. Thus, in a reversal of the well-documented

[8] Sexual tension between Aamir Khan, the quintessential Indian hero and Rachel Shelley, the Anglo Indian woman is also an integral part of films such as *Lagaan, Once Upon a Time in India* (*Tax*, dir. Ashutosh Gowariker, 2001).

eroticisation of eastern women by western men (Jordan, 2000: 525–85), Indian men entertain myths about the sexuality of 'foreign' or 'western' women. Sex workers whose physical attributes come closest to the fantasies of male clients in looking 'western', especially 'fair' Nepali women, continue to be popular with clients of different classes. They command higher prices than Indian women and are seen as more amenable to sexual experimentation. Several sex workers belonging to Nepal speak of clients asking them to wear western clothes, smoke and drink—to adopt some of the attributes of the vamp of Hindi films.[9] Not only is the 'prostitute' constructed as a potential 'vamp', but also the vamp is—not only potentially—whore-like. The sexual fantasies of Indian men are played out in Hindi films that construct the western(ised) woman as sexually available and as prostitutes and then replayed in brothels that try to realise this cinematic ideal.

Significantly, the 'real-life' prostitute is accorded the same low status socially as the westernised vamp is in reel-life; even though male clients may personally hold them in high regard. Sex workers complain of the stigmatisation of their work and point out that they play an important role in the emotional life of their clients. They also see a parallel between the covert sexuality of the work done by film actresses in Hindi films and sex work. The following excerpt from my interviews with sex workers brings this out: 'Film actresses get a lot of money for exposing themselves. No one likes to spend much money on us.'

As with the relationship between the client and the sex worker (Gangoli, 2001), sexual tension and hostility marks the interaction between the Anglo-Indian/Christian woman and the 'Indian' man in several films of the 1970s. These include: *Purab aur Paschim*, *Julie* and *Junoon* (*Obsession*, dir. Shyam Benegal, 1978). Even though the Anglo-Indian woman here plays not the vamp but the heroine, she appears to have more in common with the vamp as embodied by Helen, than the heroine. The 'West' has to be purged out of the western woman before she can be acceptable as wife-like. I look at two of these films in some detail here.

In the eponymous film, Julie, an Indian Christian woman falls in love with and gets pregnant by a Hindu boy. His involuntary absence during her pregnancy forces her to have the child secretly and abandon it. Her mother, played by Nadira, shows little sympathy. The film ends with the hero's father—seen as representing the ideal 'Indian' father figure—

[9] This paragraph is based on my fieldwork notes on sex work in Calcutta and Bombay in 1998–99 and in 2001.

accepting the 'illegitimate' child and Julie as a daughter-in-law, just as Julie's mother is taking Julie and the rest of the family to emigrate to the UK. The father castigates the mother for her anglicised ambitions. Julie's seduction and subsequent abandonment by their son calls for little chastisement by the family.

Julie's family is shown to lack the internal cohesion and patriarchal control that is the hallmark of Vikram's (hero). Her father is an alcoholic and a wastrel. Her mother is in control of the family, but the family is represented as being unhappy. Simultaneously, the demureness of Vikram's sari-clad sister contrast with Julie's sensuality and mini skirts. Julie is presented to the audience both as seductress and victim, knowing and innocent.

The film reaffirms the moral superiority of the Hindu family, first, in the contrast between the poverty and unhappiness in Julie's household headed nominally by her weak father but effectively by the dominant and unsympathetic mother; and, the cohesion and smooth running of the Hindu family headed by the patriarch. This is unspoken but no less effective. Second, the Hindu patriarch displays his magnanimity by accepting a 'fallen' Christian woman as a daughter-in-law, playing into the Hindu fundamentalist agenda of constructing Hinduism as universally tolerant and accepting.

Purab aur Paschim is based on the dialectic between the East and the West. It has been suggested that the film combines the 'attractions of consumerism with ultimately moralising voyeurism' (Uberoi, 1999: 183). A complicated story about love, friendship and duty, the film affirms the moral superiority of the (spiritual) East over the (materialist) West through the contrast drawn between an Anglo-Indian woman, Preeti, brought up in the UK and a Hindu/Indian woman, Gopi. Both compete for the love of Bharat (literally meaning India), a young man born to a freedom fighter, who dies in the national movement in the 1940s. Bharat meets the sophisticated mini-skirted Preeti—who is constantly shown with an alcoholic drink and a cigarette in her hand—when he goes to London to study science. Preeti and her brother, Shankar, though born to an Indian father, are hilariously ignorant of India. Bharat tells them about the 'real India' that he represents, in a melodramatic song, he says,

> Love is the custom in India. We don't care about the colour of anyone's skin, we may not win the world, but we know how to win hearts. There is a god in every man, a goddess in every woman. I am so proud to be born in India!

Preeti falls in love with Bharat, her father asks Bharat to marry her. Bharat agrees on condition that he goes back to India with Preeti. Preeti, though reluctant, agrees to go to India for a visit. Bharat's confidence that Preeti will fall in love with India once she goes there is, needless to say, borne out. Preeti sheds her 'western' ways, gives up her cigarettes, alcohol and short skirts and stays on in India with Bharat as an ideal wife, wearing a red sari—that she had rejected in an earlier part of the film—singing a *bhajan* (devotional song) in a temple.

A superficial reading of the film reveals to us only the 'taming' of the Anglo-Indian woman. Preeti, after an initial reluctance, is only too ready to be moulded into an ideal Hindu woman, in which there are no traces of the West. She articulates the love that she feels for India in the following words:

> I had heard that India is a land of snake charmers. There are snakes here, but people worship them. I had heard that India was full of poverty, but there are some problems in all cultures. The best thing here is the love that people have for each other, the love between parents and children. I have never stayed with my parents as a daughter should ....

This is a highly sentimentalised vision of India, one that many in the early 1970s may find a bit difficult to reconcile with the 'real' India. But like Bharat's assertion of India as spiritual, and backward only in the things that don't really matter, Preeti's change of heart reiterates the supremacy of 'Indian' values and traditions. These include the sanctity of the family and the traditional, idealised role of women within it.[10] At another, less obvious level, the film—like *Julie*—explores the sexual fascination that Anglo-Indian women hold for Indian men, and their desire to possess them.

In the next section we will see that the logic of the mainstream film changed in the mid-1970s. No longer is the hero secure in his 'Indianness' as the corruption of the 'Emergency' years created a deep rooted cynicism against the state (Gopalan, 2000: 214; Rushdie, 1991: 52). The new hero is angry, his patriotism is a little jaded and he is an insecure man often of working-class origins who makes it big in the world of crime. Here, he is seduced by the glamour embodied by and within the western(ised) woman.

[10] This has a resonance in arguments made about the public/private domain and nationalism. Historians of the national movement in India have pointed out that Indian

The Vamp/Heroine as Marginal Indian: Traces of the East

By the mid to the late 1970s, the conventional figure of the Anglo-Indian vamp was replaced by a set of heroines that combined the vamp and the heroine, the good and the bad woman. 'Action films' almost replaced family dramas. In the action films, the hero, the archetypal angry young man was emotionally withdrawn, especially with regard to the romantic lead. The conventionally demure heroine of the 1960s was replaced by the somewhat more independent, 'westernised' woman of the 1970s. The career of actresses like Helen could not survive this competition. Often, in films belonging to this genre, there is a strong parallel male lead that is teamed with a more conventional heroine. The anti-hero, embodied by Amitabh Bachchan, became popular as the rebel-with-a-cause figure that took on social and economical inequities through a combination of physical aggression and uncompromising intelligence. There has been some analysis of such iconic figures (Kakar, 1990; Prasad, 1998: 142–43; Mazumdar, 2000: 238–62; Nandy, 1998: 196–236). However, where a gendered analysis has been made, the focus has been on the male figure and his relationship with his suffering, heroic mother (Vasudevan, 2002).

An important film in this genre is *Deewaar*. It has been suggested that *Deewaar* represents the cinematic representation of the acknowledgement of the crisis of post-colonial nationalism (Mazumdar, 2000: 244). *Deewaar* is the story of two brothers, Vijay (Amitabh Bachchan) and Ravi Varma (Shashi Kapoor) and their relationship with their mother (Nirupa Roy). Their father is a union leader in a coal mine, who is forced to betray his union because the mine owner kidnaps his wife and sons. He is boycotted by the community and his older son Vijay bears the brunt of the abandonment as his arm is tattooed with the damning words, 'my father is a thief'. Vijay and the mother immigrate to the city of hope, Bombay, bring up Ravi and educate him by their hard work. Vijay then joins a smuggler's gang and becomes rich beyond his dreams. Ravi becomes a policeman and tries to reform his brother in vain. The mother and Ravi leave Vijay's mansion and the film ends with the tragic death of Vijay through the hands of his brother.

---

nationalists, many of whom had received western education, accepted that the West was superior in the public sphere of rationality, bureaucracy, and modernisation but maintained their cultural superiority in the private, spiritual and familial sphere, traditionally the domain of Indian women (Chatterjee, 1993, 35–157).

Within this tale of machismo, the women—other than the mother—have little role to play. Ravi's girlfriend, Veera (Neetu Singh), is prosperous, pretty and buxomed and arrives at intervals to comfort and romance him. Vijay's less conformist self finds comfort in Anita (Parveen Babi), a prostitute. Unlike Veera, Anita is an ambivalent figure in the film. Nothing is known of her background other than passing references to a mother, who is represented as hoping for a conventional life for Anita as a wife and mother. Anita may or may not be a Hindu woman, unlike Veera whose status as a Hindu woman is established by her name. She could be a Christian, even an Anglo-Indian, but as with a conventional vamp, the scriptwriters seem indifferent to any effort to mark her out as belonging to a family or community.[11] She never wears a sari until the last scene in which she dies. Vijay meets her at a bar, where in blatant disregard to the norms of Hindi films, where only a vamp can be so 'forward', she approaches him wearing a slinky, sexy dress, lights his cigarette and introduces herself with the words: 'You don't have to thank me. I was waiting for an opportunity to talk to you. There is no one as handsome as you in this bar, nor anyone as lonely as you.'

Her appearance and her cigarette are really signs to the audience as to Vijay that Anita is 'wanton' and whore-like (Gangoli and Solanki, 1996).[12] Vijay initially appears indifferent to her charms, as he is tense about meeting his enemies outside the bar. But intimacy develops between them, even as Vijay continues to be less than polite to her. When she reminds him that he hasn't asked her what her name is, he says, coolly: 'There's no point asking your name. Women like you change their name daily.' Anita, instead of feeling offended by this somewhat offensive statement, agrees with him. Unlike more straightforward vamp characters, Anita carries with her a sense of her stigma and appears to have internalised it. For her as for Vijay, her profession is contemptible; to be treated with contempt is less than remarkable. Anita's lack of self-esteem has perhaps a parallel in the stock character of the self-sacrificing wife and mother that is an integral part of the storyline of mainstream Hindi films. For instance, Vijay's mother accepts and explains away the abandonment by her husband as natural and refuses to countenance any criticism of her husband's

[11] The well-known vamp of the 1970s and 1980s Bindu is reported to have said: 'The vamp is usually a loner. You hardly know who her parents are, or what kind of family she is from' (Kabir, 2001: 98).

[12] Interviews with police representatives in the 1990s reveal that women have been arrested for soliciting clients if they are seen smoking in public.

behaviour that her son considers weak and insensitive. Her status as a married woman is so integral to her that through the long years of separation from her husband, she wears, rather prominently, the signs of a married woman. Not dissimilarly, Anita gracefully accepts the disparaging statements Vijay often throws at her. I suggest that Anita's lack of aggression can be seen as the effort to integrate the vamp into the heroine, to tell the audience that the sexually transgressive westernised woman can be gentle, nurturing and wife-like.

Vijay then enters into a relationship with Anita, buys her a flat and a car, and supports her financially. She becomes his confidante, he speaks to her about his troubled relationship with his mother and brother and his anguish about his father. But there is no corresponding exchange of confidence with Anita. The audience—and perhaps Vijay—knows as little about Anita and her family at the end of the film as they do when they first see her. This is quite apparent at the point when the relationship between Anita and Vijay is fairly established; he makes no effort to hide his surprise when he sees a sari in her wardrobe. For Vijay, as for the audience, presumably, the sari is an important marker of the good/chaste Hindu woman. Anita's red sari—a colour worn by brides in Hindi films—is given to her by her mother, and is a dream that is doomed to remain unfulfilled.

Anita eventually gets pregnant, Vijay agrees to marry her, but just after she changes into the red sari that her mother left for her, his enemies kill her. She dies in Vijay's arms, who, for the first time in the film acknowledges his need for her. Anita laments the end of her dreams for a husband, a child and a home, but says, 'I have been dead for a long time, I am being reborn today.' Anita's death pushes Vijay to the final act of destruction, as he goes on a rampage killing his enemies before he is shot by his brother and dies in his mother's lap.

Anita's tragedy is subsumed in the tragedy of Vijay's life and death. One can't help feeling that Vijay's death may not have been inevitable, but Anita's was. It is not inconsequential to the theme of the film that Anita dies at the very point when her hopes for a life as a wife and a mother seem to be close to realisation. Her profession and her blatant sexuality have to be punished by the script, her importance to the hero as an emotional support notwithstanding. Anita's devotion to Vijay cannot prevent her from remaining a marginal and marginalised figure in the film.

The film draws heavily on the significance of the mother–son relationship within idealised 'Indian' families. It has been suggested that a woman's status as a maternal figure is more important than that of a wife: the wife being the sexual partner is seen as less deserving of respect. As Madhu Kishwar (1997) puts it:

> Relationships with children are considered far more dependable, enduring, and fulfilling ... as a wife, a woman is expected to serve and surrender, as a mother she is allowed the right to both nurture and dominate and is supposed to be venerated unconditionally. She can expect obedience, love, and *seva* (service) from her children, especially sons, even after they grow up. Unconditional giving brings in its own ample rewards. In her role as a mother she is culturally far more glorified.

Within this paradigm, the long-suffering mother in *Deewaar* represents the true Indian/Hindu woman, whose sexuality is subsumed in her love for her children. The ambiguous and sexually charged character of Anita, despite her end, is perhaps not meant to evoke a similar sympathy.

The Indian Woman in the West: The 'Indo-Anglo' Heroine[13]

The late 1990s have seen the popularity of films known as 'family dramas'. Similar films in the 1980s celebrated lower middle-class values such as thrift and middle-class modesty, contrasting it with the vulgarity and lack of values that characterise the rich. The female protagonist is less prosperous than her lover, but embodies femininity and the ideal nurturing woman.[14] Films like *Hum Aapke Hain Koun...!* (*What do I mean to you*, dir. Sooraj R. Bharjatya, 1994),[15]

[13] By Indo-Anglo, I mean the quintessential Indian woman located geographically in the West; or, the NRI woman who retains her essential 'Indianness'.

[14] For instance, *Maine Pyaar Kiya* (*I Have Loved*, dir. Sooraj R. Bharjatya, 1989). The film tells the story of Suman (Bhagyashree), a lower middle-class girl in love with Prem (Salman Khan) a rich man, who vindicates middle-class values of thrift and hard work. Suman's father rejects the inherited riches of the young man and asks him to earn money by hard work and perseverance before he can be worthy of her hand. Prem accepts and wins the challenge. A sub-plot to this film is that the hero rejects the advances of a rich, westernised and sexy woman in favour of the quieter and domesticated charms of the heroine. Suman is shown as being the ideal homemaker winning the hearts of Prem's mother when she lives with them.

[15] *Hum Aapke Hain Koun...!* reiterates the joys of Indian (read Hindu) family life, the centrality of sacrifice for a happy life, and the pleasures that await those who conform to the values of family life. This is accompanied by a vulgar display of wealth and consumerism

Dilwale Dulhania Le Jayenge (*The Brave Will Win the Bride*, dir. Aditya Chopra, 1995) and *Kuch Kuch Hota Hai* are stories of men and women to whom being Indian is to be a part of an idealised Indian family (Uberoi, 2001: 310–12). Issues of class, caste and religion and even country are seemingly irrelevant as the emotional and romantic travails of the protagonists take precedence. Hindi films in the 1990s appear to reflect the globalisation of cultures and the creation of a new Indian identity.

The Indian woman of the 1990s film is now both western and Indian, sometimes more western than Indian, and often located geographically in the West. The effort is, however, to locate and celebrate the Indian within the western. Significantly, what is recognised as Indian may be unrecognisable to many of us located in India, but is a part of the mythicisation of India for the NRI by film-makers. The mythicisation accepts and celebrates the patriarchal family as the norm.[16] Liberalisation therefore impacts upon concepts and projections of the Indian woman in the 1990s and the early twenty-first century, she is ideally modern, yet moral and chaste (Chakravarti, 2000: WS12–17; Uberoi, 1999: 180). I focus on one of the aforementioned films—*Kuch Kuch Hota Hai*. The film gives us some pointers to how an Indian woman based in the UK is projected.

The story of the film is as follows. Rahul (Shahrukh Khan) and Anjali (Kajol) are good friends at a fantastically conceived college located somewhere in India. Anjali is tomboyish and regularly defeats Rahul at basketball. The principal of the college, Mr Malhotra is fond of Anjali. His daughter (Tina), who has grown up in the UK and is studying in Oxford, joins the college. Tina is westernised in appearance, is sexy, feminine and fair with long hair. She joins Rahul's and Anjali's college in the final year. Rahul is instantly attracted to her, but says that she's not for him as she's not 'Indian' enough; he wants a girl who he can take home to his mother.

---

that is an underlying theme of the film. The film, therefore, simultaneously celebrates an idealised version of family life, based on prescribed gender roles and valourises consumerism.

[16] *Dilwale Dulhania Le Jayenge* is located both in the UK and in India. The romance between two NRIs, Raj (Shahrukh Khan) and Simran (Kajol), in London, is thwarted by Simran's father (Amrish Puri) who wants her to go through an arranged marriage. Simran is followed to India by Raj, who tries to win her father over. When she—and later her mother—pleads with him to take her away without her father's consent, he refuses on the grounds that it would not be the right thing for an Indian to do. This denies other realities of Indian lovers that are separated, and subjected to unspeakable horrors, and for whom elopement is often the only option (for the film's reception in the UK, see also Kaur, this volume).

Once Tina proves that she has not forgotten her roots, he falls in love with her. Anjali realises that she loves Rahul at this precise moment. The film therefore reiterates, at this point, the cinematic norm that a boy and a girl cannot remain 'good friends' forever.

A heartbroken Anjali abandons her studies and returns to her mother and in the course of time, becomes a late twentieth-century version of the idealised Hindu woman, in slinky saris as opposed to her boyish jeans, and long hair in contrast to her earlier short haircut. She gets engaged to Aman, a NRI from London. Meanwhile, Rahul and Tina marry, Tina dies in childbirth and tells her daughter—also called Anjali—about Anjali (Kajol) through letters written to her. The eight-year-old Anjali and her grandmother conspire to bring the estranged friends together and succeed in making Rahul fall in love with Anjali. The timely sacrifice of the understanding fiancé, Aman, enables their marriage.

The NRI woman, Tina, becomes 'worthy' of Rahul only when she demonstrates—by singing devotional songs and visiting a temple—that she is still close to her 'culture'. This may be an effort to address the anxiety of the middle-class NRI audience that their children are becoming displaced Indians.[17] Tina demonstrates her 'Indianness' in other, subtler ways. In contrast to Miss Breganza (Archana Puran Singh), a teacher in the college, who is more overtly sensual and flirtatious than any other female character in the film, Tina remains somewhat distant and cool and is wooed assiduously by Rahul. On the other hand, Miss Breganza rings up Mr Malhotra at night and purrs, 'I hope I am not disturbing you, but I know that you won't mind being disturbed by me.' One cannot help wondering whether there is an underlying message here; Miss Breganza, who is a Christian woman based in India is westernised in a more unredeemable and perhaps negative sense than Tina, who has been geographically located in the UK.

Once in love with Rahul, Tina changes her attire to demure *salwar kameez*, rather than revealing mini skirts. The attire of the ideal Indian woman remains all important if the audience has to be reassured that Tina though initially seeming all 'western', can be 'Indian'. She asserts her right to be considered an ideal 'Hindu' wife as she is willing, if not eager, to sacrifice her life for her husband. Post-marriage, she decides to have a baby against medical advice because Rahul wants a child. Rahul

---

[17] If indeed this was the aim, it succeeded dramatically as the film was a commercial success in the UK, seen by NRIs.

is, of course, absolved of any responsibility for her inevitable death as he is kept in the dark about her medical condition. Even after her death, she continues to be a good wife by influencing her daughter through letters left to her, asking her to bring Anjali and Rahul together. Though Tina has to constantly offer proofs to the audience that she is indeed 'Indian' she comes through as the ideal, understanding and sensitive wife and mother.

Less obviously, Anjali too is westernised with her short hair, jeans and shoes. Unlike Tina, however, she is not feminine. Feminists have suggested that the film is anti-feminist in that Anjali has to become 'feminine' and sexy before Rahul falls in love with her. The point when Rahul first becomes sexually aware of Anjali is when she loses to him—very publicly—in basketball. What is missed out is that Anjali also becomes feminine in a classically celebrated 'Indian' manner. In the second half of the film she is never shown in anything but saris and *salwar kameez*. Love transforms/Indianises not only Tina, the NRI woman, but Anjali, the Indian westernised woman.

The West within India is indicated in another cameo character, that of Mr Almeida, the camp leader of the summer camp where Anjali and Rahul meet after a decade through the careful planning of the younger Anjali and her grandmother. Mr Almeida plays a ridiculous character—the late twentieth-century version of the WOG,[18] making incredible statements such as 'I love England. My father was a tailor with the British.' To add to his projection as a caricature, he sports a shirt with the Union Jack and oversees the unfurling of the Union Jack over the camp. To his horror, Rahul's mother who accompanies her grandmother to the camp, brings Hinduism within the camp, starting puja and bhajan classes, with Almeida tearing his hair out.

For all its westernised gloss, the film reaffirms the supremacy—moral and practical—of India over the West. Simultaneously, it brings out some of the anxieties of the late twentieth-century middle-class, globalised Indian. Tina is Indianised, as is Anjali, while Miss Breganza and Mr Almeida remain though not unchallenged, almost unchanged. Perhaps Anjali and Tina can be redeemed because they are indeed 'Hindu' women, while the 'Anglo-Indian' genesis of Miss Breganza and Mr Almeida make them almost irredeemable, figures of ridicule though a source of some anxiety.

[18] Westernised Oriented Gentleman (WOG), a derogatory acronym used for brown men who aped western norms.

Conclusion It has been suggested by Ashis Nandy that the Hindi commercial cinema may romanticise or even vulgarise the dilemma of those trying to survive victimhood and alienation let loose by modernisation, it never ignores or rejects it as childish or primitive (1998: 203). To deliberately oversimplify a complex argument, this worldview includes a divided image of woman that has its basis in a fractured concept of femininity: nurturing, devoted, maternal vs. unreliable, seductive, primal (ibid.: 225)—to which one may add, mother vs. whore vs. wife. There is in conjunction a fractured image of the world, the old and the new, the good and the bad.

Who, according to this perspective, are the victims of development, modernisation and the emotional and economical alienation that Nandy refers to? Are the displaced people a homogeneous category sharing a common worldview? It would seem that Nandy's victims of modernisation are primarily Hindus. As we have seen, the producers of Hindi films seem to share this view. In most Hindi films, the Hindu family—whether middle class or working class—is the normative and idealised unit. In some cases, as in *Deewaar*, they are subjected to, and fight against mechanisms of an unjust system of oppression, represented by the mill owner; in others like *Kuch Kuch Hota Hai*, the supremacy of the Hindu familial system is maintained by the recognition of the Indian with the alienated—Hindu—NRI. In all this, the audience can be complicit with myth-making if they are self-consciously, or culturally 'Hindu'.

What this approach fails to see is the heterogeneity of Indian society and that the potential audience includes a variety of displaced men and women. For instance, Ismail Merchant's film, *Cotton Mary*, a representation of the Anglo-Indian community in the 1950s in Kochi, has resulted in protests by the local Anglo-Indian community. They suggest that the film shows Anglo-Indian women as being promiscuous and men as alcoholic.[19] The protests perhaps indicate the despair of a community that has suffered such value-ridden representation in Indian and presumably western cinema.

While saying this, it may be necessary to sound a note of caution. As we have seen, there have been shifts from the representation of the Anglo-Indian woman from a sexual predator who is demonstrably dangerous and overtly sexual—Helen in *Teesri Manzil*—to a victim, willing or reluctant, to the lustful fantasies of the Indian male—Ruth in *Junoon* and the leading character in *Julie*—to the caricatured sexuality of Miss Breganza

[19] See 'Anglo-Indians oppose Cotton Mary', at http://www.indiainfo.com/cgi-bin.

in *Kuch Kuch Hota Hai*. It is, therefore, just about possible that the Indian male is coming to terms with his post-colonial status and more able to dismiss the sexuality of the Anglo-Indian woman in the late 1990s than he was in the 1960s.

However, the terms of reference continue to be set by the Indian/Hindu male. The subjectivity of the Anglo-Indian woman appears to be irrelevant. She is further marginalised by her absence as a vamp in films made in the 1980s and 1990s and replaced by a generic figure that speaks for the westernised Indian woman as much as it does for the Anglo-Indian woman. In more recent films, the globalised Indian remains Hindu, and the ideal woman combines the sensuality of the vamp that has always been seen as a western characteristic with the chastity of the wife figure.

References

ALI, FIRDAUS. 2001. 'In Search of a Vamp'. Available at http://www.rediff.com.(Accessed on 25 June 2001.)

BALLHATCHET, KENNETH. 1980. *Race, Sex and Class under the Raj: Imperial Attitudes and their Critics, 1783–1905*. London: Weidenfeld and Nicolson.

BERGER, JOHN. 1972. *Ways of Seeing*. London: BBC and Penguin Books.

CHAKRAVARTI, UMA. 2000, 'State, Market and Freedom of Expression: Women and Electronic Media', *Economic and Political Weekly*, 35(18): WS12–17.

CHATTERJEE, PARTHA. 1993. *The Nation and Its Fragments: Colonial and Postcolonial Histories*. Princeton: Princeton University Press.

GANGOLI, GEETANJALI. 2001. 'Silence, Hurt and Choice: Attitudes to Prostitution in Feminist Thought', Working Paper No. 6, Asia Research Centre, London School of Economics and Political Science.

GANGOLI, GEETANJALI and GOPIKA SOLANKI. 1996. 'The Official Discourse Around PITA', *Economic and Political Weekly*, 31(51).

GOPALAN, LALITA. 2000. 'Avenging Women in Indian Cinema', in Ravi Vasudevan (ed.), *Making Meaning in Indian Cinema*, pp. 214–37, New Delhi: OUP.

JAISINGH, INDIRA. 1986. 'The Ignoble Servility of Pati Parmeshwar.' *The Lawyers*. December 1989: 6.

JORDAN, ANN. 2000. 'Commercial Sex Workers in Asia: A Blind Spot in Human Rights Law', in Kelly D. Askin and Dorean Koenig (eds), *Women and International Human Rights Law*, Volume 2, New York: Ardsley.

KABIR, NASREEN MUNNI. 2001. *Bollywood: The Indian Cinema Story*. London: Channel 4 Books.

KAKAR, SUDHIR. 1990. *Intimate Relations: Exploring Indian Sexuality*. New Delhi: Penguin Books.

KASBEKAR, ASHA. 2001. 'Hidden Pleasures: Negotiating the Myth of the Female Ideal in Popular Hindi Cinema', in Rachel Dwyer and Christopher Pinney (eds), *Pleasure and the Nation: The History, Politics and Consumption of Public Culture in India*, pp. 286–308, New Delhi: OUP.

KISHWAR, MADHU. 1997. 'Women, Sex and Marriage: Restraint as a Feminine Strategy', *Manushi*, Issue No. 99. Available at http://free.freespeech.org.manushi/99/sexuality.html. (Accessed on 25 March 2003.)

PRASAD, M. MADHAVA. 1998. 'The State in/of Cinema', in Partha Chatterjee (ed.), *Wages of Freedom: Fifty Years of the Indian Nation State*, pp. 123–46, New Delhi: OUP.

MAZUMDAR, RANJANI. 2000. 'From Subjectification to Schizophrenia. The "Angry Man" and the "Psychotic" Hero of Bombay Cinema', in Ravi Vasudevan (ed.), *Making Meaning in Indian Cinema*, pp. 238–62, New Delhi: OUP.

NANDY, ASHIS. 1998. 'An Intelligent Critic's Guide to Indian Cinema', in Ashis Nandy, *Return from Exile*, pp. 196–236, New Delhi: OUP.

RUSHDIE, SALMAN. 1991. *Imaginary Homelands: Essays and Criticism, 1981–1991*. London: Granta Books.

SEN, INDRANI. 2000. 'Gendering (Anglo) India: Rudyard Kipling and the Construction of Women', *Social Scientist*, 29(9–10): 12–32.

UBEROI, PATRICIA. 1999. 'The Diaspora Comes Home: Disciplining Desire in DDLJ', in Veena Das, Dipankar Gupta and Patricia Uberoi (eds), *Tradition, Pluralism and Identity*, pp. 163–94, New Delhi: Sage Publications.

———. 2001. 'Imagining the Family: An Ethnography of Viewing: *Hum Aapke Hain Koun*', in Rachel Dwyer and Christopher Pinney (ed.), *Pleasure and the Nation: The History, Politics and Consumption of Popular Culture in India*, pp. 309–51, New Delhi: OUP.

VASUDEVAN, RAVI. 2002. 'Another History Rises to the Surface. "Hey Ram"—Melodrama in the Age of Digital Stimulation', *Economic and Political Weekly*, 38(28).

7

'Fight Club': Aesthetics, Hybridisation and the Construction of Rogue Masculinities in *Sholay* and *Deewaar*

KOUSHIK BANERJEA

The 1970s and the 1980s saw the emergence of the violent movie and the 'angry young man' epitomised by Amitabh Bachchan in 'Bollywood' movies such as *Deewaar* (dir. Yash Chopra, 1975), *Zanjeer* (dir. Prakash Mehra, 1973), *Sholay* (dir. Ramesh Sippy, 1975) and *Coolie* (dir. Manmohan Desai, 1983). The films have commonly been understood in relation to growing urbanisation, increasing significance of the 'Underworld' and the intense disaffection of unemployed male youth in India. The significance of elaborate fight sequences in these movies has been attributed to the increased violence of metropolitan life for the poor. Yet, just as the polysemic narratives of Bombay cinema responded to, and were produced by, the turbulent political situation of 1970s India, their representative strategies also negotiated the mobile aesthetic currency of the era. Bearing in mind that cultural production does not operate as a petrified emblem, this chapter suggests that this aesthetic dynamism may offer a vital clue as to other neglected 'meanings' negotiated through these classic film texts; indeed, to other forms of cultural dialogue taking place around the apparently surface politics of aesthetics. Crucially, it will be argued that it is the aesthetic techniques as much as the narrative solutions suggested by both films—*Sholay*, *Deewaar*—that allow for the sympathetic construction of 'rogue' masculinities—the outlaw, the outsider—at a time when to be an outsider posed considerable political risks. To that end what is proposed is a close textual reading of both films as this will also allow them to be situated in their own immediate historical context.

It is no secret that when Bruce Lee's *Enter the Dragon* (dir. Robert Clouse, 1973) was shown in India, this time produced by Hollywood, it had a profound impact on Indian audiences across the country. In this decade of increasingly authoritarian rule led by Indira Gandhi, the celluloid iconography of Bruce Lee's lean and mean stance against the villainous Mr Han found ample residue in the angry Amitabh Bachchan characters throwing off the shackles of their subaltern status to fight the henchmen of rogue *goonde* (criminal) capitalists.

This chapter considers such cross-influences in terms of masculinities, the aesthetics of violence and its philosophical undertones in film. It focuses on two classic films featuring Bombay's biggest star, Amitabh Bachchan: *Deewaar* and *Sholay*. These blockbusters are inscribed here as iconographic texts, though situated beyond the desire for an overly neat

Figure 7.1
Kung-Fu fighting: Jet Li updates the martial arts myth for a new generation of Indian cinephiles
Source: Photograph by Raminder Kaur.

historical and political context for their production. They have been chosen for a number of reasons. *Deewaar* highlights narrative shifts in attitudes towards masculine violence and the figure of the outlaw in the 'gangster' genre. *Sholay*, famously dubbed a 'curry western', highlights increasingly globalised, transnational narratives of the male outlaw, social dysfunction and violence. In its composite storylines and organic routes to production, it also embodies the transnational techniques of contemporary film-making. Additionally, it revisits the 'spaghetti western' as myth, distilling Leone's ersatz 'West' in the deserts of north India. Importantly it reworks Leone's vision of dystopic modernity at both a narrative and stylistic level. In fact, the aesthetic economy of both films actually produces heightened narratives of masculinity.

Drawing on but also updating John Fiske (1989), what is proposed here is that the meaning or significance in such film texts is not uniquely produced by their socio-political environment. Rather, these are merely one set of institutional arrangements which both films recognise. The struggle for form which they dramatise is never purely between text and metatext. What is suggested instead is that the emergence and consolidation of a hybrid aesthetic within the commercial action genre reproduces the idea of nationhood as ambivalent text. In other words, that the politics of surface which emerges in these films offers within its provisionality a critical grammar with which to explore the shifting parochialisms of culture and identity. It will be argued that surfaces matter, precisely because they elide half-truths, hidden histories. But before this idea can be developed, it needs to be located within a discourse of aesthetics as it relates to popular film cultures.

Aesthetics and Popular Film

Film technology, one of the great innovations of the twentieth century, has transformed the profile of expressive, visual culture in the modern age. Against a backdrop of rising fascism within Europe, the German philosopher and social theorist, Walter Benjamin saw culture as inseparable from, and conditioned by, technology and social class. He claimed that mass consumer commodities had liberated artistic creativity, which had crept into everyday reality. In the process, consumers had broken down the hierarchy of high and low culture, eroded the division between art and life and inaugurated the 'aestheticisation of everyday life' in which an individual's life was increasingly seen as an aesthetic or a cultural project (1992: 220). His crucial analysis indicates the contingent 'work of art in an age of mechanical reproduction' and whilst he recognises the democratic potential of new technologies—opening up social and cultural space for far greater numbers of people—he is all too aware of the dangers of re-circulating a particular fetish for the image. Indeed, he was writing as the reduction of politics to a particular aesthetics perhaps reached its apotheosis with film-maker, Leni Riefenstahl's 'Olympiad' (1936), commissioned by Hitler as the 'official' documentary of that year's Olympic Games, held in Berlin.

The premium that these developments place on visual culture is generally seen as a key feature of postmodernity, which designates a new condition which contemporary advanced industrial societies are alleged to have reached (Harvey, 1989; Kumar, 1995; Lash and Urry, 1987). It is often characterised by social fragmentation, unpredictable systems of cultural exchange, the dismantling of 'big' government, and the attendant undermining of metanarratives. Significantly, the loss of narrative certainty that has accompanied the imputed demise of the 'metatext' or 'grand theory' has led to the rise of partial texts. Where previously society or human experience could be accommodated within the folds of a totalising theory, the emphasis now is on the partiality of any given account, with the notion of historical depth supplanted by the aesthetic techniques of a 'surface' reading (Connor, 1989). This shift can have particular implications when it is a question of cinema, as Laura Mulvey has argued:

> The place of the look defines cinema, the possibility of varying it and exposing it .... Going far beyond highlighting a woman's to-be-lookedness, cinema builds the way she is to be looked at into the spectacle itself (1989: 25).

The point being made is that not only vision—ways of looking—but also visual culture—cinema—can serve political interests, and this is helpful when looking at films like *Deewaar* and *Sholay*, emerging against a backdrop of increasingly repressive state legislation in 1970s India. Equally, it is useful to remember that the act of vision itself depends on learned codes (Gombrich, 1982), is culturally conditioned (Forge, 1970; Lloyd, 1972), historically specific (Alpers, 1983; Krauss, 1985) and historically mutable (Jay, 1988).

To some extent, though, this chapter argues against Mulvey's suggestion that the visual pleasures of film narratives derive from Hollywood's relationship to the masculinised viewer, which it manufactures through the ideological apparatus of cinematic address. It is suspicious of her reading of film as inherently regressive as this appears to assume the monolithic invocation of a unified subjectivity (desirous male gaze, compliant female object) which is uniquely activated by the mechanics of the cinema as fact and process. Instead, it tries to take account of some of the pleasures of popular cinema for diverse audiences, particularly in films where heightened discourses around masculinity and violence are not simply reproduced at the level of affect, but where the film itself becomes a participatory 'text' within them. This is the case with the vibrantly rarefied worlds depicted in *Sholay* and *Deewaar*.

Walls Come Tumbling Down

By the time that *Deewar* appeared in Indian cinemas, any imputed springtime after liberation from colonial rule was well and truly over. War with Pakistan, industrial unrest, widespread corruption and the imminent declaration of a 'National Emergency'[1] by Indira Gandhi would put an end to that. Political repression against individuals and organisations who had fallen out of favour with the ruling Congress government was routine. Individuals for instance, like the legendary smuggler, Haaji Mastaan, whose rise from humble stevedore to feared gangster is allegedly paralleled in Amitabh Bachchan's celluloid portrayal of Vijay Verma in *Deewaar*.

Deewaar dramatises the epic conflict between two brothers, Vijay (Amitabh Bachchan) and Ravi (Shashi Kapoor), who choose two very different paths in life following their childhood trauma. Ravi becomes a policeman and Vijay a criminal after their father, a trade unionist, is forced to betray his workmates and subsequently his family, which he runs away from, unable to live with the shame of what he has done. His older son, Vijay, has his arm forcibly tattooed by angry former colleagues with the phrase '*Mera baap chor hai*' (My father is a thief). The father lives as a

[1] Following a period of reconstruction and hope in the decade after Independence, the political situation in India had become riven by sectarianism and infighting by the late 1960s. These divisions were compounded by food shortages, the failure of the monsoons, the Bangladesh refugee crisis and oil price shocks in the early 1970s. Rising unemployment and inflation, industrial disputes and food riots, allied to an overarching sense of government mismanagement, led to a series of industrial strikes which almost paralysed the economy in 1974. However, faced with such attempts to unseat her government, Indira Gandhi resorted to strong-arm tactics, announcing her intentions in 1975 by declaring a 'National Emergency'. It was a 19 month period of severe political repression, whereby all fundamental rights of citizens were suspended and political opponents persecuted.

destroyed vagrant, travelling endlessly on the railways as a man with no name. His family is made destitute and forced to cobble together a living in their new lives as slum dwellers in Bombay. It is only with the father's death many years later that he is reunited with the family he abandoned, the adult Vijay poignantly lighting his funeral pyre with the very arm that bears the traces of familial shame. Vijay resolves to live with the shame the only way he knows how: by rising through the ranks of the criminal underworld. Inevitably his journey to the top brings him into conflict with his brother, Ravi, who makes his arrest a personal obsession. Their great contest is for the blessing and sanction of their mother, the very model of Hindu dharmic virtue, who eventually turns her back on Vijay. This tragically sets in motion the chain of events which will end with Ravi fatally wounding Vijay at the temple where he was to meet his mother one last time. He dies in her arms and Ravi is presented with an award for his gallantry.

Many commentaries already propose the reading of Amitabh Bachchan's life as a parallel text in conjunction with the film text (Mishra, 2002) or as a metatext in itself (Sharma, 1993). Mishra et al. (1989: 52), attend to the notion of stardom and how its internal filmic inflections subsequently produce specific forms of identification and continuity of spectatorial response. In her excellent book, *National Identity in Indian Popular Cinema*, Sumita Chakravarty explores this dynamic within what she suggests is the pageant of masculinity and masquerade upholding the 'national-heroic' image in Indian commercial cinema.

> One might add that this continuity of recognition and response hinges on the notion of authenticity, on how filmic transformations metonymically evoke the actor's 'real' personality and conduct. Amitabh Bachchan and Rekha's off-screen romance, for instance, affects our reading of their on-screen performance, creating textual gaps or openings through extra-textual awareness (Chakravarty, 1993: 201).

Interestingly, the case of Bachchan's star presence largely interrupts the conventional division of interest in film stars as distinctively sociological or semiotic signifiers. Perhaps more than any of his contemporaries, Bachchan is only ever partially revealed through textual analysis as he leaps off the page and into the imagination as social fact. His actual caste and class affiliation operates in stark contrast to the harsh social milieu of his angry young film icon. He embodies film's industrial nature, working as an executive in Calcutta before becoming one of its (film's) biggest stars. Yet somehow it is still the genre which he popularised that signals the end of the civic ideal of post-Independence India and ushers in a new era of brutality, pitting the lone hero against the established forces of corruption. *Zanjeer* (*The Chain*, 1973) launches the Bachchan 'myth'—the avenging angel drawn from the lower middle classes/working classes—and no amount of textual deconstruction has managed to derail it since.

The mulitple guises—film executive, urban slum dweller, rebel hero—in which Bachchan enters the social imaginary then assume a heightened relevance regarding the male body as social-semiotic text. This is precisely because of the performative possibilities of disguise which in their visual premium demand a certain complicity of the cinema audience. Above all, as Peter Naremore indicates in his book, *Acting in the Cinema*, it is the visual repertoire of the screen actor which matters.

> Clearly films depend on a form of communication whereby meanings are acted out; the experience of watching them involves not only a pleasure in storytelling but also a delight in bodies and expressive movement, an enjoyment of familiar performing skills, and an interest in players as 'real persons' (Naremore, 1988: 2).

That Bachchan is the son of renowned Hindi poet, Harivansh Rai Bachchan, and the beneficiary of a privileged upbringing prior to his emergence on the big screen, forms part of that narrative suspension assumed of 'his' public. It is instead the ambivalent appeal of his screen rhetoric, his technical mastery of surface which counts in a specific register. It allows him to recuperate the 'lived' contradictions of scarcity and comfort into a single narrative of performance. Masks, after all, are the potential conduit for narcissism as much as mediation. They refabulate the film star's 'story' according to a system of cultural arrangements which suspend a strict linearity. Thus Bachchan's is an identity to be performed, and an ontology to be suspended precisely through the performance.

Suffice to say the lines demarcating Bachchan's screen and his 'real life' personae have increasingly blurred. Indeed, when Bachchan suffers an almost fatal accident during the filming of *Coolie* (1983), the decision is taken to include the relevant footage from the fight scene in question. In keeping with the macabre editorial tone, the scene is freeze-framed with an explanatory caption pointing out Bachchan's life-threatening injury. It is also a rare moment when the action itself appears momentarily paralysed and the narrative structure suspended in liminal animation. For those few seconds Bachchan exists in a dynamic textual space broaching cinema's aspirational qualities and its darker quotidian promise.

The cinema is recognised here in its ever-tested limit, so difficult to touch, between interior and exterior, realist image and mental image, perception and hallucination (Bellour, 1981: 128).

Lying stricken in a dusty warehouse, the Bachchan/Vijay legend is brought face to face with his own mortality. The heroic 'coolie', literally the instrument of a relentless labour, is rendered immobile, unproductive in an engine room of industrial productivity. But there is something else at stake here, the suspension of his labour as nothing compared to the temporary suspension of collective disbelief. For it is not just the Bachchan phenomenon but also the story which underpins it that lie apparently mortally wounded. Within the cinematic imagination it is no less than the potential loss of Bachchan's near-divinity that is described during this scene in the grammar of docu-drama. Chakravarty points out that: '*Coolie* makes of its hero a near-divine phenomenon, or at least one who can easily mediate between the human and the supernatural world as between classes and religious groups in India' (1993: 233).

Her metaphor of 'imperso-nation' as foundational narrative and material reality in Indian popular cinema nonetheless becomes limited by the sealed hermeneutics of a discussion on national–popular culture. Just as fact has leaked into fiction in the case of Bachchan/Vijay, so the vital statistics of transgression remain ever elusive in the need to account for an Indian 'national cinema': this is an impossible task obliging an attempted restitution of theoretical borders marked by their permeability. Her original metaphor is more potent: Bachchan as outlaw standing at the crossroads of the popular imagination. A noble figure straddling the very limits of legality, pushed too far by the shadowy forces of organised crime and laissez-faire corruption. And in that sense, Bachchan's cinema epics of manifest destiny potently dramatise many of the conventions of the classic 'gangster' film; certainly the idea of the loner battling against established social forces, even when those forces are made up of rogue capitalist *goonde*—*Coolie, Deewaar, Trishul*; the main protagonist's shift from an under-privileged or disrupted childhood to adulthood, where he has scaled the heights of his profession—*Deewaar*; or, issues of honour and betrayal, especially amongst brothers, as well as reference to family, and in particular the matriarch—*Deewaar, Sholay, Trishul, Coolie*.

> At bottom, the gangster is doomed because he is under the obligation to succeed, not because the means he employs are unlawful ... this is our intolerable dilemma: that failure is a kind of death and success is evil and dangerous, is—ultimately—impossible. The effect of the

gangster film is to embody this dilemma and resolve it by his death (Warshow, 1975).

Drawing on Robert Warshow's classic essay, 'The Gangster as Tragic Hero', it is easier to be critical of the established mapping of the fictive Indian family in Bombay cinema as a site of nationalist/anti-nationalist discourse about the state. According to this manicheanism, a story like *Deewar* works by activating then resolving familial conflict within the rubric of a proto-nationalist narrative (Kazmi, 1998). What such accounts ignore, however, are the ways in which the very conventions of the gangster genre disrupt notions of either absolute marginality or seamless integration. Thus, in a climactic moment in the film when Vijay meets his brother Ravi—a police officer—under the same bridge that was once their pavement dwelling, it is possible to hear something else in their emotionally charged encounter.

For all Ravi's (Shashi Kapoor's) talk of *adarsh* (ideals) and *asul* (principles), the exchange is never a purely dialogic one on the nature of citizenship and state. If Vijay embodies a kind of lawless anti-nationalism, which is questionable, then Ravi too is emblematic of civic disenchantment, albeit a strain produced within institutional settings. Ravi is just as much the outsider, if one clothed in state-sanctioned garb, as his criminalised brother. His poor employment prospects bely the broken promises of his education. More tragically they create the very conditions for fratricide when he is eventually assigned the task as the leading police officer in a particular investigation of 'taking down' his brother, the master criminal. And all this because 'police officer' is the only job he can find, and that in large part due to the connections of his rich girlfriend, Veera.

At such moments the soundtrack too has a talismanic potency and the ability to create complex emotional effects. Where earlier in the film, the boy, Ravi, is shown running away from his pavement dwelling and achingly watching a neatly dressed group of school children, the later scene with Vijay replays the longing for a different set of social arrangements, one which does not pit brothers on a fatal collision course. Ravi the boy watches the children troop past as the extra-diegetic music plays a famous nationalist song '*saare jahaan se achcha, Hindustan hamaara*' (the best in the whole world, this country of ours). The later scene is underscored by the same song, introducing a sardonic element to the brothers' taut meeting. It also recalls from a very different setting the ironic symbolism of Brian De Palma's 1983 remake of *Scarface*, with Al Pacino's aspirational Cuban immigrant gangster, Tony Montana, watching an airship displaying 'The World is Yours' just before his world subsides in an orgy of cocaine and bullets.

Questions of civic rectitude and anti-national practices are, as Warshow suggests, complicated by the activities of gangsters. His argument that the gangster's existence in the modern world 'as an experience of art' is universal broaches certain discomforts. The gangster's experience is ours in so much as his is not the distant folklore of the frontier, or of the mythical nation, but grounded in historical events that are familiar to cinema audiences. Be it Partition, Corruption, War or Emergency, the success of the gangster film thrives on the real-life source material which touches its paying public. Indeed, this ability to draw from the parochial and the immediate has fed into the idea that 'the genre is a cipher for narcissistic self re-evaluation' (Mottram, 1998: 4). Just as the musical score in *Deewaar* blurs certain themes and dramatic moods within the film, so one of the film's effects in its absorption within popular consciousness is a hard-boiled re-evaluation of cinematic time and space. In the desperate melancholia of Vijay/Ravi's meeting, the film seems to be suggesting that people change but things remain the same. To go back to that classic family/state paradigm, the motherland (mother) makes killers of them both, which is why in the end such a reductive mapping is short on nuance.

What is offered here by means of a slight detour is a different trajectory, one which places the Bachchan character within a global matrix of film star 'rebels'.

In the 1970s, male stars such as Clint Eastwood and Bruce Lee had a powerful impact on Indian cinema audiences. The violence of the Hollywood western and the highly spectacular Hong Kong Kung Fu films found a strong resonance in the construction of the Bachchan star text (Sharma, 1993: 172). This appears to be at odds, though, with the better known if more parochial reading. For his part the co-creator of Bachchan's 'rebel' screen persona, script writer, Javed Akhtar, grounds the Vijay character in the social and political concerns of the day.

> So the common man was experiencing upheaval ... the morality of the day said that if you want justice, you had to fight for it yourself. No one will fight on your behalf. And if you didn't fight, you'll be crushed and finished off. So Vijay, the hero of Zanjeer reflected the thinking of the time. Two years later, the same Vijay is seen again in Deewaar. By then he had left the police force, he had crossed that final line and become a smuggler. He wages war against the injustice he had to endure and he emerges the winner. You can see that the hero who had developed between 1973–75 ... reflected those times (Kabir, 1999: 75).

At face value this is fine. Vijay not only gives a name and a face, but also an attitude to the seething frustration of a generation of young Indian men. His angst and his rage mark him out as one of the people—coolie, stevedore, illegitimate son—battling the forces of corruption with just his dignity and his fists. Predictably though, the framing of his persona has also obliged a somewhat closeted discussion amongst film theorists about the impeccability or not of Vijay's Marxian credentials. Fareeduddin Kazmi typically complains that: 'The entire characterization locates the hero ... in a non-productive, non-class position. This way their possible socially creative role is ignored, their specific class-related problems displaced by their isolated, individualized problems, and all social issues depoliticized' (1998: 145).

One of the difficulties with this approach is that it overlooks the myriad ways in which Bachchan, and by extension Vijay, is produced as hybrid, transnational, ambivalent text. The calibrated fight sequences in *Deewaar* are most obviously inspired by the physical language of Hong Kong cinema, notably the recognised skill of so-called 'fight composers' (Prasad, 1998: 45). In their stylised standoff between the imputed forces of good and evil, such encounters unravel according to a balletic hermeneutics: simultaneously sealed within the graphic locus yet choreographed according to an outernational logic.[2] But the transnational resonances don't end there: at the level of narrative too there are exhortations to other celluloid imaginaries.

---

[2] Bruce Lee's presence was felt in India some years before *Enter the Dragon* (1973) established him as a major celluloid icon in the subcontinent. In the late 1960s, while working on a script for a martial arts film, *The Silent Flute*, Warner Brothers, expressing an interest in the script, sent him to India to scout out locations, before eventually turning the project down. Bruce Lee was already long dead when Warner Brothers decided to capitalise on the heightened profile of martial arts in the West and opportunistically film a version of the script, 'Circle of Iron', with a Caucasian, David Carradine, in the lead role. Bruce Lee's trip to India was a sobering one, though. Although martial arts had originally been introduced to China by the Indian monk, Bodhidharma, its profile in India had long since waned. As Bruce Thomas notes in his engaging account of Bruce Lee's life and philosophy—*Bruce Lee, Fighting Spirit*:

> When Bruce put on an impromptu display of his skills for some local martial artists, they stared in disbelief .... Wherever there was any kind of audience, Bruce Lee the entertainer would come alive .... In airports ... Bruce would attract an audience of children and put on a quick show of fighting moves or tricks. Unused to seeing Chinese people, they would gape at him as he ran through a few moves, and then burst into applause (2002: 125).

What seems important here is the way in which Bruce Lee, during his short stay in India, attains a public profile exclusively through his performance skills. It is the aesthetics of

Vijay and Ravi's sibling rivalry (for their mother's affections) recalls the fraught relationship between James Cagney's Irish immigrant gangster and his upright elder brother in the 1931 Hollywood classic, *The Public Enemy*. Vijay's desire for maternal approval mirrors that of Cagney's Tom Powers. Both men provide materially for their mothers, with Tom bringing some of his ill-gotten gains home and Vijay installing his mother in a sumptuous house acquired through the proceeds of his criminal activities. In both films, the non-criminal brother acts as a counterpoint to his sibling's imputed values, lending a moral order to a fractured urban melodrama. Both predict a criminal future for their 'unlucky' sons in the absence of a caring father during childhood. Powers' real father is a policeman who beat him, and this draws him towards a number of stand-in father figures, such as Putty Nose and 'Nails' Nathan, and a life of crime. Vijay's father is a defeated trade unionist who has to betray his comrades in order to protect his family. His humiliation is so great that he runs away from his family too, leaving them destitute and shamed. Vijay subsequently 'adopts' an old dockworker, Rahim Chacha, as a guardian figure before being adopted by the gang leader, Davar, who operates as a kind of paternal surrogate. In both films, poverty and its bitter analysis of social reality produce the underworld ambitions of Vijay and Tom. In Vijay's case he is literally scarred by the experience, when as a boy he has the following phrase forcibly tattooed on his arm by his father's embittered former colleagues: '*Mera baap chor hai*' (My father is a thief). Tom's criminality is

---

combat which assure him of such a profile. The extraordinary combat choreography which percolates his film portfolio resonates in Bachchan's dockside confrontations in *Deewaar* and *Coolie*, in terms of both narrative and method. But there are older resonances between Bruce Lee's martial philosophy and its Indian origins. It was in the teachings of Jiddu Krishnamurti, the Indian philosopher, that Bruce Lee discovered the philosophical tenets of his fighting code, '*jeet kune do*'. Its pragmatism, coupled with its streamlined aesthetics, is entirely in keeping with Krishanmurthi's assessment:

> Man is violent and the ideal of non-violence is only an immature approach to violence. What is important is to face the violence, understand it and go beyond it, and not invent an escape, an ideal called 'non-violence' which has no reality whatsoever.

Such a willingness to confront the structural inequalities of everyday life also characterises Bachchan's Vijay character and is the catalyst for several violent showdowns in *Deewaar* and *Coolie*. As film critic, Thomas Sutcliffe has noted, 'Conflict wasn't just a subject matter for cinema; it was a method' (2000: 48). This is what I mean by speaking of a fight choreography organised around the principles of an 'outernational logic': an aesthetics, philosophy and reactive currency proposed beyond the reductive limits of the nation-state and the immediate historical frame.

similarly presented against a backdrop of privations—physical (the presence of a Salvation Army band and a man with pails of beer in the opening scenes) and emotional (the lack of paternal love). Finally, in their tragic denouements, both films return their wayward sons to the maternal bosom as martyred rebels.

As a formal device the flashback structure through which the whole of *Deewaar* is coded insists upon the secrecy of an intimate narrative, shared only by the figure of Vijay's and Ravi's mother (Nirupa Roy) and the film's audience. Escorted to the podium at an awards ceremony where Ravi is being presented with a medal for bravery, she receives the medal on his behalf but appears distracted. It is her gaze, moving beyond the frame, which instigates the flashback and version of events not sanctioned by officialdom. Therein lies the film's structural ambivalence: those who 'stand behind the nation's heroes' are also the purveyors of its erased dissidence. If the nation is reproduced through the figure of the mother, then it is the very indeterminacy of the contest between morality and pain, that marks its limits.

Textual readings of *Deewaar* have tended to situate it as an allegorical history of the nation-state (Prasad, 1998: 150) or as a cathartic morality play in which social deviance is redeemed through heroic sacrifice and is but one vector in a national 'economy of desire' (Mazumdar, 2000: 250). The problem with such totalising formations is that they reinscribe the imprecision of memory, desire and origin, as embodied by Bachchan/Vijay, within a particular metanarrative of 'nation'. At an imagistic level they emphasise the self-delusional quality of the story, highlighting the incompatibility of underclass symbols (the tattoo) and an upper-class modality (Bachchan's body language).

In the end, though critical of the protagonist's search for authentic 'origins', such accounts themselves locate this desire within the ambivalent fiction of 'national unity'. Vijay dying in his mother's arms is then the precursor to some form of reconciliation with legitimate citizenship or the idea of being a good Indian. What remains unaccounted for are the complex, transnational negotiations embodied within the film's mobile aesthetic. By contrast, what is proposed here is that Vijay's dissident corporeality be seen to interrogate the limits of the national imagination precisely through his invocation of a transnational form. Hong Kong cinema, South East Asian body symbolism, the silent echoes of Clint Eastwood's 'man with no name'—Bachchan integrates all these elements into his iconographic portrayal of Vijay, the ultimate celluloid composite.

Indeed, once viewed from the perspective of rupture and displacement, Bachchan's iconoclastic performance introduces a kind of migrant metaphor into commercial Bombay films. His adaptation of Tae Kwon Do fighting styles, for instance, embodies the ways in which concepts of culture and identity are not exclusively rooted in one location. It is instead this physicality which reviews cultures as constituted across differences, rather than within a hermeneutics of self. Clearly, the lessons which Vijay has learnt from his day to day life are shaped by the forms of knowledge encoded in a set of physical practices. The subjectivity of the 'angry young man' would no longer be couched purely in notions of origin and destiny, although these remain important. Rather his sense of self moves away from an exclusive understanding of locale, and towards a scrambling optic—a way of seeing, disassembling and making sense of his world through fragments.

Bachchan/Vijay's cultural practices or performative modality scarcely distinguish one setting from another. When confronted by Samanth's (the baddie's) henchmen—the very agents of anti-national dystopia—it is the imported ethics of Kung-Fu cinema which serve Vijay well. Against a backdrop of increasing technological advancement yet industrial alienation, Vijay's physical language broaches another kind of dialogue. He speaks to the powerlessness of 'the common man' relying just on his hands, his feet and his courage to transform his working environment. The raw materials for such micropolitical redemption exist beyond the scope of the nationalist imaginary. His adversaries, initially dockyard bullies, then rival gangsters, are undermined by that ignorance. They neglect precisely Kung-Fu's potential for renewal, its mutable patterns of engagement, when it matters most: in motion, in the combat zone. During such exchanges, Vijay also violently unsettles the distinctions between citizen and stranger, and hence of the reductive parameters of 'nationalist' discourse. For if his only function is to reflect back upon the territorial integrity and mythical self-appointment of the unified nation-state, then this effectively ignores the ways in which his cultural identity exists as dynamic process rather than static emblem. In the end the potency of *Deewaar* rests on its ability to articulate the simultaneity of apparently incompatible agencies, both vitally provisional and deeply historical. This dual dynamic resurfaces in *Sholay*, released within a calendar year of *Deewaar*. It is also the year that 'the Emergency' is declared—a moment which particularises the ambiguous purchase of culture on contemporaneity.

Fanning the Flames

Following its release in 1975, *Sholay* played continuously for five years in one cinema hall in Bombay. It opened however to a dismal reception, and it was only with the release of the soundtrack containing now legendary snippets of dialogue that its box-office potential began to emerge. Only now with the benefit of hindsight does it seem odd that the film's status as a modern classic was once in doubt. It almost never made it to its second week, barely surviving an emergency meeting called by the producers, appalled by its poor showing at the box office. This was the point at which the writers and its biggest star, Amitabh Bachchan, are said to have asked the nervous father/son production/direction team of G.P. Sippy and Ramesh Sippy to wait one more week before taking any decision to withdraw the film for a substantial re-edit. Yet, even this detail has subsequently enhanced its folklore. *Sholay* is the one that got away—the film that enters the popular imagination as an article of faith. But its particular pleasures are not just found in the conditions of its production.

To some extent it can be seen as the word, the sound, the power of a truly global film grammar. From Cairo to Kingston, Bombay to Birmingham it is the dialogue and song lyrics to *Sholay* which prefigure an impressive 'economy of the same'[3]: duplicated tirelessly in a vernacular art of embodiment but irreducible to a purely local register. Jai and Viru, Gabbar and Thakur are characters whose mimetic appearance within these local registers is testament to their enduring appeal. It could be argued that their evocation at the level of memory or simply recognition operates within a transformative modality. Perhaps the point is made clearer by thinking about another global currency, football.

To walk around the streets of the Egyptian capital is to be in the presence of Bollywood; in images and gestures, socials and comedies, it is the myths of Bombay cinema that share the space between the pyramids. Young men playing back R.D. Burman songs one moment are soon lost to their favourite footballing dramas the next. There is something of *Sholay* in every street-corner kickabout, every slum tournament, enlivened by the shadow boxing of so many Beckhams, Zidanes, Peles or Maradonas. Mythologies, or rather the transformative potential of myths, are the only

[3] I borrow the phrase from Nikos Papastergiadis, who highlights in his fine essay. 'The Elastic Metaphor', the operation of an 'economy of the same' as a foundational principle of modernist strategies of incorporation. In other words, the notion of difference can be absorbed into an existing configuration, but only to reaffirm established priorities.

sponsor of such dramas. Not so much an economy of the same then as of 'the changing same'.[4] The modest suggestion here is that this dynamic is the key to unlocking the transnational magic of *Sholay*.

At its heart *Sholay* is centred around the conflict between two strong and wilful men: the psychotic Gabbar Singh (Amjad Khan) and the Thakur (Sanjeev Kumar). Their paths cross when the Thakur, who is a *zamindar* (landowner) of a north Indian village, but also a decorated policeman, is posted at the nearest big town. His village is being terrorised through draconian extortion by a gang of bandits, led by Gabbar. The Thakur takes the gang on and captures its leader, ensuring that he is sent to jail. However he breaks out and wreaks a bloody vengeance on the policeman, slaughtering his entire family. The only survivor is the policeman's daughter-in-law (Jaya Bhaduri) who is out visiting her parents when the carnage takes place. The Thakur returns and pursues the bandit, but is captured himself. Gabbar sadistically decides to chop his arms off rather than kill him outright, leaving the official threat of the law unofficially neutered. However, the film effectively begins with the Thakur hiring two small-time crooks, Jai and Veeru (Bachchan and Dharmendra) to kill the bandit. He does this after he witnesses their courage in repelling an attack by bandits on a train carrying all three men. The criminals grow attached to the villagers, both falling in love with local figures along the way, and the job becomes personal. Veeru falls for a feisty horse-rickshaw driver, Basanti, and Jai, less straightforwardly, for the *zamindar*'s widowed daughter-in-law. In the end, although a kind of justice is seen to be served, only Veeru survives the final confrontation with Gabbar's gang, Jai paying the ultimate price for vengeance. Gabbar is captured by Veeru, vowing revenge for Jai's death, and handed over to the Thakur, who is only prevented from killing the bandit by the timely arrival of the police. Veeru is reunited with Basanti but the film ends with the tragic figure of the daughter-in-law, widowed and desolate, shutting herself in behind her despair. She disappears from view behind closed windows and the credits roll.

Sholay retains many of the formal characteristics of the earlier epic, *Deewaar*. Once again, the successful Bachchan/Salim-Javed partnership combines metatextual star quality with an epic story of confrontation between established hierarchy and violent usurpers. Again the boundaries

[4] I am thinking here of the way Paul Gilroy has employed the term to describe the ambivalent strategies of 'populist modernism' in its critical interrogation of the often overlapping projects of occidental modernity and racial exclusion. The term was originally coined by African-American activist/critic/author, Amiri Baraka (aka Leroi Jones).

between criminality and legality are increasingly breached by the quasi-humanist demands of the narrative. Jai and Veeru become appendages of the law in their pursuit of the absolute criminal, Gabbar. They are recruited as the surrogate agents of the Thakur after his dismemberment by Gabbar. Quite literally they are his 'hired hands' and their extra-judicial mission is redeemable in the eyes of the law (the Thakur) given the unequivocal otherness of their prey.

The script seems to suggest that their humanity is assured by their compromised agency: on the one hand they are mercenaries, on the other emotionally-dependent beings. This dualism lends them a vulnerability in ways that never apply to Gabbar. He is shown instead as the embodiment of an absolute alterity, a howling depiction of unmediated evil. His sole motivations appear to be vengeance and sadism, although it is only in the gratuity of the latter that he differs in any functional sense from those who pursue him. By the end of the film the audience is none the wiser about the substantive location of Gabbar's desire. He has no social history, no personal biography beyond the stylistic markers of criminal excess: the howling, the tilt of the head, the mad, rolling eyes, that studded belt. Yet unlike the gang bosses in *Deewaar* it is precisely his unmediated villainy which lends Gabbar iconographic status. There are parallels with the earlier film, though, in the complex, subaltern humanism of the Bachchan character. In *Deewaar* he sides with the paternalistic criminal, Davar, against the unsympathetic Samanth. *Sholay* similarly locates him in his extra-judicial arrangement with the Thakur. Only Gabbar stands between Jai/Bachchan and true citizenship: a community of rural ideals restitutive of a feudal order.

Above all else it is against this dynamic within the film that many commentators rail. Typically, *Sholay* is located within an 'aesthetic of mobilisation' (Prasad, 1998: 153). This schema comprehends the narrative as the return of the once marginal figures of Jai/Veeru to the mainstream in their new guise as the proxy agents of an orthodox hierarchy (Thakur). Prasad's argument is that the structure of the revenge plot and rebellious cachet of the glamorous young criminals (Jai/Veeru) lend themselves to an essentially reactionary politics produced in the service, and from the perspective, of the *zamindar*. By deploying the useful criminality of Jai/Veeru, the film manages to pursue its political manifesto without alienating its primarily working-class and disaffected audiences. They too can enjoy the spectacle through the landlord's eyes. By sharing in his desire for vengeance, we are also seduced into participating in a reaffirmation of the feudal order.

> Of course, there is an attempt to provide a certain amount of political support through the mobilization of the village. But the villagers appear as the prize for which the Thakur is fighting the dacoits. It is a rivalry for the rights to political power over the villagers (Prasad, 1998: 156).

The problem with this sort of approach is that it negates so many of the contradictory impulses brought into play by an 'aesthetic of mobilisation'. It over-simplifies the structural text even as it critiques the film's apparently reductive authorisation of a feudal politics. To so neatly map the participatory/exclusionary dialectics of an orthodox social hierarchy simultaneously attaches too much importance to the filmic narrative and too little to the translocal conditions of its production. The suggestion here is that neither the narrative nor its aesthetic conventions operate according to a sealed hermeneutics. On the contrary, *Sholay* is never purely contained by its transformative character or composite form. It is here at its productive interstices that the segmentation of modernist desire starts to unravel.

Popularly regarded as a 'curry western', the appeal of *Sholay* partially lies in its ability to successfully rework a number of elements—romance, comedy, feudal costume drama—drawn from diverse sources—Japanese samurai epics, American and Italian westerns, Indian B-movies—into a scattered, shattered epic.

> The Hollywood western, which itself had drawn lessons from Kurosawa's Japanese Samurai epics, was an inspiration for both material and attitude. A sort of cowboy zeal permeated the *Sholay* unit. Ramesh and his crew were like pioneers heading out to the Wild West; warriors fighting for a just cause. They selected a barren landscape in South India, inhabited it, transformed it and against mind-numbing odds to suit their vision, and created a compelling work of art. *Sholay*'s magic comes from the sweat and courage and ardour of the unit (Chopra, 2000: 8).

In his book *Sholay: The Making of a Classic* (2000), Anupama Chopra is drawn to the translocality of both form and substance which permeate the film. Produced as the object of a methodological zeal, *Sholay* takes on some of those mythic qualities associated with 'border-crossing'. The point Chopra is making is an important one—that the film was conceived in a transgressive spirit and realised according to transnational technique.

The film's action sequences were completed using western technicians, their at-the-time cutting-edge gadgetry, and familiar male bonding techniques of whisky and friendship (in that order). Most of the post-production work was done in London and most of the opposition to the film prior to its release came from the high offices of the Indian government and its representatives abroad. At one point officials from the Indian High Commission in London arrived at the Odeon cinema in Marble Arch to seize the print of the film. Its director, Ramesh Sippy, had decided to have a private screening for friends and family, but sensing that all was not well, had cancelled at the last moment. On his return to Bombay, he was strip-searched at the airport, and customs officials instructed not to clear the prints. Only after intense politicking were the prints released and the 35 mm print premiered to a lukewarm response. However, the missing 70 mm print arrived after the official screening and was viewed by just the stragglers and the *Sholay* crew. A legend was born at the precise moment of its disavowal.

In an age of the generic Bollywood diaspora film—*Dilwale Dulhania Le Jayenge*—or East/West fusion epic—*Lagaan*—the production values and narrative of *Sholay* might appear to be nothing special. Yet, conceived in a spirit of creativity and at a moment of political closure they remain the blueprint for any subsequent cinema of desire. On one level, they have a disjunctive function, confusing and complicating the reductive critique which would equate *Sholay* with a pseudo-rebellious turn. In other words they derail the sociological impulse to root the narrative in a recuperative analysis of feudalism. Such accounts are notably silent on the organic conditions of *Sholay*'s production: so surprisingly little comment on the film's hostile reception in official quarters and popularity elsewhere; or on its elided narrative form in the late disclosure of the 70 mm print; or even on the apparent discrepancy between its imputed politics and lack of an orthodox political constituency. The suggestion here is that when questions of transnationality and subversion cut to the heart of what this film is, and how it came to be, it is insufficient to offer an analysis that is not even concerned with the materiality of the form.

That is not to say that the film's immanent characteristics are the only signifiers that matter in a struggle for meaning, merely that they need to be registered, particularly at the level of form, in any plausible concept of verisimilitude in film. This is not to diminish the importance of culturally-generated frames of understanding. Rather to emphasise that they are simply one of several interpretive devices with which films are gutted for their meaning. As one of the male interviewees recalls in Dissayanake and Sahai's enquiry into the reception of Sholay:

> Once I saw a video of *Sholay* with an American friend of mine who was a great film buff. He could identify several sequences and episodes that were copied directly from Westerns. He could also identify some background music that was taken directly from Westerns. However, overall, he felt very much that the film was Indian. This is the point I am trying to make. Some of the ideas and episodes in Sholay are definitely borrowed but the end product is very Indian (Dissayanake and Sahai, 1992: 125)!

What is of interest here is not so much the implied discourse of 'indigenisation' which is brought into play in the final sentence. Rather it is what that assumes about processual hybrids.

The ability of *Sholay* to anthologise the highlights of various genre narratives not only loosens their conventions but heightens its pleasures. It complicates the cohesive rituals of a highly physical form like the western precisely because it is inspired by abstractions of the anti-western. Director Ramesh Sippy openly admired *The Magnificent Seven* (itself based on Kurosawa's *Seven Samurai*) and writer Javed Akhtar puts a name to his inspiration:

> Sergio Leone. We were very influenced by him. I would say that there is some Mexican blood in Gabbar. He's a bandit, not a *dakku* (dacoit). So Leone's influences are there. Like in the massacre scene where Thakur comes home to see the dead bodies of his whole family on the ground—there was such a sequence in *Once Upon a Time in the West* (Kabir, 1999: 58).

The naming of Leone is not such a surprise. He pays his own stylistic debt to the ancient art of shadow puppetry early in his epic *Once Upon a Time in America*, noting in passing that the shadow play derives from Balinese theatre's adaptation of the Ramayana. In effect he returns the gaze first cast towards his ersatz West by restless eastern spirits more than a decade earlier. His Italian-made 'spaghetti westerns' reinvented the American frontier in the Spanish desert using American actors (Clint Eastwood) and crude dubbing techniques. Moreover, they supplanted the myth of the heroic frontiersman with a kind of minimalist brutalism. In a parody of the Hollywood West they restaged the national pageant as a Machiavellian drama whose main players were stone-faced bounty killers, bandits, terrorised villagers and enigmatic gunmen with no name. Stylistically, they branded the desert-scapes with their pared-down dialogue, influential soundtracks, sharp editing and sadistic violence.

Gabbar Singh, by his creator's own admission, was modelled on the psychotic, laughing villain, Indio, in Leone's *For A Few Dollars More*. Yet he enjoys the kind of uncontested authority over his men that Indio can only fantasise about. More evocative is the way that both men are situated in a moral universe where greed and revenge, violence and betrayal are the primary referents. As a counterpoint, in the Leone vehicle, one of the bounty hunters, Lee Van Cleef's Colonel Mortimer, introduces the idea of conscience, absolution and revenge as the key modalities of a quasi-legal ontology. In the end he rides off into the sunset without payment, having exacted his bounty by avenging his family honour. It is Clint Eastwood's Manco who is left to ponder the limits of his own greed. In *Sholay* the two mercenaries are shamed into changing their ways when they are caught by the widowed daughter-in-law in the act of robbing their employer's safe. Both films then hold out the promise of a kind of moral redemption within the pleasures of transgressive agency. Ultimately, *Sholay* operates at yet another level of abstraction, updating and transforming India's own 'southern westerns', themselves a sub-cultural phenomenon which reduplicated the cultural status of the spaghetti western.

Final Cut

Iconographic films like *Deewaar* and *Sholay* still resonate with a non-synchronic pulse. Although emerging within the turbulent politics of the early 1970s in India, there is a strong case to be made that the relevance and appeal of these films are not simply reducible to the context of their production. In part this is a pragmatic gesture: those conditions frequently turn out to be more translocal and unruly than their imputed location within the cultural heartlands of proto-nationalist discourse would imply. This chapter argues for a more vigilant approach in thinking about how such cultural forms might be articulated within or against competing notions of 'nationality'. My contention is that it is both at the level of narrative and form that such films demonstrate 'excess': in the supplementarity of the storylines and the global reach of their technical and stylised grammar.

Their performative pleasures, particularly the zeitgeist portrayal of 'the angry young man' by superstar, Amitabh Bachchan, reside in the annexation of heroic martial arts sequences popularised in Hong Kong cinema by its stellar exponent, Bruce Lee. The outernational tactics of this aesthetics of self refuses the reductive mapping of these films in terms of a simple national/anti-national dualism. Likewise the inscription of the dystopic, ersatz West of Sergio Leone and the Cinecitta studios hardly prepares *Sholay* for its alleged function as rabble-rouser for feudalism. This chapter concludes that it is precisely in the aesthetic choices and organic routes to production of such films that one might begin to make sense of their emotional complexity. Their anamnesis relives the trauma of loss—a son, a brother, a potential lover—even as it evokes the transgressive pleasures of the journey. There is something of metaphysics, unbounded by the compressions of time and space, in such a conception. That is why these films endure. It is also why they matter.

References

ALPERS, S. 1983. *The Art of Describing: Dutch Art in the Seventeenth Century*. Chicago: University of Chicago Press.

BELLOUR, R. 1981. 'Segmenting/Analyzing', in Rick Altman (ed.), *Genre: The Musical*, London: Routledge and Kegan Paul.

BENJAMIN, W. 1992. *Illuminations*. Glasgow: Fontana.

CHAKRAVARTY, SUMITA. 1993. *National Identity and Indian Popular Cinema, 1947–1987*. Austin: Universtiy of Texas Press.

CHOPRA, A. 2000. *Sholay: The Making of a Classic*. New Delhi: Penguin.

CONNOR, S. 1989. *Postmodernist Culture*. Oxford: Blackwell.

DISSANAYAKE, W. and M. SAHAI. 1992. *Sholay: A Cultural Reading*. New Delhi: Wiley Eastern Ltd.

FISKE, J. 1989. *Understanding Popular Culture*. Boston: Unwin Hyman.

FORGE, A. 1970. 'Learning to see in New Guinea', in P. Mayer (ed.), *Socialization: The View from Social Anthropology*. Tavistock.

GOMBRICH, E. 1982. *The Image and the Eye: Further Studies in the Psychology of Pictorial Representation*. Phaidon.

HARVEY, D. 1989. *The Condition of Postmodernity*. Oxford: Blackwell.

JAY, M. 1988. 'Scopic Regimes of Modernity', in H. Foster (ed.), *Vision and Visuality*, University of Nassachussetts Press.

KABIR, NASREEN MUNNI. 1999. *Bollywood Film*. BFI Publishing.

KAZMI, F. 1998. In Nandy (ed.), *The Secret Politics of our Desires: Innocence, Culpability and Indian Popular Cinema*, pp. 134–57, New Delhi: OUP.

KRAUSS, R. 1985. *The Originality of the Avant-garde and Other Modernist Myths*. MIT Press.

KUMAR, K. 1995. *From Post-Industrial to Post-Modern Society: New Theories of the Contemporary World*. Oxford: Blackwell.

LASH, S. and J. URRY. 1987. *The End of Organized Capitalism*. Cambridge: Polity Press.

LLOYD, B. 1972. *Perception and Cognition: A Cross-Cultural Perspective*. Penguin.

MAZUMDAR, R. 2000. In R. Vasudevan (ed.), *Making Meaning in Indian Cinema*, pp. 238–67, New Delhi: OUP.

MISHRA, V. 2002. *Bollywood Cinema: Temples of Desire*. New York and London: Routledge.

MISHRA, VIJAY, PETER JEFFERY and BRIAN SHOESMITH. 1989. 'The Actor as Parallel Text in Bombay Cinema', *Quaterly Review of Film and Video*, 2: 49–67.

MOTTRAM, JAMES. 1998. *Public Enemies: The Gangster Movie A–Z*, London: Batsford.

MULVEY, L. 1989. *Visual and Other Pleasures*. London: Macmillan.

NAREMORE, JAMES. 1988. *Acting in Cinema*. Berkeley: University of California Press.

PRASAD, M. 1998. *Ideology of the Hindi Film: A Historical Construction*. New Delhi: OUP.

SHARMA, A. 1993. 'Blood, Sweat and Tears: Amitabh Bachchan, Urban Demi-God', in P. Kirkham and J. Thumim (eds), *You Tarzan: Masculinity, Movies and Men*, pp. 167–81, London: Lawrence and Wishart.

SUTCLIFFE, T. 2000. *Watching: Reflections on the Movies*. London: Faber and Faber.

THOMAS, B. 2002. *Bruce Lee, Fighting Spirit*. London: Sidgwick & Jackson.

WARSHOW, R. 1975. *The Immediate Experience: Movies, Comics, Theatre and Other Aspects of Popular Culture*. New York: Atheneum.

8

The Consumable Hero of Globalised India

SUDHANVA DESHPANDE

> *If the 1970s hero was anti-establishment, as a yuppie I promised a better world. The yuppie doesn't bash a truckful of goondas [goons]. He's smarter. He doesn't have to kill in the battlefield, he can make a killing in the share market. The yuppie believes in capitalism, not communism. Actually, he believes in a new 'ism' every day* (Shah Rukh Khan).[1]

The more things remain the same, the more they change. Popular Hindi cinema is no longer what it used to be. The 1990s, the decade of economic liberalisation, has transformed Hindi cinema quite thoroughly, though not beyond recognition.[2] To be sure, most films still portray the struggle of good versus evil, they have eight or nine songs each, and many of the stock characters of Hindi cinema are still unchanged. Yet, beneath the

[1] Interview with Shah Rukh Khan in *Filmfare*, August 2001.

[2] The Indian government adopted an explicit reform programme of a neoliberal persuasion in mid-1991. Amongst other things, this has meant an increasing withdrawal of the state from the spheres of production and distribution, as well as the social sector. So far as the film industry is concerned, the liberalisation programme has meant that the state is no longer a viable avenue for the finance or distribution/exhibition of off-beat, non-commercial cinema. There have been other, more complex changes as well, in terms of changes in attitudes and lifestyles—what gets called, in absence of a better term,

surface similarities, much has changed. I argue ahead that amongst the important markers of this change is the figure of the male hero.[3] I seek to contrast the new, liberalised hero of the 1990s with his earlier counterpart of the 1970s. This earlier hero, personified most of all in the Angry Young Man screen persona of superstar Amitabh Bachchan, was born with *Zanjeer* (*The Chain*, dir. Prakash Mehra, 1973) and remained the ruling persona of Hindi cinema for well near a decade and a half. At the core of this persona was a poor man's anger towards an unequal and exploitative society, though this anger was expressed as personal vendetta and vigilantism and did not get channelled into any larger movement of the oppressed. In contrast, the new, liberalised hero is neither angry nor is he particularly anti-establishment. He is, on the other hand, rich and conformist in his social attitudes. This has had an important effect on the themes and narratives of Hindi cinema. I argue below that this new hero has redefined the meaning of the love triangle, a stock melodramatic situation that forms the point of departure for the plot of several Hindi films. Additionally, the new hero, for the first time in the history of Hindi cinema, is someone without a past and consequently without memory. These changes, I argue, are directly related to the changing economics of film production and distribution, and an expansion of its market not just beyond the shores of India, but also to other allied industries such as music, satellite television and so forth. In other words, the new hero cannot be looked at in isolation, but has to be seen as the projection of the fantasies of a new spectator. As a result, what sometimes seems to be the same old fare, merely suitably repackaged for our globalised times, is actually quite new stuff.

Eclipse of the *Chavanni* (25 Paise) Audience

Consider this: in the 1960s, Rajendra Kumar, star of films like *Mere Mehboob* (*My Sweetheart*, dir. H.S. Rawail, 1963), *Arzoo* (*Desire*, dir. Ramanand Sagar, 1965), *Goonj Uthi Shehnai* (*The Shehnai Resonates*, dir. Vijay Bhatt, 1959), and *Dil Ek Mandir* (*The Heart is a Temple*, dir. C.V. Sridhar, 1963), was

globalisation—and that is precisely the subject of this chapter. Thus, when I use the phrase 'our globalised times', I refer to the changes ushered in by these policies in the 1990s and beyond, and should not be construed to imply that the Indian economy and social life was free of global influences before.

[3] See Gangoli's chapter (this volume) for a discussion on changes in the image of the heroine in the post-1990s films.

called Jubilee Kumar. This was because several of his films did a silver jubilee run—25 consecutive weeks—while some went on to a golden jubilee (50 weeks), and a few platinum (75 weeks). Trend-setting films like *Devdas* (dir. P.C. Barua, 1935; dir. Bimal Roy, 1955),[4] *Awaara* (*The Vagabond*, dir. Raj Kapoor, 1951), *Mother India* (dir. Mehboob, 1957), or *Mughal-e-Azam* (dir. K. Asif, 1960), all had incredible runs of several dozen weeks. This continued well into the 1970s. I remember, quite distinctly, as a boy of eight or nine, when I saw *Sholay* (*Flames*, dir. Ramesh Sippy, 1975) for the first time, the film was already in its 23rd week, and was simultaneously running in half a dozen or more theatres in Bombay. Eventually, the film ran 140 consecutive weeks at Bombay's biggest theatre (da Cunha, 1979: 15).

You do not get those sorts of runs any more. Now, posters are put out to celebrate a film's run of a hundred days. That is just two days over 14 weeks. Notions of what constitutes a hit have changed dramatically. Let me cite a typical example: in June 2001, Satish Kaushik's eminently forgettable *Mujhe Kuchh Kehna Hai* (*I want to say something*), the launch pad for former hero Jeetendra's son, Tusshar Kapoor (pairing him with Kareena Kapoor, daughter of ex-actors Randhir Kapoor and Babita), in its third week, was running in nine theatres in Delhi. The following week saw the simultaneous release of what became the top grossers of that year, *Lagaan: Once upon a Time in India* (dir. Ashutosh Gowarikar, 2001) and *Gadar* (*Upheaval*, dir. Anil Sharma, 2001), and the number of theatres screening *Mujhe Kuchh Kehna Hai* was down to three. Yet, the film was dubbed a hit. In the following weeks, *Lagaan* and *Gadar* both proved to be genuine superhits, running for weeks on end at several theatres, eclipsing *Mujhe Kuchh Kehna Hai* from public memory quite thoroughly. But who cared? Certainly not Vashu Bhagnani, the producer of *Mujhe Kuchh Kehna Hai*, who had made a neat packet on his investment. If a film can become a hit on the basis of a flimsy four-five week run, clearly the economics of the film trade has become complex.

In earlier decades, it was relatively simple. A producer made a film after raising money from film financiers and merchants, and sold it to the distributors. Once the film was released, masses of people flocked to film halls, and over several weeks, their money found its way into the pockets

[4] The third well-known version is by Sanjay Leela Bhansali in 2002. This version actually has very little in common with the earlier two versions cited, being a garish paean to unbridled opulence. For a critique of the Bhansali version, see Sudhanva Deshpande, 'The Unbearable Opulence of *Devdas*', *Frontline*, 30 August 2002. There have been other versions as well, in more than one Indian language.

of the distributors, producers and sundry other elements. Or it did not, and led to lost empires, nervous breakdowns, alcoholism, even suicides. The financially disastrous performance of *Kaagaz ke Phool* (*Paper Flowers*, dir. Guru Dutt, 1959) resulted in the master director never again wielding the megaphone, and is rumoured to be—somewhat simplistically—one of the factors that drove him to suicide (see Sengupta, this volume). The essential point, however, is that the success or failure of a film was directly dependent upon how many people bought tickets in cinema halls. In other words, numbers mattered.

Numbers still matter, of course. But not necessarily only of people who buy tickets. You can, and do, have films that would have been considered flops by earlier yardsticks, actually raking in profits, sometimes of huge magnitude. Indeed, in some cases, films today can start making profits even before the shooting begins. Here are some examples. *Yaadein* (*Memories*, dir. Subhash Ghai, 2001), which starred the hottest young stars of that year, Hrithik Roshan and Kareena Kapoor, was made at the cost of Rs 170 million.[5] It turned in returns amounting to Rs 210 million well before it had been commercially released in theatres. Of this, Rs 82 million came from the sale of the film's music rights to Tips.[6] That the film flopped when it was eventually released was therefore of only academic interest to its producer–director Ghai. To put these figures in perspective, the superhit film *Deewaar* (*The Wall*, dir. Yash Chopra, 1975) had grossed about Rs 10 million in Bombay when it was released. *Dil to Pagal Hai* (*The Heart is Crazy*, dir. Yash Chopra, 1997) grossed eight times that in the same region. While this growth itself is perhaps not spectacular, what is notable is that in 1975, as now, Bombay was the largest territory in the domestic market, while the overseas market was negligible. This is not the case any more: *Dil to Pagal Hai* did overall business of about Rs 500 million, including overseas. Its music alone raked in megaprofits, with more than 10 million audio cassettes of its soundtrack being sold. Indeed, the sale of music rights is a very recent phenomenon. Yash Chopra insisted on, and received, an advance of Rs 10 million for the music rights for *Dilwale Dulhania Le Jayenge* (*The Brave Heart Shall Win the Bride*, dir. Aditya Chopra, 1995),

[5] At the time of writing, there are approximately Rs 48 and Rs 76 to a dollar and pound respectively.

[6] 'Going for a Song', *India Today*, 1 April 2002.

and this figure went up to Rs 45 million for *Dil to Pagal Hai* and Rs 75 million for *Mohabattein* (*Loves*, dir. Aditya Chopra, 2000).[7] Even more amazing is the case with Karan Johar's *Kabhi Khushi Kabhi Gham* (*Sometimes Happiness, Sometimes Sadness*, 2001), with the most spectacular casting coup since *Sholay*: Amitabh and Jaya Bachchan, Shah Rukh Khan and Kajol, Hrithik Roshan and Kareena Kapoor. The film, through the sale of its music rights, overseas distribution rights, and telecast rights, had reputedly mopped up a staggering Rs 350 million even before a single shot was canned.[8]

Then there is the more recent trend of selling advertising space in the movie. Pop star, Daler Mehndi, and Amitabh Bachchan danced in front of a Liberty shoes billboard in the latter's comeback flop *Mrityudaata* (*The Bringer of Death*, dir. Mehul Kumar, 1997). The logic of corporate sponsorship for films was taken to a new level a few years later by Shah Rukh Khan. When Dreamz Unlimited (a company he floated along with actress Juhi Chawla and director Azeez Mirza) produced *Phir Bhi Dil Hai Hindustani* (*Still the Heart remains Indian*, with the first two starring and the third directing), the company raised a fair amount of money from corporations, which in the bargain got entire scenes devoted to their products. So, Shah Rukh Khan woos Juhi Chawla in front of a Swatch kiosk and drives around in a Santro car, and so on. This takeover of space by corporations is called 'synergy' between industry and entertainment. In Hollywood, entire films have been produced by corporations (*You've Got Mail* is a recent example), and this trend is set to grow in Mumbai, where Pantaloon produced *Na Tum Jaano Na Hum* (*Neither do you know, Neither do I*, dir. Arjun Sablok, 2002) with Hrithik Roshan in the lead.

The equations have changed dramatically. According to producer Tutu Sharma, the overseas distribution rights for a big budget film are roughly

---

[7] To put these figures in global perspective, *Dil to Pagal Hai* did business of about US $12 million, while *Titanic* grossed over $600 million in its first 40 weeks and made a total of $1,214 million worldwide. In India itself, *Titanic* made in excess of Rs 560 million (US $12.5 million) at the box office in its initial 10 months. All figures are from the India Infoline.com website (http://www.indiainfoline.com/sect/mefi/cont.html) accessed in September 2002.

[8] Admittedly, these advances have been negotiated in a boom period. It is unlikely that such inflated figures will become the norm and already in 2002 there are reports of music companies backing out of, or cutting down on, promises of large advances they had made to film-makers. Thus, Sony is reported to have backed out at the last moment before signing a Rs 250 million deal for the overseas rights of *Kabhi Khushi Kabhi Gham* (*India Today*, 1 April 2002). Even so, the overall trend towards increased advances is unmistakable.

double that for the largest Indian territory, Mumbai.[9] In other words, if a distributor forks out Rs 35 million to buy the rights for the Mumbai territory, he will pay about Rs 70 million for the overseas market. In a case like this, the price for all-India rights (including Mumbai) will be about Rs 120 million; that is, the financial returns to the producer from distribution in an overseas market of about 20 million people is roughly 60 per cent of the volume realised from distribution in the entire Indian market of 1 billion people.

Aggregate the revenues from all sources including music and telecast rights and the returns from the domestic viewing public (which we always think of as the primary market) as a proportion of total revenues shrink pretty drastically. Sharma estimates that only about 35 per cent of the revenue earned by a film is from the sale of tickets in the domestic market. Subhash Ghai's company Mukta Arts has put out nearly identical figures:

> Until the early '90s, the mainstream revenue profile was comprised of domestic theatricals, contributing 79 per cent, and music rights contributing the balance 21 per cent. Currently, the breakdown has been altered with domestic theatricals contributing only 34 per cent and music rights contributing 16 per cent. The new categories of revenues include satellite rights, accounting for almost 20 per cent of the total revenue, and the distribution rights of overseas territories, accounting for 30 per cent of the total revenue.[10]

The total turnover for the industry as a whole is also set to grow. Arthur Andersen's study on the entertainment industry commissioned by the Federation of Indian Chambers of Commerce and Industry (FICCI) says that the entertainment industry as a whole is projected to grow from Rs 130 billion in 2001 to Rs 293 billion by 2006. The report estimates the size of the film segment at Rs 25 billion in terms of costs in 2001, and predicts a steady growth at 15 per cent to Rs 50 billion by 2006.[11] The UK-based Dodona Research predicts that:

> India's film business is set for a period of sustained growth ... production investment will rise 70 per cent by 2006, the Indian film

[9] I wish to thank the actress Nandita Das for procuring these estimates for me from Sharma.

[10] Quoted from the Mukta Arts website (http://www.muktaarts.com/), accessed in September 2002.

[11] FICCI, *Indian Entertainment Industry: The Show Goes On and On ...*, March 2002, pp. 4–5.

industry's export revenues will climb 120 per cent over the same period, foreign films' theatrical rentals in India will also rise steeply.[12]

Those who think that the money dished out by the rickshaw-puller, the industrial worker, the vegetable vendor, the domestic servant, the urban unemployed, is what accounts for the turnover of the Hindi film industry could not be more wrong. 'What matters today are "A" grade centres—about 15–20 big cities—and the overseas centres,' points out director Azeez Mirza.

> Who cares about the rest? Even Pune is now a 'B' grade centre. When the overseas centres gross 15–16 crores [Rs 150–160 million], why would a town like Bathinda be important? The time is past when people made films for the *chavanni* [25 paise] audience.[13]

Hindi cinema is funded today in overwhelmingly large proportions by the rich, whether in India or abroad.

The rise of multiplexes is part of this development. Multiplexes have numerous benefits for the few: exhibitors and distributors earn more per film because of higher ticket prices; by breaking the one-film-per-week model, and shuffling the number and timings of shows of particular films, investment is made to yield the highest possible revenue; a certain kind of niche film (such as the English film *Hyderabad Blues* [dir. Nagesh Kukunoor]) now becomes commercially viable; by exhibiting six or seven films per week, the chances of a flop resulting in a big loss to individual exhibitors is minimised; and socially, by targeting and catering to a niche audience, the multiplex becomes an extension of the home theatre, where the rich can watch films in the privacy of their own class. Increasingly, Hindi cinema is turning into a party of the rich, and the rest of India is invited as voyeurs.

However, one should also keep in mind that Hindi cinema is not a homogenous category. The trajectory of these big-budget, high-profile, large-revenue films aimed at the hyper-consumerist audience is very different from that of the more modest productions, made by the residual segment of the industry, which are geared towards a 'lesser audience' with limited disposable incomes. The Hindi film industry produces

[12] From the Dodona Research website (http://www.dodona.co.uk/bollywood.htm), accessed in September 2002.

[13] Interview with Aziz Mirza, *Udbhavana*, 16(56), July 2000. Translated into English by the author.

'A' grade, 'B' grade, 'C' grade, and even 'D' grade films, each category having its own class-defined market, and hence its own aesthetic assumptions—or to put it the other way, the varying degrees of the lack of aesthetics in all these follow from somewhat different commercial compulsions.

One way to capture this difference is to chart the career of actor Mithun Chakraborty. He started out with director Mrinal Sen in the film *Mrigaya* (*Mirage*, 1976), and then came to Bombay. Here, he became a star with a large following among the lower middle class and the urban poor. This was in the 1980s, when he had assumed a screen persona that was a mix of Amitabh Bachchan, James Bond and *Saturday Night Fever*'s John Travolta. In the late 1980s he starred in a few Amitabh Bachchan films as well: *Ganga Jamuna Saraswati* (dir. Manmohan Desai, 1988) and *Agneepath* (*Path of Fire*, dir. Mukul Anand, 1990). By now, however, his days of glory were over, or so everyone thought. Mithun Chakraborty thought otherwise, and all through the early to mid-1990s, he became more prolific than ever. Between 1990 and 1995, he starred in at least 51 films—8.5 films a year, or a film every 42 days! None of these, however, was a hit in the conventional sense.

Without a single hit, how did Mithun Chakraborty manage to get so many films over so long a period? He shifted to the south Indian hill station of Ooty, and built a hotel there. So, a producer would land up at Ooty, stay with his crew in Chakraborty's hotel at concessional rates, shoot a film with him and an aspiring or failed starlet, finish shooting in three weeks flat, do post-production in Mumbai over the next fortnight or so, and inside two months, a film would be ready with six or seven songs, several fight sequences, one rape, fiery dialogues, and a weepy mother. The producer would then release the film in the less classy theatres in the big cities and in smaller cities like Patna, Indore, Benaras and Bathinda. The actor's loyal front-stall fan following ensured a decent run for a couple of weeks. Low investment, short gestation, moderate returns, and guaranteed break-even: many producers were very glad to take this package.[14]

The New Hero of Globalised India

It is not the poor, then, but the globalised rich who, for the most part, create the profits for commercial Hindi cinema. The projection of their fantasies has produced a new kind of hero. Who is this new hero of globalised India?

[14] Since film financiers lend money at 3–4 per cent interest *per month*, the length of the gestation period can often be the difference between profit and loss.

Typically, this new hero in the Hindi film tends to be Punjabi, rich and upper caste. It was not so earlier.[15] Erstwhile heroes were rarely given an explicit regional and linguistic affiliation. Even if the actors were not all Hindu, their roles were implicitly so, and one could guess that they were not Dalit (low caste), but beyond that the film itself did not locate the hero very specifically in social or temporal terms, the idea being to reach out to a pan-Indian viewership. Actors such as Raj Kapoor, Dev Anand, Dilip Kumar, Rajendra Kumar and Dharmendra, all spent a lifetime playing characters who got introduced, a trifle ludicrously, as 'Mr Amar', or 'Mr Anand', or 'Mr Raj'. Even Amitabh Bachchan, as the angry young man, was normally just Vijay. True, in some films he played the Muslim, or at least carried a Muslim name: *Muqaddar ka Sikandar* (*The Emperor of Fate,* dir. Prakash Mehra, 1978) and *Coolie* (dir. Manmohan Desai, 1982) spring to mind. His famous Christian persona is the lovely street-smart guy in *Amar Akbar Anthony* (dir. Manmohan Desai, 1977). Carrying the logic of this hit further, Manmohan Desai, in *Naseeb* (*Fate,* 1981), gave him simultaneously three names, Hindu, Muslim and Christian: John Jaani Janardan. The logic in all these cases is to not specify the regional and caste affiliations of the hero too precisely, so that his persona could appeal to viewers across regions, languages, and castes.

This is no more: the 'Rahuls' and 'Prems' of the 1990s are very much Malhotra and Khanna, and the Anjalis and the Simrans they fall for are Oberoi and Grewal—in other words, the heroes as well as the heroines are all clearly rich, upper-caste Punjabis. Earlier heroes were either poor and had the rich girl fall for them—*Lawaaris* (*Orphan,* dir. Prakash Mehra, 1981)—or were rich and fell for the poor girl—*Sharabi* (*Drunkard,* dir. Prakash Mehra, 1984). Or, sometimes, they were poor, and unsuccessfully coveted the rich girl—*Muqaddar ka Sikandar*. In any case, usually there was a threat—or promise, depending on how you look at it—of violating or transgressing social and economic boundaries. Not that such boundaries were really transgressed. Far from it: a variety of tricks were devised for this purpose. Either the hero just died, as in *Muqaddar ka Sikandar*, or it was revealed (to the hero, that is, that the audience knew all along) that he is in fact the long-lost son of a rich man, as in *Lawaaris*. This made matters simple—through the film, you could have the poor hero mouthing populist rhetoric against wealth, and in the end, when it really mattered, he ended up with oodles of it.

[15] For the most part, in what follows, this new hero is contrasted with the angry young man persona of Amitabh Bachchan which dominated the decades of the 1970s and 1980s.

Even when the hero was not poor himself, he needed to identify with the poor in a variety of ways. There are several films of earlier times (particularly of the 1950s and 1960s) where the hero is a qualified professional, an engineer or a doctor, who fights, or at least speaks, for the poor. Or if he is rich, then he often has a poor friend who he looks upon as a brother. Sometimes, he is the son of a rich industrialist or landlord who doles out largesse to poor workers or peasants, much to the chagrin of the father and the old and irritating *munshi* (account keeper). Or, if he is Amitabh Bachchan, he realises utopia by simply leading the poor into the rich man's house and asking them to occupy it—*Lawaaris* and *Coolie*.

This need to identify with the poor masses was most endearingly encapsulated in a typical convention of the Hindi film: the male solo number early in the film which introduces the hero. Typically, the song would establish the hero as a hopeless romantic, on the lookout for the right one to give his heart to, and one would see a Shammi Kapoor or a Rajesh Khanna driving in an open-top careering down idyllic hillsides and lush fields where doll-like peasant girls would coyly wave at them. Hindi cinema has never been naturalistic, so there is no point complaining that the girls look anything but peasant-like. Today, however, the heroes do not have any peasantry—real or unreal—watching their passage. This signals a larger change in song picturisations. In the films of the pre-globalisation period, one can list any number of hit songs—for instance 'Ramaiya vasta vaiya' in *Shri 420* (*Mr 420*, dir. Raj Kapoor, 1955) and 'Khaike paan Banaras wallah' in *Don* (dir. Chandra Barot, 1978)—that have rural or urban labouring classes dancing and singing with the hero(ine). The films of the 1990s have banished labouring classes from song picturisations altogether. Forget about the rich boy teeny-bopper romance films of Shah Rukh Khan and Salman Khan, this is even true of Aamir Khan films like *Rangeela* (dir. Ram Gopal Verma, 1995), *Ghulam* (*Slave*, dir. Vikram Bhatt, 1998) and *Raja Hindustani* (dir. Dharmesh Darshan, 1996), where he plays the poor boy. The exception has perhaps been Govinda, the only truly comic hero since the 1950s and '60s singing star Kishore Kumar. In *Coolie No. 1* (dir. David Dhawan, 1995), Govinda is, well, a coolie. But after his delightful portrayal of an intransigent youth who refuses to move his roadside *dhaba* (small eatery frequented by the poor) from in front of Kader Khan's five-star hotel in *Dulhe Raja* (*The Bridegroom*, dir. Harmesh Malhotra, 1998), even Govinda seems to have pretty much shed his lumpen proletarian image.

This is why Aamir Khan's home production, *Lagaan*, in which a bunch of villagers take on the might of the British empire is so refreshing. What is particularly interesting is that it is the peasant-dalit-Muslim (Bhuvan-Kachra-Ismail) combine that eventually turns the match for the Champaner eleven. But does the film mark the return of the peasant to the Hindi screen? Almost certainly not. Those who now account for the profits of the industry are simply not interested in watching sweaty peasantry. Why then has *Lagaan* succeeded? Of the many factors, two important reasons are the superb music of the film and its cricket-as-nationalism theme which, as in real life, managed to unite passions across classes and international borders.[16] Indeed, how much of an exception *Lagaan* is can be seen from the example of *Shakti* (*Power,* dir. Krishna Vamshi, 2002). In this, a young woman (Karisma Kapoor) gets married in Canada to the son (Sanjay Kapoor) of a village potentate (played with characteristic brutishness by Nana Patekar). Visiting her husband's village, not only is she repelled by the dirty, smelly and uncouth villagers, but loses her husband in a bloody internecine family feud. Subsequently, she has to fight with her life to rescue her young son from his own grandfather, who wants to bring the boy up 'like a tiger' to avenge his father's murder. In a depiction that would put Kipling to shame, the Indian villagers in *Shakti* are cruel, barbaric, bloodthirsty, while the NRI is civilised, decent, gentle. Interestingly, the woman, on the run from her father-in-law, is helped by a small-time bootlegger (a delightful cameo by Shah Rukh Khan), who helps her after she offers him cash (dollars, not Indian rupees). He eventually dies gazing longingly at the dollars, but not before ensuring that the woman has escaped her tormentors. The native, then, is moved to heroic deeds, but only after contact with higher civilisation—which comes in the garb of hard currency, of course.

Of a piece with the banished peasant is the way the very look of the heroes has changed. The joke about actor Salman Khan is that he is the only Gandhian star in India: he has vowed not to wear a shirt so long as the hungry millions in India go shirtless. Indian heroes of the past did not have physiques like his. Actors like Dilip Kumar, Shammi Kapoor, or Rajesh Khanna never displayed their biceps. Even the angry young man persona of Amitabh Bachchan was not premised on a muscular physique. Only a real washout, like the wrestler-turned-actor Dara Singh, survived by showing off his muscles. This is not the case any more. If actors Jackie Shroff and Sunny Deol, compensated for their limited acting talent with macho looks in the 1980s, Sanjay Dutt discarded drugs and his actress mother Nargis's delicate looks to reinvent himself as a hunk in the early 1990s. Just in

[16] For an interesting range of articles on *Lagaan*, see *Udbhavana*, No. 62, August 2002.

time, too. For the 1990s was the decade of the biceps—Salman Khan, Akshay Kumar, Sunil Shetty, Akshay Khanna and the many others who came and went. Even Aamir Khan, arguably the best actor amongst the '90s stars, has a good enough physique to look a convincing small-time boxer in *Ghulam* (dir. Vikram Bhatt, 1998).

The exceptions to this macho brigade, of course, are Shah Rukh Khan and Govinda, the one wiry and the other, thank god, fat. But even they are feeling the pressure, and in his home production *Ashoka* (dir. Santosh Sivan, 2001), Shah Rukh Khan shows more muscle than one thought he had. The new century has also brought forth Hrithik Roshan, with a physique so perfect, it seems somehow unreal and plastic. Welcome to the age of the consumable hero who does what the dancer-vamp Helen did earlier—he dances like a dream, and his body itself, rather than his persona, is the object of consumption, much to the delight of the advertising world. It is only fitting, then, that this new, consumable hero wears Gap shirts and Nike sneakers, and when he dances, it is in front of McDonald's outlets in white man's land, or Hollywood studios, or swanky trains, and has white girls—not Indian peasants—dancing with him.

Indeed, the fact that the hero dances is by itself a huge change. Ashok Kumar, Raj Kapoor, Dev Anand, Dilip Kumar, Rajesh Khanna, Dharmendra—all these major stars of the yesteryears danced, if at all, embarrassingly badly. Shammi Kapoor danced very well, of course, but looking at his films today, one is struck by how little he actually *danced*. He made faces, contorted his body, flicked his head, and he did all this with consummate grace, but he danced very little, if *dance* is what we are talking about. The only male star I can think of who *really* danced is that most underrated genius, Kishore Kumar. It is telling, of course, that Kishore Kumar could afford to dance as he did, because he was looked upon as a comic singing hero, and his dances were an extension of his fooling around. Things began changing in the early 1980s with Mithun Chakraborty, Jeetendra, Rishi Kapoor and others beginning to dance. But even those dances look distinctly amateurish compared with the very complicated steps that modern heroes are routinely made to go through today.

Much, then, has changed. Some of it has been noted and commented upon, such as the celebration of the Hindu undivided family. *Hum Aapke Hain Koun...!* (*What am I to you*, dir. Sooraj R. Barjatya, 1994; hereon *HAHK*) is of course the best and the most analysed example.[17] Anyone

---

[17] See, for example, Rustom Bharucha (1995), Mukherjee (1995) and Patricia Uberoi (2001).

who has been watching films in the second half of the 1990s will have become bored to death with those countless marriage sequences full of suited and turbaned men, and heavily bejewelled and made-up women, not to mention the mandatory *karva chauth* sequence.[18] But the point of the formula that *HAHK* put in place went beyond mere repetition of marriage sequences and songs. It was almost as if the family—often expatriate—*becomes* a family only through the observance of ritual. And once film-makers ran out of ritual from the real world, they began inventing their own. An example is the Abhishek Bachchan-Aishwarya Rai starrer *Dhai Akshar Prem Ka* (*Two and a half Syllables of Love*, dir. Raj Kanwar, 2000). The hero, mistakenly assumed to be the heroine's husband by her family is made to go through the ritual of being turbaned while a priest chants incoherently. This ritual, which takes place sometime after their presumed marriage, marks his entry into his wife's family. To the best of my knowledge, no such ritual exists anywhere in India.

The other major change is the increasing communalisation of the Hindi film since the late 1980s, as the movement for the construction of a Hindu temple at the site of a (now demolished) mosque in Ayodhya picked up on the one hand, and the right wing Hindu party, Shiv Sena, became stronger not just in Mumbai, but also the film industry.[19] The most obvious index of this is the change in the depiction of the Muslim: from being the hero's friend, the Muslim metamorphosised into the villain in an increasing number of films. *Tezaab* (*Acid*, dir. N. Chandra, 1988), famous for the scintillating '*Ek do teen*' number by Madhuri Dixit was an early film that depicted the Muslim as villain. Since then, there have been many. In *Ghatak* (*Fatal*, dir. Rajkumar Santoshi, 1995), Sunny Deol, a brahman from Banaras, appropriately named Kashi, takes on and defeats a very Muslim-looking villain and his many brothers. *Shool* (*The Thorn*, dir. E. Nivas, 1999) has a thakur-brahman alliance taking on a Muslim-backward caste combine in small town Bihar. *Pukar* (*The Cry*, dir. Rajkumar Santoshi, 1999), a jingoistic film made right after the Kargil war between India and Pakistan, plays on the easy association of Muslims with Pakistan, and thus got for its hero, Anil Kapoor, the National Award for acting conferred by a jury which included the editor of *Panchajanya*, mouthpiece of the fascist Hindu organisation, the Rashtriya Swayamsevak Sangh (RSS). *Gadar*, the biggest hit in recent years, uses the backdrop of the sub-continent's Partition to say some very vicious things about Muslims.

[18] *Karva chauth* refers to a ritual, increasingly popular in north India, wherein married women fast for a day to pray for the long life of their husbands.

[19] On the rise of the Hindu right wing, see A.G. Noorani (2001).

All these are important developments, and need careful study and analysis because of the sheer power of Hindi movie on both the elites and the masses of South Asia. However, there are two other matters that stand out, which have escaped critical and political attention. One is how the new hero has redefined the meaning of the love triangle, and the other is that for the first time in Hindi cinema, the hero is someone without a past, and consequently without memory.

The New Love Triangle

The love triangle is the classic formula, with countless variations. At its most basic, however, the triangle traditionally had either one man and two women, or two men and one woman. The history of the love triangle is so dense with associations and allusions, that it is difficult to generalise. Let me, therefore, simply cite some of the best known examples. In *Devdas*, we see the hero unable to claim his childhood sweetheart and unwilling to accept the golden-hearted prostitute. At a larger level, the film depicts the feudal aristocracy's inability to cope with the transition to capitalism. The two women, then, represent the unattainable aspirations of this class contrasted with its sordid and decadent reality. This formula is reworked in Guru Dutt's *Pyaasa* (*The Thirsty One*, 1957) where the rich heroine (Mala Sinha) spurns the poor poet (Guru Dutt) who in turn is loved by the prostitute (Waheeda Rehman). The formula here is used to critique bourgeois society which puts monetary value on everything from love to art. The same formula was reworked to fit the angry young man films of the 1970s: in *Muqaddar ka Sikandar*, Amitabh Bachchan as the poor orphan cannot bridge the social divide to express his love for the heroine (Rakhee) who is in love with his best friend (Vinod Khanna), and therefore turns to the courtesan (Rekha), whose former lover is the villain (Amjad Khan). Here, the angst and the frustrations of the lumpen proletarian hero reinforce, in the end, a comfortably class compliant framework. The other triangle with one woman wooed by two men is seen in films like *Andaaz* (*A Matter of Style*, dir. Mehboob Khan, 1949) where the heroine (Nargis) eventually murders the manager of her estate (Dilip Kumar) when her husband (Raj Kapoor) suspects her fidelity. This complex psychological melodrama moralises that the newly independent nation, somewhat contradictorily, should embrace capitalist modernisation while retaining feudal family structures and values. In Raj Kapoor's *Sangam* (*Confluence*, 1964), the formula is used to tell what is essentially a love story between two men (Kapoor himself and Rajendra Kumar), interrupted by the woman (Vyajanthimala). However one looks at it though, the love triangle is premised on the assumption that one of the three has to lose out in the end.

Now, consider some of the scenarios of the love triangle of the 1990s. *Kuch Kuch Hota Hai* (*Something or Other is Happening*, dir. Karan Johar, 1998): Girl 1 (Kajol) is in love with Boy (Shah Rukh Khan), but Boy loves Girl 2 (Rani Mukherjee), who loves him in return. Boy marries Girl 2, they have a child, and Girl 2 dies, but not before realising that Boy was actually made for Girl 1. So the spirit of Girl 2, using the child as mediator between the worlds of the dead and the living, brings about the union of Boy and Girl 1.

Judaai (*Separation*, dir. Raj Kanwar, 1997): Boy (Anil Kapoor) and Girl 1 (Sridevi) are married, though not happily, because Girl 1 nags him incessantly about their lack of wealth. Girl 2 (Urmila Matondkar), fabulously rich, makes the indecent proposal: husband in exchange for wealth. Girl 1 accepts. With wealth, Girl 1 becomes ever more insufferable, but Girl 2 turns the perfect Hindu woman, ever obedient, ever suffering. In the end, though, the sanctity of the marriage is maintained, and Girl 2 walks away carrying Boy's baby in her womb.

Chori Chori Chupke Chupke (*Secretly, Quietly*, dir. Abbas Mastan, 2001): Boy (Salman Khan) and Girl 1 (Rani Mukherjee) are happily married. But Girl 1 suffers an accident during pregnancy, loses the child, and cannot conceive again. The couple and the extended family are desperate for a child, so adoption is suggested by the Boy, but ruled out by Girl 1. She forces him, instead, to look for Girl 2 (Preity Zinta), who will bear his child in return for cash. They live together as a happy threesome during pregnancy, and even though Girl 2 for a while contemplates not giving up the child, eventually she goes away with a beatific halo, leaving baby and cash behind.

Kunwara (*Bachelor*, dir. David Dhawan, 2000): Boy (Govinda) and Girl 1 (Urmila Matondkar) meet in New Zealand, fall in love, but become separated. Boy comes back to India, saves pregnant Girl 2 (Naghma), abandoned by her lover, from committing suicide. He agrees to masquerade as her husband in front of her family, but Girl 2 turns out to be Girl 1's sister. So Boy lives in their house, pretending to be Girl 2's husband, but loving Girl 1.

One can cite more such examples. How are these versions of the triangle different from the earlier ones? Without going into the details of the plot, the essential difference is that in all these cases we find two women wanting one man—*and he gets them both!*[20] This development is basically a post-*HAHK* phenomenon. *HAHK* is the landmark film which, by playing out the desires of unbridled consumerism, ritualism and religiosity through the fantasy of the contradiction-free Hindu undivided family, became a massive blockbuster. *HAHK's* formula was picked up with lightning speed by the industry, and a whole avalanche of feel-good happy family films followed. Film scholars and sociologists have showered attention on *HAHK*, but an unremarked fact is that at precisely the time that the new hero was becoming conformist and seemingly upholding family values, he was also turning bigamous. The consumerism of the new globalised hero, then, extends as much to the sexual realm as it does to the economic.

Why are Young Men Angry no More?

The other question, that of history and memory, is more complex. Manmohan Desai has been celebrated as the original postmodernist Bombay director,[21] with a thorough (and often delightful) contempt for logic and meaning. He made a fortune by casting Amitabh Bachchan in lost-and-found potboilers: *Amar Akbar Anthony*, *Parvarish* (*Nurture*, 1977), *Suhaag* (*Auspicious Mark*, 1979), *Naseeb* (*Fate*, 1981), *Mard* (*Man*, 1985). It is tempting to think that the brothers-separated-at-birth theme was in some ways perhaps a subconscious response to the trauma of a nation partitioned at birth. What is interesting is that this particular formula has completely disappeared from the Hindi films of the '90s. It is not clear why this has happened, but what is certain is that the hero's past itself has disappeared. This may seem like a baffling disappearance, since it had always been memory which drove the Hindi film hero to aggrandisement, revenge, vigilantism, crime, murder, or all of these. The examples are many and well known, so let us just stick to Amitabh Bachchan. If one were to ask what makes the angry young man angry, the answer will surely be memory: the memory of his parents' murder in *Zanjeer*;

[20] An interesting case is Shyam Benegal's film *Zubeida* (2001), in which Karishma Kapoor plays a divorced woman who marries a prince (Manoj Bajpai), who already has a wife (Rekha). While the film dwells on Zubeida's emotional insecurities in this triangular relationship, it does not condemn bigamy *per se*. Even more surprising is the nostalgic, almost heroic, treatment of the prince. This is surprising to say the least, coming as it does from the maker of *Bhumika* (*Role*, 1976), a film which was a radical statement for its depiction of the independent woman.

[21] See, for instance, the entry on Desai in Ashish Rajadhyaksha and Paul Willemen's *Encyclopaedia* (1999).

of his being an illegitimate child in *Trishul* (*Trident,* dir. Yash Chopra, 1978) and *Lawaaris*; of his childhood sweetheart in *Muqaddar ka Sikandar*; of his own betrayal under trying circumstances in *Kaala Patthar* (*Black Rock,* dir. Yash Chopra, 1979); and, most famously, of his being branded as a thief's son in *Deewaar*. Memory, after all, was what gave that high voltage intensity to the stunning screen persona of Amitabh Bachchan.

None of this is true any longer about the Rahuls and the Prems of today's Hindi films. None of these young men are any longer 'angry'. Forget about being enraged by social inequalities, they do not even run away with their beloveds in the face of parental opposition. On the contrary, like the hero of *Dilwale Dulhania Le Jayenge*, they celebrate their conformism as valour. But more striking still is the fact that they do not have childhoods any longer. Let me recall some of the films that have defined the consumable hero: *Dilwale Dulhania Le Jayenge*, *Kuch Kuch Hota Hai*, *Dil to Pagal Hai*, *Hum Aapke Hain Koun...!* *Pardes* (*Overseas,* dir. Subhash Ghai, 1997), *Kaho Na Pyar Hai* (*Say that there is Love,* dir. Rakesh Roshan, 2000), etc. In all these films, you never see the hero's past, his childhood, the circumstances of his birth and upbringing. Why?

The consumable hero is the creation of the liberalised market. To the extent that liberalisation itself is a relatively recent phenomenon, having been set in place only in 1991, the consumable hero has no history. His class acquired jobs with perks, high disposable incomes, a jet-setting lifestyle and shopping holidays overseas only from the mid-1990s or so. The person who has no history, has no memory. More precisely, he has no history that he cares to recall. A generation before liberalisation, his father was solidly middle class, the type the actor Amol Palekar excelled at playing in low budget films on the urban middle class by Basu Chatterjee (*Rajnigandha* [*Tuberose*], 1975; *Chhotisi Baat* [*A Little Tale*], 1976). This is a past the new liberalised yuppie, whether in India or abroad, disdains rather intensely.

There exists a strong connection between the bigamous consumable hero with neither memory nor anger, liberalisation and the rise of new markets (NRIs, DVD sales, telecast rights, merchandising), and the celebration of family values and ritual. The average NRI carries a great nostalgia for an imagined home that is governed by familiar and secure family ties and ritual observances that emphasise as well as enforce those ties. In having to cope with a system that grants greater prosperity while taking away family ties, servants, grandma-babysitters, the servile office boy, and all the other cushy paraphernalia of middle-class life in India, the NRI starts treasuring that imagination, embellishing it to the point where it becomes totally fetishised. With the rise in the NRI population (and their ability to pay hard currency, which grows by a factor of about 50 when converted to the Indian rupee), Hindi cinema has become an active manufacturer of such fetishes.

The script and songwriter, Javed Akhtar, has likened Hindi cinema to a state of India, whose language is not the language of India, different, yet not alien (Kabir, 1999). Indians understand that language, as they do that culture. In the decade of the 1990s, however, much has changed. That state called Hindi cinema is seceding, and it has already started speaking a language that seems more and more alien. The party of the rich shows no signs of winding up; on the contrary, as it swings with greater abandon, the keyhole of our voyeurism gets only narrower. No happy endings here.

References

BHARUCHA, RUSTOM. 1995. 'Utopia in Bollywood: *Hum Aapke Hain Koun*', *Economic and Political Weekly*, 15 April.

DA CUNHA, UMA (ed.). 1979. *Indian Cinema 78/79*. New Delhi: Directorate of Film Festivals.

KABIR, NASREEN MUNNI. 1999. *Talking Films: Conversations on Hindi Cinema with Javed Akhtar*. New Delhi: OUP.

MUKHERJEE, M. 1995. 'The HAHK Phenomenan: Appeal of Permanence and Stability', *Times of India*, 22 May.

NOORANI, A.G. 2001. *The RSS and the BJP: A Division of Labour*. New Delhi: LeftWord.

RAJADHYAKSHA, ASHISH and PAUL WILLEMEN. 1999. *Encyclopaedia of Indian Cinema*. New Delhi: OUP.

UBEROI, PATRICIA. 2001. 'Imagining the Family: An Ethnography of Viewing *Hum Aapke Hain Koun*', in Rachel Dwyer and Christopher Pinney (eds), *Pleasure and the Nation: The History, Politics and Consumption of Public Culture in India*, New Delhi: OUP.

Part III

Travels

9

The Scattered Homelands of the Migrant: Bollyworld through the Diasporic Lens

CHRISTIANE BROSIUS

The topography of South Asian migrant communities in the heart of a German city like Frankfurt is one made up of different overlapping maps and movements. Clusters of shops offer real and soul food for those people living away from the overwhelming flow of scents, music and visual stimulation of which their 'home countries'—be it Pakistan, India or Sri Lanka—have so much to offer. Between these diasporic pockets, other sites shape the urban landscape: the high-rise buildings of international banks and elegant cafés, supermarkets selling items under 5 Euros, Turkish mosques and tea houses, and shopping windows clad in velvet red, with signs announcing that inside, sexual pleasures are for sale. The South Asian shops are somewhat condensed illuminations of a parallel world: alongside trays filled with triangular henna tubes, samosas and wedding garlands, shelves offer film magazines such as *Stardust* or *Filmfare*, and postcards of film stars Shah Rukh Khan and Kajol. Walls are covered with posters announcing classical and pop concerts, lectures on religious issues, as well as the screening of the latest blockbuster. It is here, where my journey into 'Bollyworld' began in August 1998 when I set out to interview South Asian shop-owners on their perception of India's Independence Day. But most of all, it is here where countless Bollywood films begin their journeys into the lives of a variety of people, where 'Bollyworld's' cartographies cover visible and invisible spaces.

This chapter does not focus on a discussion of particular Bollywood film narratives or modes of film production. Instead, it looks at the ways in which films and the images and narratives they disseminate may function as sites of identification for particular audiences in specific contexts. In each context, concepts like the family and the nation, being 'at home' and being 'out of place', religion and culture, are shaped differently. The chapter explores the ways in which various media technologies—cinema as well as video and Internet—work both as sites and tools for practices of representation. It examines practices of identity formation among members of the South Asia diaspora in Germany in a web of global flows of images and ideas related to Bollywood narratives. Perceived as zones of cultural contact, the social and media milieus framed here allow for an analysis of media events as sites of identity constitution. One of the key questions here explores how, despite Bollywood's highly ideological and normative, homogenising narratives, strategies of reading them can also disrupt the process of identity fixation.

In proposing a discussion of Bollywood as a 'contact zone', I aspire to circumvent the idea of a singular cultural space from which transnational identities emerge.[1] Contesting the binary geographic and metaphorical model of 'homeland' and 'exile', that suggests that members of transnational communities fall victim to this dichotomy, I favour a more critical view on the assumption that there is only one privileged space of belonging (see Brah, 1996). Instead, the notion of 'homing desire' seems more adequate since it embraces both the myth of return (to one's origins) *and* the 'lived experiences of a locality' (ibid.: 192). This view is further supported by Smadar Lavie and Ted Swedenburg's claim to recognise the existence of 'many geographies of identity' (1996: 4). Such geographies partly overlap with each other, have lucid or oscillating borders, but also create tensions, where temporary borders are established in order to 'recreate a culture of diverse locations' (Amitav Ghosh, cited in Clifford, 1997: 249), of creolised identities rather than clearly shaped entities. Finally, following Ulf Hannerz' argument that identities are shaped by overlapping, partly competing social milieus, I propose a discussion on intertwined geographies

[1] James Clifford employs the term 'contact zone' in his discussion of museums as 'borderlands between different worlds, histories, and cosmologies .... [They are] places of hybrid possibility and political negotiation, sites of exclusion and struggle, ... places of encounter and passage' (Clifford, 1997: 212–13). I propose to understand 'Bollyworld' as mapping practice, archive (selection, preservation) and stage (performance).

that come to constitute parallel models of identity as well as alternative modernities.[2] In this context, particular images and narratives figure as meaningful signifiers for identification. Like people, they journey from one zone or space to another; and in this process, different meanings are attributed to them. It is here, where Bollywood becomes Bollyworld, where it enters into, and is shaped by, the diverse cartographies of diasporic communities, unfolding complex ways and locations of meaning.

Three such cartographies of Bollywood's 'mediatisation' and negotiation of identities will be discussed. First, there is the 'institutionalisation' of film screenings in the wider mediascape of Germany's 'indigenous media' (Ginsburg, 1995). Second, 'homing' concerns, fears and desires of social agents will be analysed with respect to a recent Hindi film in connection to its public screening as well as the everyday life worlds of the agents, in particular, their varied notions of cultural identity.[3] Third, the debate on Bollywood films will be investigated by focusing on a 'virtual community' of second generation Indians on the Internet. They allow us to discuss another angle of looking at Bollywood 'from below', revealing a different engagement with film and identities. Alongside these three milieus, media impacts are analysed in terms of: (*a*) media as 'container of Indianness'; and, (*b*) media as canvass for negotiating a fractured sense of 'Indianness' and 'Westernness'.

The idea of 'Bollyworld' as an offspring of 'Bollywood' appeals to me for various reasons. It expands the realms of the material world by transgressing into the complex ecologies of representation as a performative and signifying practice (Hall, 1997). Like the changes of costumes and localities in a song-and-dance scene of a Bollywood movie, the meanings produced in these acts of representation are constantly changing, shifting or simultaneously at work on different levels such as the local and global, national and transnational, personal and collective, etc. 'Bollyworld' requires us to analyse the relation between viewer and viewed, the extent to which social agents define the sites of meaning production themselves, or are drawn to them because they seem to provide consensus. 'Bollyworld'

[2] Ulf Hannerz' (1992) concept of milieu ranges from the individual to the global sphere and suggests that an individual agent takes up different roles and positions in different spheres and networks. The idea of alternative modernities acknowledges different forms of (diasporic) agency responding creatively to the experience of modernity instead of assuming a static, modular model of predominantly western modernity imposed from above as with elite groups.

[3] With one exception (Hasima K.), interviews in this chapter were conducted in German. Names of all informants have been changed, or abbreviated.

thus deviates from a vision of Bollywood as an ideological and normative source of hegemonisation and authentification in that it associates with, and is made up of, various open networks and flows. Within these broader categories of transnational movements, the notion of 'India', projected in many Bollywood movies as the 'real' centre and homeland of migrant hearts and minds, as anchor and harbour for the 'scattered' people, even becomes marginalised and 'unreal' (see Figure 9.1).[4]

Let me briefly outline the social milieu in which I conducted interviews with members of the South Asian diaspora in 2001. As mentioned earlier, the locale is Frankfurt, a city of about 700,000 people, known for its international airport and its role as a global finance centre, and my hometown. Frankfurt and its surroundings are home to the largest number of South Asians in Germany.[5] In several parts of the city, in particular those

Figure 9.1
An Indian shop in Frankfurt
Source: Photograph courtesy C. Brosius.

[4] 'Scattered' is derived from the Greek term diaspora, *dia*, 'through' and *speirein*, 'to scatter' (Brah, 1996: 181).

[5] Currently, 43,600 Indians and 35,000 Pakistanis are registered in Germany (Bundesamt für Statistik), not counting those already holding a German passport as compared to almost 2 million Turkish citizens. This is roughly a third less than in the UK (Statistisches Bundesamt, 2004). According to Census Statistics, 2,038 Indians, 1,624 Pakistanis and

in close vicinity of the central railway station, many offices and shops as well as restaurants run by Pakistanis, Afghanis, Sri Lankan Tamils and Sinhalese and Indians (mainly from Gujarat, Punjab, Kashmir, Tamil Nadu and Kerala) have been established in the last decade. The airport is most probably the reason for the high density of South Asian population, as well as a liberal immigration policy of the regional state of Hessen in the 1980s

The range of migrants from South Asia is diverse, ranging from single men to families. Most of the members of the first generation still aspire to return to their home-country in the future, a phenomenon that has been labelled as 'myth of return', for in most cases, the return to the land of origin is generally only temporal. Second generation members generally do not share that desire. Their desire for homing is mostly linked to Germany or other western countries. Migrants of the first generation settled down here for various reasons: educational, business purposes and seeking political refuge. The milieu is made up of first and twice migrants, that is people coming straight from South Asia or via another country where they made a living. Most of their children were born here. Some hold the citizenship of South Asian countries, others of the UK, or hold German passports. With respect to my informants, there is Ashraf H. who, together with his partner Arshad K., organises Hindi film screenings in local cinema halls across Germany. Ashraf was born in Afghanistan, and came to Germany (via India) in the late 1980s where he studied film at Munich's renowned Film School. Then there are the Khans, a couple with four children aged between eight and 20 years. The mother, Hasima, was born in Pakistan but grew up in London where a part of the extended family still lives. After her (arranged) marriage, she and her husband Parvez moved to Germany. Parvez comes from the Indian part of the Punjab where his parents still live. He works for an international airline which facilitates frequent visits to India and Pakistan. In the early 1990s, Hasima opened her own video, food and clothes shop in the city centre. She rents out Hindi films and Pakistani dramas on video and claims to have about 200 regular video customers. There are other shops, like Bobat's, that keep not less than 25,000 videos and, increasingly DVDs, for sale and rent (see Figure 9.2).[6]

2,899 Afghanis have registered in Frankfurt. This does not count those with a German passport (Source: Census Frankfurt. Bürgeramt, Statistik und Wahlen, 2001). Approximately 6,000 Indians, 12,000 Pakistanis and 16,000 Afghanis live in Hessen (Goel, 1998).

[6] Bobat was the first Indian shop set up in Frankfurt in the late 1970s. The owner, a Gujarati, is a twice migrant: born in colonial Burma, he moved to India as a child.

Figure 9.2
Views of the interiors of an Indian shop in Frankfurt
Source: Photos courtesy C. Brosius.

The wide range of film customers indicates that Bollywood is popular across the Indian borders and enjoyed in countries like Pakistan, Afghanisthan and even Russia and the Middle East. The focus in the last section is on visitors of a website named theinder.net, none of which I have personally met and who are spread across Germany.[7] In discussion forums, they engage in commenting on recent releases from Bollywood, their views often mirroring complex navigation between alienation from and fascination with Bollyworld narratives.

Distributing Bollywood to Transnational Audiences

How does Bollywood reach its dispersed audiences? The largest and most visible source in Germany are the video shops. On Saturdays in particular, these shops become a social meeting point, where South Asians from Frankfurt and the surrounding regions do both their shopping and exchange information. The shopping windows flag out posters of the latest Bollywood releases and illustrated catalogues inform the customer about the videos and DVDs available for sale or rent. Most customers rent videos and DVDs on a weekly basis (at 2–3 Euros per item). A shop like Bobat's caters for almost every taste, from *Mother India* (dir. Mehboob Khan, 1957) or *Sholay* (*Flames*, dir. Ramesh Sippy, 1975) (with English, but sometimes also Arabic, Korean, French, Japanese subtitles) to a more recent release such as *Ek Rishtaa—The Bond of Love* (*One Family*, dir. Suneel Darshan, 2001). Bollywood films are certainly the most popular entertainment medium, the majority imported from Pakistan, Dubai or London through well-oiled distribution networks. The DVD market is rapidly expanding, also via the Internet, offering better replay quality than pirated videos. Besides Bollywood films, Pakistani television serials (mostly family dramas) in VHS-format enjoy a high popularity among Muslim and customers from other religions. In addition, major cricket games, footage of Miss World competitions, documentary films on Eid celebrations, and other spiritual programmes can also be rented. Some video and DVD shops in Frankfurt also specialise in Tamil language films. Many of their customers are political refugees from Sri Lanka who sought asylum in the 1980s.

[7] theinder.net was launched in June 2000. The web site targets a German-speaking audience. More than 100 users per day visit the site, many use the chatroom and discussion forums to exchange ideas about India, film, love, politics, etc. See also www.mixedmasala.de, www.munichmasala.de.

Increasingly, members of the diasporic South Asian communities in Germany are coming to own satellite dishes and receivers through which they can extend and diversify their access to indigenous media, Hindi films in particular. Private satellite channels like B4U (Bollywood for You),[8] Sony, Star TV and Zee TV compete for middle-class audiences with evenings full of old and new Bollywood films, music programmes or news from India and Pakistan. However, the annual rent of satellite television programmes is costly (each channel charges c. 120–200 Euro p.a., as of summer 2001).

Within this diverse media landscape, where Hindi films are basically consumed at home, going to the movies has very much become a part of outdoor leisure life for many South Asian families in and around Frankfurt in the past two to three years.[9] Ashraf is one of the organisers of Bollywood film screenings who have successfully mapped out an itinerary that covers the map of Germany by carefully choosing local cinema halls according to the presence of large and active South Asian communities.[10] Ashraf states that the early days of marking the new media landscape were difficult ones. First of all, a community of movie-goers had to be established who sought the attraction of a social outing paired with the offer of 'good films'—that is, films of high quality in terms of film projection as well as narrative. Their effort paid off. Meanwhile, those movie halls in Frankfurt and the outskirts where Bollywood films are screened on a Sunday, are packed despite the cost of 8–10 Euros per ticket. Some people even travel from places as far as 60 km away to view a film show. Ashraf and Arshad get the film reels directly from the UK. They tour them through Germany, often accompanied by family members who help out at the front desk while Ashraf and Arshad talk to visitors and watch the audience carefully in order to keep out potential boozers and make sure that the cinema visit is a 'safe' and pleasurable experience for the audience. According to Ashraf, the audience is largely made up of Pakistanis, Indians and Afghanis. With respect to the consumption of media, the Afghanis are clearly part of Bollyworld's transnational reach. Many of them migrated to Europe through Pakistan and India, creating new associations with cultural, religious and also political spheres, no matter whether they are

[8] A UK-based entertainment channel with Hindi song and film programmes, see www.b4utv.com.

[9] Screenings of Tamil films take place in different local cinemas.

[10] Other cities of public Hindi film screenings include Berlin, Hamburg, Munich, Ludwigshafen, or Mannheim (personal communication between author and Ashraf H., August 2000).

Hindu or Muslim Afghanis. In Frankfurt, one of the most frequented shops selling Bollywood films is owned by Ashraf's father.

What about the films themselves? Asked about the categories of success of a Bollywood film among diaspora audiences, and whether there were particular markers that might differentiate such an audience from one in India, Ashraf states:

> They are not concerned whether a film flopped in India or was a blockbuster. As long as they know that the films feature stars like Aishwarya Rai or Shah Rukh Khan, they don't worry about the plot. Certainly, everyone has access to the Internet and what you do is to get your information about the film from there. *Hey Ram* was a complete flop in Germany.[11] ... Next week's film will be a big hit, starring Aishwariya and Anil Kapoor.

To what extent 'everyone' has access to the Internet, or whether Ashraf is only referring to the professional middle classes, cannot be discussed here. Comparing it to home video, he counts on the auratic power and social appeal of the 'big screen'. However, besides stars, the narratives come to be important when Bollywood films are 'tested' according to their representation of moral values and cultural identity, thus the term 'clean movie' used by many viewers. This counts in particular for members of the first generation who, I argue, in the main consider Hindi films as a 'fortress' and agents of authority for generating and enforcing ideas of a paradisical homeland and notions of an authentic culture. However, we shall see that this is part of the imaginings of many homelands, of which Bollyworld dreams form but a part.

Watching Movies: Between Pleasure Dome and Danger Zone

The movie hall is not plainly entertainment, a bridge to the 'lost' homelands, or a reminder of 'authentic' culture to the 'alienated', 'westernised' youth.[12] Ashraf recalls the many times he had to assure his audience that the films would be screened in a socially

[11] *Hey Ram* (dir. Kamal Haasan, 2000) is centred around Mohandas K. Gandhi's assassination in 1948.

[12] I use the term 'authenticity' as part of a discourse of power in which agents aspire to attribute 'truth value' and primordial categories to identity (gender, ethnic, class or else). 'Authentic' is thus not 'natural' but constructed.

conflict-free zone. The last point has caused organisers and audiences concern because in the recent past, tensions among, and because of, drunken single men occurred that led to both the heightening of security control and the tendency to screen films in local halls that provided, very much like in Indian movie halls not long ago, a balcony for families, and lower circles for the young men.[13] A mixed social and communal space would be associated with an uncontrollable, thus 'dangerous' space.

The local Bollywood movie shows are an event–space: most of the shows take place on a Sunday, usually two per day, between lunchtime and the early evening. Members of the mixed audiences know each other and use the film event as a platform for a social gathering. Yet, for the Khans, the visit of *Ek Rishtaa* was the first time they went to the public screening of a Bollywood film in Germany. Normally, they would watch films at home or at a friend's place. I had planned to visit film shows with their two older daughters (aged 20 and 17) before. Even this family visit had been difficult to organise. The reason why the girls would not get permission to watch a Hindi film in public on their own was that their father worried both about their safety, *and* the honour and reputation (*izzat*) of the family. The girls were still unmarried, and besides, could not go out on their own without male company. At first, Laila (20) argues,

> because my father knows how the Indian and Pakistani men are, he thinks we would be hassled by some stupid blokes .... But my parents have also heard that there are Afghani guys who may argue with the Pakistanis, and this leads to fighting. Because of this, he [the father] won't allow us to go (personal conversation, December 2000).

She then adds: 'The fact that we might engage in a friendship ... no father would want that, no matter whether Pakistani or Indian.' The movie screenings become a site where parental control may be subverted, where status and origin may be transgressed or remain anonymous, thus leaving individual players more freedom for agency. The danger in this transgressive, or 'liminal', space enhances the notion of the movie show as a 'risky' contact zone of uncontrolled encounters, possibly even of serious

[13] Ethnic tensions are rare. However, about the film *Border* (dir. J.P. Dutta, 1997), the owner of the Bobat shop reports that Pakistanis demonstrated in Frankfurt to ban the screening of the film as well as its rental in video shops (personal conversation, December 2000). This is due to the film's alleged anti-Pakistan and anti-Muslim bias.

flirtation. Morally and physically, the public movie event runs the danger of becoming a place single women must not enter—not so much because they become vulnerable, but because the family's, particularly the men's respectability derives from the girls' chastity and conduct.

Nonetheless, the films themselves provide a canvas for the playing out of issues to do with sexuality that cannot be avoided/circumvented even under the parents' protective wings. This brings us back to the Khans' first visit of a publicly screened Hindi film, *Ek Rishtaa*. Since it is shown in a cinema hall, it is proclaimed a 'clean' and entertaining family movie, safe for families to watch it with their children. The main narrative is how the happily united family of industrialist, Vijay Kapoor (Amitabh Bachchan), is dramatically torn apart by business problems provoked by an 'alien' intruder into the family, who marries Preeti, the oldest daughter of the Kapoor clan (Juhi Chawla). Finally, the family is reunited under the banner of eternal compassion, the symbolic power of kinship and respect for the elders. Throughout the film, stereotypes of modernity and tradition remain peacefully intertwined, even though it is a relationship based on tradition's alleged superiority and its capacity to assimilate, or 'tame', modernity (rather than vice versa). Thus, even the notion of modern romantic love requires the patriarch Vijay's blessing: what Patricia Uberoi (1998) pinpoints as an instance of an 'arranged love marriage'.

However, on that Sunday in May, sunk into the comfortable chairs of the movie hall, covered in the velvet embrace of darkness, and carried away by the colourful spectacle of big screen family affairs that move the plot towards its resolution, the atmosphere was suddenly loaded with tension. A sequence of a few seconds only was montaged into the flow of moving images surrounding the wedding night of Nisha (Karisma Kapoor) and Ajay (Akshay Kumar). In this sequence, the viewers could witness Nisha lying on her back, her hands holding firmly onto the bed's iron railing behind her, with eyes closed in utter joy, her naked torso covered by Ajay's naked body as they make love. No birds. No fountains. No fireplace. No wet saris caught in thunderstorms (Dwyer, 2000). Among the Khan family, I witnessed eyes wide open, faces staring at the other to check each others reactions, the parents' faces freezing, the expressions in the girls' faces sheer puzzlement, close to laughter caused by deep embarrassment. It took several minutes and filmic scenes of distraction to melt the invisible ice that seemed to have frozen the viewers in their seats. After the film, we all drove back to the Khans' home without mentioning the scene at all.

Protecting One's Culture

Later, at the Khans' home, I conducted separate interviews with the daughters and the mother. The conflict lingering behind the curtains of silence turned out to be one of different ways of seeing 'morality' from the perspective of first and second generation migrants.

Bollywood films here come to constitute and intertwine various moral spaces. The conversations revealed that the marriage night scene had created an almost tactile contact zone. It was highly loaded with somatic metaphors linked to moral sentiments and values that were instantly linked to cultural identity. Both Laila and Fatima stated that the scene had instantly created embarrassment. Had they been watching *Ek Rishtaa* as a video at home, so they remarked, they would have automatically forwarded the scene because their parents would not allow them to watch such things. When viewing Bollywood films, they explained, violent scenes were never at stake, only the 'erotic' ones. Furthermore, even with American and Pakistani films on television, the family would follow a rigid practice of switching channels. Narrated Laila, the older daughter:

> They (the parents) have taught us that whenever such scenes appear on the screen we must not watch them, that's forbidden. Why we have to switch channels, why we have to do that, we don't know. We only know that it's forbidden. We don't talk about that.

The reason was given by Hasima, the mother, in a separate interview half an hour later. Stating that she felt equally embarrassed about the love scene, she added: 'If you're sitting there for yourself, it's okay.' This comment indicates that the perception of a film partly depends on the viewing context: watching a film collectively in a cinema hall can definitely be more fun. Yet, there also seems to be a transfer of meaning in that personal roles transgress into public roles, controlled by the 'social gaze'. Fathers become representatives of families in public who must protect their daughters as objects of male desire. Pleasure can turn into discomfort.

I argue that *Ek Rishtaa* 'shocked' because by departing from the standard depiction of love scenes in Bollywood films, it challenged the audio-visual media literacy of the viewers because the film moved outside the common narrative and style of popular cinema. The private gaze was transformed into a social gaze, as if the audience was witnessing something 'real'. The tension raised by the new situation was increased when, by entering the cinema hall, the Khans left both the secure privacy of the living room and the relative (remote) control over the images on their television screen. The public space of the cinema hall, knowing that the images were simultaneously seen by everyone in the hall, plus the fact that the audience had expected a 'clean family movie', increased the feeling of tension and vulnerability. It was as if the parents saw it not with their own, but with their children's and the rest of the community's, eyes. For a brief moment, the closed world of the film narrative introduced an unconventional set of images that immediately triggered off associations of what love-making looks like and 'how it's done' in public. Suddenly, the borders between the expected and the unexpected, filmic reality and physical experience, collapsed. It is this breakdown of, or oscillation between, fantasy and actuality that led Hasima to come to the conclusion that with respect to visiting a Hindi film on a Sunday, 'most of the families with their kiddies, they will think twice about it .... Even though the kiddies don't understand, they saw you doing *it*.' At this point, Bollyworld's authority as a trustworthy speaker of selfhood collapsed temporarily, becoming a morally irritating, if not threatening factor in that the film media came to be perceived as 'containers' conveying both permissible and not permissible fantasies (Kasbekar 2000; see also Halstead, this volume). The depiction of a wedding night has to follow certain conventions in order to preserve the idea of the wedding as a morally 'clean' ritual as opposed to the personal sexual pleasures enacted by the film figures of Nisha and Ajay.

Besides being a container of 'Indianness'—that is, idealised cultural values—film also works as a canvas for negotiating a fractured sense of 'Indianness' and 'westernness'. The way in which the wedding night is read by Hasima reflects her personal concern to position herself, her family and their notions of a homogenous cultural identity within a space that can, like a treasure box, be filled and glanced at with 'our things', safely secluded from 'their things' by closing the lid. This signifying practice attempts to fix meaning and enhance stereotypes that can then be employed as alleged essences within cultural identity's repertoire. Listening to Hasima's elaboration on Bollywood films' 'duties' evokes ideas of an idealised viewer who can follow the narrative almost like a *flaneur* walking through a theme park. The projected ideal is that the viewer is at once both entertained and educated, that he or she can dwell in certain permissible fantasies while being firmly positioned in a moral universe. In this context, selection can be practiced on the basis of elaborating categories like 'us' and 'them', 'normal' and 'abnormal', 'inside' and 'outside'.

Particularly among members of the first migrant generation, these categories are explicitly centred around ideas, images and metaphors of the woman and family, both identified with tradition's continuity, honour and status in the (imagined) community. To heighten these notions, Hasima introduces another spatial category by extending the zone of control over the depiction of sexuality-as-morality into the mediascape of US films, thereby juxtaposing 'Indianness' with 'westernness'. Hasima criticises the fact that in *Ek Rishtaa,* 'they just show love so loosely ... they show you exactly how it goes. Like in an English movie ....' In the light of the shortness of the scene this assumption seems somehow over-interpreted. Nevertheless, it must be taken seriously as it indicates that different regimes of the gaze and of realism are applied here: certain things can be watched in 'English' films because they are 'naturalised' as culture-specific. Yet, they must not transgress into the 'clean' world of Hindi (family) films. Hasima elucidates that her family loves to watch Western films, 'because, hey, come on, the stories are really good, of these American movies, so you want to see the film as well. But at the same time, you don't want to see all this rubbish.' In this context, the West is stereotyped, and thus distanced, as a spectacular but essentially immoral Other. Notions of 'indigenous' evolve in the *act* of creating chains of juxtapositions.

The idea to keep one's own cultural identity 'clean' both derives from, and results in, a constant act of imagining (South Asian) culture as a homogenous entity, by giving 'homing' a privileged place away from allegedly threatening western influences. This becomes evident when Hasima refers to the filmic depiction of sexuality in a non-Bollywood film on India that was made for a predominantly western audience. As owner of a video shop, Hasima used to bring home new releases on VHS—whether from India or Pakistan. Talking about *Fire* directed by Deepa Mehta (1996), she critiques the film's address of homosexuality as something 'abnormal' and alien and thus offending those who are considering themselves as representatives of 'normality'. Again, the notion of a traditional family is idealised as a marker and guarantor of cultural stability and identity. Commenting on lesbian love as a threat to 'authentic' morality and values, Hasima argues:

> The kids know [that it exists]. The kids know. What do you think?! Even Amir [her son aged 15], he knows all that .... In the Pakistani films, I used to tell them, look we Muslim people *we don't do that*, okay? I didn't mind if the kiddies watched Pakistani movies, because it was *really* clean. But *now*, even in the Pakistani movies, they're showing them [women] with half-sleeve dresses and their scenes are really vulgar. So I don't even bring that anymore! Because that was our way of telling the kiddies, listen, this is our culture, do you see anything in the movies like that!? But you can't even do *that* anymore. So I think it's the same with the Indian movies. I think all the other families, they do the same thing ... but if they're showing all this, you can't tell your kiddies, we don't do that! They say, 'how come they're doing that!?'

Here, the Bollywood film (but also Pakistani media) is deployed as a 'helping hand' for first generation migrants to communicate that 'culture' is a given, something one has to keep and appreciate like family photographs. This invocation steps in when institutions, such as schools, and networks, such as cultural and religious centres, in the diasporic context are seen as failing to provide adequate socialisation. Migration as such becomes a 'danger zone' in which essentialised values and ideals are felt to be constantly challenged, destabilised and thus weakened. The film media serves as a backdrop for negotiations, dramatisation and dichotimisation of 'we Muslims don't do that' versus 'they are doing it'. The idea of 'crisis' as a response conditioned by location reflects fears of a westernisation (infiltrating even Pakistani films) that is identified with a dilution of a notion of authentic identity and parental authority. Hasima's remark points at the dilemma: her legitimacy to draw upon indigenous media as provider for a 'clean' identity is discredited by what she refers to as vulgar elements in both Indian and Pakistani media. The collapse of clear distinctions, thus her fear, enables the children to question the authority of both parents and 'tradition'. What crops up time and again in Hasima's negotiations is the controlling gaze of the Ahmadi community of which the family is a member.[14] It is for the sake of this internalised social control that personal desires and pleasures, particularly of the second generation, must be tamed.

---

[14] Members of the Ahmadi sect are part of a minority community in Pakistan who have been declared as 'non-Muslims' in several amendments of the Pakistani constitution in 1974, 1982 and 1986.

A similar wish to establish sound identities in the youth through somatic metaphors was articulated by a Pakistani shop-owner and movie-goer (A) to the author (CB) before the public screening of a Hindi film in a local cinema hall in the outskirts of Frankfurt:

> CB: I would like to know whether these Indian films represent a culture that is important to your kids too. Is it important that they display different values than in western films?
> A: No. We like to watch other films. But you can say that it's my desire that they don't watch [western] romances, *naked films*, or something alike (August 2000).

This view echoes the idea of films as a moral authority and relates it to the notion of 'nakedness' as an index for immoral western values.

The fact that popular films can be both great pedagogical tools and sources of misrepresentation shows that for Hasima (HK), 'indigenous media' does not equal 'good media'. In her view, even 'home products' cannot be trusted any more.

> CB: [If *Fire* or *Ek Rishtaa* are not 'clean'], how do you show your 'own culture'?
> HK: *Now*, after that film [*Ek Rishtaa*], I don't know ....
>
> CB: No more Hindi films?
> HK: Not even Pakistani films, unless they are [clean].... There's one film, that's a very clean one, that's a very good story. It's about Sharia [Islamic law]. *Then* I know it's a very good, clean film, then I say, okay, I take it. Otherwise, I don't bring it [from the shop] myself. I don't even bring the Pakistani films anymore.
>
> CB: And spiritual programmes?
> HK: We don't have many like this. And the kiddies are not interested.
>
> CB: But what is your worry? That the children would think badly about Pakistan or India?
> HK: Yes, of course!!! About the culture! Look Christina [sic], we're living in Europe, right?! We want our kids to keep their own culture. That's natural, right?! Like, when you go to (India) ... it will be the same. So this is the only way we can teach them. No matter how much I try, I told you, they don't get to see the *real* culture. How many weddings will they get to see, how many birthdays, how many

funerals—they won't get to see that here, right?! So we try to get them to see it through the films, or the dramas or that .... But if they're trying to show all these vulgar things, then you can't do that anymore.

CB: But are you worried about them being influenced by American films?
HK: No, because I think that at the same time we're also brainwashing them. We say 'listen, we're not those people, this is not our religion, this is not our culture. We can't do that!' But if they're starting to show that in our own culture, we're stuck, we can't explain to the kiddies anymore. They will only turn around and say 'they do!' How come you people don't know that?

A source of danger is thus not only the 'alienation' of the children through school but the fact that the films from home, once perceived as trustworthy, become agents of unintended change and enhance the blurring of imaginary and real territories and identities.

For Hasima, Bollywood films and Pakistani dramas are part and parcel of a culture that is otherwise 'invisible' and 'out of touch' for diasporic communities. To her, they have the potential to collapse geographical distances and provide the space for a virtual and yet sensual face-to-face communication with the homeland. This is particularly important in the context of an underdeveloped migrant infrastructure in terms of cultural centres or South Asian neighbourhoods the way diaspora communities in the UK, and also the USA, have done. Weddings and other public rituals are rare events for *in situ* social encounters. In between these 'real' plays, Bollywood films provide props and plots for the performance and constitution of South Asian community life. In that, they are vital for the display of evidence that one has managed to be both economically successful and to preserve one's link with home abroad (*des pardes*). Thus, the filmic depiction of a wedding, for example, contributes to the elaboration of a vocabulary of a 'transnational realism',[15] joining a whole 'range of geographical sites, monuments and symbols to create a powerful visual rhetoric of (trans-)nationality' (Mirzoeff, 2000: 2). Bollyworld is the universe through which transnational realism becomes 'second nature',

[15] The term refers to Arjun Appadurai and Carol Breckenridge's concept of 'nationalist realism': 'an array of images, symbols, scripts and plots in which the nation is figured as central to the project of modernity. The nation, sometimes as figure, sometimes as ground, is never absent from this transnationally constituted visual field' (1995: 9, see also p. 13).

a stage on which 'authentic' cultural practices turn into commodities.[16] Yet, the previous examples have also shown that the trust in Bollywood as second nature has been overshadowed by local contexts and multiple ways of 'reading from below'. Thus the endeavour to use films to create 'controlled spaces' through which moral values of an alternative modernity can be generated and taught, seems to have only partially worked.

Arranged Marriages and Mini Skirts

Hasima Khan perceives popular family films, and wedding films in particular, as a substitute 'picture book' for something seen as lacking in the diasporic context. Interestingly, religious identity does not dominate her judgement: whether Hindu or Muslim, the centrality of wedding as a community event in which the concepts of family and tradition are celebrated, subsumes everybody under the spectacle of Bollywood. Specifically, it is the celebration of respect for the elders as those who have legitimately chosen the match for their daughter or son that is placed centre stage.

Yet, at another level, an interesting distinction is made between Pakistani and Indian culture. The first is defined as more conservative and traditional while the latter is connoted as 'modern' and more materialist. This applies particularly when it comes to the question of dress as a marker of identity, an issue taken up by Hasima to attribute morality to particular ethnic groups and norms:

> *Pardes* was a clean movie. The only thing you could say was that they wore mini skirts and all that. But then, because we are Muslims, we think like that .... With the Hindus, it's no problem, they can wear that and they do .... They changed a lot, the Indians [in urban India of the 1990s].

Interestingly, *Pardes* is a Bollywood film centred around the question of how to preserve and protect one's (Hindu) identity in the diaspora. In this process, the woman is stereotyped as chaste, carrying not only the responsibility to represent her husband and his family's honour, but also

[16] According to Lavie and Swedenburg, second nature is the mimetic creation of an 'imagined pure form ... and its process of construction .... [These] reproductions ... inspire or provoke a search for an uncontaminated and unruptured original' (Lavie and Swedenburg, 1996: 11).

the nation's (India's) integrity. With a few exceptions, the film's narrative is dominated by women wearing traditional dress (*sari* or *salwar kameez*). Yet, in order to emphasise the fact that some women have come to neglect their 'essential' role in the diaspora, Hasima recollects *Hindu* women in mini skirts. It seems as if her communal perspective is part of an attempt to prevent her (Muslim) daughters from drawing upon those figures to legitimate a change of outfit.

Wearing, displaying and talking about clothing is thus very often a means of disciplining the body, especially, sexuality. However, Laila responds positively to her mother's desire to teach the children what 'their real' culture is through Hindi films. Yet, her alignment with 'real' culture evolves from a pleasure of consuming romance and spectacular festivity. In terms of tradition and festivals Laila's (LK) reading of filmi wedding scenes turns India into a utopian site. Here she talks to the author (CB).

> CB: Do you learn about [Indian] culture through films?
> LK.: Yes. Take, for example, weddings. We don't know what weddings are like in those [diasporic] countries. And it's really tremendously beautiful to see what it's like *in reality*. It's interesting that one learns about one's own culture—a culture that doesn't exist here —through the films. And that one can learn a lot!

Laila's diagnosis of a lack of 'one's own culture' sidelines morality and highlights spectacle. To her, Bollywood represents the grand lifestyle of professional middle classes, a celebration of family, love and material wealth. Indian (Hindu) weddings are filled with dance, joy and laughter, where women dance freely with men. She juxtaposes this with what she describes as boring Pakistani weddings, an endless chain of gatherings without any mixing of gender. For Laila, Bollywood sets the standard for what she wants her wedding to be like. In this context, it should be pointed out that 'filmi' weddings have gained an inflationary popularity in the wake of a growing middle class and economic liberalisation in India in the early 1990s, and many 'clean' family films are centred around wedding narratives.[17]

Although national identity does not play a major role in the informants' articulation of concerns and ideas with respect to film, the notion of communal difference, the subtle difference between Hindus and Muslims,

[17] The path-breaking icon of the genre of the 'wedding film' is *Hum Aapke Hain Koun...!* (*Who am I to you*, dir. Sooraj R. Barjatya, 1994). See, for example, Uberoi, 2001.

Indians and Pakistanis, is part of an ongoing interpretation of modernity. Difference is constituted with respect to collective identities as well as personal identities, and gender plays an important role in this process. Since Hasima's family comes from Pakistan, and Laila's future groom—who has been chosen by the parents—is from Karachi, the children have been exposed to Pakistani culture in some way or another. At the same time, their father's family ties in India have simultaneously provided them with symbolic capital of 'things Indian'. The second generation has a different view upon it. Laila and her sister perceive Pakistani films and weddings as old-fashioned while Indian equivalents are labelled more 'liberal' and 'trendy'.

> CB: Is it important to you whether you're watching a Hindi film or a film from Pakistan?
> LK: Yes, you notice the culture.
>
> CB: Is there a difference?
> LK: Yes, there is. With the Indian films it's generally that they are somehow more liberal, the youth enjoy more freedom and one gets the impression of living in a dream world. They have the better life, what one eventually hopes to have too. I would say that's not the case with films from Pakistan.
> FK [Laila's sister]: I would say that they are more open, those Indian films. You come to notice that [Pakistani serials] are so 'Muslim-like'.

For Fatima and Laila, Pakistani serials convey the idea of closure and fixation when it comes to public expressiveness. They privilege the conservative celebration of traditional Hindu families and values in popular films because they find, within this hegemony, traces of liberal and modern attitudes. Clothing is a central source of identification for the sisters and both wear western fashions, yet nothing that would display their knees, or have a plunging neckline. In some way, Bollywood seems to be a welcome compromise as it becomes both a liberating force ('you may wear mini skirts') and restricting moral authority ('until you get married').

In a film like *Ek Rishtaa*, modern and traditional ways of life find reflection in the dress codes. Gendered role models are negotiated in a scene where one of the heroines appears at a wedding dressed in a white mini dress, a (unconscious) gesture of disrespect for which she is looked and laughed at. Nevertheless, Laila interprets 'Hindus' as moving more easily between, or even fusing tradition and modernity.

CB: When you see those modern girls, like in today's film, one gets the feeling that they can live in both worlds, in the family, but also move around freely in mini skirts.
LK: I think that's fascinating.

CB: Would you say that this film represents an ideal. It shows me what I'd like to be, both traditional and modern?
LK: Certainly! To be *both* .... To wear traditional clothes at home, for the parents, really good, and then, when being outdoors with friends, dress up in trendy clothes, to wear what one feels comfortable in, where you like yourself.

'To be both'—to comfortably navigate between two or maybe more worlds without breaking with tradition—that is a cultural competence of highest value for Laila. The notion of self changes according to the specific situation, and is marked by the changing sets of clothes. When we talked about the fact that with her marriage, a heroine will refrain from wearing western clothes altogether, Laila stated that she never noticed this transformation: 'I always felt sympathetic to that situation and tried to imagine that if I would get married and enter a new family, that I would also try to assimilate .... To generate a good impression of myself.' This is partly based on the ideal typical roles performed in the Hindi films. At least, that's what Laila proposes:

CB: Do you consider these figures as important to think about yourself?
FK and LK: Absolutely!
LK: In such a moment one imagines—what would *I* do, how would *I* react? Then you see how the story continues and, I guess, one compares oneself to the actress. Now she did it the way I did it.

Laila acknowledged that there are rules and obligations for every context. However, this view was given different value when she tried to negotiate the imagined with the 'real' everyday life in Germany, when, for example, suddenly the idea of her own arranged marriage metamorphosed her into a bird in a golden cage. With respect to her marriage, Laila claimed that she will never undergo such a rapid transformation:

He [the future husband] has nothing to say in that respect. But I know, I wouldn't wear anything he opposes to .... I don't want to provoke. But I've been wearing tight clothes almost all my life—I can't imagine that just because he's there, everything will be changed for him only.

This indicates that Bollyworld's moral universe—or according to Rosie Thomas (1995), what is permissible—is a world of different interpretations, negotiated, floating and stretchable, moving into or opposing actual everyday worlds, depending on the context. Certain narratives are pulled into descriptions of personal lifestyles and ways of seeing. Romantic Bollywood films, according to Laila, follow one pattern:

LK: When two people are in love, someone always has to intervene, either the parents or someone else.
CB: And you think that's a reflection of reality?
LK: Yes, as much as I have experienced it, yes. I guess the films show what's happening in reality, it's not like they're just fantasising.

Laila's patterning of Hindi films and her sensitivity towards the genre of 'tragic romance' and respect for parents is intertwined with her own experiences. Only a year before this meeting, she was secretly dating another man, a second generation Muslim from Morocco. They wanted to marry, but her father opposed the match and refused to even meet the man. He was a Muslim but not Ahmadi, and he was not Pakistani but a Moroccan. Here, the parents appropriated a racist stereotype quite common among Germans who identify Moroccans with drug dealers and potential criminals. Quickly, the parents finalised Laila's arranged marriage. Laila was forced to give in, under threats that the family would otherwise break ties with her—quite like in *Ek Rishtaa*. The key argument was that the family's reputation within the Ahmadi community would otherwise be ruined. Laila recalls the internalisation of social control of the community:

My mother grew up in Europe, my father lives in Germany since twenty years. But I wouldn't say that they have assimilated to European culture. They haven't forgotten their culture. And that's what they try to pass on. To tell us, we must not forget this, to give us something on our way. They don't give us freedom the way most other [youth] enjoy it .... My parents are very aware about what the other people think. There are many, and I see it in the case of my parents, who

> don't live for themselves but for the community. Thus they watch us so that we don't make any mistakes, because the community should not hear anything wrong, they don't want to loose their reputation. That's why they try to keep control over us somehow.

In part, Laila seemed to subordinate her views to the parents' will and the authority of the community's religious leaders. But she also seeks to establish her own position in the diaspora context which has very much coloured her perceptions of cultural identity, personal freedom, family loyalties and obligations. Despite this recognition, and incredible personal conflict, she herself 'broke' the bonds with the family in order to live with her Moroccan boyfriend.

Bollyworld as Homeland

The imagination of India and Pakistan as homelands, idealised in audio-visual media such as Bollywood films, becomes almost a counter-world to what is actually a loss of the 'myth of return' particularly for first generation migrants. In this process, 'homing' comes to signify an ambiguous identity, one of navigation between integration and rejection. Narrates Laila:

> When I hear my parents talk about living in Pakistan ... it doesn't work. My father tells me he could never return to India, not for always, okay, for holidays. But they know what life is like there, it's really hard. Why should they give up what they have here? .... It's better there, that's really true .... In Pakistan one could live well, if one had enough money. My father says, if we have enough money he would go to India. If you don't have money, you're lost.

But what seems even more relevant than the economic factor is her experience of being labelled as Other wherever they go:

> What I find strange is that when we go to Pakistan, then they don't consider us to be Pakistanis, for them we are Europeans. Here in Germany, we're foreigners, and there too, we are seen as foreigners .... I sometimes wonder, 'where's actually our home?' To learn about our culture is important: it's important because one day we want to return to *our* home.

Displaced and alienated at home, despite the desire for homing: this is one of the ghosts haunting many migrants, forcing them to generate both fragile and multiple images of the self as well as sound visions of Indianness disseminated by Bollywood. It is here that a discourse of fear takes place and narratives of crisis are elaborated on fertile grounds: crises of loss, lack, dismemberment, pain, etc. The experience of being foreign at home (*pardesi*), invokes 'tensions [that] may arise when places that have been imagined at a distance must become lived spaces' (Gupta and Ferguson, 1997: 40). Maybe that is one reason why 'Bollywood's' invocation of family plays an important role for migrants for it remains a reminder and harbour of 'home' even when chances for a return to the homeland decrease.

Ek Rishtaa is one such film where, visions of the homeland are transposed onto the family. After a major family crisis, the family reunites and rituals of forgiving are performed. Laila affirms this moral power of the 'Bollywood family':

> I believe that reality is like that. This happens to me frequently, that something like this happens in reality, that there are tensions in the family, that problems occur and that finally, everyone comes to the conclusion that, okay, problems come and go, but the family has to stick together, always .... I guess that's life. In life everything revolves around the family .... I don't know what it's like with others. But in our case, that is, among the Pakistanis, or our family, even when they argue or when they have a real big fight, when each and every person is hurt, and when the argument has real consequences, finally, most of the people practice forgiveness.

Laila said this months before she decided to leave home, and when she was still negotiating possible solutions to get out of the arranged marriage and convince her parents of her love for her Moroccan boyfriend. Her comments indicate that Bollywood films can be interpreted for the creation of ideological resolutions. However, the 'idea of India' enhanced through a mediascape and industry like Bollywood is negotiated by social agents bearing different kinds of symbolic capital and underlines the fact that ways of looking at and relating to Bollywood are not at all homogenous. So far, I have discussed identification processes by focusing on members of middle classes that have not enjoyed higher education. I propose that they produce different discourses about commercial Indian film and identity than the Indian youth that I will present in the following section.

Bollywood and 'Pop Patriotism' on the Internet

The web site www.theinder.net reflects a particular kind of packaging of 'Indian culture' (and of Bollywood as a significant part of it) for an audience of young Indians coming from a professional middle-class background of lawyers, nurses, engineers, academics or diplomats, often with one German parent.[18] These youths reflect upon India and her culture as an 'imagined homeland', but in a different way from that of Laila or Fatima. 'India', and Bollywood films in particular, serve as props of a montaged, exotic spectacle, ready-made and enjoyed for playful consumption. The youth on the net seems to navigate playfully and confidently between the familial and the public world, without displaying too much concern with Bollywood narratives of family traditions and values. 'To be both', at home in South Asia and Germany, does not cause the moral dilemmas articulated by Hasima or Laila.

www.theinder.net links and creates virtual (online) and actual (offline) communities. It is a contact zone and social catalyst for diverse members of Indian communities dispersed across Germany, many of whom are students. Writes Sherry K. who regularly places his comments on the web site: 'This is the forum for a real virtual community. We exchange views about India and I have come to make some *real contacts* too.' Many face-to-face contacts are then established at New Asian Underground and Bollywood parties that are organised by second generation Indians in various German cities and which increasingly appeal to non-Asian youth too (see Sharma et al., 1996). The popularity of Bollywood events since 2002 underline the commodification of Indian popular culture. This greater visibility is often identified with a new kind of recognition of migrant groups (as representatives of a 'trend'). At the same time, Indian youth have started criticising the superficial and purely commercial attraction of Indian culture in this context.

Using nicknames such as 'TheKeralaBoy', 'KamasutraBoy' or 'amitabh bachchan', the agents entering the discussion forum on the web site remain behind a 'virtual' mask. The fact that they explore subjects related to Indian film in a 'real virtual' community points to another difference relating to Hasima's or Laila's articulations. The latter display a strong concern to consider film in relation to what members of their family and the transnational community of Ahmadis might think and expect, thus

[18] Thanks to Urmila Goel who provided me with information on the web site. See also footnote 7.

acting out identities with an emphasis on an internalised social gaze. The first group, the users of the web site, imagine their identities as part of a more anonymous para-community that does not have a great impact on the lives they lead in the diaspora. The comments (written in German) selected for this chapter show that their authors relate to Bollywood with a much more playful, elitist and partly orientalist view on India. They openly critique Bollywood films as 'tacky' or 'superficial' and thus show that the reception of the films is by no means homogenous but rather based on ruptures and fissures. Here, popular films—and the vision of India they stage—are seen through 'westernised eyes', as cheap and escapist 'kitsch', noisy and colourful spectacles with embarrassing (traditional=backward) narratives and special effects (see Thomas, 1985: 118). Writes Amitabh Bachchan:

> I think these bollywood films are rather bad: crap singing, crap plot and always this brutal, shabbily made-up violence. *Bumm baff bang* ... good against evil, good finally winning in the last moment, the hero always conquering the gal ('*tussi*'). Yawn. ... where are the demanding films with content??? (discussion forum, www.theinder.net, 9.12.2000).

And Bijon's opinion on Bollywood is this:

> bollywood-films are bread and games for the people, a dream world .... Intellectual requirements: nill; entertainment: 100 per cent. Not my cup of tea ... bengali films are certainly different. Satyajit Ray's films lasted about two hours and were socio-critical—he was the first indian who received an oscar for his life-work (ibid.).

www.theinder.net also has an entertainment section where 'diasporic film critics' like 'Assma', distinguish a film like *Chori Chori Chupke Chupke* (*Secretively and Quietly*, dir. Abbas-Mustan, 2001) from formula films by pointing out that

> there is no song in which hero and heroine dance in the rain and jump from one hill to another. Each song is well-placed and seems to flow with the narrative, not isolated from it, as in so many other films (ibid., April 2001).

This view on Bollywood as backward and childish is highly ambiguous. At the same time, the glamour and 'authenticity' factor of Bollyworld almost works like an exotic veil through which these members of the second generation communicate and negotiate their alliance to what they understand as 'typically Indian'. Proportionally, with Bollywood's international recognition, their own status improves. This indicates a shift from the internalisation of controlling community eyes to a concern for what 'the world' thinks about and recognises as 'Indian'. Thrilled by Bollywood's transnational networks and international popularity, TheKeralaBoy writes:

> It's amazing that 'Bollywood' unites people from all classes .... Most of the 'foreign' Indians (Auslandsinder) don't recognise this. I know many Turks, Africans, Indonesians, Arabs and other nationalities who freak out when they watch Bollywood films, even if they don't grasp their meaning ... go and watch *Mohabbatein*, *Kutch Kutch Hota Hai* [*sic*], *Dil Se*, *Gulham* [*sic*] (www.theinder.net, 10.12.2000)!

The commentary on some of the most popular, and also internationally recognised Hindi movies in the past years denotes that socialisation of youth in German cities takes place in multicultural milieus and that consensus is constituted in this multi-perspectival context. The suggestion here is that while Indians have still not recognised the appeal of Bollywood films, members of other transnational communities have, and thus work as eye-openers for Indians' distant relationship to their homeland. However, the emphasis in this comment is rather on Bollywood's entertainment value than on narrative and ideology. Another reason why the Indian film industry is received in a more gentle light is because of stars like Amitabh Bachchan or Aishwarya Rai—people who have made it on the international market—be it through Bachchan's 'waxification' in Madame Toussaud's Cabinet or Rai's nomination as Miss World ('our Indian women are the most beautiful in the world', www.theinder.net).

The international recognition adds light and appeal to the (un)popular image of India as a backward country. But it also enhances the development of an Indian version of transnational nationalism that is to a great extent based on a commodification of Indian heritage. Writes MotherOf TheNations: 'Yah man, our India is great! We can really be proud of it. All the clever and good people generated by *us*, shaping revolutionary ideas of today's world .... *Mera Bharat Mahan*! [My India is great, C.B.]' (www.theinder.net, 17.12.2000). The latter-day genre of 'clean' Bollywood films is appreciated because of its placing of the professional middle classes and nouveau riche at centre stage, highlighting only those segments of society that 'have made it' in India or abroad. The fetishisation of Indian heritage and tradition is covered with a layer of cosmopolitanism and cultural nationalism. The rigid corset of Bollywood's moral universe thematised earlier transposes itself onto a colourful backdrop. Bollywood's consumption on theinder.net takes place in light of such an elitist and eclectic approach, thereby coming surprisingly close to Hindu nationalist discourses.[19] As long as they come along in trendy make-up, even Hindu nationalist arguments are 'sociable'. This articulation of a new pride of India can be compared to the packaging of Bankim Chandra Chattopadhyaya's *Vande Mataram* (*Hail to Mother India*, 1880s) in a multimedia spectacle commemorating 50 years of India's Independence in 1997 where (Hindu) nationality appears to be glorified and stylised as a metanarrative of utopia, another theme park of logos and gestures reflecting national affiliation without political and moral commitment. Srirupa Roy argues that this is part of a '"new" nationalism ... (that) can harmoniously coexist with official nationalism'. The multimedia production marked the entry of 'pop patriotism' (Roy, 2003) packaged for a young audience in India, but certainly also enjoyed much popularity among Indian diaspora.[20] This pop patriotism which appeals to the imagined audience seems in line with many recent Bollywood films displaying and celebrating 'authentic Indianness' as aesthetically attractive, economically powerful and morally superior (from *Pardes* via *Phir Bhi Dil Hai Hindustani* [*But the Heart remains Indian*, dir. Aziz Mirza, 1999] to *Ek Rishtaa*). This presents a further difference to the ways of reading Bollywood by Hasima and Laila Khan: their statements underline a discourse about ethics and community to negotiate morality and sexuality by creating dichotomies such as 'modern' and 'traditional', 'normal' and 'abnormal'. The virtual pop patriotism of members of theinder.net shows less concern with these categories and displays a more confident appropriation, or rejection, of Bollywood Indianness into creolised identities of the diasporic youth.

Discussions on theinder.net convey a critical reception of 'Indian' nationality, sexuality and morality, stigmatising it as corrupt and misleading. This becomes evident in a debate about the controversial non-Bollywood

[19] See www.hinduunity.org, a Hindu extremist web site, that seems to appeal to a great extent to Hindus living abroad.

[20] Bharatbala Production also engaged in the multimedia presentation of the Indian national anthem *Jana Gana Mana 2000* (see Roy, 2003. See also http://www.janaganamana.satyamonline.com).

production of Deepa Mehta's film *Water*, the last part of a trilogy, following *Fire* and *Earth*. Here, organisations aligned to the Hindu Right disrupted the shooting of the film in Banaras in 2000 by claiming that the film production would 'pollute' not only the sanctity of the holy city but also the image of women (the film script addresses the subject of prostitution). Writes mother of all films:

> I think it's crap and incomprehensible that radical hindus can always blockade these alternative and liberal films. That's not according to Indian culture. Haven't the Indians (hindus, sic.) developed the kamasutra, the first pornos in the world were displayed on temple walls ... what the swedish [*sic*] were in the sixties was already celebrated by us 2000 years ago. The radical hindus are brain-dead, inhibited, colonial traumatised fuckers of the cow who uphold the inhibited manner of victorian england [*sic*] as an Indian virtue (www.theinder.net, 9.12.2000).

What is criticised in this context is that the projection of morally upright and tolerant Hindus is counter-posed by a no-objection policy of Hindu Right organisations when it comes to Bollywood's open display of violence: 'But with all those Bollywood films, where violence and other things are idealised, [the Hindu Right, C.B.] remains silent' (TheKeralaBoy, ibid., 8.12.2000).

This second generation of Indians living in Germany defines the relationship towards the homeland of its parents anew. States KamasutraBoy in the discussion forum:

> In some ways we haven't even disappointed our parents, despite the fact that we might not live according to Indian tradition, tradition is always in us and it will always be passed on and will therefore, at least I hope so, never be lost. *Proud to be an Indian*![21]

This statement does not carry the weight and struggle imbued in Laila and Fatima Khan's perceptions of media as containers of identity and lifestyles. With the Khan family's interpretations of Bollywood and creation of Bollyworld, the conflict to come to terms with almost juxtaposed ways of seeing Indian culture—as well as westernness—as moral universes indicating different regimes of pleasure. With the discussions prevalent amongst

---

[21] Italicised words are the original language.

the upper middle class world of www.theinder.net, such a crass juxtaposition does not prevail. Bollywood dilutes Indianness-as-nationality in terms of a geographic connotation and authorisation of the modern nation-state insofar as, in the diasporic context, the state as a source of primary loyalty and thus, identification, moves to the periphery. Nevertheless, Bollywood remains homogenising in that it affirms and translates the nation-state's most favourite child, the idealised (middle class) family, as a 'shining emblem' for global consumption. In this respect, nationalism and transnationalism come to share certain values and significatory strategies for identification.

Conclusion

In this chapter, I observed that as a 'contact zone' and space of identity constitution and performance, Bollyworld shapes and is shaped by diverse agents, desires, fields of consumption and spheres of meaning production. In this course, homogenising narratives of the films at times become reinterpreted, translated and appropriated into agents' lives, and even subverted and criticised. The discussion of Bollywood films as moral universes of nationhood, familial values and notions of sexuality enables us to understand that a clear separation of homeland and 'exile' is neither feasible, nor desired by the representatives of diaspora communities in Germany as represented in this chapter. Instead, different 'homing strategies' and imaginings of homelands are deployed and created to localise and, at the same time, re-territorialise identities. In this context, the role of film screenings in local cinema halls was analysed as both a 'social event for community constitution' and a 'danger zone' in which the private and public gaze shape the film reception. Furthermore, the role of Bollywood films in the context of two groups and two generations of South Asian migrants were discussed to explore different ways of seeing and production of identity discourses. While all the informants shared the desire to have pride in Indian/Pakistani culture and nationality, the members of lower middle classes displayed a need to consider what members of their community might think and interpreted Bollywood narratives according to rather rigid norms, values and given identities. Bollywood could be read as a representative of a transnational South Asianness to all those with backgrounds in the region. It could thus serve as a 'teaching tool' to invoke notions of authentic identity along the lines of 'clean' and 'vulgar', restricting and liberal. Youth members of professional middle-class families critically challenged primordiality with respect to the expression of individual desires, sexuality and Bollywood's depiction of traditional family life. The internalisation of the 'local' or personal community gaze is sidelined and more emphasis placed on the recognition of 'Indianness' as a commodity, to be acknowledged by an imagined international community. The search for homelands in Bollyworld is thus an ongoing process of mapping and remapping roots and routes.

References

APPADURAI, ARJUN and CAROL BRECKENRIDGE. 1995. 'Public Modernity in India', in Carol Breckenridge (ed.), *Consuming Modernity. Public Culture in a South Asian World*, pp. 1–20, Minneapolis and London: University of Minnesota Press.

BRAH, AVTAR. 1996. *Cartographies of Diaspora: Contesting Identities*. London and New York: Routledge: 178–210.

CLIFFORD, JAMES. 1997. *Routes: Travel and Translation in the Twentieth Century*. Cambridge (Mass.) and London (UK): Harvard University Press.

DWYER, RACHEL. 2000. 'The Erotics of the Wet Sari in Hindi Films', *South Asia*, XXIII(1): 143–59.

GINSBURG, FAYE. 1995. 'Mediating Culture: Indigenous Media, Ethnographic Film and the Production of Identity', in Leslie Devereaux and Roger Hillman (eds), *Fileds of Vision: Essays in Film Studies, Visual Anthropology and Photography*, pp. 256–91, Berkeley: University of California Press.

GOEL, URMILA. 1998. *Citizenship and Identity among Second Generation South Asians in Western European Countries*. Unpublished MA thesis, London: SOAS.

GUPTA, AKHIL and JAMES FERGUSON (eds). 1997. *Culture Power Place: Explorations in Critical Anthropology*. Durham and London: Duke University Press.

HALL, STUART (ed.). 1997. *Representation: Cultural Representations and Signifying Practices*. London: Sage Publications.

HANNERZ, ULF. 1992. *Cultural Complexity: Studies in the Social Organization of Meaning*. New York and Oxford: Columbia University Press.

KASBEKAR, ASHA. 2000. 'Hidden Pleasures: Negotiating the Myth of the Female Ideal in Popular Hindi Cinema', in Rachel Dwyer and Christopher Pinney (eds), *Pleasure and the Nation: The History, Politics and Consumption of Public Culture in India*, pp. 286–308, New Delhi: OUP.

LAVIE, SMADAR and TED SWEDENBURG (eds). 1996. *Displacement, Diaspora and Geography of Identity*. Durham and London: Duke University Press.

MIRZOEFF, NICHOLAS (ed.). 2000. *Diaspora and Visual Culture: Representing Africans and Jews*. London and New York: Routledge

ROY, SRIRUPA. 2003. 'Moving Images: The Postcolonial Indian State and Visual Representations of Nationhood', in Sumathi Ramaswamy (ed.), *Beyond Appearances: Visual Practices and Ideologies in Modern India*, pp. 233–64. New Delhi: Sage Publications [*Contributions to Indian Sociology*, Occasional Studies 10].

SHARMA, SANJAY, JOHN HUTNYK and ASHWANI SHARMA (eds). 1996. *Dis-Orienting Rhythms. The Politics of the New Asian Dance Music*. London: Zed Books.

Statistisches Bundesamt. 2004. *Ausländische Bevölkerung nach der Staatsangehörigkeit am 31.12.2003 in Deutschland* Nr.VIB-176 [Statistics on foreigners listed according to citizenship as of 31.12.03], Wiesbaden.

Thomas, Rosie. 1985. 'Indian Cinema: Pleasures and Popularity', *Screen*, 26(3/4): 116–31.

———. 1995. 'Melodrama and the Negotiation of Morality in Mainstream Hindi Film', in Carol Breckenridge (ed.), *Consuming Modernity: Public Culture in a South Asian World*, Minneapolis and London: University of Minnesota Press.

Uberoi, Patricia. 1998. 'The Diaspora Comes Home: Disciplining Desire in DDLJ', *Contributions to Indian Sociology*, 32(2): 305–36.

———. 2001. 'Imagining the Family. An Ethnography of Viewing *Hum Aapke Hain Koun*', in Rachel Dwyer and Christopher Pinney (eds), *The Nation and its Pleasures: The History, Politics and Consumption of Public Culture in India*, pp. 309–51, New Delhi: OUP.

10

In Search of the Diasporic Self: Bollywood in South Africa

THOMAS BLOM HANSEN

The Hindi film, *Kuch Kuch Hota Hai* (*Something or Other is Happening*, henceforth *KKHH*, dir. Karan Johar), was released in South Africa in late 1998 riding on the back of its huge success in India and in the UK and the US. The rumours of its success among 'mixed audiences' in the US, convinced the manager of a large cinema complex in Durban's Musgrave shopping centre, the heart of upper middle-class whiteness in the city, that it would be feasible to screen the film in one of the smaller halls. A few months later in December, the manager Mr Shaffie Mohammed, received what he called 'a request from one of our white patrons to acquire a subtitled copy of the film'. He succeeded in getting one via Mauritius, which during the years of India's cultural boycott of the apartheid regime had been an important supplier of cultural products from the Indian subcontinent to South Africa's 1.3 million people of Indian origin. For the next six months the cinema hall was continually sold out.

Meanwhile, other copies without subtitles ran in the suburban Indian townships to half-empty halls. The screening was stopped there after a few months, which is normal, even good for a Hindi film. But in Musgrave, the craze continued for more than eight months. This was the first Bollywood production ever to be shown in a formerly white area in the city, and also the first Bollywood film ever to be shown with English subtitles. The overwhelming majority of spectators were of Indian origin, quite a few whites had their first encounter with Bollywood, whereas very few Africans were to be found in the audiences. Unlike many other African countries where Hindi cinema has drawn mass audiences for decades, Indian films and other cultural products from the subcontinent have been 'racialised' in South Africa and confined to Indian areas and audiences. The film became a cultural phenomenon that revived and redefined an otherwise declining interest in Indian films among Indian South Africans. Many filmgoers saw the film three, five, even eight times, and its success was intensely covered and discussed in the local Indian press. Local journalists repeated the fact that the film ran longer than, and was seen by more people in Durban than, *Titanic*. At the same time, local Indian papers and radio programmes ran features where psychologists warned against the damaging effects of repeating viewing and obsession with film stars on young and tender minds.

So what was there about this film which made it so popular? Why did it evoke such a huge response, at this juncture, and what does that possibly tell us about the conditions of possibility for articulating various forms of identity and ethnicities in the new South Africa? In order to address some of these issues, let us first look at the film itself, its style of address and themes, and second, look at the structures of recognition that produce the Indian 'community' in South Africa, and in particular the way in which Bollywood films for a long time have been a type of 'mega-signifiers' of Indianness in South Africa (and elsewhere). Finally, I link this phenomenon more directly to the larger discourses of the nation, citizenship and loyalty in contemporary South Africa.

'What does this film make of me?'

Following the film theorist, Christian Metz (1982), I will suggest to see reception and viewing of films as an experience suspended between two viewer positions: the 'inscribed' viewer constructed by the film's style of address, its storyline, its register of references, etc., and the 'actual' viewer—that is, those who actually sit in front of the screen. Unlike in theatre, the performance and the reception do not presuppose each other in the cinema hall, and the 'actual' viewers of films have the freedom to attend or not attend to the film, or to move in and out of various dimensions of the inscribed viewer position. Metz' argument is that the viewer does not identify with the persons on the screen, who obviously are fictive, but with herself as someone inhabiting this inscribed position created by the address of the film. What is judged and negotiated in the process of viewing is, as Ashish Rajadhyaksha (2000) argues, what the film makes of the viewer, and whether that is seen as an acceptable, enjoyable or insulting position.

Anyone familiar with Hindi films and the culture of film viewing in India will know that this indeed is far removed from the serious atmosphere of total attention and identification with the screen as is the ideal in modern realist art cinema. Hindi films are constructed around a set of easily recognisable conventions, particularly song-and-dance sequences, often predictable plots and stereotypical characters. There is, in other words, a strong ritualistic element in the viewing of Indian films, a light-heartedness, a tongue-in-cheek mimetic relationship to all kinds of styles and genres derived from western cinema, and a certain disarmingly over-the-top quality to dialogue and the style of acting. Knowledge of these genre conventions and the ability to appreciate films in this relaxed, repetitive, intensely social form is crucial to the larger 'reading competence' that characterises the average, often extremely film-literate spectator in India. By reading competence, I mean a visceral familiarity with styles, songs and the legacy of older films that may be alluded to, rather than any formal knowledge. Hindi films such as *KKHH* are obviously judged on the basis of how they speak to these discerning sensibilities of such ordinary Indian film literati.

Some have suggested that this culture of film viewing is derived from *darshan,* the Hindu practice of viewing an idol or image of a deity for hours (Mishra, 1985; see also Chatterjee, this volume), while others, such as Tejaswini Niranjana (1997), have suggested that the 'Indian spectator' over the last decades has become a global phenomenon, a form of relationship between film and viewing that are integral to the cinematic culture in countries with populations of Indian origin; for example, South Africa. Based on the evidence given ahead I will suggest, however, that the *KKHH* phenomenon in South Africa may be understood, at least in part, as a consequence of *the relative absence* of this 'Indian spectator' in contemporary Durban.

But let us first look at how this film addresses its audience, what it makes of its spectators, or how it inscribes them as spectators. The address of the film is clearly middle class and aspiring to be both cosmopolitan and diasporic, displaying a range of strangely de-localised series of styles, dress, and a style of dialogue and interaction that draws heavily on Hollywood teenage movies.

Plot Summary

The film is basically a love triangle between the hero Rahul (played by teenage idol Shah Rukh Khan), his friend, the tomboy Anjali (played by Kajol), and their common friend Tina (Rani Mukherjee), a sophisticated NRI-girl who, in a set of scenes caricaturing a brash 1970s style, enters the prestigious college St. Xavier's, directly from Oxford. She 'cannot even speak proper Hindustani', as Rahul initially remarks. He is enticed by Tina's amply displayed bodily shape, and the friends drift apart as he decides to marry her while leaving Anjali behind, unhappy and devastated. Rani dies of complications after having given birth to their daughter, who she as a last wish wants to call Anjali, in memory of their lost friend.

The film's present is with the child Anjali, living with her father Rahul and her grandmother. One of the high sentimental points occurs when little Anjali, at a talent contest at her elite school, is supposed to give a little speech over the theme 'Mother' but is unable to say anything.

The remainder of the plot unfolds at a summer camp where the lost friend Anjali, the tomboy-turned-woman, is one of the instructors and which the little Anjali is attending. Here, Rahul meets Anjali again in her new and more desirable feminine incarnation and their love is renewed. Anjali is going to get married to another man, played by Salman Khan, but he decides at the last minute at the wedding to give her up and let her be reunited with Rahul, her true love.

The film takes place in a setting which is completely westernised/ Americanised, in clothing that constantly is on display, in display of body-culture, sports, rock music, beach volleyball, basketball, etc.—the West implanted onto India: a pure fantasy space, a fantasy of an India minus squalor, dirt and the lower classes. The film is also about the disciplining of women, or rather their self-disciplining, as well as the negotiation of the family. The cultivation of the true femininity in Anjali makes her a desirable object—no longer wearing jeans and T-shirts as in the first part of the film, but dressed in a sari as a proper Indian woman (see Gangoli, this volume).

Another striking thing about the film is the absence of any paternal authority as well as the absence of jealousy and conflict between lovers. The film clearly depicts its main characters as unfettered individuals whose actions are guided by their own feelings and impulses, their conscience and inner goodness—nowhere are conventions, culture, or moral injunction presented as restraining or intervening except as benign principles of goodness and moral principle—as in the very improbable respect of pure and true love.

As I shall return to in a moment, the film's celebration of romantic love and of 'clean' relationships between individuals—that is, no sex, no pressure, no violence was one of the points that many viewers cited as its greatest feature. A 20-year-old girl put it across by saying: '... the beauty of this film is that it leaves you with a sense of being clean'.

Signs of the Indian

Since the late nineteenth century there has been a keen and growing interest among educated Indians in South Africa in representing the 'Indian community' in proper terms to the surrounding society. Incessantly in conflict with the white authorities, Indian organisations strove to create physical and social spaces for leisure and cultural performances and to facilitate frequent visits of cultural performers and religious preachers from the subcontinent. What was at stake was the right to practice and perform Indian culture *within* 'community spaces' and a desire to represent a unified community to wider society, whereas the issue of recognition of the aesthetic qualities of Indian culture from the supremacist, or at best paternalist, white culture, hardly was an issue at this juncture.

The late 1940s was a defining moment for Indians in South Africa. Apartheid became the ruling ideology after 1948, and the National Party began to revive older repatriation schemes for Indians as they were viewed as 'alien' to Africa. On top of this, serious riots in Durban in 1949 where African workers attacked Indian homes all over the city and left more than a hundred casualties and thousands homeless, dealt a blow to the expanding and vivacious Indian culture in Durban. Faced with a cultural boycott that severed the ties with India; a hostile urban policy that systematically destroyed the sprawling Indian neighbourhoods and relocated Indians to new townships south and north of the city; and, with legislations that made interracial interaction very difficult, the Indian community seemed to 'cocoon' and close ranks.

However, as the apartheid state began to develop and implement the doctrine of separate development in the late 1950s, the issue of Indians as non-indigenous was played down and Indians were now to be governed through culturally-specific institutions. Not only were Indians for the first time in the history of the country granted citizenship in 1961, they were also 'Indianised', allotted space and institutional arenas for classical culture, airtime for Bollywood film music on the radio, a radio station for Indians was created, religious practices and performances were encouraged and subsidised, as was the study of Indian classics—religious texts, music, theatre, etc.—at the educational institutions designated for Indians. This project of converting race into space, of physical separation of race groups, and of separate governance was systematically implemented. Separate development ethnicized the races, it sought to produce its own cause, and orientalised the Indians, not by viewing them as belonging to the subcontinent anymore, but as specifically South African and thus more modern and rational in their cultural and religious practices than those in the Indian subcontinent.

It was indeed the policy of the apartheid state to create a conservative Indian elite that could act as a junior partner to the whites, and thus the promotion of a classical, aesthetic 'taste-culture' in the rapidly growing Indian middle class was integral to this strategy. This resonated well with deeply ingrained notions of cultural and social supremacy on part of the so-called 'merchant class', the wealthy and successful descendants of the Gujarati and north Indian passenger Indians vis-à-vis the often dark complexioned lower-caste descendants of indentured labourers who constituted the bulk of the Indian working class in Durban.

The sheer weight and determination of the apartheid project and the worldwide resistance against it meant that most writings on identity in South Africa, at least until recently, have been influenced by a critique of official categories and attempts to repudiate widely held and authorised stereotyped knowledge of ethnic differences in the country. This has meant a relative paucity of explorations of the complex structures of recognition and everyday mythologies through which ethnic and racial groups have been reproduced for decades.[1] This silence has been reinforced by the relatively strong trend among Indian intellectuals to identify with the wider ideology of non-racialism and thus downplay, if not explain away, racial-cultural differences as mere smokescreens covering up real issues of state repression and capitalist exploitation. For the very articulate group of Indians who opposed apartheid and resolutely 'de-ethnicised' themselves (and some of whom today play a significant role in the African National Congress [ANC]), the reproduction of Indian ethnicity was always a source of embarrassment.

Debates among Indians in Durban and elsewhere in the country concerning the recognition, or lack thereof, of Indians in South Africa seem, in other words, suspended between two forms of recognition. Externally,

---

[1] For a good history of the Indian working class in Durban with a predominantly economic/materialist perspective, see Freund (1995). Ashwin Desai's passionately argued *Arise ye Coolies* (1996) focuses on the deep class divides in the 'community'.

there is the contradictory desire of performing in what we can call the 'white gaze'—that is, to be accepted, or at least acknowledged by what is still called a 'dominant' or even 'mainstream' white culture. This desire is compounded by a longstanding fear of what is widely regarded among many Indians as the intrinsic violence and aggressive sexuality of Africans, combined with often racist and sometimes supremacist contempt for everything African.

Internally, one finds a set of debates in community organisations, in the 'Indian public sphere'—the web of Indian newspapers, radio stations and local weeklies—about transformations internal to the 'community', revolving around issues such as the imaginings of the 'motherland', the erosion of proper cultural practices, the divides between generations, worries about westernisation of the youth and the corruption of sexual mores, the internecine struggles between religious communities or Tamils and Hindi speakers, although hardly anyone uses Indian vernaculars as home languages anymore, and so on.

The separation of these two types of concerns and dynamics among Indians in South Africa has to do with the profound sense of enclosure and minoritisation that prevails and imposes itself as a dominant agenda on any discussion of what it means to be Indian in the country. The public arena in the Indian community is truly closed to the gaze of other groups. It is unknown, but not hidden—just not considered interesting, let alone appealing to people outside. To many whites it is still the murky world of the 'coolie', or an exotic but alien world of customs and practices; while the world of the *charou* (a derogatory Afrikaans slang for Indians that now is used as an affectionate and culturally intimate term) neither appear friendly, nor open to Africans.

As I moved to Durban in 1998 and wanted to subscribe to the city's two Indian weeklies it was difficult to convince the woman (herself an Indian) at the front desk of Independent Newspapers of Kwa Zulu Natal that it was not a mistake. I tried to explain that I was not just an ignorant foreigner understanding nothing, but actually wanted this newspaper brought to me. 'But you will find it very Indian, sir—you know, dance, films, recipes and all.' 'Yes, exactly', I said. She smiled, half embarrassed, accepted my money but clearly had doubts about my mental condition.

Sheltered by this dismissive or hostile indifference, Indians have developed traditions, musical forms, slang and a whole set of socio-cultural codes that are quite unique. Most see themselves as authentically Indian, but many cultural practices are far removed from the cultural practices and traditions of Bihar and Tamil Nadu which the indentured labourers brought with them in the nineteenth century. The modern Indian urban culture in Durban, Johannesburg and Pietermaritzburg is heavily structured by white working-class culture, linguistic influence from Zulu and Afrikaans and of course English—more so than most Indians would like to admit.

A glance inside the large Indian townships around Durban reveals a popular life that is not in accordance with 'Eastern' culture per se. It is, rather, a working-class culture appreciating products of the lower end of the commercial Indian film and music market—and from the 1960s increasingly western pop music, and later American TV shows and soaps. The leading Indian newspaper in the country, *The Post*, started in the 1950s as *Natal Post*, a hard-hitting tabloid with crime, sensation and pin-up girls catering mainly for the white working class. It became immensely popular with Indian workers, and gradually emerged into an Indian family newspaper in the 1980s. Much of what is considered Indian—family structure, vernaculars, ways of dressing, observance of religious rituals, and appreciation of Indian cultural products—have been vanishing over the last decade to be replaced by a more commercially packaged consumer culture with an occasional Indian tinge.

One of the few media that consistently transcended class and language and remained the mega signifier of Indianness in this context is, however, Bollywood productions. Film music played a central role in the gradual production of modern, urban Indian communities in the Durban region. It still constitutes the core of the experience of community through film viewing. Orchestras such as the Ranjeni orchestra were heroes in Durban for decades, copying Hindi film songs from cinema halls and performing them at functions and weddings in ubiquitous community halls. Repeated viewing of the same revered films produced an 'insider culture', though far from being as intense as in India, it made Durban's Indian cinema halls important meeting places where young people and families indulged in the intense experience of the sound and the music.[2] In some ways the film songs became the true secret of the community, something that required a command over colloquialisms and insider perspectives—unlike classical culture which was open to the white gaze and ears. Film music marked a zone of the truly ethnic-popular, a zone of enjoyment and *jouissance*, a license to indulge in things Indian without excuses, a strong sense of marking 'our space' and 'our tunes'—an indulgence in the ethnic always

[2] For a treatment of this period see Vashna Jagarnath (2002).

more associated with the working class, but also shared by the nascent Indian elite and middle class.

To my mind, Herzfelds notion of 'cultural intimacy'—the inside of the lives and practices of the nation or the ethnic group that are 'ours' but also somewhat excessive, too ethnic or too crude and thus a source of embarrassment—fits rather nicely here (Herzfeld, 1997: 1–36). It is a cultural zone that is open and yet closed, something many Indian South Africans are a bit ashamed of. To be a *charou* is associated with superstition, gullibility, funny accents, ridiculous submission to the white *baas*, etc.—something that forms the staple of humour at the Indian community theatre I have written about in a different context (Hansen, 2000).

The interest in Indian films declined in the 1970s along with the decline of Indian vernaculars as home languages. Today, less than 4 per cent of Indians, mainly Muslim Gujaratis report that they use Indian vernaculars as home languages. The decline in the viewing of Indian films was squarely linked to generations, as most of those who viewed Indian films and enjoyed the music were middle-aged or above, while the interest among young people in Bollywood was on a steady decline in the 1980s and 1990s.

Previously, the Indian part of the city had four big cinemas, but now only one cinema, Isfahan, is left in the city centre. This was linked to the video revolution and one finds a broad range of Indian films on offer in video shops in Indian neighbourhoods. However, the cinema complexes in large Indian townships of Chatsworth and Phoenix screen the standard Hollywood fare as elsewhere in the country. The interest in Indian films has continued to decline also after 1994 when restrictions on trade between India and South Africa were formally lifted. But *KKHH* changed this longstanding trend dramatically.

The leading retailer of Hindi film cassettes and other Indian cultural goods in South Africa, Roopanands, informed me that even huge Hindi blockbusters only sold a mere 500 cassettes all over the country. By contrast *KKHH* sold 5,000 in only two months. It was as the owner said, '... truly extraordinary, something we hope is the beginning of a trend that can reverse the decline, but we are not sure'.

When one reads Indian newspapers one gets an impression of wide interest in Indian cultural products. But until quite recently most Indians did not listen to Radio Lotus or watch Indian films. Many younger Indians did not like to think of themselves as particularly Indian as their parents used to do, but were rather more fond of either African-American music styles or the contemporary Indian dance music and aesthetics emanating from places like London, Toronto or Melbourne. As we shall see ahead, this has begun to change over the last few years and *KKHH* has played an important role in this change.

In the Gaze of the Other

The public culture of post-apartheid South Africa is still deeply racially segmented but at the same time governed by a new sense of the careful use of language, symbols and phrases and a range of attempts at approaching the 'others' through their cultural artefacts, food, art and music. Many changes are underway, particularly the ways in which African-American styles of music, dress and language seem to provide an emerging cultural lingua franca among younger people—whites, blacks, coloureds and Indians—in the country.[3] Derogatory terms as 'curry muncher' or *charou* are used with a humorous twist in advertisements for restaurants. Formerly, 'white newspapers' abounded with recipes of Indian food and connoisseur advice on spices that previously only could be found in the 'extras', the weekly inserts catering to Indian concerns and taste in the 'mainstream' Sunday papers—maybe in themselves arresting metaphors of the situation of Indians in South Africa.

The interesting thing about *KKHH* was the way in which it bridged the well-established patterns of cultural consumption among Indians—the 'high' and classical taste culture also appreciating western quality products, and the 'low' culture, either too westernised and culturally illiterate in the eyes of the elite, or too ethnic, too Bollywood, known as the 'masala of the aunties'. *KKHH* was a modern Indian film, the West implanted to India, recognisable in dress, forms of school, of dance, of music, summer camps, everyday slang and thus suited for a quest for recognition from white culture by being white, but not quite, and with a tantalising Indian tinge. One of the many 'public secrets' (see Taussig, 1999) in Durban is that many Indians have developed a strong identification with white culture, and share many white fears and phobias in connection with Africans. This elective affinity with whiteness which is a 'social fact' but difficult to debate or articulate has produced a heightened sensitivity to any derogatory remarks from whites in public. Indian identity dynamics are, again more pronounced than in many other places, structured around what Hegel called 'the desire of the desire of the other', in this case the desire of a favourable white gaze.

[3] In South Africa, coloured is an official category for the 'mixed race' people (Khoisan, Malay, Whites, Africans). During apartheid, this group was governed separately, with their own townships, institutions and areas.

In Alexander Kojève's reading of Hegel's master-slave dialectic (Hegel, 1977: 111–119), he emphasises that what is desired by the slave is 'the desire of the desire of the other'—that is, the recognition (*annerkennung*) of his humanity, and thus his desirability, by the master. The slave asks the master, 'See me as who I am', and constitutes his own identity through this confrontation with the other. In Kojève's dramatic and teleological reading, it is the slaves—that is, the ordinary human beings—who move history and are the truly creative figures *qua* their tremendous drive towards recognition and freedom. The masters (the élites, the aristocracy) on their side are doomed as they have nothing to strive for, the recognition they strive for may be easily given but worthless because it is given by slaves and only reproduces the master as what he already is (Kojève, 1969: 45–55).

As it has been pointed out by Jacques Lacan, this compelling logic of identity is always incomplete. If the subject is born in the encounter with the desire of the other, its identity depends on the character of this desire, that is, the gaze of the other, understood here as what Lacan terms the symbolic order or 'the Law': authorities, dominant discourses, social conventions, etc. This gaze, the other's desire, cannot be fully fathomed and understood and the subject is therefore bound to be a subject of radical doubt and uncertainty (Lacan, 1977: 293–324). Slavoj Zizek argues that this uncertainty defines the subject and suspends it between anxiety and desire.

> Anxiety is aroused by the desire of the Other in the sense that 'I do not know what *objet a*[4] I am for the desire of the other'. What does the Other want from me, what is there—in me more than myself—on account of which I am the object of desire of the Other (Zizek, 1994: 71).

What is posed to the other is therefore not 'see me as what I am' (because I cannot know), but rather the probing and anxious question, *ché vuoi?* 'What do you see in me?'

Subjectivity is bound to take shape in this gaze, or desire, that cannot be fully fathomed and the answer to this dilemma is what Zizek terms 'anticipatory identification'—that we become what we think we are in

[4] In Lacanian usage, the *objet petit a* stands for the irreducible sign of the Real—that is the frightening and fascinating dimensions which cannot be symbolised and encompassed within a prevailing social-cultural order, and therefore prevents the closure of identities and cultural horizons.

eyes of the other. Instead of waiting anxiously for a symbolic mandate to arrive, to be hailed and thus become subject, as Louis Althusser would have had it, human beings often anticipate the signs by which they are known to, and desired by, the other.

> Anticipatory identification is therefore a kind of pre-emptive strike, an attempt to provide in advance an answer to 'what I am for the Other' and thus to assuage the anxiety that pertains to the desire of the Other (Zizek,1994: 76).

KKHH and the way it inscribed its viewers as Indians, but modern and middle class, offered Indians in South Africa an opportunity to make such a pre-emptive strike and to inhabit more comfortably the identity space that they already had been assigned by dominant orientalising discourses in South Africa. Consider this letter from a retired school principal to the editor of *The Post* regarding *KKHH*:

> For the enjoyment of non-Indians who have already developed a palate for Indian cuisine and have begun to notice the beauty of Indian belles, Kuch Kuch Hota Hai ought to be televised. It would help to modify the negative perceptions some people have of Indians (from letter to the editor, in *The Post*, 20–23 January 1999).

A part of the thrill of *KKHH* was that it presented images of a supposedly Indian form of modernity that many local Indians felt comfortable with, and that it displayed female beauty and elegance of designs and sets—essentially commodities marketed as India's contribution to the global cultural economy (see also Brosius, this volume).

In the debates unfolding around the phenomenon an exuberant reader of *The Post* referred to *KKHH* as, 'a thousand times better than most of what passes as entertainment in mainstream cinemas—no sex, no copulation, violence—only pure love and true emotions'. Some defended the simplicity, if not banality, of the plot by pointing out that '... even Shakespeare used simple stories', while others stressed the important emotional appeal such films has to Indians living abroad. A letter to the editor went:

> It gave me goose bumps and made me feel proud to be an Indian. It is of particular significance to an ex-patriot (sic!) Indian such as us who live out of the motherland and sometimes lose touch with values that should be dear to all true Indians (*The Post*, 17–20 March 1999).

Another part of the exhilaration had to do with the occupation of formerly white spaces. The Kings Park stadium was hired for a show with the four stars of the film, marketed as the *Awesome Foursome* doing the dance routines and playback songs. An excited journalist wrote '... usually Kings Park is full of biltong munching and beer drinking rugby fans, but soon it will be the scene of a colourful and exotic world class show'. The space normally occupied by unsophisticated white working-class men would now give way to the Indian middle class enjoying a 'world class show'. Indians flocked to Musgrave centre to watch the movie in a formerly 'white' and elite space, often along with whites, despite the fact that it was difficult to get tickets. Throughout its run, the film was screened in a small hall which explains why it was sold out most of the time—the rumour of which again had the self-perpetuating effect of attracting even more viewers.

The address of *KKHH* was part of a wave of Indian music and films successfully catering to communities of migrant Indians and larger audiences around the world. Bollywood, in this tailor-made and utopian fashion, provides a space wherein images of the modern city, 'westernised' habits and bodily gestures can be reconciled with romantic notions of India, and thus domesticated as acceptable ways of being Indian.

The importance of this film lies, therefore, in the intersection of the two dynamics I have outlined: the internal circulation and debates on what proper Indianness is and should be, and the external dimension, the representation of the community, of India and Indian culture as such to a larger South African audience. The film was welcomed by so many because it served to make the Indian community visible and recognised on the basis of its distinct cultural heritage, suitably modernised, de-ethnicised and packaged to suit the tastes of so-called cosmopolitan audiences.

The ANC's official denouncing of ethnicity and its simultaneous celebration of an 'African renaissance' that officially embraces the cultural diversity of the country is deeply contradictory. One paradoxical effect is that assertions of 'Indianness' and signs of 'Indian culture', have acquired new importance. This has been picked up by, amongst others, cultural organisations, business operators and a whole host of shows, musical performances, dresses, who use the music, the names of stars, etc., to launch entertainment, fundraising and so forth. When the Hindi Shiksha Sangh, a reputed organisation promoting Hindi language and north Indian classical culture, celebrated its 50th anniversary in 1999, the highlight of the show was a copy-band playing the *KKHH* songs. Many others took it up, including political parties around the general elections in 1999. Ela Gandhi, granddaughter of Mohandas Gandhi, and today an MP for ANC recorded an election song on the *KKHH* song, called *Kuch Kuch ANC*. Ela Gandhi who sang the tune with a somewhat thin voice, stated:

> There are a lot of freedom songs in African languages but nothing really in English or for the Indian community .... The movie did so well, people identify with it and it conveys important themes of sacrifice, love and non-violence. It also brought out the colonial mentality that some people suffer from which make them think that only the white man can do things (*The Post*, 23 May 1999).

The problem with this new exhibition of 'Indian culture' was, and still remains, that many Indians cannot really fathom what the new nation expects from them, how they should behave like proper citizens in the gaze of the new politically-dominant African elite. South African public culture is clearly no longer just white. Public discourses on nationhood and patriotism are strongly influenced by the Africanist rhetoric promoted by President Mbeki, but also by more conservative and nativist stances represented by traditional leaders and the Inkatha Freedom Party, among others. There is, as Jean and John Comaroff (2001) have pointed out a noticeable move towards linking notions of autochthony and assumed proximity to nature directly to rights to the land and to the nation. Different Indian quests for recognition seem to be haunted by an immense insecurity and an acute awareness of not being autochthonous people of Africa. The question that implicitly is asked all time is 'what do you want from me?'

Do Indians have a claim to citizenship and belonging because they too were non-white and therefore oppressed by the apartheid regime, as Indian organisations have argued? Or because they, or at least some Indians, also participated in the struggle against apartheid? Or should they, as Mbeki requested a group of Indians during the election campaign in 1999, try to become 'African' first, and then Indian. 'Why can't you just call yourself African Indians?', he asked and assured the audience that such a gesture would make a major difference. Nobody in the audience seemed, however, to seriously believe that assurance. Even in ANC circles this attempt to rename Indians never carried any success.

Other Indians try to consolidate their position by strengthening links to diasporic networks and with India, or in the case of Muslims to global Muslim organisations, partly in the vain hope of some protection from the xenophobic and clearly anti-Indian atmosphere that conservative organisations like the Inkatha increasingly espouse. In March 1999, the leading Zulu language newspaper *Ilanga* ran an editorial with a rabid anti-Indian content. The editorial ended with the rhetorical question: 'When will a new Idi Amin be born from the womb of a Zulu woman?' In the face of an impending election, the editor lost his job, but it became clear to many Indians that such sentiments indeed existed and occasionally were articulated within the 'Zulu public sphere'—a network of newspapers, radio stations and publishing houses that, by virtue of language, is effectively closed to most whites and Indians. The fears of Zulu hostility were once again fuelled when the well-known 'struggle-poet' and song-writer Mbongeni Ngema, in May 2002, released a song called *amaNdiya* (Zulu for Indians). In rather crude lyrics the song accuses Indians of being oppressors and worse than the whites.[5]

But let us take a look 'inside' the community first.

Who are we Indians, after all?

In the vivid debates unfolding around the film the earlier rift between a 'classicised' taste culture and a popular enjoyment of film tunes was displaced and reconfigured around another rift, partly gendered and partly generational. On the one side were elderly or middle-aged men criticising the depletion of true Indian values by the film, or denouncing it for being too silly, banal, and displaying the worst sides of Indian culture. On the other side were younger women, and some men, who had strong feelings and attachments to the fantasy space that *KKHH* had offered them. They reacted strongly against criticism of *KKHH* in letters to the editor and the various talk shows and radio debates on the phenomenon.

'Don't criticise our heroes just because they are not yours (...) you don't understand our world', a young girl said angrily to a university intellectual who criticised what he saw as an unbearable lightness in the film's story line. 'It touched our hearts, brought tears to our eyes (...) that is enough for me', said a middle-aged housewife. And another women said 'I'm glad

[5] In the English translation, the lyrics go: 'Oh, brothers, oh, my fellow brothers/ We need strong and brave men to confront the Indians/This (situation) is very difficult/ Indians don't want to change/ Whites were better than Indians/ Even Mandela has failed to make them change.' The incident received intense press coverage, see, for example, newspaper archives at www.iol.co.za.

I saw it (...) it brought me a happiness and warmth I hadn't experiences for years ....'

Even a former hard-nosed Trotskyite and labour activist, who hosted the popular talk show, *Viewpoint*, at Radio Lotus had to give in after he saw the film. He started an hour-long debate on air by saying, 'I felt the warmth of this story, it made you believe in real values again, that there indeed is true love and friendship to be found out there.' Then the floodgates opened. Masses of people called in, mostly women, some men as well—sometimes critical of 'the mass hysteria' as one said, others defending the right of women to be sentimental about such things. 'I went with my mum and sister', a young man said, 'I thought the film was well made, as good as any American film, but I did not cry like her. But she was happy afterwards, so what is wrong in that?' he asked.

Unmistakably and often unstated, the debate revolved around the painful negotiation of the nuclear family and its ideal foundation in enduring romance between two unattached individuals. The heavily mythologised institution of 'the Indian family'—joint, comprising several generations, tight-knit, controlled but warm and giving and at the heart of any claim to 'Indian culture'—has been breaking down in Durban's Indian townships for several decades. The ideal of the nuclear family has become the norm among younger people along with higher levels of education among both men and women. In addition, a new and more hedonistic and promiscuous youth culture has emerged among all communities in the liberal post-apartheid society. Yet, strongly patriarchal structures still pervade most cultures in the country and rape and other forms of sexual violence against women have become the most widely reported crimes in South Africa. Among ordinary *charous* in the Indian townships, however, ideals of the submissive Indian woman still persist in the face of the rapidly changing gender relationships. In combination with the widespread ownership of guns among Indians, this tends to produce staggering rates of so-called 'love-murders'—mostly men killing their wives/lovers/ex-girlfriends. Although these and other domestic crimes are ubiquitous in South Africa, the phenomenon of 'love murders' has become particularly widespread in the Indian townships.

Another part of the debate was about whether the film was typically Indian or not. For some, *KKHH* was a typical Indian film and thus represented a long overlooked genre with universal messages—comparable to Shakespeare, as several participants in the debate claimed. To critics it was exactly the fact that it was typical, its unbearable ethnicity and connotations of gossiping aunties and Indian 'backwardness', superficiality, etc., which was its main problem and limitation. A male schoolteacher told me:

> I find this film tasteless and crude. Don't you think that Indians can do better than that? We have been telling our kids for years that there are as good as any white kid … then people praise this film which shows Indians as, well, amateur clowns, if you ask me.

Others welcomed the film because they thought it was atypical, that now, at last, there was an Indian film one could relate to and enjoy because of its western frame. Yet, for others of a more conservative persuasion this was precisely the problem of *KKHH*—what commentator Yogin Devan called its 'cheap aping' of a western form:

> While the pastel-coloured sari's [*sic*] and blouses worn by Tina were beautiful to admire, the fuddy-duddy in me would not easily accept the clothes worn by the students at Xavier's College. Who in Mumbai goes to college in a silver lame miniskirt or tight disco hot pants ... the actresses resorted to cheap clingy western clothes. I quickly blamed it all on India's recently adopted open economic policy and free trading (*Tribune Herald*, 24 January 1999).

The core audience of the film, those who saw it several times were mainly younger people, generally disinterested in politics and with rather vague ideas about what Indian culture was supposed to mean. For them, the main novelty was that, because of the subtitles, they could for the first time understand and follow the dialogue of a Hindi film. A young man said to me, 'Now we understand a little better the gibberish of the aunties.' Riashney, a student from a Tamil background told me:

> We grew up with both Hindi and Tamil films but I rarely watched them. They were on the video when the family was together, my mother and aunts would sing some of the old songs and talk about their youth, but it meant nothing to me. To be honest, I always found the old films terribly silly. I never understood their humour.

Many younger people enjoyed this new sense of understanding of a medium they had experienced throughout their lives as series of images, music and words, mostly unintelligible, as a part of the family home, family gatherings, etc.—a sphere of Indianness, whether Hindu or Tamil, belonging to an older generation. But with *KKHH*, this Indianness was no longer a source of embarrassment, no longer a sign of a backward, working-class and excessively ethnic and alien culture displaying aesthetics and heroes out of tune with western taste. The new type of Indian male stars also appealed to broader audiences. *KKHH* was, in the words of a 15-year-old girl, '... a film I could invite my white classmates to see with me. They liked it, especially to look at Shah Rukh Khan.'

Another interesting thing was the absence of discussions on the content of the film. Was it too simple or banal, or was the storyline unimportant? It seemed to me that the storyline and the characters were much less important than the atmosphere, the state of mind, the sentimentality and visceral register evoked as such by the film, not least the music and the songs. The reliance on viscerality rather than on plot, on music and songs rather than on characters is a well-known facet of the 'culture of viewing' in India. In South Africa, however, this 'reading competence' was not in existence among the younger audiences. Besides, the sentiments evoked by *KKHH* related to other and more specifically local dimensions. First, the desire to inhabit the 'white gaze' in a favourable way. Second, because it spoke to what I will call the 'People of Indian Origin' fantasy of India,[6] not Indians in the western world, but the fourth and fifth generation descendants of indentured labourers and others who had no experience of, or active relations to, India.

KKHH was an enticing sign because it spoke to a fantasy of India widely held among Indians in South Africa, an India devoid of squalor, dirt and chaos. Paradoxically, this fantasy seems actually to be nurtured by the South African Indian's confrontations with the real India through travel and roots-tourism. These encounters either produce hyper-rationalist and utterly insensitive statements about what India is like, how dirty it is, how much damage the modern world has done to Indians in the subcontinent, etc., or as spiritual sublimation of India into a huge exotic sign under which everything is imbued with a special significance (see Hansen, 2001).

To inhabit the fantasy space of *KKHH*, or the two weeks air-conditioned whirlwind tour of India, seemed at least to elicit surprisingly parallel

[6] People of Indian Origin (PIO) is a category that was defined in 1989 by the Global Organization of People of Indian Origin (GOPIO) an organisation created by businessmen and public figures with Rightist and Hindu nationalist leanings. The government in India dominated by the Hindu nationalist BJP began in 1999 to issue so-called PIO cards, kind of quasi-passports giving a range of rights to PIOs in India, barring the right to vote.

commentaries and emotions for some. Consider the affinity between the following two statements about India as an experience: Neena who had been to India many times as a devotee of Sai Baba told me:

> For me everything in India is wonderful, the pace of life, the landscape, the way people go about life—there is something spiritual about it, as if people are at peace with themselves. After some days in India, I also get this feeling of being calm and relaxed and happy. This is the spirituality we lack in this country and in our community people have nothing but petty envy and jealousy to put instead.

And this statement from Uma, a college student, about why she had seen the film nine times:

> I have seen this film nine times, and I know every detail in it. But I would not hesitate to go a tenth time because it brings me such good feeling of hope, of goodness, a feeling of being at ease with myself—something that lasts for days after I have seen the movie.

I am not suggesting that the film functions as an illusory dream escape from the hardships of everyday life. My suggestion is simply that the film feeds into the ongoing search for ways of being Indian in South Africa that does not appear as 'un-patriotic', or overly 'ethnic', another term with negative connotations. The inherent discrepancy between the 'inscribed viewer' position of the easy-going modern diasporic Indian and the 'actual viewers' of young and anxious South African Indians in the townships simply opened a space for this negotiation of identity. *KKHH* gave a glimpse of the possibility of being a modern 'diasporic Indian' in contemporary South Africa. The success and approval of the film from non-Indians gave hope that distinctly non-autochthonous cultural practices could be respected in a country where multicultural policies, notions of 'minority' as well as Indian ethnicity have been compromised by apartheid.

Between Autochthony and Diaspora

It seems clear that a film like *KKHH*, produced in India to cater both to domestic and diasporic tastes and fantasies, works as a complex screen upon which very diverse ideas of Indianness and modernity are projected. In India itself, it is rather obvious that this and other films in the genre have little if any relationship to the actual lived reality of the country. When I discussed the *KKHH* phenomenon with a well-known writer on Hindi cinema, he said jokingly, 'Oh, but these people in Durban have taken this film far too literally.' His point was, of course, that the absence of a 'reading competence' among young Indians in Durban made them see this film, produced within the conventions of a rather light-hearted and 'over the top' genre, as a grand story of true love and romance, loaded with significance and signs of Indianness.

Second, the phenomenon also raises the by now old question of what 'diasporic' means. Some, like the Indian intellectual Tejaswini Niranjana, who have worked with literature and artistic products, regard South African Indians as diasporic because there are groups actively involved in interactions and exchange of goods, signs and symbols with India—which would be a possible definition of a 'diasporic' relationship. This is indeed true of elite groups, particularly Gujarati communities who throughout the twentieth century built and maintained networks in Africa and across the Indian Ocean. It is not true, however, of the average Indian middle-class family in Durban (more than half of all Indians in the country today live what could be defined as a middle-class life)[7] who also provided the crucial audience for *KKHH*. For them, India is immensely distant—at best a part of a family history, and the true signs of ethnicity lie in local religious practices and institutions, of pressure for arranged marriages, food habits, and the cultural preferences of their parents and older people, including Hindi or Tamil films. While many Indians have tried to de-ethnicize themselves in the last decades, to adopt 'white' lifestyles, the immense insecurity and new possibilities opened in the last decade in South Africa have also brought about a quest for the re-marking of bodies, territories and social practices in cultural terms. But India is nowhere in the picture as an object of identification, and even less as a destination of emigration. India is widely conceptualised as a destination for sentimentalised roots-tourism, for shopping in Mumbai or for visits to ashrams by individuals belonging to neo-Hindu movements like the Ramakrishna Mission or devotees of Sai Baba.

[7] Every available statistical evidence supports this. Although masking deep class differences, the data on the Indian community as a whole shows that Indians have average incomes only slightly lower than whites, that they are the best educated group in the country, and that the frequency of ownership of houses, cars, telephones, etc., is high and only second to the very high material standard of living of white South Africans (*South Africa Survey 2000/2001*, South African Institute of Race Relations, Johannesburg, 2001).

KKHH portrayed a dreamy and hazy but also more attractive space of recognition: a global Indian diasporic space imagined to be more hospitable and generous than South Africa, yet distinctly Indian and modern. The fascination of *KKHH* thus correlates closely to the fact that the numerous young Indians leaving South Africa each year do not merely follow 'white' emigration. They head for the big centres of 'diasporic' Indian culture—Melbourne, Toronto, London and New York. South Africa is increasingly experienced as an 'alien-nation', as Comaroff and Comaroff (2001) have put it, and this pushes South African Indians in the country towards identifying with other entities. The virtual, floating and rather abstract sense of being Indian articulated through sensuous and visceral signifiers such as films, music or religious devotion appear much more attractive and non-controversial than conventional notions of lineage, blood or political loyalty. This resonates more clearly with what Steven Vertovec (2000) calls 'diaspora as a mode of cultural production' which nonetheless also revolves around themes of renewing and recasting the meanings of 'Indian culture' in the face of its absence in everyday life.

Subsequent developments in Durban have corroborated the significance of the transformation *KKHH* brought about in the reception and circulation of Indian films in South Africa. Both the large cinema corporations dominating the distribution of films in the country now screen subtitled Indian films in the large 'mainstream' cinema complexes in Durban, Johannesburg, Pietermaritzburg etc. Blockbusters such as *Lagaan: Once Upon a Time in India* (dir. Ashutosh Gowarikar, 2001) and *Ashoka* (dir. Santosh Sivan, 2004) attracted massive audiences—white and Indian. A large newly-opened cinema complex in Durban's northern suburbs depends heavily on the four to five Indian films it constantly screens. Hindi cinema has become an integrated part of Durban's urban culture that today is effectively shared by Indians and some whites. Indians are now preponderant in formerly white institutional and commercial spaces and much more accepted by the whites in the city than ever before. In large parts of the Arab world and Africa, Hindi cinema has become a vital and integral part of popular culture and the producer of narratives of morality, gender and family values (see Larkin, this volume). Yet, the deep running racialisation of cultural practices in South Africa mean that there are few signs of Indian cinema becoming a similar medium of entertainment and visceral engagement between the city's Indian and African world.

COMAROFF, J. and J. COMAROFF. 2001. 'Naturing the Nation: Aliens, Apocalypse and the Postcolonial State', *Journal of Southern African Studies*, 27(3): 627–51.

DESAI, ASHWIN. 1996. *Arise ye Coolies: Apartheid and the Indian 1960–1995*. Johannesburg: Impact Africa Publishing.

FREUND, BILL. 1995. *Insiders and Outsiders: The Indian Working Class of Durban 1910–1990*. London: James Currey.

HANSEN, THOMAS, B. 2000. 'Plays and Politics: Cultural Identity and Politics among South African Indians', *Journal of Southern African Studies*, 26(2).

———. 2001. '"Why can't They Clean the Streets?" Roots-tourism and Notions of Modernity among South African Indians', paper given at the Conference Migration and Modernity in South Asia, University of Sussex, 8–9 January 2001. An abridged version of this was published under the title 'Diasporic Dispositions', *Himal*, December 2002, pp. 12–20.

HEGEL, G.F. 1977. *The Phenomenology of Spirit*. Trans. A.V. Miller. Oxford: OUP.

HERZFELD, MICHAEL. 1997. *Cultural Intimacy: Social Poetics in the Nation-State*. New York: Routledge.

JAGARNATH, VASHNA. 2002. 'Indian Cinema in Durban: Urban Segregation, Business and Visions of Identity from the 1950s to the 1970s', in P. Kaarsholm Roskilde (ed.), *City Flicks: Cinema, Urban Worlds and Modernities in India and Beyond*, Occasional Paper No. 22, International Development Studies.

KOJÈVE, ALEXANDER. 1969. *Introduction to the Reading of Hegel*. New York: Basic Books.

LACAN, JACGUES. 1977. *Ecrits. A Selection*. Trans. A. Sheridan. New York/London: W.W. Norton & Co.

METZ, CHRISTIAN. 1982. *Psychoanalysis and the Cinema: The Imaginary Signifier*. London: Macmillan.

MISHRA, VIJAY. 1985. 'Towards a Theoretical Critique of Bombay Cinema', *Screen*, 26(314): 133–46.

NIRANJANA, TEJASWINI. 1997. 'Left to the Imagination', *Small Axe*, 1(2).

RAJADHYAKSHA, ASHISH. 2000. 'Viewership and Democracy in the Cinema', in Ravi S. Vasudevan (ed.), *Making Meaning in Indian Cinema*, pp. 267–96, New Delhi: OUP.

TAUSSIG, MICHAEL. 1999. *Defacement: Public Secrecy and the Labour of the Negative*. Stanford: Stanford University Press.

VERTOVEC, STEVEN. 2000. *The Hindu Diaspora: Comparative Patterns*. London: Routledge.

ZIZEK, SLAVOJ. 1994. *Tarrying with the Negative*. Durham: Duke University Press.

11

Belonging and Respect Notions vis-à-vis Modern East Indians: Hindi Movies in the Guyanese East Indian Diaspora

NARMALA HALSTEAD

Respect notions provide a significant framework for how Bollywood Hindi movies speak to the contradictions of belonging in the Guyanese East Indian Diaspora in Guyana and New York.[1] Guyanese East Indians see the *role* of the Indian woman in these movies to be personified, in particular, by the themes of duty and respect, specifically, but not exclusively to

[1] The data is drawn from ethnographic research in Guyana on the rural West Bank Demerara and the city, Georgetown between 1995 and 1999; and in Queens, New York, between 1999 and 2002. I began to visit Queens on a regular basis from 1990. In both Guyana and New York, I met with families in their homes. Further, I participated in public functions and social gatherings and met with East Indians in business settings. I was also able to draw on prior understanding of the use of Hindi movies in Guyana, as a Guyanese East Indian who has lived in Georgetown for many years (see Halstead, 2001). I also draw on my experiences from my involvement in a family television station in Guyana.

I discuss the data in relation to both young and old men and women which also allows for different conceptions of the modern to emerge. The different localities provided for varying approaches to how East Indians considered themselves as 'modern' and the ways an idea of America resided alongside 'Indian culture'. These differences could be conceptualised in terms of 'status' which was also the common theme between the East Indians in all these localities. In 'Better Prospects', on the West Bank Demerara, status

her husband.[2] Their emphasis on respect notions, however, provides for key patterns which encompass not just women, but also men and children and where prayer and duty are projected as central to their performance of culture. Many Guyanese East Indians see the Hindi movie focus on respect notions as providing a collaborative role model for how they want to be Indian. The issue of authenticity is, in this context, expressed in the need to perform rituals in the correct way (see Halstead, 2000, 2001; Jayawardena, 1980).

However, this professed role of the Hindi movie is in itself a point of departure in terms of how these East Indians understand themselves as modern, act for and against culture, and where they see themselves as part of the 'West'. The contradiction in this representation and role of Hindi movies is evident in the way East Indians move in and out of an ethnic identity, where they perform for and against culture and where authenticity is about how well they can claim the 'foreign' (Halstead, 2002). This is a contradiction which also allows the Hindi movie to similarly move in and out of its ethnicised identity. It is seen to be 'too modern' to represent Indian culture. Further, those who belong as 'modern people' rely on this ambiguity to inhabit a home that is imagined elsewhere (Lovell, 1989; Olwig, 1998; Rapport and Dawson, 1998). In these contradictory forms of belonging, the representative capacity of the Hindi movie becomes transformed from signifying Indian culture to personifying 'western decadence'. This explicitly representative role is also mediated through a *filmi* culture, where people want to behave like the superstars of the Hindi screen, in terms of 'romancing' and performing the song-and-dance routines.

Being modern has to be problematised in terms of an idea of progress and specific competence and knowledge and as decadence where the

---

performances depended both on how well East Indians maintained 'respect' and their connections with a global network. Negating 'bad behaviour' and emphasising global connections became particularly important to de-emphasise the 'repute' of this 'squatting area'. There is not the same public urgency in displaying status in the Georgetown localities, but this is also very central to their inter-group and intra-group interactions as well as to their emphasis on outward migration. Status is also achieved in Guyana through the category of becoming a migrant and facilitated through various exchanges and gifts in various settings.

[2] The term 'Indian' is in more general use among them. East Indian is the official categorisation, used in the Census and meant to distinguish 'East Indians' from 'West Indians'. It is also used by Indians as a 'cultural' description, to show public distinctiveness and their difference from others. Guyanese East Indians are also referred to as Indo-Guyanese.

'West' is imagined as other. The notion of the modern has to be considered then in terms of contextual forms of belonging and as plural (Knauft, 2002; Trouillot, 2003). In one instance, it relates to how East Indians understand themselves as persons who are competent in global settings and have knowledge and expertise beyond the local. The modern becomes situated in opposition to restrictive 'local identities', which may be seen as backward. But the term is also used to mean those who are 'wild' as imagined in a decadent western sense. This dichotomy is further expressed in terms of how East Indians seek the foreign as part of their identity: in this instance, the western identity is prized (Halstead, 2002). Further, claiming the foreign contrasts with the representative role of the Hindi movie vis-à-vis Indian culture.

Different migration histories and resettlement patterns influence the varying ways in which East Indians belong in the post-colonial diaspora. East Indians first came from India to then British Guyana in 1838 under the indentureship system and enmeshed in a myth of return (Bhachu, 1985: 3–4). The idea of return would eventually be translated by their descendants as geographical and social journeys *in* the 'West', where belonging in relation to India had to be understood in terms of how they would seek the foreign in Guyana and New York. Links with India were partly construed through these Bombay Hindi movies which they watched. In post-colonial Guyana,[3] both their claiming of the Hindi movie and their self-critique of its representative space also have to be examined in relation to how they were politically marginalised by the elite black dictatorship of Forbes Burnham (1964–85), even though they were the majority ethnic group in Guyana. In this setting, East Indians are distinctive where it is important to be seen to be Indian for the benefit of the outsider's gaze. The need to project a distinctive Indian identity could be read as an instrumentalist approach to combat political and cultural marginalisation (Banks, 1997: 39–43). This instrumentalist approach obscures how East Indians also act against culture where both 'Indian' and 'non-Indian' performances locate them as modern.

Indian distinctiveness was professed where different groups of East Indians came to be seen as one ethnic group with a common culture (see Seecharan, 1997). This was despite the way East Indians came to the British West Indies from diverse 'cultures' in India (see Vertovec, 1992: x). Inherent in this understanding of culture was an emphasis on *Indian* moral values and Hindu and Muslim traditions linked to India and understood

[3] Guyana became independent in 1966.

to contrast with what other ethnic groups do in Guyana (Depres, 1967: 58; Jayawardena, 1963: 24–25). But this 'commonality' also has to be understood in terms of a great deal of intra-group differentiation and where Guyanese East Indians' emphasis on status and claiming and disclaiming *matiness* (equality with each other) affects the notion of community (see Baumann, 1998).

These contradictions relate to how they interact with the Hindi movie. Following its importation in the 1930s, Hindi movies were proclaimed to lead to a 'cultural re-awakening in Trinidad among Indians' (Samaroo, 1987: 44–45) and a 'cultural revival' in Guyana, helping to preserve and develop the 'Indian' way of life (Persaud, 1979: 209). They provided visual representations of India and interacted with ideas of how people wanted to be Indian in relation to this homeland (cf. Lutze, 1985: 6). East Indians' understandings of Indianness linked with the emphasis on traditions and morality as inherent themes in Hindi movies (Sarkar, 1975: 8; Thomas, 1985: 126), but also allowed for the growth of a filmi culture (Dickey, 1993: 42).

There is an ongoing outward migration movement from Guyana, with North America as the preferred destination: East Indians relate to an idea of America which becomes located in how they belong in the foreign and their status performances. Outward migration, by itself, becomes a significant achievement. In these status enactments, the Hindi movie also *becomes simplistic*. This perception by East Indians allows a scrutiny of the Hindi movie as 'non-modern' in contrast to how they are modern as knowledgeable people. A comparison arises with media such as Hollywood movies, where viewing these movies is an activity of 'modern people'.

However, the complexity of the representative space of the Hindi movie sees a shift. East Indians, in turn, lament the Hindi movie's decline into 'western decadence'. In this changing role, it is the hugely popular American soap opera, *The Young and the Restless*, also seen as widely immoral by Guyanese, that becomes 'neutral' programming, where Indian women can justify their usage of this soap opera by contrasting it to the newly decadent Hindi movie. These various interactions are interwoven with the Hindi movie's filmi culture and their everyday interactions with music. Hindi movie songs are often used for Hindu religious functions. They supplement the prayers and are casually sung and replayed by people who have 'limited' knowledge of Hindi. The non-Hindi *speaking*[4] East Indians will sing in Hindi and narrate the storylines.

[4] There is, nevertheless, a good understanding of the language among those who watch Hindi movies.

The song-and-dance routines of the movie resonate with courtship rituals among the young, are part of various Indian musical competitions and more recently have become 'local talent' on television. The Hindi movie superstars become heroes of the Guyanese East Indians. Hindi cinema as a medium of pleasure and entertainment (Dickey, 1993: 175–76) also allows East Indians to derive enjoyment through satire and irony. But that 'pleasure' can be facilitated in the ways the Hindi movie is located both inside and outside Indian culture. The narratives of the movies become part of various social interactions both in Guyana and New York. I consider these interactions as forms of belonging, where East Indians use the Hindi movie as modern people. How they belong remains in the idea of constant travelling and provides for the contradictions of Indianness: these forms of belonging rely on a 'social journey' in the West. This is expressed through their desire to be *authentic*. This notion of authenticity relates not only to essentialist ideas about culture, but is also about how they claim particular forms of knowledge beyond the 'local' which render them as 'cool' and modern both in Guyana and New York. Crucially, what is the authentic is mediated by their varying relationships to respect notions.

Decadence, Representation and Women's Role

Respect notions require East Indian women to be the 'upholders of culture' (see Jamieson, 2000: 311; Sidnell, 2003). Their behaviour allows for various forms of respect between young and old. The way these notions have to be upheld sees a stated separation between decadence and purity. Decadence becomes attached to a notion of the West which is in opposition to the idea of proper Indian behaviour.[5] But there is another striking contrast: the Guyanese East Indians also see the West as part of their identity (Clifford, 1997: 4–5; Drummond, 1980; Halstead, 2002). The 'West', however, is occidentalised as decadent in relation to the representative role of Hindi movies (Carrier, 1995). Thus, the West is both the other and the self in different contexts of how East Indians relate to the foreign as part of their identity and the ways they are modern. This further becomes reflected in their interactions with Hindi movies.

[5] See De Boeck (1989: 31) for an interesting application of 'West' in the Luunda's use of place, where the direction East (where the sun rises) is the origin of the 'cultural order' in opposition to the West, associated with death and the underworld.

The representative role of Hindi movies vis-à-vis 'western decadence' is reflected in Rosie Thomas' discussion (1985: 126), where the movies offer a space which allows for respect of a number of Indian ideals. These include those relating to kin, friends, duty, obligations, destiny and religion and the privileging of good over evil (see also Sarkar, 1975: 8). Thomas pointed out:

> Evil or decadence is broadly categorised as 'non-traditional' and 'Western,' although the West is not so much a place, or even a culture, as an emblem of exotic, decadent otherness, signified by whisky, bikinis, an uncontrolled sexuality and, what is seen as lack of 'respect' for elders and betters, and (from men) towards womanhood (1985: 126).

In the first instance, it is the 'absence' of this sexuality vis-à-vis East Indian women's role which has to be projected by men and supported by women in certain contexts (see Strathern, 1981: 166–67). In the second, men are also constrained to act in particular ways in relation to the issue of women's sexuality, but their constraint is not evident in the same form as that of women, who could easily be seen as *the* subordinates. Here, I consider material on both Guyana and New York to show how these approaches to sexuality are about respect conventions and how they mediate the way East Indians belong in the modern. I start with examples from Better Prospects, a squatting area on the West Bank Demerara in Guyana, and will compare this with data on Georgetown, Guyana and on Richmond Hill, New York, USA.

The issue of considering different localities is significant in terms of how these places are envisaged by the East Indians. However, locality here does not allow for homogenous groupings where there are wealthy people in one location and poor in another, for instance. The emphasis on outward migration allows for an inward flow of goods and services so that people in impoverished areas can be wealthy. Also, there is a public emphasis on everyone being equal to each other: this has been described as *mati*, people who are equal under common conditions of hardship (see Jayawardena, 1963). The commonality is around the issues of public distinctiveness and status, which the East Indians understand and scrutinise in varying ways. This scrutiny may also be related to how different understandings of the various localities relate to, or produce, status. Further, locality has to be probed in terms of how East Indian migrants use place to perform their changing ideas of respect in relation to 'America'. It is how the East Indians inhabit the *modern* (rather than a specific physical location) that is significant to their use of Hindi movies and which, in turn, allow for insights into the contradictions of this distinctiveness.

In Better Prospects, the switching of identity was particularly evident: this is where people describe themselves in categories of Indian and non-Indian, as movements between ethnic and non-ethnic identities. The modern embraces both Indian and non-Indian as discussed in Halstead (2000): non-Indian is where they move out of ritualistic performances or acknowledge that they are not behaving in an essentialist way, i.e., perform a self-critique. Some East Indians felt it necessary to stress the need to uphold ideals of Indian culture and will decry bad behaviour in others noting that they did not have 'culture'. The attitude of Lalji,[6] a male East Indian, who is a constant visitor to Better Prospects, demonstrates how men expect women to behave in terms of Indian culture, even though the men also act against Indian notions of respect. Lalji talks about a particular Hindi movie, where the *sindoor* (red dot on forehead to indicate married status) worn by a married woman was the most significant factor in her life (see Gokulsing and Dissanayake, 1998: 77). He notes that even when the heroine became separated from her husband, a physical injury allowed a red dot (of blood) on her forehead. This signified that she was still married and devoted to her husband.

The conversation shifts to his estranged wife who was 'teaching the right thing and doing the wrong thing'. This returns to the issue of respect. She was *failing* to perform her duty and had left him. He contrasts his wife's behaviour with the attitude of the Hindi movie heroine, noting that his wife could learn to uphold Indian culture from viewing Hindi movies, which showed the right path and had meanings, particularly for older Indians. It emerges that Lalji has a *sweetwoman* (lover). But the existence of this lover does not affect how he views his wife's behaviour.

Despite his own 'everyday' non-Indian actions and that of his wife, he was ready to show how Hindi movies fitted into Indian notions of respect. These were standards of behaviour which he himself expected from his wife and others in his understandings of what was Indian culture. Yet, it was permissible to liase with a sweetwoman, where he could in another cultural context effectively situate himself outside of these notions of respect. For East Indians like Lalji, newer Hindi movies could be blamed for 'letting down the culture'. These movies were like those people who go against Indian notions of respect and behave in 'wild, modern' ways

[6] I use pseudonyms.

and now occupied a space in relation to western decadence as well. In these newer movies, heroines dress in short skirts and exhibit behaviour not fit for family viewing as Hari, a resident in Better Prospects notes. These changes to Hindi cinema resonated with the contrasting ways heroines were expected to behave over different decades from demure to provocative (Gokulsing and Dissanayake, 1998: 9; Kazmi, 1998: 21–23).

Hari considers himself addicted to old Hindi movies and amuses his two young daughters with this interest, as they feel these movies are of the past. But he says that he feels ashamed to view the newer movies, particularly in the presence of his daughters. The idea of shame about the stars' behaviour in the newer Hindi movies is very much located in the representative role of Hindi movies and Hari's notions of respect. Thus, the 'shameful' behaviour has to be identified, separated from that fixed notion of Indian culture and linked with western decadence. Hari's wife, Asha, feels it necessary to monitor her children's viewing of Hindi movies. This may be compared to audiences who scrutinise Tamil cinema-going for positive and negative influences (Dickey, 1993: 43). While these East Indians obtain pleasure through ridicule of the Hindi movie, this is often about scrutinising it for its representative capacity. Where this approach is situated by some women as a denial of their role as 'culture carriers', it is one overshadowed by the greater cultural expectations which privilege the role of East Indian women as 'upholders' of the culture.

Asha herself prefers to view the American soap opera, *The Young and the Restless*. She, however, feels that she can view it because it has nothing to do with Indian culture unlike the representative Hindi movie which, in turn, 'fails' this role. Asha is among a number of women who separate the American soap opera from Indian culture; this attitude is not shared by many East Indian men who feel that watching the *The Young and the Restless* is shameful, since it is against Indian notions of respect.

Similarly, Rajni, a widowed Guyanese East Indian woman and a grandmother in Richmond Hill, New York, considers the Hindi movie in terms of its representative role to act as censor if the scenes become too 'westernised'. She would sit before her television to view a Hindi movie daily, but exercise self-censorship in terms of the standards of these movies. This censorship is not extended to *The Young and the Restless*, which she also views daily, and where women dress in 'sexy fashions' and have scandalous affairs. Rajni noted that it was acceptable for her to view this programme because it was 'nah true story', and that the 'stories were based on their own traditions (not hers)'. Rajni noted that the newer

Hindi movies had too many 'short skirts'; these movies failed to show the 'right traditions'.

This may be further examined in relation to Rajni's view that Hindi movies were about her 'own traditions' (see Swami Agehananda Bharati, 1977: 263). Rajni considers herself a traditional East Indian woman. She prays daily at home, carries out religious work and contributes to the maintenance of her *mandir* (temple) in Guyana. Hindi movies which emphasise prayers and good deeds are of particular interest to her. She noted that in the movie, *Karan Arjun* (names of the stars in the movie), the stars prayed to the deities for help. She said that one of the heroines benefited from praying to *Durga* (a Hindu deity) that it was 'the prayer she pray, help her'. She noted that the viewers of these movies also obtain help because it showed the power of prayers and good deeds. She noted, 'Don't believe in no evil. When problem meet you (this is not the time to) *do something*. Do you regular prayer. Every single day must go to you altar in you house.' What people need to learn from these movies, as Rajni saw it, were the 'right traditions'.

But when Rajni wanted to express her disapproval of the ways in which young people today publicly romance in contradiction of Indian notions of respect on Liberty Avenue in Richmond Hill, New York, she compared them unfavourably to the romantic scenes in Hindi movies. This reference to a Hindi movie is also about filmi culture around Hindi movies and the ways the young imagine themselves as the 'superstars' of the Hindi screen. Their image as superstars is subsumed in how Rajni sees the representative capacity of the Hindi movie. She noted that whenever she and her employees saw couples kissing and embracing each other, they would say '*Sawan Ko Anne Do* (*Let Spring Come*, a 1979 Hindi movie) was on the Avenue', and 'collapse' in laughter.

What is interesting is that she refers to an old movie to condemn the wild behaviour of the young people. Rajni reveals her own embarrassment with these romantic scenes and her public separation from filmi culture even though the scenes in these older movies were presumably both 'demure' (in terms of how East Indians now criticise newer movies) and still allowed the heroine to follow the 'right path'. This embarrassment speaks to the different space of the Hindi movie in filmi culture and as representative of Indian culture. *But Rajni unveils a tension between the expectations of women's role in Indian culture and their projected lack of sexuality in these older movies as well.* How the representative role of women is imagined also provides for a domestic space where the notion of respect is privileged over the conjugal sexual role (Bannerji et al., 2001; De Boeck, 1989: 35–36). This tension informs social interactions between men and women and the ways they act for and against culture (Ortner and Whitehead, 1981: 24–25). The romantic clinches of the young become placed in relation to the Hindi movie despite all the talk in Richmond Hill about the young, in particular, falling under the influence of western decadence and about the older Hindi movie representing the right traditions.

The idea of western decadence is defined in opposition to respect notions in terms of how Hindi movies position women in relation to respect. The possible departure of women into 'wild behaviour' has to be ignored for Hindi movies to be representative of Indian culture. How Hindi movies can also be disparaged and further seen to occupy a non-Indian space through negative western influences still does not allow for a publicly *permissible role* where women act against culture. *That must be left to non-Indian programming such as* The Young and the Restless, *which also serves to emphasise the way Hindi movies are seen as belonging within Indian culture.* Thus, the communal viewing of Hindi movies including those which are seen as 'letting down the culture' is not considered as contradictory to Indian culture in a way *The Young and the Restless* is considered to be. The East Indians will not generally find it acceptable to converge in a communal setting around a public screening of the 'immoral' *The Young and the Restless* in Guyana. Where flaws are to be found in that representative capacity of the Hindi movie, it is to be blamed on the newer movies, but without the kind of condemnation directed at the 'decadent' *The Young and the Restless*.

Some women will openly acknowledge that the portrayal of their role in Hindi movies is laughable and this was evident in their viewing. Several women in Guyana and New York also declared that they view the Hindi movie so they can 'cuss' or ridicule some of the storylines or stars' behaviours. The irony and dismissal is situated, in particular, in the unrealistic expectations which are depicted of women's roles (Vasudev, 1988: 107–9).[7] Their critical approach engages with cultural expectations of their role as presumed upholders of culture and how these link with actual experiences.

Yet, the Hindi movie in its capacity of representing Indian culture and where *this can be a politicised setting is not seen to offer a credible space to*

[7] This dominant perception of women's role in Hindi movies may be compared with how heroines of newer movies have to participate in stories of victimhood and vengeance involving rape scenes (see Gokulsing and Dissanayake, 1998:106). How women emerge from these plights, however, confirms with their role as representative of certain ideals.

question these expectations.[8] This is unlike *The Young and the Restless*, where promiscuous relationships are the norm and where, in Guyana, the public viewing of this soap opera by East Indian women is condemned by other East Indian women, men and youths. In a way that the Hindi movie cannot do, public usage of this soap opera is seen to redefine what is visible of women's behaviour: they emerge from the 'public confines' of the household and its projection around respect notions, moving beyond particular public expectations of their role. In doing so, they display authority around other aspects of their daily experiences.

Respect Notions, Gender and 'Modern People'

Men also position themselves against Indian notions of respect and are redefined in the viewing of 'action movies' (see also Banerjea, this volume). Their viewing of action movies from Hollywood does not merit the same kind of self-censorship and scrutiny as does the viewing of *The Young and the Restless* by women. Consider the example of Boyo and his extended household who live in Better Prospects. This household is an inter-religious group, of Hindus, Christians and Muslims and where lavish Hindu religious ceremonies are held. The groups which congregate at this house can behave in a disorderly fashion. The male group is sometimes joined by one of Boyo's daughters-in-law. The daughter-in-law is *seen* to act in a 'non-Indian' context, when she is part of this group, unlike the other daughters-in-law who do not join in the viewing activities of the group. Among this group, Hindi movies often suffer in comparison with Hollywood films. But what this usage also brings out is the subtleties of upholding respect notions in relation to gender and how this gendered interaction is negotiated in the non-Indian context, where East Indians see themselves as acting outside of specific ideas of Indian culture.

Boyo, who is in his 40s, noted that in his youth he had been an ardent fan of Hindi movies. Now, he preferred to view what he described as 'action films' from Hollywood. It is clear that men rather than women (the 'upholders of culture') can 'comfortably' view 'realism' and 'sex scenes'.

[8] This may also be compared to social gatherings around the viewing of Hindi movies at the cinemas. Young people meet in a *respectable setting* that is not seen to be offered in the same way by cinemas which screen movies from both Hollywood and Bollywood or just the former. The emphasis in this cultural context is on decency and respectability, which fits with notions of what it means to be Indian in a specific setting.

But men also move out of particular respect notions, where the expectations which 'bind' women in public asexuality also constrains the men to express public and communal uneasiness vis-à-vis sexuality. Gender does not *publicly* allow men greater sexual freedom. This may be seen as distinct from how they can view 'action' movies with its 'western decadence' theme and the way they are uneasy about women viewing the 'immoral' *The Young and the Restless*. Thus, despite the onus on women to uphold idealised notions of culture, men also play a role in relation to these respect notions. This observation may be considered in terms of Marilyn Strathern's (1981: 169–70) point about other issues around gender analysis. Relating these models of analysis to Hageners' behaviour, she noted:

> In what they sometimes set up as a 'problem of women,' Hageners—of both sexes—are also spelling out certain implications of personhood, of the alignment between self-interest and group action, in short, what is to them a 'problem of people' (ibid.: 170).

The readiness of men to view the action movie is also about the way they are non-Indian: this provides for specific forms of sophistication and knowledge and the *contextual disregard* shown by both men and women of the notions of respect. The issue of respect becomes transformed in terms of forms of belonging linked to being modern and where this also questions particular constructions of their gendered roles.

These forms of belonging resonate with the dismissal of the Hindi movie for lacking western sophistication. The dismissal finds an echo in a dominant Hollywood discourse which positions these movies as secondary (Gillespie, 1995: 83; Thomas, 1985). Arguably, that discourse, in itself, ignores the wide popularity of Hindi cinema and as Thomas (1985: 116–17, 128) notes has to be seen as problematic in terms of output, global usage and audience interaction. Nevertheless, this discourse lends itself to the way the East Indians seek to distance, deny or critique their usage even while being avid viewers. At the same time, the huge popularity of Hindi cinema speaks to the ways in which the East Indians engage with an imaginary created by the filmi culture of Hindi cinema and how the Hindi movie mediates their belonging as modern people. In this setting, the East Indians can generally maintain a distance while viewing the Hindi movie. They find it necessary to be critical as part of their enjoyment. This resonates with Thomas' point about the tremendous public and distinctive audience interaction in Indian cinemas, where, for instance, viewers will clap, boo or sing (Thomas, 1985: 129). She notes:

> Despite what middle-class critics imply, it is clear, if one experiences an Indian audience irreverently clapping, booing and laughing with the films, that they know perfectly well that the films are 'ridiculous', 'unreal' and offer impossible solutions, and that pleasure arises in spite of—and probably because of—this knowledge (ibid.: 128).

Both in Guyana and in New York, in the familial setting, much criticism is readily voiced while the movie is aired. This ability to provide critical running commentaries is often the declared reason for viewing the movie.[9] This critical approach also unveils Hindi cinema as both simplistic and unrealistic, a point also made, for instance, by Kobita Sarkar who in 1975 noted that Hindi movies' representations of cultural values could be deemed outdated in India (Sarkar, 1975: 4; see also Swami Agehananda Bharati, 1977). The East Indians also become critical of the Hindi movies; their 'simplicity' affects their modern identity. Conversely, from the examination of the newer Hindi movie as being 'too modern', the position, particularly expressed by the young, but also by older East Indians, is that it detracts from *how they want to be modern.*

The perception of the Hindi movie as part of Indian culture is often the cited reason for its popularity. One woman, Reshma, living on the outskirts of Better Prospects, noted 'Me ah Hindu and me ah watch Hindi movies.' Yet, persons from other ethnic groups also view Hindi movies (see Gokulsing and Dissanayake, 1998: 101). This representative role of Hindi movies *within Indian culture* is not immediately obvious in the polyethnic Guyanese society. Thus, Hindi movies were not targeted in the same way as the staple diet of *dal* and *roti* of the East Indians, when yellow split peas and wheat flour were banned by the Forbes Burnham administration in the 1980s, and which the East Indians felt were hostile acts by this government against them. In the inter-ethnic setting, the obvious locating of the Hindi movie in Indian entertainment also situates it publicly aside from ritualistic and religious practices which are seen as

[9] Sara Dickey discussed how the notion of entertainment as pleasure can be probed to show its positioning in daily lives. Cinema viewing is seen as a 'process of negotiation' to allow for meanings to be made in relation to viewers' worlds (Dickey, 1993: 13–14).

more representative of the East Indians in Guyanese society. The representative role of Hindi movies was specifically demonstrated in how some East Indians located the *initial* televising of Hindi movies in 1992 as a public representative space in the inter-ethnic setting.[10] This was seen as a dramatic reversal of their political marginalisation under the dictatorship of Forbes Burnham. At the same time, as noted, this representative capacity is subsumed, where the Hindi movie is seen to be simplistic.

While Hindi movies were seen to provide linkages to India and facilitate a cultural revival in the colonial era, this role shifted to accommodate changing notions of the 'homeland' and what it meant to be Indian. Despite the representative role of Hindi cinema in Guyana, it does not provide direct links to the homeland of India. The notion of India being 'home' was significantly eroded, although some linkages were maintained through merchandising by Indian merchants and cultural activities facilitated by the Indian High Commission in Guyana. The East Indians also became 'at home' in the migrant land, yet continued travelling raises the notion of home as an involvement in diasporic wanderings, where home is a continual quest for the foreign. Thus, the idea of Indian culture whilst reliant on 'authentic practices' linked to India and where Hindi movies can confirm Indian notions of respect is also performed in relation to non-Indian ways and an explicit emphasis on *being modern*.

A Muslim viewer, Feroze, and his Christian wife, Nita, were diffident about their interest in Hindi movies and denied regular viewing. Yet, they subsequently noted that they would view these movies on television in Guyana about thrice a week. On the various occasions I visited them at their home in Better Prospects, they were invariably watching a Hindi movie on television. One Hindu university student, Radha, from a village near Better Prospects, and the first woman to be educated in her extended

[10] Prior to its televising, public access to Hindi movies was through cinemas. Social events surround cinema-going activities at the various cinemas which show only Hindi movies in Guyana, in particular, Liberty cinema in Georgetown. On Sundays, in particular, large crowds of Indians would queue to gain admission to these often three-hour long movies (see Pfleiderer, 1985: 82). Often, they would view a movie more than once. This was exemplified in the case of the hit movie, *Hum Aapke Hain Koun...!* (*Who am I to you*, dir. Sooraj R. Barjatya, 1994), which had a record run in Guyana in the mid-1990s. The way this Hindi cinema going was seen as part of a social gathering was demonstrated by the attention paid to appearance, where women used it as an occasion to 'dress up'. The queues would include members of an entire family and also young couples who were courting.

household, displays a 'cultural capital' (Bourdieu, 1980) which enacts distance between her forms of knowledge and how the Hindi movie mediates identity.

Radha noted that people wanted to kill themselves for the Hindi movie superstar, Amitabh Bachchan, when he visited. Radha herself found it necessary to distance herself from this 'frenzy'. She noted that she could not understand why people were so crazy to see 'Amitabh'. Radha is critical of Hindi movies. She is also critical of the *The Young and the Restless.* Both are programmes which have to be distant from her knowledge and expertise. This may be linked with how Boyo (discussed earlier) and his group chose 'English movies' over Hindi movies: this rejection of Hindi movies in favour of 'English movies' is also *becoming modern* in a particular way. Similarly, the son of a *pandit* (Hindu priest) working in Georgetown talked about how he had come of age by switching from the viewing of Hindi movies to 'English' (Hollywood action) films much to the dismay of his 'traditional' mother who felt that he was straying from his culture to learn 'wild English' ways. Unlike Hindi movies, these so-called English movies could not be seen to belong in the same way within the framework of Indianness despite the fact that Guyana is a former British colony and its first language is English. The youth showed how these boundaries of Indianness were being redefined to encompass that which was seen as explicitly 'non-Indian'. He felt he was attaining status by being seen to be modern vis-à-vis 'English' media.

How the East Indians are modern, in this instance, resides with an insider space of self-critique. It also speaks to how they want to be foreign, where this is both about knowledge, sophistication, and conversely, 'western decadence'. Young people inhabit the modern in particular ways by being 'cool': this is by knowing how to belong in an inter-ethnic setting as part of their modern identity. Here, it is commonalties rather than differences that are relevant to an acceptable 'brand image' (see Halstead, 2002). While in one context the Hindi movie is still not modern enough, in another, the filmi culture of entertainment and romance can also be part of being cool as a *youthful space* of the modern. How the Hindi movie and its filmi culture become transformed in relation to what is cool is also about how it travels with people engaged in a social journey. This then mediates how the East Indians move in and out of an ethnic identity. The changing role of women and how the young participate in a filmi culture, in particular, demonstrates these movements.

Rituals of Courtship and Pleasure

The imaginary of filmi culture, i.e., how East Indians interact with the music, song-and-dance routines and romance themes provides for a different form of interaction with the Hindi movie. The East Indians as modern may rely on the representative space of Hindi movies, but this is through a public engagement with its filmi culture. Here, criticism of romantic scenes in Hindi movies has to be contextualised in the East Indians' identification with the stars and in their emulating musical performances. There remains a strong linkage between these scenes and the representative role of Hindi movies. These love scenes are often framed in moralistic values and in intricate storylines where good eventually triumphs over evil, with the stars being heroic and courageous. In turn, these movie stars are role models for the Guyanese East Indian diaspora and become part of the filmi culture of song-and-dance performances and other social interactions intertwined with ideas of Hindi cinema. Hindi movies become the centre of courtship rituals and fit into people's desires to engage in romance as this is imagined in relation to the performances of the superstars of the Hindi screen.

Filmi culture becomes intertwined with expressions of Indo-Caribbean music, or *chatni* performances,[11] where people want to be like the stars through localised performances. With the coming of Hindi movies on television, and the televising of local Indian talent in Guyana, children and youths, in particular, find opportunities to practice their filmi talents, and I met with many who performed on television. I also met with a number of young girls of 5–10 years of age in Georgetown and on the West Bank Demerara who were practising dancing before their home television screens in imitation of televised Hindi movies' musical sequences. These children include Boyo's granddaughter whose ambitions, like the other children I met, are to go on television to show off her talents in filmi dancing. This ambition is also nurtured by one of the youngster's in Boyo's household who generally prefers to view 'action' movies over Hindi films. How the young perform and want to publicise their filmi talents allows for a further appreciation of the way Hindi movies are also located outside of their representative capacity in relation to Indian culture. At the same time, televised performances are subjected to similar scrutiny for 'letting down the culture' or lacking sophistication, where 'modern East Indians' also want *Indian culture to be seen as sophisticated*. This becomes a necessary

[11] Also known as 'chutney' which , in this case, signifies 'hot music'.

scrutiny where the East Indians' emphasis of the representative space of Hindi movies is also about ensuring *that this does not detract from how they are modern.*

In New York, usage of Hindi movies also fits with the various ways the young, in particular, interact with different forms of media to move in and out of the 'ethnic identity' and to be 'cool'. From Liberty cinema in Guyana to Liberty Avenue in New York, this interaction with Hindi movies and filmi culture fits into varying and contradictory notions of Indian courtship and the representative space Hindi movies occupy in Indian culture. Several youths who were involved in listening to dubbed tunes and had scant interest in Hindi movies or in being seen as *Indian* acquired an interest in filmi music in their efforts to impress their girlfriends. For them and others, it is important to have a stock of music CDs and cassettes. These youths also play popular music in English and *chatni* tunes. This public involvement with filmi culture links with how some East Indians in Guyana acknowledged that their courtship was facilitated through regular attendance (Pfleiderer, 1985: 82) at the cinemas to view Hindi movies. While the way filmi culture fits alongside the youths' various interests may be critiqued as a functional device to impress potential girlfriends, it is more about what is popular and where this usage becomes part of their modern image in a specific setting. Thus, the imaginary of filmi culture becomes aligned with other popular forms of youth expressions. This differs from the earlier example of the youth in Guyana, for instance, who saw Hindi movies as backward and had to claim 'English' movies to come of age.

Additionally, New York migrants are seen to have gained particular access to the modern as part of the myth of being an American migrant. By migrating the East Indians are considered to have achieved a positive benefit of 'westernisation'. But this then has to be negotiated in a different way and in relation to the idea of *more freedom* for the young, particularly where this can be seen to conflict with Indian respect notions. Thus, young people ostensibly have more 'freedom' to engage in romantic relationships in the New York setting. There is general dismay and concern over unplanned pregnancies by single young women and over how women and children call in outsiders (policemen) to settle domestic disputes. Young people are seen to behave in wild ways through these relationships. This is a setting where migrants feel constrained to act in non-traditional ways in efforts to adjust where they often need to have more than one job to survive. The efforts to disengage this 'negative modernity' see new emphasis on Indian distinctiveness, where Indian ceremonies of worship and youth activities in the religious environment are meant to counter negative American influences.

This traditional/contra-traditional setting allows for the young to identify with respect notions for reasons which have to do both with Indian culture and with what makes them 'cool'. The idea of 'purity' re-emerges in relation to what is popular among the young. This is epitomised in the way one woman in Richmond Hill, New York, felt that the movie *Kuch Kuch Hota Hai* (*Something or Other is Happening*, dir. Karan Johar, 1998) was a clean offering, a story which made one feel good. She noted that some East Indians felt so good about it that they went to see the movie more than seven times in the Long Island cinema in New York (see Thomas, 1985: 130; see also Hansen, this volume). Another New York resident, Shulah, noted: 'That movie touched everybody ... (it was about) young love, innocence, finding love again.'

The notion of purity is also evident in how filmi culture is incorporated into religious activities. Filmi songs are a regular part of *mandir* (temple) ceremonies and other public *puja* (ceremonies of worship) in New York. A well-known *pandit* (Hindu priest) in Queens, New York, was able to facilitate his departure from Guyana by winning a singing competition. His award was a ticket out of the country. In New York, he would subsequently become part of a singing group where he and his friends met to perform songs from Hindi movies. These gatherings were intertwined with devotional sessions. Eventually, the *pandit* co-established a *mandir* in Brooklyn, where songs from Hindi movies are also part of the programme.

Pandit Gossai was a senior microbiologist at the Georgetown hospital in Guyana when he sought to join the many leaving Guyana at the height of the black elite Forbes Burnham dictatorship in the 1980s. At the time, the 1981 Mukesh Memorial singing competition was being held in honour of Mukesh, a famous Hindi movies' playback singer. Gossai won a trip to Canada. He then journeyed to New York where he obtained employment as a teacher. He began to 'do a bit of singing in my house,' in New York. A few friends were also doing the same thing. Eventually, a friend provided a basement where they met as a group to perform and listen to songs from Hindi movies and *bhajans* (religious songs). Gossai and another key member of the group spoke of a 'purity' of expression in the songs and the Indian ideals represented therein which allowed for the sessions to be extended into religious meetings. In addition to singing, Gossai began to preach Hinduism. He noted: 'I have touched a lot of people because of my teaching, songs, messages.'

The group subsequently acquired a building to set up a *mandir*, the Bhuvaneshwar Mandir in Brooklyn, New York. Services are held there every Sunday. In addition to Hindu hymns, songs from Hindi movies are also offered. Gossai himself has become very well known. He describes himself as a 'Hindu missionary'. He is regularly invited to seven countries including Canada and various states in the USA to perform *pandit* work. The linkage with religion shows how filmi culture resides with the representative capacity of Hindi movies. This is also cultural where the idea of entertainment is incorporated into respect notions.

While the East Indians, particularly older migrants seeking to highlight an ethnicised identity, make meanings of these movies in relation to Indian culture, there is also the interaction at the filmi level. This filmi and religious interaction fits with, and is part of, people's emphasis on 'authenticity' and performing traditions in the migrant setting (Strathern, 1992: 37). In this context, where the idea of authenticity is about how they can become 'more Indian', particular linkages with India are sought. This is exemplified through usage of goods for rituals, fashions and travel. People come to purchase ethnic food imported from Guyana, but they also buy the religious goods and ethnic wear brought from India. This allows for a 'community' which becomes visible in religious and cultural activities and in daily trading and other activities on Liberty Avenue, particularly over weekends. Liberty Avenue has a cluster of shops which offer videos of Hindi movies and filmi music on CDs and audio cassettes (for the case of the South Asian diaspora in Frankfurt, see Brosius, this volume).

The general interaction with Hindi movies becomes inserted into these renewed links with India, where Indian movie stars are regularly in New York, both in casual settings allowing for street encounters, and for extravagant shows. These shows are well attended and tickets, as was the case with a Bollywood awards ceremony in New York in May 2000, are sold out well in advance. This engagement is also about popular entertainment and links with how the East Indians explore filmi interactions alongside *chatni* and 'less Indian' forms of music. The East Indians' success as migrants and how they see themselves as modern people links with their desire to be more 'authentic', as Indians, but authenticity is also about belonging, in part, of the redefined West, where they can be 'cool'.

The issue of authenticity replays itself into these contradictions of Indianness. In New York, the East Indians' relationship with the Hindi movie has many similarities with the interactions in Guyana, but in New York there is a specific *renewed emphasis* on displaying traditions. The emphasis exists alongside the way women and children, in particular, are seen to have greater freedom to act against these traditions and how the East Indians can reject the idea of an 'Indian community'. This tension, where the East Indians distance themselves from the community, is not immediately evident in the projection of Indianness in Queens, New York. But it flows into the intensity of this display of Indian distinctiveness where religious and cultural activities are carried out vis-à-vis a 'western decadent' setting.

Where authenticity is about disowning this community and examining it for its contradictory behaviour, distinctiveness becomes mediated by critical scrutiny. This also relates to how 'western decadence', can be desired. Further, it considers forms of knowledge and expertise understood to be gained outside of a politicised ethnic identity. How migrants become critical of the emphasis on ethnic activities situates the 'renewal' with India as commercial or nostalgic, but this scrutiny is mediated by the ways they are also 'non-Indian' in both Guyana and New York. As modern people, these movements allow them to engage in a 'social journey', that is constantly being constructed in relation to the new and changing ideas of the foreign. The Hindi movie is seen as representative of Indian culture and western decadence, being simplistic and at the same linking with what is popular with the 'modern young'.

Conclusion

How the East Indians belong in relation to Hindi movies not only provides insights into their understandings of themselves as modern people where they form a distinctive Indian collective, but also acts against the notion of Indian culture. This observation was also examined in terms of how the Hindi movie was representative of Indian culture, but linked to western decadence. In turn, the idea of western decadence was probed to examine the contradictions of these forms of belonging and where being cool is about a resultant filmi culture. Significantly, these varying approaches rendered visible ideas about respect notions. How the East Indians enacted or acted against these notions were demonstrated through different notions of homeland and of home.

In their engagement with authenticity, the East Indians found it necessary to privilege an ethnicised Indian identity, but also to disparage it. As modern East Indians their desire to be authentic in different settings resonated with the way Hindi movies fit into certain specificities of diasporic media and explicate the contradictions and ambiguities of the diasporic condition. The contradictions of people who find it necessary to travel were reflected in the differing approaches to Hindi movies as disaporic media. The modern East Indians belong by imagining and claiming home in different ways, in particular where they felt it necessary to continue the journey from India to the Caribbean to North America and where this journey is also socially constructed in relation to the foreign. Their constant reclaiming of home mediates a journey where authenticity becomes how they are distinctively Indian and also seek the foreign.

Acknowledgements

I thank Eric Hirsch, Raminder Kaur, Darshan Ramdhani and Bobby Small for their comments at varying stages in writing up the data. Versions of this paper were presented at the conference 'Writing Diaspora' in Swansea 2000 and at the LSE South Asian seminars in 2001. I am very grateful to the participants of both forums for their critical comments.

References

BANKS, MARCUS. 1997. *Ethnicity: Anthropological Constructions*. London: Routledge.

BANNERJI, HIMANI, SHAHRZAD MOJAB and JUDITH WHITEHEAD (eds). 2001. *Of Property and Propriety: The Role of Gender and Class in Imperialism and Nationalism*. Toronto: University of Toronto Press.

BAUMANN, GERD. 1998. *Contesting Culture: Discourses of Identity in Multi-Ethnic London*. Cambridge: Cambridge University Press.

BHACHU, PARMINDER. 1985. *Twice Migrants: East African Sikh Settlers in Britain*. London: Tavistock Publications.

BOURDIEU, PIERRE. 1980. 'Aristocracy of Culture', *Media, Culture and Society*, 2(3): 225–54. Trans. Richard Nice.

CARRIER, JAMES (ed.). 1995. *Occidentalism: Images of the West*. Oxford: Clarendon Press.

CLIFFORD, JAMES. 1997. *Routes: Travel and Translation in the Late Twentieth Century*. London: Harvard University Press.

DE BOECK, FILIP. 1989. 'Place as Cultural and Natural Texture', in Nadia Lovell (ed.), *Locality and Belonging*, London: Routledge.

DEPRES, LEO. 1967. *Cultural Pluralism and Nationalist Politics in British Guiana*. Chicago: Rand McNally and Co.

DICKEY, SARAH. 1993. *Cinema and the Urban Poor in South India*. Cambridge: Cambridge University Press.

DRUMMOND, LEE. 1980. 'A Cultural Continuum: A Theory of Intersystems', *Man* (n.s.), 15: 352–74.

GILLESPIE, MARIE. 1995. *Television, Ethnicity and Cultural Change*. Routledge: London.

GOKULSING, MOTI and WIMAL DISSANAYAKE. 1998. *Indian Popular Cinema: A Narrative of Cultural Change*. Stoke-on-Trent, UK: Trentham Books.

Halstead, Narmala. 2000. 'Switching Identities: Movements between "Indian" and "non-Indian" in Guyana', *Anthropology in Action*, 7(1–2): 22–33.

———. 2001. 'Ethnographic Encounters: Positionings within and Outside the Insider Frame', *Social Anthropology*, 9: 303–17.

———. 2002. 'Branding Perfection: Foreign as Self; Self as "Foreign-Foreign"', *Journal of Material Culture*, 7(3): 273–93.

Jamieson, Mark. 2000. 'It's Shame that Makes Men and Women Enemies: The Politics of Intimacy among the Miskitu of Kakabila', *Journal of the Royal Anthropological Institute*, 6(2): 311–24.

Jayawardena, Chandra. 1963. *Conflict and Solidarity on a Guianese Plantation*. London: The Athlone Press.

———. 1980. 'Culture and Ethnicity in Guyana and Fiji', *Man*, 15: 430–50.

Kazmi, Nikhat. 1998. *The Dream Merchants of Bollywood*. New Delhi: UBS Publishers' Distributors Ltd.

Knauft, Bruce. M. (ed.). 2002. *Critically Modern: Alternatives, Alterities, Anthropologies*. Indiania: Indiania University Press.

Lovell, Nadia (ed.). 1989. *Locality and Belonging*. London: Routledge.

Lutze, Lothar. 1985. 'From Bharata to Bombay Cinema: Change in Continuity in Hindi Film Aesthetics', in Beatrix Pfleiderer and Lothar Lutze (eds), *The Hindi Film: Agent and Re-agent of Cultural Change*, New Delhi: Manohar.

Mishra, Vijay. 1985. 'Towards a Theoretical Critique of Bombay Cinema', *Screen*, 26(3–4): 133–46.

Olwig, Karen Fog. 1998. 'Epilogue: Contested Homes: Home-making and the Making of Anthropology', in Nigel Rapport and Andrew Dawson (eds), *Migrants of Identity: Perceptions of Home in a World of Movement*, Oxford: Berg.

Ortner, Sherry B. and Harriet Whitehead. 1981. 'Introduction: Accounting for Sexual Meaning', in Sherry B. Ortner and Harriet Whitehead (eds), *Sexual Meanings: The Cultural Construction of Gender and Sexuality*, Cambridge: Cambridge University Press.

Persaud, Paul. 1979. 'Indians in the Caribbean', in I.J. Bahadur Singh (ed.), *The Other India: The Overseas Indians and their Relationship with India*. New Delhi: Arnold Heinemann Publishers.

Pfleiderer Beatrix. 1985. 'An Empirical Study of Urban and Semi-urban Audience Reactions to Hindi Films', in Beatrix Pfleiderer and Lothar Lutze (eds), *The Hindi Film: Agent and Re-agent of Cultural Change*, New Delhi: Manohar.

Rapport, Nigel and Andrew Dawson (eds). 1998. *Migrants of Identity: Perceptions of Home in a World of Movement*. Oxford: Berg.

Samaroo, Brinsley. 1987. 'The Indian Connection—The Influence of Indian Thoughts and Ideas on the East Indians in the Caribbean', in David Dabydeen and Brinsley Samaroo (eds), *India in the Caribbean*, London: Hansib.

Sarkar, Kobita. 1975. *Indian Cinema Today—An Analysis*. New Delhi: Sterling Publishers.

Seecharan, Clem. 1997. *Tiger in the Stars: The Anatomy of Indian Achievement in British Guiana 1919–29*. London: Macmillan Education Ltd.

Sidnell, Jack. 2003. 'An Ethnographic Consideration of Rule-following', *Journal of the Royal Anthropological Institute*, 9(3): 429–45.

Strathern, Marilyn. 1981. 'Self-interest and the Social Good, Some Implications of Hagen Gender Imagery', in Sherry B. Ortner and Harriet Whitehead (eds), *Sexual Meanings:*

The Cultural Construction of Gender and Sexuality, Cambridge: Cambridge University Press.

STRATHERN, MARILYN. 1992. *After Nature: English Kinship in the late Twentieth Century*. Cambridge: Cambridge University Press.

SWAMI AGEHANANDA BHARATI. 1977. 'Anthropology of Hindi Films', *Folklore*, 18: 258–66.

THOMAS, ROSIE. 1985. 'Indian Cinema: Pleasures and Popularity: An Introduction', *Screen*, 26(3–4): 116–131.

TROUILLOT, MICHEL-ROLPH. 2003. *Global Transformations: Anthropology and the Modern World*. Hampshire: Palgrave Macmillan.

VASUDEV, ARUNA. 1988. The Woman: Myth and Reality the Indian Cinema', in Wimal Dissanayake (ed.), *Culture and Cultural Identity: Reflections on Films from Japan, Indian and China*, London: University Press of America.

VERTOVEC, STEVEN. 1992. *Hindu Trinidad: Religion, Ethnicity and Socio-economic Change*. London: Macmillan Caribbean.

12

Bandiri Music, Globalisation and Urban Experience in Nigeria

BRIAN LARKIN

Beside Kofar Nassarawa, a gate to the mud wall that once ringed the Muslim heart of Kano, northern Nigeria, there is a *mai gyara*, a mechanic who repairs scooters and motorbikes. On this atrophying wall in the 1990s there was a poster of Ibrahim El-Zakzaky, a radical Islamic leader, and next to him one of Ayatollah Khomeini, the Shi'a leader Zakzaky championed. No doubt the mechanic or one of his assistants was a fan of Zakzaky, a somewhat charismatic figure among the Muslim youth of the north, but the fact that someone else had tried to tear off the poster of Khomeini registered the wider suspicion that Hausa Sunnis have for Shi'a worship. Once, while my vespa was in a line waiting to be repaired, one of the assistants switched cassettes on an old tape player and started playing a bandiri tape. As he did so one of the customers started to hum along, recognising the Indian film tune on which the song was based, but not knowing the words of this Hausa variation. Bandiri singers are Hausa musicians who take Indian film tunes and change the words to sing songs praising the Prophet Mohammed. This action sparked an immediate response from two customers who looked with distaste—clearly uncomfortable at being subjected to this music while waiting for their bikes to be repaired. Their discomfort provoked a mild but clear debate splitting the mechanics and customers—all from the old city of Kano—into three discrete groups: those who wanted to hear the bandiri music; those, who included the man humming along, who did not care one way or another; and the last two customers who asked that the music to be stopped.

Knowing the controversy around bandiri music because of my research on Indian film in Nigeria I found it interesting that the two customers reacted, not with anger but with a palpable sense of distaste, a sort of weary disappointment, as if the music like cigarette smoke in a restaurant was a repugnant physical presence being forced on them. It emphasised the ambivalent quality of a musical form such as bandiri which, with roots in a secular realm of entertainment, is also religious. It partakes of the elaborate Sufi tradition in which recitation of praises to the Prophet carry with them spiritual and sometimes magical benefits and sound has tangible properties beyond the aural. The distaste against bandiri may well have been motivated by a dislike of the migration of Indian films into Hausa popular culture. But while one may not like Indian music it does not make the same claims on one's spiritual well-being and mode of honouring God. It was the ability of bandiri to compromise its orthodox religious listeners by creating an unorthodox, Sufi environment that generated unease. This is an anecdote about the everyday reproduction of music and while being a marginal, fleeting moment it captures in that evanescence three themes that govern the production and circulation of bandiri music: the flow of Indian films to Nigeria, providing the raw symbolic material from which bandiri is fashioned; deep-rooted practices of Sufism which have marked West African Islam for hundreds of years; and, the recent spread of an anti-Sufi Wahhabi movement generating the contested religious space in which bandiri operates.

By singing live at public ceremonies such as weddings, or selling cassettes through local markets, bandiri[1] singers who sing Hausa praise songs to Indian tunes effect a transformation from the profane to the sacred. The popularity of the genre rests, however, on the common cultural competence of listeners who recognise their favourite Hindi film songs. By doing so these listeners see through the mask, so to speak, as the profane original haunts the sacred copy. As suggested above this is a contested phenomenon in a Muslim society undergoing an Islamist revival. Is it really Islamic, many Hausa Muslims ask, to use songs taken from sensual, un-Islamic origins for religious purposes? Moreover, the controversy over bandiri music is not just about Indian love songs. Bandiri is named after

[1] Bandiri is also known as *mandiri* in Hansa.

the drum—the *bandir*—used in ritual practice by Sufis to enter into trance. Is it really Islamic, many Hausa Muslims ask, to enter into trance, or to use drums inside the mosque, indeed to be Sufi in a world where Wahhabi belief moves provocatively across the Muslim world? Bandiri sits at the nexus of these very different sorts of transnational flows, Islamist revival and Indian popular culture that meet and make sense in northern Nigeria, in the context of a spatial configuration of culture, media and religion.

My aim in this chapter is first to analyse the workings of a cultural form like bandiri with its complex intertwining of sacred and profane, remembering and repressing. Second, I wish to use the example of bandiri, and of the three networks or sets that it exemplifies: the history of Sufi adherence, the flow of Indian film to Nigeria and the recent rise of a new legalistic Islamic movement to make a larger argument about the construction of urban space in Africa. Focusing on Kano, Nigeria, the city where bandiri began, and following Henri Lefebvre (1991), I argue that space is produced and organised over time by the penetration and transformations in capital which insert any particular place into wider networks of exchange that facilitate the flow of cultural and religious forms. Urban areas such as Kano are made up of congeries of overlapping networks. When new cultural and religious forms emerge they do so in an urban crucible that is already overdetermined according to the particular structure of those networks as they exist in a city like Kano. These networks provide the structural precondition that shapes the symbolic form and social meaning of a phenomenon like bandiri and it is the articulation of these networks together that creates the raw material from which urban experience might be fashioned.

Producing Urban Space in Africa

Recent analyses of urban space in African studies and anthropology have stressed urban space as a crucible for the flow of cultural forms across borders (see, for example, Appadurai, 1997; Gaonkar, 1999; Inda and Rosaldo, 2002). The theoretical move here has been to argue that the West and the non-West have mutually constituted each other in a structurally uneven, but nevertheless two-sided process. This is clearly aimed at asserting the agency of African or Asian societies, that while the traffic in culture from the West is prominent in African societies, as Jean-Francois Bayart remarks, this is always an act of reinvention and appropriation rather than simply domination (Barber, 1997; Barber and Waterman, 1995; Bayart, 1993; Hannerz, 1992). James Ferguson has recently made a persuasive argument that we ought to examine the nature of urban (and rural) identities in Africa as modes of cultural style: poles of signification that people can move between depending on wealth, education and cultural competence. Ferguson is mobilising an idea of urban space as defined by a syntagmatic chain of difference. To be 'rural', 'urban', 'local' or 'cosmopolitan' are not temporally distinct states of being where one evolves into another, but rather are produced in relation to each other within the same social field. Urban life, as represented here, is the matter of choosing between differing stylistic modes: whether to speak a European language or an African one; whether to dress in traditional clothes, in the bureaucratic attire of suits and ties, in baggy jeans and football shirts or in the hijab. The danger here is that the urban is defined as an arena in which a free flow of symbolic forms clash and compete without stepping back to address the issue of how these forms arrived in the first place.

Ferguson is well aware of this danger and warns against it though his central aim is not to analyse how cultural forms emerge from specific political–economic contexts.[2] Rather, for the Copperbelt urban dwellers he examines, western clothing, Congolese rumba, South African theatre and West Indian reggae comprise the established forms of urban space out of which cultural style is fashioned. By probing into the background of this space—how it comes to be organised in the way that it does—my aim is to unite this concern for hybrid cultural exchanges with a sense of the material underpinnings that make those exchanges possible.

Kano is a large sprawling city on the edge of the Sahelian desert. If the city is an event, as Georg Simmel has argued, and urban experience the outcome of a ceaseless series of encounters, then those encounters in this city are constituted within the limits of the networks that bump up against each other. Sufi religious brotherhoods, Lebanese businessmen, Ibo traders, and Hausa politicians are based in Kano but embedded in their own discrete networks that extend in different directions over the world. Space in this account is not something that is simply there but, as Lefebvre (1991) argues, is something that is the outcome of capitalist relations of

[2] Ferguson derives his concept of cultural style from performance theory and specifically the work of Judith Butler, but he argues that this work can suffer from lack of attention to wider fields of political–economic structures. He cites Kath Weston's work as a corrective to the tendency in performance studies to construe identity as in part a play of signification without due concern to the material constraints that shape the possibility of performance (Ferguson, 1999: 98–101). Ethnographically he supports this with a keen sense of the political–economic contexts in which Zambian migrants (and return migrants) operate.

exchange and those relations create the peculiar sets of networks that exist in any particular urban place. For the movement of cultural goods to occur—be they Indian films, hip-hop from the US or high fashion from Europe and Japan—a formal and informal infrastructure has to be established for creating the material channels that allow transnational cultural flows to move. These infrastructures connect certain points in a network, ranking and separating one place from another, enabling the possibility of certain connections while foreclosing other linkages. 'Flows' for all their seemingly disembodied nature (Tsing, 2000) require material conduits and they appear because a place—in this case urban Kano—is embedded in precise networks of social relations built over time.

Infrastructures are the material forms that bind and knit urban spaces into wider sets—forcing us to think of space not in terms of discrete buildings or isolated moments on a landscape, but as networked amalgams of built space connected physically by railways, shipping lanes and air routes. As capital depends on infrastructure that facilitates the circulation of goods, successive regimes of capital build the infrastructures necessary for that mode of exchange, in the process making over the urban space in their own image (Graham and Marvin, 1996, 2001; Harvey, 2000; Lefebvre, 1991). The location of markets, the siting of districts for business and residence, and the layout of roads, railways stations, airports, are all fundamentally affected by the waxing and waning of different infrastructural forms. Related to this is the fact that the physical links created by infrastructures—which places get connected into a network—has huge effect on the cultural life of a city. It shapes which migrants arrive there, which languages become commonly used, and which cultural forms become part of an urban arena.

Lefebvre argues that as space is continually reformed by the necessities of capital, newly developed networks do not eradicate earlier ones but are superimposed on top of them creating a historical layering over time. As he memorably put it, this makes space seem like the flakiness of a *mille-feuille* pastry rather than homogenous and discrete (Lefebvre, 1991: 86). At any one point, then, urban space is made up of the historical layering of networks connected by infrastructures. These are the conduits that dictate which flow of religious and cultural ideas move and therefore which social relations get mobilised in their wake. Their historical layering helps explain why dormant cultural, religious and economic forms can suddenly gain purchase again, be reawakened and re-energised in a new situation.

Urban spaces such as Kano can be seen as assemblage of different sets that connect Hausa to other networks. By set I am loosely using the mathematical definition of a set as the combination of different elements interlinked to form a totality. Infrastructures—both material and immaterial —are the connecting tissues that bind these elements to the whole. They are material in the obvious sense of the construction of air routes, railways etc., that join one place to another. They are immaterial in that they require linguistic competencies, professional expertise, and educational styles and cultural philosophies that facilitate the exchange of information and goods across cultural boundaries. Islam, for instance, is one such set integrating Kano Muslims into a wider totality of the Muslim *umma* by means of shared religious practices, pilgrimages, education, Sufi adherence and so on. Islam itself can be broken down into multiple sub-sets only some of which the Hausa are involved in. When we refer to the 'urban experience', partly what we are referring to is the particular assemblage of sets that forms the unique configuration of a city. These are layered over time and the introduction of new layers interacts with previous ones, re-energising some, closing off others, but always creating the unique configuration of a city. This evolution orients Kano internally toward southern Nigeria but also across the Sahara to North Africa and the Middle East, across the Atlantic and increasingly over the Indian Ocean to Asia (Bayart et al., 1999). Northerners chase modernity through Muslim connections to Saudi Arabia, Dubai and other Islamic centres, as well as through connections to the West. All this makes Kano integrated yet distinct from its sister cities in the south and it is out of this Kano-based configuration of Islamic and Western modernity, that the unlikely synthesis of bandiri music, with its roots in Sufi worship and Hindi lovemaking, is possible.

Set One: The Lovers of the Prophet

In 1996 I was taken by the bandiri singer Lawan 'Dan Yaro Magashi to a bandiri performance in the Magashi quarters of the Kano *birni* (old city). Magashi is an area in the old city of Kano, for Muslims the traditional moral heart where Islamic values and lifestyles are maintained (Barkindo, 1993; Larkin, 2002; Tahir, 1975). It is an overwhelmingly Sufi area, predominantly Tijaniyya but with a large and powerful minority of Qadiriyya followers (Anwar, 1989; Paden, 1973). Outside a house where a naming ceremony was being performed the group had tied loudspeakers to the walls across the narrow alleyway. The singer held the microphone and sang Hausa words to Indian film tunes and behind him four youths sang back in response, each of them beating the bandir, the large black tambourine-like drum from North Africa. In front of them all were another seven or so youths dancing a Sufi dance, punching their arms back and forth in time to the music. In the doorways young girls listened, laughing, their bodies covered in brightly coloured prints and their heads encased by large scarves while the alleys around were packed with a mob of boys listening, shouting and sometimes singing to the song being played. Older men looked on, somewhat sceptically, from a distance. As the song finished another youth took the place of the singer pitting his skill at lyric writing and singing against the one who came before (and who would come after).

In a way, bandiri could only have emerged in areas like this in Kano, or similar areas in sister Sufi cities such as Sokoto and Zaria in the north.[3] Kano was one of the urban areas where Indian films first emerged in the 1950s and today it remains the distribution centre for pirated video cassettes of Indian films (the main way they circulate in the north). In the second half of the twentieth century it has been a font for the introduction of new modes of Islamic education thereby paving the way for the emergence of a cadre of modernist religious scholars that have gone on to lead new anti-Sufi Islamist movements. But, most famously, Kano has been known for nearly a century as a dominant centre of Tijaniyya Sufi affiliation and learning.

Bandiri music developed from the religious use of the bandir drum by Qadiriyya Sufi adepts. Every evening in Kano, Qadiriyya Sufis gather at certain mosques for the public performance of the *dhikr*—the ritual that uses the bandir drum to regulate the speed of chanting litanies (Loimeier, 1997). Roman Loimeier highlights the importance of repetition: '... where

[3] Sufism is based around the charismatic authority of a founding saint whose knowledge is passed down in a direct line of descent from sheikh to disciple. As orders mature over time they extend over space, generating dispersed networks linked by common ritual practices, pilgrimage and education. Kano has long been famous as an economic centre of the trans-Saharan and trans-Sudanic trade routes and there has been a long connection between Sufism and the dominant Kano trading families. These families are associated with important Sufi sheikhs and many have produced their own lineages of distinguished religious scholars. Many scholars have pointed out that the common religious affiliation of particular Sufi orders has been key to the creation of non-kin based trading networks that rely heavily on credit and trust, and that the success of Sufism is an example of the clouding of religious and economic activities (Paden, 1973; Tahir, 1975). In Kano, the success of the Sufi order Tijaniyya is strongly linked to its role in producing patron–client networks that are seen as central to the order's reputation for economic success. It is this crucible of Sufi affiliation that lies behind the success of bandiri.

through the constant chanting of a short phrase like Allah Allah [...] the participants breathe in or against the rhythm of their chanting' (Loimeier, 1997: 60), leading to the invoking of trancelike states (Buba and Furniss, 1999). This is a public phenomenon that arose in the late 1950s as part of the effort by a Qadiriyya Sheikh, Nasir Kabara, to turn Sufi practice from an elite, secret movement into a mass movement. As Loimeier observes, the regular public ritual of bandir drumming has become a public spectacle of Qadiriyya affiliation in that 'the presence of the tariqâ [Sufi order] in the city is underlined not only visually but also acoustically from day to day and night to night' (ibid., see also Paden, 1973).

As a musical practice, bandiri derives significance from this ritual use but is different in key ways. For the most part it is played at events such as wedding parties and naming ceremonies which have both a religious and a non-religious dimension (Buba and Furniss, 1999). Often, different singers will come together with the same backing group. They will take a particular Indian film, such as *Kabhi Kabhi* (*Sometimes*, dir. Yash Chopra, 1976) and divide up the songs between them, each one responsible for translating a different song from the film into a Hausa praise song. Then, during the performance, the singers will take turns, each competing with one another for the best performance. There is tremendous excitement around this, in the energy of the dancing, the sound of the drums, and the reaction of the crowd gathered around. While the audience is mostly young, certain songs are chosen from 1950s and 1960s Indian films to directly appeal to older people in the audience. Bandiri is seen by both performers and audience as a religious form, but it clearly borders many of the activities and genres of secular music.

Bandiri orginated in the practice of youths studying at Islamiyya schools, the new schools in Nigeria that teach Islamic subjects in a western pedagogic framework. Students at these schools got together to sing songs in Hausa on how to obey parents, or translated short *hadith* (the record of the sayings and deeds of the Prophet Mohammed) and turned them into songs, or simply sang praises to the Prophet. The first songs were religious versions of popular songs by Hausa musicians such as Mamman Shata or 'Dan Kwairo and after a while youths began to adapt Indian film songs (it was and remains common for Hausa youth to sing Indian film songs in school). Their aim was revivalist, to introduce a more religious dimension to popular activities such as wedding parties and naming ceremonies and to attract youth back to religious contemplation through the form of popular mass culture.

In the late 1980s as bandiri began to take off in popularity, societies such as *Kungiyar Yabon Manzon Allah* (Society for Praising the Messenger of God) and *Kungiyar Ushaq'u Indiya* (Society for the Lovers of India) were created to formalise the coming together of young Hausa singers performing bandiri music. *Ushaq'u* is an Arabic word meaning a passionate or ardent lover and is derived from the world *'Ishq* meaning passion or yearning. In Hausa (as opposed to Arabic) the word is associated with a religious register in contrast to the more familiar term for romantic love. As one singer explained to me *'ishq*, in the Hausa usage at least, refers to the deepest possible love. While singers do sell cassettes that are sold generally on the market, bandiri is still primarily a live performance genre. Groups are sponsored by individuals to perform at specific ceremonies and they often try to translate their prestige from bandiri performance into a patron–client relation with prominent Sufi *malams*[4] or religious teachers (Buba and Furniss, 1999). As bandiri gained in popularity singers started to sell cassettes through specialist dealers at the market. The first tapes were compilations of different bandiri singers and grouped under the heading of the Society of Ushaq'u singers and labelled *Ushaq'u Indiya 1*, *Ushaq'u Indiya 2* and so on.[5] The tapes themselves contain an opening prayer and a brief introduction to the singers. Some tapes address the audience as 'My brothers, Lovers of the Messenger of Allah (S.A.W.)' implicitly constructing the audience as fellow Sufi members (likely to be the case) and reasserting the religious intention to the music.

Set Two: The Rise of Anti-Sufism

Bandiri music grew and developed in an arena of overt conflict. Those who perform bandiri realise that this is a controversial activity. As one told me, 'You know religion in our country. One man's meat is another man's poison', and that while many people are against

[4] Singers do attempt to make money through the commodification of bandiri by selling cassettes, but for the most part the material benefit of bandiri comes through prestige which can be used within the Sufi network itself. The most prestigious activity, for instance, is to be invited by an important sheikh to perform at *maulud* celebrations that celebrate the birthday of the Prophet Mohammed or of important Sufi saints. These celebrations are deeply controversial in Hausa society as many Wahhabi's attact these acts of commemoration as unIslamic. Despite such reactions, the celebrations remain central rituals in the Sufi calendar.

[5] Each tape has a brief introduction which reaffirms the religious intent of the cassette and introduces the society and particular singers. I quote here from the opening to the cassette *Ushaq'u Indiya na sha biyu* (Ushaq'u India number 12)

bandiri music many more find it hugely attractive. This conflict does not just derive from the software of bandiri—the songs and their borrowing from Indian films—but the hardware itself—using the bandir drum—and the drum's significance as a symbol of Sufi adherence. The identification of bandiri with Sufism has made it deeply controversial in Nigeria, piggy backing onto the wider religious conflict that has pitted established Sufi orders against the rise of a new Wahhabi oriented movement—Izala (*Jama'at Izalatil Bid'a wa Iqamatus Sunna* or The Movement Against Innovation and for a Return to the Sunna)—and its intellectual leader Abubakar Gumi (Barkindo, 1993; Gumi, 1972, 1992; Loimeier, 1997; Umar, 1993).

The rise of Abubakar Gumi is significant because his figure represents the shift to a new configuration of Hausa economy, politics and society. Gumi was one of the first Islamic scholars to be educated by the British within the colonial education system and certainly the first major religious leader to come to prominence through his participation in the colonial and post-colonial bureaucracy. Before him Sufi scholars were linked to aristocratic elites and to old trading families who were deeply suspicious of western education and the *boko* (western) lifestyle. Gumi's support network was different, it relied on his alliances within the post-colonial bureaucracy and his close relations with elected politicians, military figures and bureaucrats. And for Gumi it was precisely his bureaucratic colonial links—as a scholarship student to the Sudan, and as Nigerian Pilgrims Officer to Saudi Arabia—which helped him travel widely within the Muslim world. Gumi was especially known for his close relationship with Saudi Arabia, one that began with his stint as Pilgrim's Officer but was cemented by his role as religious leader to the Sardauna of Sokoto, the Premier of the Northern Region of Nigeria at independence. Gumi adopted the legalistic, anti-Sufi brand of Islamic belief prominent in Saudi Wahhabism and it was this which he brought back to Nigeria.

In the name of Allah the most gracious and most merciful, may peace be upon the Prophet Muhammad and may God bless him and his family. My relatives, lovers of the Messenger of Allah, we are now going to introduce Ushaq'u India cassette number 12. The singers are:

Muhammad Lawan Yaro Magashi
Muhammad Abubakar Baffajo
Marmara Auwalu Iguda Takasai
Balarabe Musa Kabada
Sani Garba S/K Dan/Dago

Mallam Inuwa Bala is the person to beat the drum.

In the early 1970s, Gumi began to outline a critique of Sufism in a variety of fora from tafsir (Qur'anic exegesis) at the mosque, to newspaper articles and radio broadcasts. This critique followed orthodox Wahhabi lines: he attacked Sufism as an innovation *(bid'a)* in Islamic practice in a religion where innovation in matters of faith was not allowed; he criticised the veneration of Sufi saints and the practice of Sufi orders; and, in its stead he argued for a return to the key texts of Islam—the Qur'an and the hadith—which were available to everyone through education and reason. In 1972 his critique was centralised into a book *The Right Belief is Based on the Sharia* which caused an uproar in Nigeria. Gumi's strategy was to take central ritual symbols of the prominent Sufi orders in Nigeria—the Tijaniyya and Qadiriyya—and to argue that they ran contrary to the teachings of the Qur'an. In the case of Qadiriyya the tactic was to take on one of the central rituals of the order—the use of the bandir drum in the mosque—and to argue that it was an illegal innovation. Most shockingly he did so using sharp, inflammatory language claiming that 'those who combine drumming with religion [...] reduce their religion to a plaything [...]. They will taste the punishment which they disbelieve' (Gumi, 1972: 43).

The effect of this attack was electric. The history of Islam in Nigeria has been rent with religious conflict but to this point this had always been conflict within and between Sufi orders. Gumi was now claiming that they were all 'imposters in islam' (Gumi, 1992: 142) sparking an intense backlash that spilled over into armed conflict between the followers of the different camps. The use of the bandir was defended by Nasiru Kabara the Qadiriyya sheikh with which the practice was most identified.[6] Gumi's attack, and Kabara's defence, meant that the use of the bandir drum came to be a defining symbol of Sufi belief or deviance. It became a dense symbol of the conflict between Sufis and anti-Sufis, something to be championed or rejected but never ignored.

It is no accident that the use of bandiri music, with its evangelical goal of using popular Hausa songs and Indian film tunes to bring youths back to religious practice, arose at a time when Sufi practice itself was under unprecedented assault from a Wahhabi inspired anti-Sufi movement. The activity of singing praise songs, even of calling the singers 'lovers of the prophet' is an implicit attack on the condemnation of praise singing by the transnational spread of orthodox Wahhabi ideas to Nigeria. These themes are often explicitly dealt with in the songs themselves when singers

[6] For an account, see Loimeier, 1997.

assert their right to praise the Prophet despite 'whoever is against him',[7] a dark warning neatly conflating non-Muslims with followers of Izala, the movement led by Abubakar Gumi. The background of the Sufi–Izala conflict provides the cultural and religious reason why Indian film music was taken up—both in this way and at this time. By drawing on the massive popularity of the film style and the already existing practices of singing Hindi films songs, Sufi followers managed to establish a powerful and popular new music genre, the significance of which lies in the layering of social relations and space: the position of Kano as the node of two very different circuits of cultural and religious flows—one reaching out across the Sahara and the other across the Indian ocean.

Set Three: Indian Films in Kano

Indian music saturates the popular culture of northern Nigeria creating a landscape of desire and spectacle and a field for nostalgia and memory. This nostalgia derives from the long historical popularity of Indian films among Nigerian audiences dating back to the 1950s, which has imprinted generations of Hausa with the songs, narratives and stars of Indian film (Larkin, 1997). Bandiri taps into these emotions, creating an intertextual play with romance and devotion, charisma and stardom and traditional culture and modernity. It is a form of mimicking whereby the 'copy' draws from the power and symbolic richness of the original but only at the cost of raising questions of cultural authenticity and cultural erosion. The tunes that bandiri singers borrow bring with them memories and tastes of the original context of reception. A song about the love of the followers of the Prophet Mohammed for him is shadowed by an image of the actor Salman Khan doing press-ups in the film *Maine*

[7] Take this example: a version of a song by Sidi Musa from the Indian film *Hum Dono*.

S: Praising Mustapha is necessary for us, whoever is against Him, the Prophet is ours …

S: In the name of God I intend to long …
I going to praise my Mustapha …
If they like it or if they don't like it …
Our Messenger is in front …
Because he is the one that we love my Mustapha …

A: Praising Mustapha is necessary for us, whoever is against Him, the Prophet is ours.

S: I swear I love you O Sayyadi …
And I love to choose you O Sayyadi …
O my life, O my Mohammad …

Pyar Kiya (*I Have Fallen in Love*, dir. Sooraj R. Barjatya, 1989); other songs are haunted by the actors and actresses symbolically superimposed over every song of praise. Nigerian Sufi followers resignify this music into devotional songs, syphoning and transforming charisma from one context to another. Bandiri thus relies upon a dialectic of similarity and difference. The copy has to be similar enough for the original to be recognised, to recoup the profits of mimesis, but yet it has to be transformed, religiously and culturally. Its original context must be obliterated at the same time as it is invoked, in order to take on sacred meaning. This is the aura that local Hausa singers bring to a devotional tradition of praise singing with a long, elaborate history. At the same time as redefining Indian films in a Hausa context, then, they are redefining Sufi praise music in terms of its association with the glamorous modernity of Indian films. And they project, through mimicry, Hausa popular culture into the prestigious and alluring world of global cultural flows.

One of the interesting features of the popularity of Indian films in northern Nigeria is the dialectic of similarity and dissimilarity and the ways that cultural borrowing involves elaborate acts of remembering and repressing. For instance, I have previously discussed the complicated way in which Hausa people see Indian culture as 'just like' Hausa culture: in its depiction of relations between the genders; in the negotiation between a reified 'traditional' culture and an equally reified 'westernisation'; and, in the mise en scène and iconography of everyday life (Larkin, 1997). This is one aspect of the ways in which Indian films benefit from a perceived similarity and a strong identification between the two cultures, one based on cultural practice, moral ethics and linguistic similarity. Many Hausa, for instance, argue that Hausa and Hindi are descended from the same language—an argument also voiced to me by an Indian importer of films in accounting for their popularity. While 'wrong' in terms of linguistic evolution, this argument takes into account the substantial presence of Arabic and English loan words in both languages, a key factor in creating this perceived sense of similarity. Hausa and Indians have also been linked through the common denominator of the British empire and it is interesting to specu-late on the mediating presence that the empire had in creating a sense of commonality that helps account for the popularity of Indian films.[8] All this feeds into the cultural background of the Indian

[8] In many ways the British empire can be regarded as a set that placed diverse societies into articulation via the historical experience of colonisation. When the British took over northern Nigeria they brought with them principles of governing that had been first

post-colony and explains part of the identification of Hausa audiences with Indian culture in the common historical experience of the British empire and the perceived tension between traditional culture and a modernising western one.

The powerful sense of identification between the two cultures is also explained in terms of Bollywood's alterity from American and British film and television and its depiction of moral problems that are simply absent from most western media (Larkin, 1997). This was brought over to me in a discussion about the film *Maine Pyar Kiya* starring Salman Khan, a hit in Nigeria as elsewhere. My male friend identified hugely with the central tension of the films—Salman Khan's father forbidding his son to marry a poor girl and attempting to force him to marry the rich daughter of a business friend. The overt sentimentality was not seen in terms of fantasy but as something that emerges out of the historical experience of common people, a historical experience common to Nigeria and India: the power of elders over youth and the corruption of traditional relations by the pursuit of money. As my friend commented:

> So the film is educative in fact. I have never watched an Indian film very interesting like this one. Because I shed tears, tears in watching the film [...] though knowing the film is fiction but I still shed tears, because it just showed a real dedication to what is happening in the world.[9]

This comment is common in northern Nigeria where people see Indian films as representing real, everyday problems and not in the terms of kitsch fantasy with which they are greeted in the West. This is what makes them educative. Bashir made this explicit:

> American films are based mainly on [...] either action, war or just a show, like documentaries, so that is it. But Indian films on the other side, they base their films on their problems and on the problems of the masses, their masses. Anyway I don't watch much American films.[10]

elaborated in the crucible of South Asia. Certainly, there was traffic in administrative personnel, modes of bureaucracy, in language (English) in educational principles, cultural styles, fashions and evening forms of ritual. It is interesting to speculate whether this common historical experience may account for the Hausa sense of similarities with Indian society.

[9] Interview, Sani Bashir, November 1995.

[10] ibid.

When the Hausa refer to Indian films being 'just like' Hausa culture—a sentiment echoed here by Bashir—they actually mean the films are *more like* Hausa culture than the other two dominant mass cultural fields the Hausa engage in—southern Nigerian and American media. Indian films are more sexually demure than American films but they are far more transgressive than everyday Hausa culture and as much as reflecting problems inherent to that society they are potentially threatening and destabilising of it. This tension between like and unlike, similarity and distance is the key to the appeal of transnational cultural forms as it allows imaginative play which is tolerated *precisely because it is different*. The Hausa can watch Indian films and appreciate their similarities while easily downplaying the differences. This has been recently dramatised by the rise of a Hausa video film industry in the late 1990s. Unlike their southern counterparts Hausa film-makers have explicitly borrowed from Indian films moving away from themes of magic, witchcraft, corruption and money that mark southern Nigerian videos and emphasising instead the theme of love. The alterity of Hausa videos from southern Nigerian ones and their similarity to Indian films is most marked by the song and dance sequences between the actor and actress which heavily borrow from Indian films. These sequences follow the generic conventions of Indian films: songs stand as a proxy for physical love and for intense emotions that cannot be expressed in everyday language; they take place outside of the diegetic space of the story in areas of picturesque natural beauty; and this fantastic, extra-real environment is accentuated by frequent costume changes within the same song sequence. While massively popular these sequences have caused huge controversy in Hausa society for initiating what is seen as an un-Islamic, and un-Hausa mode of courtship into Hausa film. In the wake of the introduction of Shari'a law in 2001 and in response to the public outcry, the making of these Hausa videos were banned in Kano state (the prime site of production). Later the ban was eased so that film-making could continue as long the song sequences did not include sexual intermixing. Interestingly enough, during this controversy neither did the new Islamic state see any need to ban Indian films, and nor does the new censorship board censor Indian films which continue to be popular. The tension arose when styles of love and sexual interaction from Indian films were dramatised in a Hausa context. What could be tolerated while safely confined to the practices of another culture (however 'like' Hausa culture it may be) was simply too controversial when the necessary gap for cultural borrowing was collapsed. Indian films are more demure than Hollywood ones, less explicit than recent southern Nigerian videos, but they are still sexually transgressive for an orthodox Islamic society, and like all cultural flows the popularity of Indian film depends on the maintenance of a safe distance, a stable alterity, the lack of which can be powerfully threatening.

Bandiri

Emerging out of the long Sufi tradition of singing praise songs to the Prophet, bandiri partakes of that tradition in using a language of erotics whereby mystical arousal is linked to emotional arousal. In ritual use, trance can be used to provoke mystical love culminating in ecstasy whereby the person possessed can mystically communicate with God or the Prophet (Qureshi, 1995). In bandiri, Mohammed is often the focus of intense love and longing and bandiri singers (and Sufi adepts) refer to themselves as 'lovers of the prophet' the emotional excessive realm of secular love being used to convey to quite different but equally emotional parameters of religious love. Take this example sung by Sidi Musa and adapted from the film *Geet Gata Chal* (*Go Singing a Song*, dir. Hiren Nag, 1975):

M: My heart is longing for you, my soul loves you, me, I am longing for my messenger, the Prophet of God.
A: My messenger the Prophet of God.
M: My heart is longing for you, my soul loves you, me, I am longing for my messenger, the Prophet of God.
A: My messenger the Prophet of God.
M: Owo You are the one I am longing for Mustapha na Sayyadi. You are the one longing for Habibi, Prophet of God.
A: Habibi, Prophet of God.
M: I am longing ... O ... I am continuously longing for you. I am longing more and more.
A: O Mohammad Prophet of God, O my lover.[11]

Here M = *Mai wak'a* (singer) and A = *Amshi* (reply).

In this Hausa song the vaulting strings of Indian film songs are absent as is the western and Indian instrumentation leaving only the beating of the drum. Where the original film song is based around a duet between a man and a woman each singing verse, Sidi Musa, in turn, uses the more familiar African form of call and response played out between him and his backing singers. What is shared between Musa's song and the original is the melody

[11] See also Buba and Furniss, 1999: 39.

and the sense of emotional excess, with Sufi followers using the ecstatic enactments of love in Indian films and stripping them of their secular trappings. Bandiri creates a play of similarity and difference, like and dislike, profane and sacred. We can see this process at work better by examining a Hausa song, '*Zumar zuma bege*', by the bandiri singer Lawan 'Dan Yaro Magashi. '*Zumar zuma*' is an adaptation of a famous song '*Jumma chumma de de*' (Jumma give me a kiss) performed by Amitabh Bachchan in the film *Hum* (dir. Mukul Anand, 1991).

The song sequence from which '*Jumma chumma*' is taken is set in an Indian shipyard warehouse where a petty rogue, Tiger, dances with his docker friends singing to his girlfriend demanding that she give him a kiss. Jumma refuses as she sashays across a platform above them, raising her long red flamenco dress and revealing her black stockinged legs while her breast heaves in and out. Tiger and his friends dance in choreographed ecstasy, their pelvises thrusting back and forth. Finally, Tiger, impatient with her denials, picks up a hose large enough to represent the symbolic ejaculation of the dockers and drenches Jumma, tearing off her dress, knocking her from her platform into the midst of the gyrating men below. The distance between them collapsed, she dances with the men, her body wet and uncovered. Still she refuses to kiss her lover maintaining the teasing distance between them until finally she and Tiger are engulfed by the dancing men and when Tiger emerges his face is covered with the bright red marks of her lipstick.

'Dan Yaro Magashi took the song from this sequence and wrote a Hausa version in honour of the Prophet Mohammed. In this version Tiger's song to Jumma is transformed into an African call and response between 'Dan Yaro Magashi and the bandiri drummers providing accompaniment. The skill here lies not just in copying the Indian tune or the quality of the singing, but also in the cleverness with which 'Dan Yaro chooses Hausa words which closely mirror the original Hindi.

Jumma chumma de de		***Zuma zumar bege***
Jumma chumma de de	M:	*Zuma zumar bege*
jummaa chumma de de, jumma		*zuma zumar bege mu sha*
jumma chumma de de	A:	*Zuma zumar bege*
	M:	*Bege bege*
	A:	*Zuma zumar bege mu sha*
Jumma chumma de de jummaa	M:	*Zuma zumar bege ... bege*
		zuma zumar bege mu sha
	A:	*Zuma zumar bege*

	M:	*Bege bege*
	A:	*Zuma zumar bege mu sha*
Jumma ke din kiyaa chumma kaa vaadaa	M:	*Zumar yabo ta gurin dan Amina,*
Jumma ko tod diyaa chumme kaa vaadaa		*manzo masoyi masoyina na raina*
le aa gayaa re phir jummaa-chummaa		*ko yar kadan ni ina so na kurba in sha ...*
Jumma chumma de de	A:	*Zumar zuma bege*

Here M = *Mai wak'a* (singer) and A = *Amshi* (reply).

'*Jumma chumma de de jumma*' (Jumma [a girl's name] give me, give me a kiss) becomes '*zuma zumar bege mu sha*' (honey, honey we are longing to drink). Similarly, the verse line '*Jumma ke din kiyaa chumma kaa vaadaa*' is transformed into '*Zumar yabo ta gurin dan Amina*'. The purpose of bandiri music is to strip the Indian song of its original lyrics, thus symbolically divorcing it from its original filmic context. Here that context is a song sequence famous within Indian films for its raunchiness. Amitabh Bachchan plays a docker (Tiger) and Kimi Katkar (Jumma) the object of his desire. The sequence opens with Katkar parading down a runway above a band of seething dockers alternately raising and lowering her red flamenco dress. The wide shots of the group are intercut with medium close-ups of Tiger and his cronies thrusting their pelvises in and out. Here the Indian film plays with the boundaries of the gendered moral universe of Indian film. As Sunita Mukhi points out Katkar repeatedly says 'no no' to Bachchan while her actions mime 'yes yes'. It is striking that a song with such a sexualised origin could be seen as fodder for religious meditation, but this is part of the ambiguous place Indian films play in the landscape of northern Nigerian culture.

Remembering and Repressing

As much as bandiri rests upon the dialectic of similarity and difference it intimately engages emotions of remembering and repressing. For copying to be successful the original tune has to be recognised and the Hausa lyrics are tied physically to the Hindi originals. But every moment of copying carries with it the anxiety produced by the immoral origins of the song. This immorality is heightened when we consider the ambivalent place of cinema within the conservative social arena of northern

Nigeria. There, cinemas used to be largely all male places, the few women who did attend were seen as prostitutes and sexual desire was to be found both on and off the screen (Larkin, 1997). Since the introduction of Islamic law in 2001 women have been formally banned from these places and strict sexual segregation enforced. It is in this context that Indian films, the aura of relative sexual freedom they display and the teasing independence of actresses (shown well in Kimi Katkar's flirtation with Bachchan) gain sexual and moral purchase. Indian actresses are often seen as quintessential prostitutes not because they are immoral but because their deportment and relative freedom in interacting with men, their sexual freedom and their glamour are all attributes associated with *karuwai* (prostitutes) in Nigeria. It is therefore not uncommon that important female and male homosexual prostitutes in Kano name themselves after favourite film actresses, playing with these identities and borrowing from the aura of Indian stardom in a way that is analogous to bandiri music, but morally inverting its use. In the context of Hausa society then, Indian films can be sexually transgressive, their erotic display, their sexual intermixing and the use of music for carnal and not religious purposes combine to keep them beyond the pale of orthodox Islam. For bandiri singers these origins must be repressed at the moment they are invoked, forgotten (so to speak) just at the time they are remembered for the transformation from secular to sacred to occur. This action is often addressed in the songs themselves as in this example from Sidi Musa's song from *Geet Gata Chal* cited earlier:

M: My heart is longing for you my soul loves you. I am longing for my messenger the Prophet of God.
A: My messenger the Prophet of God.
M: Oh whenever I start translating an Indian song leave me this work and I shall finish it.
A: Ai you are the one to finish it.
M: Those who are longing for women should stop it. They should long for my Messenger the Prophet of God.
A: My Messenger the Prophet of God.
M: Those who are longing for women should stop it. They should long for my Messenger the Prophet of God.
A: My Messenger the Prophet of God.
M: We should forget about Indian songs, they are useless.
A: They are useless.

M: I am saying, in Indian songs I heard them singing Geet Gata Chal, but I am singing the Prophet of God.
A: The Greatest.
A: O Mohammed, Prophet of God, O my lover.
M: Sidi Musa, son of Sidi, I am the one who composed this Praising of the Prophet of God.

Here M = *Mai wak'a* (singer) and A = *Amshi* (reply).

Here you get a prime instance of the ways in which the original context is repressed in the moment of its mimesis. The association between songs and longing for women sets up the undesirable, unIslamic, nature of Indian songs—*ba shi da amfani*—it is useless. But at the same time the song carries the intense emotions familiar from Indian films. As in western musicals, songs in Indian films are often timed to appear as proxies for powerful feelings characters cannot convey in everyday conversation. Bandiri singers wish to maintain that intensity of emotion, to copy it, but then to divorce it from its original context leaving only a heightened state of being.

Mimicry then, lies at the heart of the social meaning of bandiri music. Taussig (1993: xiii) argues that 'the power of mimesis lies in the copy drawing on the character and power of the original, to the point whereby the representation may even assume that character and power'. What is occurring here is a siphoning of charisma, as Sufis are harnessing the glamour and transnational prestige associated with Indian films to the quite different charisma of religious devotion.[12] But in this case, bandiri can only be successful if the meanings generated through mimicry can be limited. Whether this can be completely achieved is an open question. Certainly older Hausa and non-Sufis who look down on bandiri music and some who criticise it fiercely believe that the shadow of its original filmic performance haunts the reproduction, undermining it and making it either detrimental to Hausa culture (because of foreign borrowing) or unIslamic, depending on your point of view. Peter Manuel (1993) observes that the same tension operates in the performance of parodies in the Indian context, especially devotional ones where 'the borrowed melodies may remind listeners of the specific cinematic scenes in which they were picturized' and that these 'extra-musical' associations can never be

[12] Meg McLagan provides an interesting discussion of the tension between religious charisma and media celebrity in her discussion of the resignification of the Dalai Lama in the Tibet movement. See McLagan, 2002.

divorced, and perhaps threaten to overwhelm, the transformed meaning of the copy.

This suggests the difficulty, previously mentioned, of being able to 'repress' the filmic origins of particular songs to the degree necessary to make them sacred and no longer profane. The singer Lawan 'Dan Yaro Magashi explained to me that he always sings 'classic' songs from older films because it takes the older generation by surprise when they recognise a song from their youth. He talked of how old people would come up and reminisce about seeing the film from which the original song was taken, suggesting that he explicitly aimed to evoke the original moment of reception in order to draw upon it to give the Sufi version emotional resonance and meaning. Sudhir Kakar (1989) has written about the important ways that the common cultural competence of youths immersed in Indian films (or any other sort of films) such as my aforementiond Hausa friend, creates a common memory that provides a field of nostalgia later in life. Writing of himself, Kakar recalled the sexual pleasure he experienced in his early childhood at watching wet saree scenes. When he saw such a scene recently,

> I felt grateful to the world of Hindi movies for providing continuity in an unstable and changing world [...] When I was a child, the movies brought the vistas of a desirable adulthood tantalizingly close; as an adult, I find they help to keep the road to childhood open (ibid.: 26).

Remembering and repressing, mimesis and alterity are the oppositions that provide the productive tensions thus making bandiri work.

Indian Songs, Copies, Originals, and Copies Again

If Bandiri music is a copy it brings up the question of what is the original of which it is a copy? This can be a significant question in the case of Indian film songs which, as many observers point out, are nothing if not rapacious in culling melodies and rhythms from religious, folk and popular musics of the world. One famous source of Hindi film songs, for instance, are qawwalis, the rhythmic chanting, drumming and clapping performed by Sufi followers in India and Pakistan, intended to stimulate intense emotions (Manuel, 1993; Qureshi, 1995). From the inception of Indian cinema qawwali was subsumed to the secular needs of the new medium. Instrumentation was made more diverse, emotional intensity was retained, but the focus was shifted to include romance as well as religion. Regula Qureshi points out that over time there has been a feedback loop between live qawwali performances and filmic qawwalis. Film music has borrowed heavily from the religious genre, but then the transformations it has introduced have fed back into live qawwali performances. Moving across space to northern Nigeria, Hausa Sufi followers, unaware of the Sufi roots to some of the songs they listen to, nevertheless recognise the emotional intensity (that first attracted music directors to qawwali) and re-resignify that emotional ecstasy back into an 'original' Sufi context. Which one is the copy? In the case of '*Jumma Chumma*' this is all the more byzantine in that, unknown to Lawan 'Dan Yaro Magashi the Hausa singer of '*Zuma zumar bege*', '*Jumma Chumma*' is itself an adaptation of '*Yeke Yeke*', a West African song sung by the Malian singer Mory Kante.

When, between 1970 and 1983, the Nigerian government banked $140 billion from the boom in oil revenues the surge of these oil monies through the urban networks of cities such as Lagos, Port Harcourt, Onitsha and Kano had similar and dissimilar effects. On the one hand all of them experienced the 'fast capitalism' of oil wealth: rapid urban growth, a flood of consumer goods, and a shift toward a consumption based economy (Watts, 1992). But, in many ways, these monies set in motion different effects. The south's long-standing interaction with the West led to an increased penetration of evangelical Protestantism into southern Christianity and this meant that more people than ever before began to travel, work and be educated in Europe and the United States. In the north of Nigeria, the arrival of oil monies hugely intensified Hausa interaction with the wider Islamic world. Oil enabled the Hausa to invigorate pre-colonial and colonial participation in Sufi networks. It facilitated mass participation in the hajj, intensifying the educational, financial and political links between Nigeria and Saudi Arabia that were crucial to the rise of Wahhabi ideas and movements.

In this way the structural reorganisation brought about by the oil boom set in motion both similar and dissimilar effects in Nigerian cities. The reason for this lies in the historical residue of social practices, the layering of social spaces, which accumulate in any particular place. Transformations in capital energise the historical layers embedded in a city, facilitating the intensification of some and initiating others while closing down still more. It helps explain why dormant cultural, religious and economic forms can suddenly gain purchase again, be reawakened and re-energised in a new situation. As Lefebvre (1991: 73) argues, 'itself the outcome of past actions, social space is what permits fresh actions to occur, while suggesting others and prohibiting yet others'.

Bandiri emerges out of the urban crucible of Kano in northern Nigeria and the specific historical configuration that creates the conditions for the Kano urban experience. In Kano, air routes link the metropolis to Beirut, Jeddah, Lagos and London. Stickers of Sufi preachers contest with Osama Bin Laden, Sani Abacha, Shah Rukh Khan, Tupac Shakur, and Ali Nuhu for space on Kano buses and taxis.[13] The recent revival of Shari'a law is contemporaneous with the jump in popularity of gangsta rap and hip hop available on VCD and satellite television. As an urban centre, Kano is the node of overlapping sets of cultural, religious and economic networks that provide the skeleton around which Kano urban life is built. They provide the raw material that cultural actors use to express identity. Cultural and economic ties to the West are countered by the increasing orientation of Nigerian traders toward the Middle East and Asia and the pilgrimage to Mecca has become the context for legal and illegal trade as well as for religious observance.

The bricolage of culture inherent in a phenomenon such as bandiri is not a free-floating event. It is the fashioning of cultural performance from the availability of cultural forms in a particular given space—urban Kano. The media generates urban forms by activating connections in a network, placing Kano Hausawa (Hausa people) into material and immaterial connections with movements and ideas from over the world making the urban arena 'a multiplicity of spaces crosscutting intersecting or aligning with one another, or existing in relations of paradox or antagonism' (Massey, 1994: 3). In this way bandiri can be seen as an epiphenomenon of an historical trajectory that brings certain social sets into articulation in the crucible of Kano bringing about the historical conditions of possibility from which something like bandiri might emerge. Urban possibilities are formed out of the unintended juxtapositions of different sets present in urban space. Bandiri music highlights how much Hausa audiences are avid and longtime consumers of a transnational circulation of Indian images and music for which they are the unintended recipients. For 40 years an information flow has been persistently diverted off the mainstream of its distribution circuit to other places south of the Sahelian desert. It is there that it rubs against an Islamic society in the midst of religious revival and out of that experience a new form of music—bandiri—emerges.

---

[13] Osama Bin Laden is the Islamic terrorist; Sani Abacha is a former dictator of Nigeria; Shah Rukh Khan is a famous Indian film star; Tupac Shankar is the late African-American rap artist; and, Ali Nuhu is a star of Hausa video films.

Acknowledgements

The research for this article was provided by the Wenner-Gren foundation. I am very grateful to Lawan 'Dan Yaro Magashi, Alh., Alh. Rabi'u B.K. and Yusufu Hamid for introducing me to the world of bandiri music. Translations were provided by Usman Aliyu Abdulmalik and *Al-haji*. Presentations of this work at the University of Iowa, and Columbia University seminar in South Asian Studies provided me with valuable feedback as did the comments of numerous people: Meg McLagan; Teja Ganti; Birgit Meyer; Rafael Sanchez and Sudeep Dasgupta. I thank them all. This article was originally published in *Cahiers d'Études Africaines* (2003), XLII (4): 168.

References

ANWAR, A. 1989. *The Struggle for Influence and Identity: The Ulama in Kano, 1937–1987.* M.A. Thesis. University of Maiduguri. Maiduguri, Nigeria.

APPADURAI, A. 1997. *Modernity at Large: Cultural Dimensions of Globalization.* Minneapolis: University of Minnesota Press.

BARBER, K. (ed.) 1997. *Readings in African Popular Culture.* Bloomington: Indiana University Press.

BARBER, K. and C. WATERMAN. 1995. 'Traversing the Global and Local: Fùjí Music and Praise Poetry in the Production of Contemporary Yoruba Popular Culture', in D. Miller (ed.), *Worlds Apart. Modernity through the Prism of the Local,* pp. 240–62, London: Routledge.

BARKINDO, B.M. 1993. 'Growing Islamism in Kano City since 1970: Causes, Forms and Implications', in Louis Brenner (ed.), *Muslim Identity and Social Change in Sub-Saharan Africa,* pp. 91–105, Bloomington: Indiana University Press.

BAYART, J.F. 1993. *The State in Africa: The Politics of the Belly.* London: Longman.

BAYART, J.F., S. ELLIS and B. HIBOU. 1999. *The Criminalization of the State in Africa.* Oxford: James Currey.

BUBA, MALAMI and GRAHAM FURNISS. 1999. 'Youth Culture, *Bandiri* and the Continuing Legitimacy Debate in Sokoto Town', *Journal of African Cultural Studies,* 12(1): 27–46.

FERGUSON, J. 1999. *Expectations of Modernity. Myths and Meanings of Urban Life on the Zambian Copperbelt.* Berkeley: University of California Press.

GAONKAR, DILIP (ed.) 1999. 'Alter/Native Modernities,' *Public Culture,* 11(1).

GRAHAM, S. and S. MARVIN. 1996. *Telecommunications and the City: Electronic Spaces, Urban Places.* London: Routledge.

———. 2001. *Splintering Urbanism: Networked Infrastructures, Technological Mobilities and the Urban Condition.* London: Routledge.

GUMI, A.M. 1972. *Aqidah Al-Sahihah Bi Muwafiqah Al-Shari'ah* (*The Right Belief is Based on the Shari'ah*). Ankara: Hilal Publishing.

———. 1992. *Where I Stand.* Ibadan: Spectrum Books.

HANNERZ, U. 1992. *Cultural Complexity: Studies in the Social Organization of Meaning.* New York: Columbia University Press.

HARVEY, D. 2000. *Spaces of Hope.* Berkeley: University of California Press.

Inda, J.X. and R. Rosaldo. 2002. *The Anthropology of Globalization: A Reader*. Oxford: Blackwell.

Kakar, S. 1989. *Intimate Relations: Exploring Indian Sexuality*. Chicago: University of Chicago Press.

Larkin, B. 1997. 'Indian Films and Nigerian Lovers: Media and the Creation of Parallel Modernities', *Africa*, 67(3): 406–40.

———. 2002. 'Materializing Culture: Cinema and the Creation of Social Space', in F. Ginsburg, L. Abu-Lughod and B. Larkin (eds), *Media Worlds: Anthropology on New Terrain*, pp. 319–36, Berkeley: University of California Press.

Lefebvre, H. 1991. *The Production of Space*. Translation by D.N. Smith. Oxford: Blackwell.

Loimeier, R. 1997. *Islamic Reform and Political Change in Northern Nigeria*. Evanston: Northwestern University Press.

Manuel, P. 1993. *Cassette Culture. Popular Music and Technology in South India*. Chicago: University of Chicago Press.

Massey, D.B. 1994. *Space, Place and Gender*. Minneapolis: University of Minnesota Press.

McLagan, M. 2002. 'Spectacles of Difference: Cultural Activism and the Mass Mediation of Tibet', in F. Ginsburg, L. Abu-Lughod and B. Larkin (eds), *Media Worlds: Anthropology on New Terrain*, Berkeley: University of California Press.

Paden, J.N. 1973. *Religion and Political Culture in Kano*. Berkeley: University of California Press.

Qureshi, R.B. 1995. 'Recorded Sound and Religious Music: The Case of Qawwali', in L.A. Babb and S. Wadey (eds), *Media and the Transformation of Religion in South Asia*, pp. 139–66, Philadelphia: University of Pennsylvania Press.

Tahir, I.A. 1975. *Scholars, Saints, and Capitalists in Kano, 1904–1974: The Pattern of Bourgeois Revolution in an Islamic Society*. Ph.D., Cambridge University.

Taussig, M. 1993. *Mimesis and Alterity: A Particular History of the Senses*. New York: Routledge.

Tsing, A. 2000. 'The Global Situation', *Cultural Anthropology*, 15(3): 327–60.

Umar, M.S. 1993. 'Changing Islamic Identity in Nigeria from the 1960s to the 1980s: From Sufism to Anti-Sufism', in L. Brenner (ed.), *Muslim Identity and Social Change in Sub-Saharan Africa*, pp. 154–78, Bloomington: Indiana University Press.

Watts, M. 1992. 'The Shock of Modernity: Petroleum, Protest and Fast Capitalism in an Industrializing Society', in A. Pred and M. Watts (eds), *Reworking Modernity: Capitalisms and Symbolic Discontent*, New Brunswick: Rutgers University Press.

13

Cruising on the *Vilayeti* Bandwagon: Diasporic Representations and Reception of Popular Indian Movies[1]

RAMINDER KAUR

A friend of mine was once sitting with a well-known Indian film director on his Mumbai patio drinking tea, talking about popular cinema and its successes overseas. At one point in the discussion, he turned round to him and said, 'Tell me, what do NRIs really want?'[2] The NRI market has enthralled and irked Indian film-makers alike. This was particularly the case since the 1990s when it became glaringly clear that there were many profits to be made overseas, even more so than with the home market. It is such global orientations that have become an almost obsessive preoccupation with many of these film-makers.

As we have argued throughout this volume, since its emergence at the turn of the twentieth century, Indian cinema has been a regionally diverse, transnational and hybrid media that has been often channelled into nationalist narratives. We have learnt about aspects of this complex history

[1] *Vilayeti* literally means foreign.

[2] Non-Resident Indian (NRI) is technically used for people who are Indian nationalities living abroad. It is also popularly cited for all diasporic people even if they are of another nationality. The Indian government had recently tried to construct the category of PIO—People of Indian Origin—but this has not become as popular as NRI.

with Rosie Thomas' accounts on two early film actresses, with Kajri Jain's focus on the significance of locality in the making of an indigenised Indian cinema, with Gayatri Chatterjee's chapter on a globalised visual culture for what she calls 'pre-cinema', and with Shuddhabrata Sengupta's narrative on the imprint of the cameraman and his diverse technical and aesthetic expertise. Such varied dynamics have informed the growth of Indian cinema from the outset, and we have seen how this has affected representations of women, with Geetanjali Gangoli's consideration of the metaphor of the 'vamp'; and, equally, representations of men through the transnational genre of 'action movies', as explicated in Koushik Banerjea's focus on the films, *Sholay* and *Deewaar*.

Sudhanva Deshpande's chapter took us into the 1990s where the global travels of Bollywood movies have taken on yet another inflection. Representations of the Indian diaspora as well as the increasing use of non-Indian filming locations have accompanied economic drives to target potentially lucrative markets particularly amongst diasporic communities abroad. Earlier, there had been six territories for film distribution—five in India and one outside the country. The latter was seen more as an appendage—external markets reached by Indian films such as East and South Africa (Barnouw and Krishnaswamy, 1980: 145). This situation began to change with the rise of technically competent films with their slick production and editing, and their new storylines centring on the gentrified middle classes, trendy youth and rampant consumerism. Outside of India, UK-based Asians form one of their biggest target audiences with 55 per cent of Hindi movie ticket sales. Venturing into the third millennium, the overseas market is less of an afterthought for it has the potential to bring in substantial earnings to film-makers and distributors. Indian popular films have become big business to the point that the Underworld has taken to demanding a percentage of sizeable profits abroad. To deny them, as film entrepreneurs such as the actor-director Rakesh Roshan found out in 2000, is to risk death.

This last section of the volume accounts for how Bollywood has been received across various communities around the world. Several of the contributors note that there has been a re-mapping of the 'Indian' subject in the process, considered to be located not just within the confines of India but also outside the nation-state where countries of actual residence appear to matter little next to the diasporic character's 'essential' identity premised upon origins. The phenomena has been variously analysed for situated contexts in Frankfurt (Germany), Georgetown and the West

Bank Demerara (Guyana), New York (US) and Durban (South Africa). The diasporic subject has become central not just to economic targets, but also to the making of a national, Bollywood cinema.

The post-1990s globalisation of Indian cinema is distinct to earlier transnational gestures. Indeed, the consumption of film amongst non-South Asians as amongst the Nigerian Hausa people (accounted for by Brian Larkin), hardly gets a mention in modern-day film-makers' discussions. Despite the longstanding appeal of Indian cinema across the globe, the more lucrative markets of Europe and the US with their relatively successful Indian diasporas are targeted for their economic capital. Representations of the 'foreign' in Bollywood have also accelerated in leaps and bounds—from sporadic 'travels' through Euro-America in films like *Sangam* (*Confluence*, dir. Raj Kapoor, 1964) and as Geetanjali Gangoli's chapter recounts, in *Purab aur Paschim* (*The East and the West*, dir. Manoj Kumar, 1970) to its almost normative inclusion in virtually all contemporary Indian film plots. Here, I go on to further investigate the current scenario with a focus on diasporic representations in, and reception of, the film hits of the 1990s. I chart out a dual carriage of imaginaries: on the one hand, investigating the kinds of characters and narratives that configure Indian conceptions of its diaspora as portrayed in Bollywood movies; and, on the other hand, focusing on how such films have been received and reviewed by a sample audience based in London. Thus, the interface between production and reception, representation and consumption of Indian and transnational identities is critically examined.

Concomitant with the accelerated distribution of Indian popular films across the globe, has come a rise in the literature over the last decade commenting on the 'new' phenomena of the transnational Indian positioned outside of India yet 'yearning' for his/her homeland—an argument proposed by observers based in India and elsewhere. Maithili Rao, for instance, comments:

> As for the yearning NRIs all over the globe, the Hindi film is the umbilical cord that anchors them to their past, to Indian culture and its norms. One might think the second and third generation of NRI kids—often dubbed ABCDs (American born confused *desis*) in the US—would have moved away from the staple fare of their parents, since they have grown up with Hollywood and MTV, but their fractured psyche seems to hang on with even greater passion to the easiest form of bonding with the mother country (Rao, 2001: 159).

Figure 13.1
Diasporic Indians in front of department store celebrating 'Bollywood culture' in London's Oxford Street, 2002
Source: Photograph courtesy Raminder Kaur.

On a less assertive note, Sumita S. Chakravarty proposes:

> ... Indian commercial cinema has come to symbolise an order of psychic investment for immigrants of Indian origin all over the world ... in a fundamental sense, [it evokes] the problematic scenario of originary desire: the desire for origins (with the accompanying discomfort, pain, and guilt) that lies at the very heart of the attempt at new identity formations on the part of displaced peoples (1993: 3).

It is apparent that, on the one hand, reports of the popularity of Indian films overseas is too easily read off as indices of nostalgia. On the other, diasporic youth are overwhelmingly seen as 'between cultures' and the source of much mirth for their supposed 'confusion'. This is despite the fact that MTV and Hollywood are probably just as avidly consumed in the cities of India than anywhere else.

Nostalgia is also notable in Patricia Uberoi's relatively more considered article (1998: 312). However, Uberoi does qualify such presumptions by recognising the caricature of the nostalgic NRI (ibid.: 328). Such films, she asserts:

> ... register an important site of ideological transformation and contestation as popular culture comes to terms with the new reality of middle-class diaspora and its challenges to national identity—for those at home, for many of whom the West is now the desired destination, as well as for those '*pardes*', nostalgically recalling the imagined homeland (ibid.: 334).

Uberoi goes on to investigate the differentials in films about diasporic Indians in a context of 'the internationalisation of the middle-class family and the consequent problem of the cultural reproduction of Indian identity in transnational locations' (ibid.: 307). With her comparison of two films, *Dilwale Dulhania Le Jayenge* (henceforth *DDLJ*, *The Brave will take away the Bride*, dir/script Aditya Chopra, 1995), and *Pardes* (*Overseas*, dir. Subash Ghai, 1997), she notes:

> ... where DDLJ proposes that Indian identity can survive translocation, albeit requiring renewal and replenishment through periodic return to the homeland, *Pardes* discloses a deep ambivalence with respect to diaspora—glamourising its material benefits and enabling possibilities, while condemning its moral consequences (ibid.: 310).

Below, I go on to investigate the reception of *DDLJ* amongst members of the British Asian diaspora, whilst proposing a slightly different argument. I suggest that some of the more obvious summations of the success of commercial Indian films abroad, especially for the UK, are somewhat misguided. As Christiane Brosius and Narmala Halstead have also variously concluded for their respective studies, it is too glib and cursory to say that Bollywood enables a religion-like nostalgia for people of the Indian disapora; or that it serves some kind of identity orientation in the midst of a West-induced anomie and that film provides an emotional and material link that needs to be reaffirmed due to the distance from their so-called homeland, India.[3] It is also specious to presume that Indian

[3] This argument is familiar in the literature on race/ethnicity and diaspora, but to date has not affected upon the literature on film. For critiques of diasporic South Asians'

popular films provide a 'shared culture' that links everyone who is ethnically Indian as a general rule. Each case need be qualified in terms of, amongst other themes, gendered identities, generational groups and the histories of particular diasporas. Here we find that with the relatively more assured and confident South Asian diaspora in Britain as opposed to Germany, for instance, there is a playful and parodic relationship amongst the spectators of Indian cinema. It appears that when cultural identities are siphoned through a variety of activities in education, bureaucracies, a lively popular culture and regular travels to the subcontinent, the burden for Indian cinema to channel notions of Indianness to its diaspora are considerably lessened. The relative longevity of Indian film consumption amongst the British Asian diaspora in the public sphere (Kaur and Terracciano, 2005) and differences in socio-political environments may also go some way to explaining the differences noted by Thomas Blom Hansen amongst South African Indian spectators in Durban.

Stored away with the dusty suitcases of Indian migrants to Britain were memories of Raj Kapoor and images of Nargis. Less obviously these early, post-World War II diaspora populations reinvented a sense of 'the old country' through a patchwork quilt of filmic, musical and festive events. Family members back in South Asia anticipated monthly remittance payments from the 'lucky ones' who had managed to gain a passage overseas—this proved no small burden to the mainly working-class Asian migrants, for whom food and shelter were still the major priorities in the land of Rolls Royce motors. Notwithstanding the conversion of many disused premises into thriving cinemas, serving up a diet of Bollywood classics and contemporary Hindi fare was a significant development from the 1960s. It was an early example of the entrepreneurial flare now so readily associated with a diasporic Asian business class. Perhaps, more significantly though, it marked the beginning of a transformation that was to take place over the next few decades in every major metropole with a significant Asian population. The proliferation of these cinemas in all such sites left indelible marks upon urban social spaces in Britain. Film was being reappropriated as a cultural resource and invested with a multifaceted Asian diaspora consciousness. The 1980s signalled a reversion back to the homes when video technology meant that less and less people went to the cinema to view Indian movies. But, by the 1990s, despite the growth in Asian satellite and cable channels, group trips to multiplexes to watch the latest Bollywood offering saw a resurgence again.

dreams about the homeland and the 'myth of return', see volume edited by Raminder Kaur and John Hutnyk (1999).

In this chapter, I want to focus in particular on the idea that ingredients designed with the so-called NRI/'diasporan' in mind do not necessarily lead to a concerted series of identifications from British Asians. In fact, it is often the case that it leads to the obverse—a disidentification albeit momentary and contingent, a disassociation that could nonetheless rest side by side with, though in tension, the emotional and enjoyable affects of films as it relates to performative excesses, romance, songs, and the star appeal of prominent actors/actresses—something that Richard Dyer (1979) has described as the charismatic 'supplement'. These are the factors that more often than not translate into box-office successes in the UK. Thus, my main point is that box-office successes and ratings cannot be uncritically translated into a discourse about NRI nostalgia—which tends to be the case amongst many of the film critics, scholars and indeed, Indian-based film-makers.

Second, in this fetishisation of the figure of the NRI, I argue that there is a kind of new hegemony created, albeit from a particular perspective, where capital and distributive networks leads to the hegemonic authorisation of what it means to be a 'proper Indian'. This is an image that sits very comfortably with the arguments of conservative and Euro-centric opinion on the nation with regard to the position of the migrant and their offspring in countries of the North.[4] Even though Bollywood films portray the relationship between the diasporic and Indian subject as 'exploitative and predatory, ones in which the feminine nation is taken advantage of by the masculine diaspora in the form of the capital-wielding NRI' (Desai, 2003: 58–59), I argue that this entails a projection of anxiety from the point of view of powerful film financiers, directors and producers. Such global aspirations could be described as an instance of 'pax Indiana'—between powerful representatives of Indian cinema and their corporate partners in the West. It is a phenomenon that emerged in the post-1990s neo-liberalised carnival of trade-offs where Indian film-makers set out to control the world market of Indian popular cinema, striking deals wherever convenient. Thus, despite India's comparatively weaker role in global geo-politics and the supposed affluence of diasporic Indians,

[4] In an interview, film-maker Aditya Chopra explains:

> I have shown that the character of Amrishji [i.e., played by Amrish Puri] could be shown to be far away from his roots. In a sense he is a displaced person and yet his outlook is very stubborn. Without intending to, I touched upon the issue of the major generation gap that exists between Indian immigrants and their children (Mohamed cited in Uberoi, 1998: 328).

I want to offer another equally valid perspective pertaining to the regime of global filmic representations of Indians abroad. With the emergent interest from non-South Asians, it is Hindi film, with its centre firmly implanted in the subcontinent, that is beginning to authorise accounts on the identities of those diasporans who do not necessarily see India as the centre of their psycho-political imaginaries. Despite decades of struggle to be recognised as citizens with rights and resources in Britain, such assumptions relocate them back in the subcontinent.[5] Once again, it appears that culturalist discourse allies with conservative and Eurocentric opinion that migrants from the South 'do not quite fit' in the West and where the specificities of diasporic histories and the cultural politics of that area are elided.

A Kinship Across Continents?

Popular Bollywood movies of the 1990s include stories about the limits and possibilities of young love. An eponymous case being *Maine Pyaar Kiya* (*I Have Fallen in Love*, dir. Sooraj R. Barjayta, 1989). This was alongside the spectacle of festivities and family celebrations, *Hum Aapke Hai Koun...!* (*Who am I to you*, dir. Sooraj R. Barjatiya, 1994)—a film heralded for its 'clean family fun' centring on festivities around a wedding. Another popular theme concerned films about NRIs living abroad. *DDLJ* is a case in point amongst others such as *Pardes, Chori Chori Chupke Chupke, Kaantein, Kuch Khatti Kuch Meethi*—the list may well be endless.

The 1990s was also an era of resurgent nationalism and wariness about the 'terrorist', often portrayed as an anti-national traitor and Pakistani agent, who appeared time and time again in movies such as Mani Ratnam's *Roja* (1994) and John Mathan's *Sarfarosh* (*Brave Hearts*, 1999). The disputed territory of Kashmir provided the rationale for numerous films about past and present border disputes (example, *Border*, 1997; *Kohram* [*Chaos*] 1999; *Hindustan ki Kasam* [*Swear by the Name of India*] 1999; and *Mission Kashmir*, 2000). Although this subject is outside of the purview of this chapter, it is perhaps worth making a small point—it is not necessarily the case that the 'saccharine love movies' are the antithesis of such 'war/terrorist movies'. In fact, both types of film reveal a fundamental conservatism where the family becomes a metonym for the nation, and vice versa.

[5] See work by Centre for Contemporary Cultural Studies (1982), Stuart Hall (1996), Paul Gilroy (1992), and the edited volume by Ashwani Sharma, John Hutnyk and Sanjay Sharma (1996) for accounts of diasporic populations' struggles to create homes in Britain through the use of popular cultural forms.

On this note, Chakravarty provides a discussion on what she calls 'war romances' of the 1960s (1993: 219–24). In these films, war tended to figure more as the background to the main storyline of romance between two people. Such movies represent another genre of films enjoyed abroad, touching upon political issues and are deemed to make a more serious point. A prominent 'civil war romance' (popular more so amongst the diaspora than in the subcontinent) in the 1990s was a film about the threats posed by Assamese separatists, *Dil Se* (*From the Heart*, dir. Mani Ratnam, 1998).

I want to focus on two of these films, in particular, for the kinds of viewing narratives that they generated—*DDLJ* and *Dil Se*. In *DDLJ*, the story revolves around a London-based petrol station owner who, pinning for his native Punjab, tries to marry off one of his daughters to the son of an old friend resident in India. The film is, as Patricia Uberoi observes,

> ... one of a new series of popular movies in which the NRI is positioned as hero. This *in itself* seems to be a social trend worth watching and reflecting on—a testimony at once to the enabling opportunities of the liberalised economy of the 1990s, and to the emergence of a new transnational Indian elite class as the reference group for the upwardly mobile Indian middle classes (Uberoi, 1998: 325).

DDLJ shows the authoritative father figure who wants to return to his 'roots', and marry off his daughter, Simran (played by Kajol) to the son of an old friend, Shah. The father may well be part of the diaspora, but his allegiance to India, concomitant with values of traditional patriarchy, adheres him to India. On the one hand, the film narrative fulfils a curiosity about its presumed 'cousins' abroad for Indian-based audiences. On the other, for those located overseas, the story appears to act as a conduit to maintain emotional and material (financial) links to the subcontinent. Yet, if we were to look more carefully at the kinds of responses the movie received, we can see some finer ruptures in such sweeping brush strokes.

I considered the responses of five London-based British Asians, between the ages of 25–40, four of them female. They were all second generation Asians whose parents were born in India, but who themselves were not, at the time of writing, parents. They all enjoyed watching Hindi movies—be it by way of cinema, satellite television, videos—but their responses seemed to be bristling with contradictions. Their inclusion here cannot of course be fully representative, but their comments do allude to some interesting dynamics which I go on to develop ahead.[6] Concerns about the socialisation of children into Indian values and culture, which characterise some of the findings of Brosius', Halstead's and Hansen's chapters, are not of a premium here, and I think this is one significant reason for diverging from the theme of the 'nostalgic NRI'. The discussions generated here (with author) concentrated on Indian films as a conduit of pleasure and material for the constitution of individual diasporic identities in Britain. One respondent, Nina (aged 29, an accounts administrator), stated:[7]

> That Shah Rukh is cool. He's not like the others who take themselves too seriously like Salman, or who don't take themselves seriously at all, like Govinda. He's got the balance. Although I think his accent for this film was unnecessary. Is that how they think we talk over here?

Another woman, Asha (31, a pharmacist), opined:

> The songs are great. They're what really make the film. That and the Shah Rukh-Kajol combination. I must admit some of the stuff is ridiculous, like going to Hounslow on a tourist bus, or walking past the Queen's palace on your way to work. I don't know many people who do that.

A man, Mohan (33, an IT consultant), pointed out:

> I suppose there's a level at which the story is trying to be realistic, and the idea about going to Europe—we all try and do that in our youth, but we do it on the cheap with a backpack, staying in some poxy youth hostel, not those chalets they show.

---

[6] These viewings were conducted after the general release of the film with video showings of the film and discussions thereafter, from May to August 2000. The film *Dil Se* and the New Wave independent movie, *Bombay Boys,* were also viewed on separate occasions, but space does not permit me to account for these discussions at length other than to provide evidence for my main argument here. As Hansen's chapter also reveals with his focus on the film, *Kuch Kuch Hota Hai* (*Something or Other is Happening*, dir. Karan Johar, 1998), repeat viewing is a practice that is not uncommon for successful Bollywood movies. Thus, their responses were interwoven narratives with memories of the movie viewed in the cinema and its home viewing.

[7] The names have been altered.

A woman, Indu (26, a youth worker), profused: 'Yes, it's the same old I love you, you love me ... Oh shit there's my dad! .... But it's enjoyable, done with style and the film's memorable because it's a different setting to the usual.' Finally, a woman, Kieron (36, a journalist), admitted:

> I don't like being compared to a pigeon, nor the dog of a washerman.[8] I don't need to be lectured by someone who just doesn't know. I let them off because the songs are good and I suppose, I got emotional towards the end.

All in all, the characters were read in a realist manner as travesties, where England is seen through the filter of Bollywood rose-tinted glasses. The Indians appear as if in 'diasporic drag', like much else with Hindi cinema, an identity that they consume, play with, and not compelling enough to even 'appear as genuine'. Nina said: 'The hero and heroine—they might have been born in England but they're like those in *Goodness Gracious Me* when the Indian students go on an outing to England.'[9]

What's interesting about such viewpoints is that the phenomena which the novelist, Samuel Taylor Coleridge, once described as a 'willing suspension of disbelief', is there for the fantasy elements of the films—that is, for the songs, the star aura. However, the rest of the film narrative is engaged in a realist manner that is then compared to the social world as they knew it. We may compare this proposition of a 'suspension of disbelief' with arguments made about viewing Indian audiences framed in the discourse of darshan. Whereas scholars such as Lawrence Babb (1975) and Diane Eck (1985) imagine viewers within a religious modality, to be gullible believers, Prasad (1998) proposes a more reflexive argument for the hierarchy implied between the believers and a non-believing, en-lightened scholar in such scholarly views:

> A.K. Ramanujan, the late poet and scholar, is reported to have remarked once: 'I do not believe in god; I believe in people who believe in god .... This formulation has the distinct advantage of providing, in its very syntax, a glimpse, in miniature, of the

[8] The father (in the film) says in a moment of rage against disrespectful youngsters: 'Call themselves Indian (Hindustani). They give India a bad name. No shame, no honor. Don't even know how to respect elders. They've become like the dogs of washermen—no good for the home, nor for the riverside.'

[9] *Goodness Gracious Me* was a popular comedy sketch show produced for the BBC after its earlier incarnation as a Radio 4 programme. It was mainly conceived and showcased by British Asian talent.

articulating, structuring effect of this act of suspension of disbelief. The caesura that separates the two segments of the formulation is also the link that reveals the structured, hierarchical relationship between them. We notice here a syntactical relay across the gulf of the caesura, of a subjectivity that first posits and then suspends itself in order to make place for the concluding phrase: 'those who believe in god' (Prasad, 1998: 7).

Reflexive darshan may be compared with a notion of reflexive spectatorship—that is, spectatorship that both immerses itself in the film and also distances itself so as one can adopt a more critical stance—a discourse that also informs the narratives of film-makers. Unlike critics such as Ashis Nandy (1998) and Sudhir Kakar (1980) who argue that Hindi cinema is about another universe, a repetitive mythic order that audiences indulge in, we must also highlight the caesura which momentarily suspends them in disbelief. From the point of view of film-makers, post-1990s movies are increasingly engaging with realist modes, so that we find a rationale for song-and-dance sequences, attempts at forging new narratives within the stock of Bollywood characters and narratives.[10]

It appears that, on the one hand, songs, stars and emotional excesses (what may be called performative excesses) are qualitatively engaged with in terms of a centrifugal effect moving outwards—enjoyment and losing oneself in the music or star aura. On the other hand, the surrounding narrative is understood in terms of quite literal substitutions of centripetal 'meanings'—moving inwards in an attempt to fix the terms of reference. For example, the latter concerned issues such as the film location, how characters move from one place to another, the matter of sequential continuity, what one would do in a certain situation, and so forth. The disposition to have a willing suspension of disbelief is less so for the familiar, the mundane, particularly if it pertains to an area that the spectators recognise and is firmly implanted as part of the narrative, rather than couched as a backdrop for a song routine. There are, of course, points where this dichotomy breaks down: for example, the incredulity that met Kajol performing, instead of a wet sari number, a wet ra ra skirt number in the backyard of a suburban garden whilst her mum takes down the washing. But such reactions to novel representations tend to be the exception rather than the norm.[11]

---

[10] See also Ravi Vasudevan's analysis of the film, *Andaz* (dir. Mehboob Khan, 1949) made with middle-class Indian audiences in mind who were used to watching Hollywood films.

[11] Nonetheless, even here, respondents were willing to give her the benefit of the realist doubt by enjoying the song for what it was worth, and for the men, 'a flash of leg'.

Overall, there are qualitatively different levels of engagements. There tends to be a realistic reception for the narrative which is concerned with the linearity of events, settings and viability of characterisations in a space occupied by spectators used to viewing various different types of films—something that I call reflexive spectatorship. It transpired throughout our discussions on the films that there is a triple consciousness to reflexive spectatorship. This triple orientation comprises reception:

(*i*) in relation to Hindi films;
(*ii*) in relation to themselves as Indians/Asians in the West and the symbolic value that the Hindi film connotes—that is, as a cultural repository of alterity, but not necessarily a total identification or immersion in the film texts; and,
(*iii*) in relation to a larger repertoire of filmic references that made the film comparable to other filmic traditions and exemplars, which we shall explore in more detail ahead.

Spectatorship is very much about partaking in the film in a present modality, that is, engaging in the sequence of events as the plot unfolds. At other times, spectatorship is more about immersion—as in the song and the charismatic supplement of the film and actors. This level of engagement compares with the supra-realist immersion for the songs, creating a kind of 'intermezzo' (Deleuze and Guattari, 1986, 1987), a momentary loss of identities in the process of identification, moments caught between the past and the future or in Roland Barthes' words, 'pregnant moments' (1977: 73).[12]

I do not wish to draw out absolute differences, but qualitative emphases—where the realm that might be described as the performative explores the topography of desire and its vicissitudes. It is also where the star presence can be seen to split between, as Laura Mulvey (1989) puts it, 'ego ideas' particular to the screen presence of the stars (as opposed to the screen story/character that they play). Evidently, the production of meaning is not only derived from the internal articulation of the text, but also from its relationship with the spectator and his/her personal histories and experiences of film viewing. Rather than the searching for meaning from within the film text, I suggest that meanings are conjured that draw upon earlier knowledge of films and actors. Indeed, the receptive process

[12] See also Les Back's (1996) invocation of Deleuze and Guattari's work to consider performances of the 'bhangramuffin', Apache Indian, amongst a mixed race audience.

is less about ascertaining meaning, and more about affect, which seeks corroboration from outside the text. By this, I refer to the way the performative is in a sense 'pre-learnt'. This is done through various routes:

(*i*) in relation to the particular film being watched;
(*ii*) the familiarity with songs that are generally released before films come out, and along with music programmes, visualised and therefore enjoyed for their performative power; and,
(*iii*) the extra-textual magnetism of the star—a reputation crystallised through the popularity of earlier films, gossip, good looks and so forth.

This formulation has implications for diasporic representations of Hindi films abroad. It is indeed this aspiration to 'represent' the diasporic by Bollywood film-makers that has lead to a striking disidentification from many of the diasporans I talked about. This is not to say that the Hindi film is totally dismissed by diasporic Asians, but that it is negotiated on a shifting terrain of love and disdain. My respondents were willing to put this aside if the overall effect is greater than, as Kieron put it, the 'cringe factor that all Hindi films have to have'. In these instances the narrative becomes less significant than the amalgam of views, sensations and performances.

The phenomena of disidentification is also there for what has been described as New Wave cinema that emerged in the 1990s, that is, films that have been produced in India by a younger set to meet the needs of the worldly-wise youth market. The new 'Turks of Bollywood' include Kaizad Gustad, Rahul Bose and Nagesh Kukunoor. They grew up on a diet of Hollywood movies, MTV and Hindi films and, more often than not, were trained abroad (Desai, 2003). Their films are slickly packaged with the latest modcons and designer wear, but holding on to a kernel of 'Indian' values of family, dignity and emotionality somewhere in their narratives. In Gustad's spoof, *Bombay Boys* (1998), for instance, ciphers of diasporic nationalities from all over the world are used to represent moral excesses gone astray. The story revolves around a UK-born homosexual man on a quest to 'find himself' in India, the US-born narcissist/actor out to make it big, and the Australia-born neglectful Asian who has come to find his long-lost brother. With this film, the age-old disdain-desire relationship of the West against the non-West is inverted for the East's perception of the West. The West is seen, on the one hand, as a place of progress, and on the other, as a place of hedonistic excesses and licentiousness, both played out not through the presence of the western man/woman, but through the signifier of the *westernised* Indian abroad—the NRI. The kinds of NRIs represented in Indian films tend to be the well-to-do north Indian, middle-class families overlooking the diversity of class and ethnic positions of diasporic Indians. On the whole, the NRI, even though born abroad, remains essentially an Indian abroad, uprooted from his/her real homeland, 'contaminated' by the West, and needed to be taken back into the fold in what might be called a nationalist missionary project. This homogenising tendency of seeing all diasporic Indians as practically the same is implicit within the term Non-Resident Indian, that is, someone whose main orientation is Indian even if s/he was not born there, which a few of my respondents took exception to. As Asha quipped in our discussions of this film: 'NRI according to them really means Not Really Indian.'

Indianness in this context becomes a measure of authenticity in the persistent legacy of Orientalism, this time from the East, but one that combines well with views originating in the West.[13] To transplant these anxieties and ambivalences onto the NRI instead of the generalised terrain of the West (Chatterjee, 1994) is also to chart out territories that could also be claimed as part of the Indian 'empire'. As Chandra Talpade-Mohanty (1998) argues, how one understands and defines home is a profoundly political exercise. To posit India as the authentic homeland from which all other 'homes' are inauthentic is also a profoundly problematic assertion. Dressing up the 'homeland' with intoxicating imagery of peasants dancing in lush fields does not camouflage the fact that this too is a political, and for some, a contentious point of reference. The multiplicity of locations—literally and metaphorically—and the fluidity of positionalities

---

[13] Inner struggles between modernity and tradition or between East and West in a context of uncertain globalisation are externalised and remapped onto the diasporic Indian. Ashis Nandy (1983) has explored the deep ambivalences held by Indians towards the West which are projected onto types, earlier examples being the oversexed vamp (westernised) and the self-effacing heroine destined to be a good housewife (see Gangoli, this volume). Here the West is replaced by the westernised or overseas Indian. As Uberoi argues:

> ... DDLJ had introduced an element of novelty in this practice by its attempt to define Indian identity for Indians both at home and abroad through the emotional travails of a young NRI couple in love, rather than through the more conventional confrontation of Eastern versus Western cultures and values (1998: 326).

are totally thrown out of the window in the Hindi film.[14] The upshot is that notable films produced elsewhere, outside of India representing diasporic Asians—*Handsworth Songs* (dir. John Akomfrah, 1986), *My Beautiful Launderette* (dir. Stephen Frears, 1985), *The Buddha of Suburbia* (dir. Roger Michell, 1993), *Bhaji on the Beach* (dir. Gurinder Chadda, 1994), the Canadian produced *Masala* (dir. Srinivas Krishna, 1991) to name but a few—become marginalised as 'inauthentic', as *too* hybrid (where hybridity in Bollywood cinema is naturalised and nationalised).[15] These diasporic film products become understood here as mongrelised, bastardised and therefore inauthentic from a range of perspectives parallel to perceptions of them as subjects of intrigue and mirth.

Straight from the Heart

A film that was admired both for its content and its storyline, particularly in the UK, was *Dil Se*. What was surprising about *Dil Se* was that it flopped in India only to be revived by an enthusiastic response from overseas (UK) where it stormed into the top 10 UK film charts on release in 1998. It was widely reported in the press that in the Feltham Multiplex, West London, the film was more popular than Steven Speilberg's *Saving Private Ryan*, even in its unsubtitled form. For the first two months, the film was shown on five screens, five times a day to sell-out capacity. This phenomena almost impelled the Indian middle-class in particular to sit up and take notice, effectively reviving interest in this first-time flop to make it a success again.

Dil Se is a story about Amar, a journalist for All India Radio (played by Shah Rukh Khan), who is sent to Assam, a border state in north-east India. Whilst there, he encounters Meghna (played by Manisha Koirala), at a train station, falls in love with her, and later goes back to the area to find her. Eventually, he tracks her down and together they go through a series of adventures as she proves to be an Assamese separatist. Amar goes

[14] These observations are not exclusive to diasporic representations. Representations such as these follow in the footsteps of the fetish of the bhai-bhai Hindu-Christian-Mussalman (Muslim) triumvirate, the parody of the south Indian, the sirdarji (turbaned Sikh man), the virtuous wife/heroine and so forth, all of which are by now staple parts of the Indian popular film.

[15] However, there are odd exceptions, odd being the operative term where films such as *Bend it like Beckham* (dir. Gurinder Chadda, 2002) have been globally enjoyed for not only their diasporic characters, but also the novelty value of an Asian woman playing football. The film's associations with a world-class footballer, David Beckham, is not, however, insignificant to the movie's exceptional success.

back to new Delhi, loses contact with her, and his family arranges a marriage for him. Nearly a year later, Meghna turns up at his doorstep out of the blue with another woman. She wants shelter and safety and he takes her in. Unknown to him, the two women are planning a big bomb attack on a national parade in New Delhi. The police come to Amar suspecting his involvement in the affair. He is eventually let off and goes to see Meghna to confront her but also one suspects to warn her that the police know about the attack on the parade. At the end, there is a face-off between Amar and Meghna. She stands strapped with bombs and makes an impassioned appeal for human rights. Amar reminds her of the innocent who would also die. She asks him for the way out. He says 'Love. I can't live without you.' Finally, the bombs explode blowing the lovers up into each others arms.

Publicised as: 'A film about real people. About you and me', the success of this film abroad left many Indian film-makers aghast: why this film, they asked themselves? It is neither 'clean' family fun (it has a sad ending), nor does it represent diasporic subjects. Well, why was it enthused about in the UK? My respondents had this to say. Nina suggested that: 'Manisha Koirala's character is interesting. She's strong, got a mind of her own. And she's not trying to be like an innocent lamb, like they show for women in other Hindi movies.'[16] Asha reflected: 'The filming was brilliant. I'd never seen such scenes before in a Hindi movie.' Mohan compared it to other films of which he was a fan: 'It wasn't just fantasy, but trying to make a point. At some points it was hyperreal like a Takeshi Kitano movie, other times fantastic elements—ranked with the best and the cinematography was comparable to the best of Bertolluci.'

Indu opined: 'It was not embarrassing to see it with my English friends. It holds its own with anything produced over here'. Kieron commented: 'It wasn't just jingoistic but level-headed. Even brave of him [the director] to film it the way he did' and later, 'It's not only a successful film, but a cult film like that of Sholay—with its epic qualities.'[17]

What emerged in our discussions was that it was not important to have signifiers of the transnational or the diasporic agent in the validation of the movie. In fact, if that was going to lead to yet another clichéd representation of the 'foreign' and the 'non-Indian', the film could indeed

[16] Space does not permit me to consider the question of gendered responses. See Purnima Mankekar's (1999) work for a study of gendered responses to television and films in contemporary New Delhi.

[17] See Koushik Banerjea's chapter for an analysis of the film *Sholay* as an intertextual cult film.

lead to a conspicuous disidentification, its performative excesses then left with the task to compensate for the distancing created by the characters and storylines. What was more important than diasporic representations was the originality of the script, the conviction of the actors, and the look of the film. A fine balance was needed between the extra-real dimensions—the song-and-dance sequences, the melodrama—and the realistic, that is, where the film was set, what happens next, the integrity and intentionality of the characters and so forth. This balance was almost perfectly poised in the picturisation of the title song, 'dil se', which gripped everyone's attention for not only the melodic poignancy of the song, but the innovative blend of romance against a background of separatist and army violence. Asha had this to say about the clip: 'It said a lot about the romance. To have it pictured next to the army and the bombs going off. It's like saying that love is a difficult path and can be explosive.'

Shadows of the Authentic

Clearly, representations of particular identities need not lead to a confirmation of those particular identities amongst spectators. Rather, the engagement can lead to a marked disidentification. This is particularly so where representations of the diasporic are essentialised as types. In Hindi cinema, India is reinscribed as a hegemonic centre, where the Bollywood metalanguage is invoked everywhere. One is therefore led back to India as the fount of all identities. Diasporic then becomes a shadow of the authentic. This process reinscribes the hegemonies of Orientalism, but this time from the totalising dynamics of an auto-Orientalising East (Mazzarella, 2003).

Now, with the acceptance of Bollywood in the mainstream in the West, there is a certain complicity where capital and power come together to marginalise further those that are already marginalised as minorities. Bollywood film-makers and those working in Indian television are now avidly shaking hands with multinational corporates such as Columbia, Tristar, Polygram, Sony, Fox, and Star. They are also in cahoots with several key figures in British-based entertainment institutions as vindicated by Andrew Lloyd Webber's production of *Bombay Dreams* in London's West End, now shifted to New York's Broadway (the musical was indeed inspired by the film, *Dil Se*). At the time of writing, the Royal Opera House is planning a production which is a mix of Puccini's *Turandot* and Bollywood. Even the Hinduja brothers talked about getting involved in

Figure 13.2
Sunset at Indian film and music festival in Trafalgar Square, London, 2002
Photograph courtesy Raminder Kaur.

film and invoking the likes of Michael Jackson, Phil Collins, Santana or Elton John in the project. The phenomena seems to implicate a pax Indiana where national elites become the representatives of Indianness and particular histories are all too easily effaced to represent comfortable and often essentialising visions of Indians everywhere.

If the latter is to be avoided, Bollywood films need not only continue with the performative excesses or the fantasy elements, but also in the tradition of its masala ingredients, it needs to incorporate a more diverse grammar with which to deal with the very particular histories of diasporic South Asians, rather than persist in authorising them with the dualistic scripts of nationalism and its deviants. Some may argue that this suggestion runs counter to the simplifying, stereotype and formula-obsessed traits of commercial cinema, but tried-and-tested formulas without any innovation need not always make a recipe for success each time. Less than 15 per cent of the 800 or so movies made annually in Mumbai have had any measure of success amongst audiences (see Thomas, 1985: 120–21). Perhaps such a foray into what may be deemed the unknown and the unexpected without entirely losing its anchoring in the performative excesses adored across the globe is what NRIs would really want from Indian popular cinema.

Acknowledgements

Thanks to the people who shared their views and opinions with me; to Henna Rai who corrected me when I was wrong; to Ajay Sinha for his meticulous comments; and, to commentators at the Association for Asian Studies, Chicago, 2001, and the University of Sussex, 2004, where I presented versions of this paper.

References

BABB, L.A. 1975. *The Divine Hierarchy: Popular Hinduism in Central India*. New York: Columbia University Press.

BACK, LES. 1996. *New Ethnicities and Urban Cultures: Racism and Multiculture in Young Lives*. New York: St. Martin's Press.

BARNOUW, ERIK and S. KRISHNASWAMY. 1980. *Indian Film*. Second edition. New York: OUP.

BARTHES, ROLAND. 1977. *Image-Music-Text*. London: Fontana Press.

CENTRE FOR CONTEMPORARY CULTURAL STUDIES. 1982. *The Empire Strikes Back: Race and Racism in 1970s Britain*. London: Hutchinson.

CHAKRAVARTY, S. 1993. *National Identity in Indian Popular Cinema, 1947–87*. Austin: University of Texas Press.

CHATTERJEE, PARTHA. 1994. *The Nation and its Fragments: Colonial and Postcolonial Histories*. New Delhi: OUP.

DELEUZE, GILES and FELIX GUATTARI. 1986. *Nomadology: The War Machine*. New York: Semiotext(e).

———. 1987. A *Thousand Plateaus: Capitalism and Schizophrenia*. Trans. B. Massumi. Minneapolis: University of Minnesota Press.

DESAI, JIGNA. 2003. 'Bombay Boys and Girls: The Gender and Sexual Politics of Transnationality in the New Indian Cinema in English', *South Asian Popular Culture*, 1(1): 45–61.

DYER, RICHARD. 1979. *Stars*. London: BFI Publishing.

ECK, D. 1985. *Darsan: Seeing the Divine Image in India*. Anima Books.

GILROY, P. 1992. *'There Ain't No Black in the Union Jack': The Cultural Politics of Race and Nation*. London: Routledge.

HALL, STUART. 1996. *Stuart Hall: Critical Dialogues in Cultural Studies*. London: Routledge.

KAKAR, S. 1980. 'The Ties that Bind: Family Relationships in the Mythology of Hindi Cinema', *India International Centre Quarterly*, 8(1).

KAUR, RAMINDER and ALDA TERRACCIANO. 2005. 'South Asian Performance Arts in Britain', in Bobby Sayyid, Virinder Kalra and Nasreen (eds), *Asia-Nation*, London: C. Hurst and Co.

KAUR, RAMINDER and JOHN HUTNYK. 1999. *Travel Worlds: Journeys in Contemporary Cultural Politics*. London: Zed Books.

MANKEKAR, PURNIMA. 1999. *Screening Culture, Viewing Politics: An Ethnography of Television, Womanhood and Nation in the Postcolonial India*. Durham: Duke University Press.

MAZZARELLA, WILLIAM. 2003. *Shovelling Smoke: The Production of Advertising and the Cultural Politics of Globalisation in Contemporary India*. Durham: Duke University Press.

MULVEY, LAURA. 1989. *Visual and Other Pleasures: Theories of Representation and Difference*. Bloomington: Indiana University Press.

NANDY, ASHIS. 1983. *The Intimate Enemy: Loss and Recovery of Self under Colonialism*. New Delhi: OUP.

———. 1998. 'Introduction: Indian Popular Cinema as a Slum's Eye View of Politics', in A. Nandy (ed.), *The Secret Politics of Our Desires: Innocence, Culpability and Indian Popular Cinema*, New Delhi: Zed Books.

PRASAD, M. MADHAVA. 1998. *Ideology of the Hindi Film: A Historical Reconstruction*. New Delhi: OUP

RAO, MAITHILI. 2001. 'Heart of the Movie', in Lalit Mohan Joshi (ed.), *Bollywood: Popular Indian Cinema*, pp. 137–69, London: Dakini.

SHARMA, ASHWANI, JOHN HUTNYK and SANJAY SHARMA. 1996. *Dis-orienting Rhythms, the Politics of the New Asian Dance Music*. London: Atlantic Highlands, N.J., and ZED Books.

TALPADE-MOHANTY, CHANDRA. 1998. 'Critical Feminist Genealogies: On the Geography and Politics of Home and Nation', in Ella Shohat (ed.), *The Age of Globalization*, University of Massachusetts Press.

THOMAS, ROSIE. 1985. 'Indian Cinema: Pleasures and Popularity', *Screen*, 26(3/4): 116–31.

UBEROI, PATRICIA. 1998. 'The Diaspora Comes Home: Disciplining Desire in DDLJ', *Contributions to Indian Sociology*, 32(2): 305–36.

About the Editors and Contributors

The Editors

RAMINDER KAUR is Lecturer in Anthropology at the University of Sussex. Dr Kaur's research interests include public culture, aesthetics and politics in Western India; and the South Asian diaspora, race/ethnicity and expressive cultures. Dr Kaur has previously co-edited *Travel-Worlds: Journeys in Contemporary Cultural Politics* (1999), is the author of *Performative Politics and the Cultures of Hinduism: Public Uses of Religion in Western India* (2003), and a co-author of *Diaspora and Hybridity* (2005).

AJAY J. SINHA is Associate Professor of Art History and Chair of the Film Studies Program at Mount Holyoke College, USA, where he has taught courses on Asian art and Indian films since 1993. He has previously published *Imagining Architects: Creativity in Indian Temple Architecture* (2000) and contributed numerous articles on ancient Indian religious architecture as well as contemporary Indian art to edited volumes and journals.

The Contributors

KOUSHIK BANERJEA is Lecturer in Cultural Studies at Birbeck College, University of London. He has published in *Theory, Culture and Society*, *Postcolonial Studies* and *Ethnic and Racial Studies*, and is a contributor to *Dis-orienting Rhythms: The Politics of the New Asian Dance Music* (1996) and *Travel Worlds: Journeys in Contemporary Cultural Studies* (1999).

CHRISTIANE BROSIUS is currently Lecturer in the Department of Anthropology at the South Asia Institute of the University of Heidelberg. Dr Brosius is co-editor (with Melissa Butcher) of *Image Journeys: Audio-Visual Media and Cultural Change in India* (1999), and has authored *Art as Think-Space: On the Notion of Pedagogy in Aby Warburg's Work* (1997). Dr Brosius is also the author of *Empowering Visions: The Politics of Representations in Hindu Nationalism* (forthcoming).

GAYATRI CHATTERJEE has been a film scholar since 1986 and is associated with the Pune Film Institute. She is the author of *Awara* (1992) for which she received the President's Gold Medal in 1993, *Mother India* (2002), and of *Sant Tukaram* (forthcoming). She has contributed numerous articles to leading national and international journals on film and cultural studies and has subtitled over 50 Indian films.

SUDHANVA DESHPANDE is an actor, writer and director who has been a member of the New Delhi based theatre collective Jana Natya Manch, best known for its radical street theatre. Mr Deshpande has written for various newspapers and journals as a theatre/film critic, and works for LeftWord Books, New Delhi.

GEETANJALI GANGOLI is a Lecturer at the University of Bristol. Dr Gangoli is the recipient of the Panos Reproductive Health Fellowship (1998–99) and the Sir Ratan Tata Fellowship at the Asia Research Centre, London School of Economics (1999–2000) to work on issues relating to sex work, sexuality, and the law and reproductive health in India. Dr Gangoli has published widely in leading journals such as *The Economic and Political Weekly*, *The Indian Journal of Social Work* and *Issues in Medical Ethics*.

NARMALA HALSTEAD is a Lecturer at Cardiff University. She has carried out ethnographic research in Guyana and New York and her research interests include nationalism; ethnicity; globalisation and identity; forced migration; anthropology of media; anthropology of conflict and violence; and, reflexivity. Dr Halstead has published as a novelist and has also worked as journalist and editor in print and broadcast media.

THOMAS BLOM HANSEN is a Professor at Yale University. He is the author of *The Saffron Wave: Hindu Nationalism and Democracy in Modern India* (1999) and is the co-editor (with Chrisophe Jaffrelot) of *BJP and the Compulsions of Politics* (1998) and (with Finn Stepputat) of *States of Imagination: Ethnographic Explorations of the Postcolonial State* (2001). Dr Hansen is currently engaged in research on identity politics, diasporic practices and cultural transformations among Indians in South Africa during and after the era of apartheid.

KAJRI JAIN is currently Australian Research Council Fellow at the School of Communication and Creative Arts, Deakin University, as the co-recipient of an Australian Research Council Large Grant to conduct research on Television, Globalisation and Social Change in India. Dr Jain has been Knapp Chair in Liberal Arts at the University of San Diego and a Getty Fellow, as well as teaching in departments of art history and cultural studies in Australia. She has also worked as a graphic designer in New Delhi and Sydney. She has authored a book on calendar art titled *Gods in the Bazaar* (forthcoming).

BRIAN LARKIN teaches at Barnard College, Columbia University, where he writes on issues of media technologies and urbanisation in northern Nigeria. He is co-editor (with Faye Ginsburg and Lila Abu-Lughod) of *Media Worlds: Anthropology on New Terrain* (2002) and is editor of the Symposium 'Media and the Design for Modern Living' in *Visual Anthropology Review*.

SHUDDHABRATA SENGUPTA is lecturer, documentary film-maker, media practitioner and writer based in New Delhi. He is a member of the Raqs Media Collective and an initiator of SARAI: The New Media Initiative at the Centre for the Study of Developing Societies (www.sarai.net). Dr Sengupta is co-editor of *The SARAI Reader 01: The Public Domain* (2001) and *Double Take: A Second Look at the Documentary* (2000). Dr Sengupta has published widely in journals and magazines.

ROSIE THOMAS is a Reader in Art and Media Practice and Director of the Centre for Research and Education in Art and Media (CREAM) at the University of Westminster, London. Her research interests include documentary theory and practice, and Indian cinema history. Dr Thomas' early research as a social anthropologist was on the Bombay film industry and, since 1985, she has published widely on Indian cinema, contributing to books as well as journals such as *Screen* and *Quarterly Review of Film and Video*. She is also an independent documentary television producer and, since 1990, has made more than 30 programmes for the British Channel Four on a range of subject matters, from health and mental health issues to South Asian politics, arts and culture.

Index